William Galt

Railway Reform

Its importance and practicability considered as affecting the nation, the shareholders, and the government

William Galt

Railway Reform
Its importance and practicability considered as affecting the nation, the shareholders, and the government

ISBN/EAN: 9783337295301

Printed in Europe, USA, Canada, Australia, Japan

Cover: Foto ©Suzi / pixelio.de

More available books at **www.hansebooks.com**

RAILWAY REFORM:

ITS IMPORTANCE AND PRACTICABILITY

CONSIDERED AS AFFECTING

THE NATION, THE SHAREHOLDERS, AND THE GOVERNMENT.

BY

WILLIAM GALT.

"The roads of a country, from the very nature of things, are public concerns; they are as necessary to a people as the air they breathe."—*Second Report of the Select Committee of the House of Commons*, 1846.

"Should we live to see fully developed all the powers and energies of this system, we have no doubt we shall also live to see it recognized as one of the very greatest benefits that either art or philosophy has conferred on mankind."—*Quarterly Review.*

"If I entertained any feeling on the subject of the interference of Government, it is one of regret that they did not, in the first instance, take a more active and prominent part, that they did not themselves lay out for consideration what appeared to them the best general scheme for accommodating the traffic throughout the metropolis, without having the slightest reference to this company or that."—*Speech of the Earl of Derby in the House of Lords, February 12th, 1864.*

LONDON:
LONGMAN, GREEN, LONGMAN, ROBERTS, & GREEN.
1865.

ADVERTISEMENT.

THIS treatise was written for private circulation in the early part of last year; it underwent revision in the parliamentary recess; and since the subject attracted public notice, the author has added, with a view to publication in a complete form, the last three chapters. This explanation is necessary to prevent a confusion of dates in the mind of the reader.

Mr. Gladstone has given notice, "That it is the intention of Her Majesty's Government to advise the Crown to appoint a Commission to inquire into the economical question connected with our railway system: that is to say, the cost of conveyance on railways, and into the charges which are made by railway companies to the public."

Without an accurate knowledge of these important facts, it would be utterly impossible for the Legislature to deal satisfactorily with our railway system: it could neither comprehend the extent of the evil it has inflicted on the country on the one hand, nor devise the necessary remedy on the other. Government having determined " to begin with the beginning," there is every reason to hope that the movement now so well commenced may terminate in an equally satisfactory manner.

16*th February*, 1865.

PREFACE.

In 1844 an Act of Parliament was passed for the purpose of enabling Government to purchase on certain specified terms all railways in the United Kingdom that from that time forward should be constructed.

To protect, however, the interests of the shareholders, and give ample time to the nation and the Legislature to have full experience of the management of our railways by companies, it was enacted, that *twenty-one years* should elapse before our present system should become subject to any change, or the rights of proprietorship or management of the directors be in any way interfered with. It will, therefore, be seen that in 1865 this Act comes into operation, and *five-sixths* of the existing railway mileage will eventually become subject to its provisions.

This measure was introduced into Parliament by Mr. Gladstone, then President of the Board of Trade, in Sir Robert Peel's administration, and passed through under his charge. For a considerable time previous to its introduction there had been not only great dissatisfaction on the part of the public with railway management, but also to some extent with the system itself. The belief was universal that the country did not derive as much benefit from its railways as some continental countries did from theirs, where they had been constructed by the State, and were managed under the immediate control of their respective Governments.

On the opening of the Parliamentary Session of 1844 a

committee, composed of some of the leading members of the House of Commons, was appointed " to consider whether any or what new provisions ought to be introduced in such railway bills as would come before the House during that or any future session, for the advantage of the public and the improvement of the railway system." This committee was nominated and presided over by Mr. Gladstone, and there were examined before it nearly all the principal men of the country connected with railways. The evidence of these gentlemen formed the groundwork on which the committee framed its reports, and the measure subsequently introduced into Parliament was in accordance with the recommendation of the committee.

Although there were clauses in this bill relating to other matters connected with railways than their purchase by Government, yet to enable the Government at a future time to effect this object was the main purpose for which the Act was passed. "The question," said Mr. Gladstone, on introducing it to the House, " of the whole bill is the purchase or option of purchase on the part of Government: if we agree about that we shall not quarrel about the rest; on the other hand, if we differ about that, it will be a question for our consideration whether we will take the rest, or postpone the whole till a future period."

Sir Robert Peel likewise took a warm interest in the success of the measure. He was not prepared, he said, on the second reading of the bill, "to advise the immediate purchase of railways, nor did he wish to see the Government, or part of the Government, the directors of railway concerns; but, seeing that there was a monopoly with respect to conveyance and communication, the Legislature should have the power of purchasing, after a certain period, after giving due notice thereof to the parties concerned. They were about to say to the railway companies, '*You shall not have a permanent monopoly against the public,* but after a limited number of years we give you notice we shall have the option of purchasing your property.'" Such were the opinions held by Sir Robert Peel on this subject, which induced his Government to bring forward, and carry through Parliament, the bill in question. The second reading was opposed, but carried by a majority of nearly two to one; and on the third reading, matters having been satisfactorily arranged, all opposition was withdrawn.

The law is therefore complete that enables the Legislature to take the initiatory steps in the next session of Parliament, for the purchase of our railways; but where is the life and spirit to give that law effect? I am compelled to answer, that they do not exist. Neither in the community at large, nor in any section of it, great or small, has there ever been expressed a desire to carry out the object for which this Act was passed. Whatever may be the dissatisfaction with the manner in which our railways are managed, and however loudly that dissatisfaction may at times be expressed, it has not extended to any complaint against the system itself, still less to a demand for that great organic change for which the Government of Sir Robert Peel thought it so necessary to provide. The Railway Act of 1844 may therefore be said to be quite forgotten at the very time it ought to be remembered, and to have become obsolete before it even could be brought into operation; for all practical purposes it is at present a dead letter. Whether or not it can or ought to be revived, is the matter we have now to consider.

It would be difficult in the whole course of our legislative history to find another instance in which a Government measure has been treated with such utter neglect as has fallen to the lot of this unfortunate Act. A committee, composed, as we have seen, of the most eminent men of the House of Commons, after a thorough investigation of the subject, recommended it to the Legislature; after a full discussion in Parliament, the bill passed the third reading without a dissentient voice, and is then—forgotten. Surely such a lame and impotent conclusion, on a matter of such vital importance to the best interests of the country as our traffic on railways undoubtedly is, was never before heard of. One might reasonably have supposed it would have been otherwise. The name of Sir Robert Peel is not yet quite forgotten among us; nor can Mr. Gladstone be called an unknown man; and yet that Act, on which these two certainly not undistinguished men expended so much care and trouble, is virtually defunct. There are scarcely twenty people, perhaps, in the country, unconnected with railways, who have any recollection of it; and very probably those few persons have now very little wish to remember anything about it. Although I shall have frequent occasion to refer to it, and will treat it with every respect, just as if its provisions were to be brought into full force next session of Parliament, it must, nevertheless, be understood, that in doing so I do not differ from others, as to its real position: and when I speak of "the Railway Act of 1844," it will be only for the purpose of rounding a period or giving point to an " idea," as the case may be.

The administration, however, of that day must have been deeply impressed with the importance of the subject, and the necessity of providing a remedy for anticipated evils, when it succeeded in having this Act passed by the Legislature. But why is it despised or forgotten? It may be said in reply, that the very fact of its being in such a position is a sufficient answer to the question; but I altogether demur to such an answer as satisfactory; there may be causes, and in this case I think it will be found that there are causes, which have prevented it from receiving that consideration to which, as I contend, it is justly entitled.

In order more fully to comprehend the motives which induced the Government of Sir Robert Peel to bring this measure forward, it is right to recall to mind not only the principles on which that administration was founded, and the general policy that it carried out, but also the peculiar circumstances that have been in operation having the tendency to render the law in question practically obsolete.

The railway monopoly had in 1844 become very powerful. It had possessed itself of the main channels of communication throughout the country; it had superseded the ordinary means of conveyance; it was to a great extent independent of the Legislature and Government; its abuse of power had become altogether intolerable; and the more the system under these circumstances was extended, the more was this monopoly consolidated and confirmed.

But the subject was one in every respect exceedingly difficult to deal with. In accordance with that traditional policy of this country which leaves to private enterprise the execution and management of our great industrial works, the construction of railways had been, as a matter of course, undertaken by joint-stock companies, and the Legislature, in giving them powers to construct their lines, conferred on them a virtual monopoly of the traffic in the several districts through which their lines ran. But the companies that, up to this time, had obtained their Acts and invested their capital in the works on the faith of Parliament, had constructed upwards of two thousand miles at an expenditure of nearly one hundred millions sterling; hence the impossibility of any attempt to impose obligations on the companies not in accordance with the original agreement.

The public feeling on the management of railway affairs at home was not much gratified by a comparison with the way in which they were managed abroad. Belgium was the first of the continental kingdoms to establish a railway system; the railways were constructed by the State, and a very low and nearly uniform tariff, at about *one-third* of the average English rates, was adopted.

As the Legislature was debarred from passing an *ex post facto* law in regard to the companies that had already been incorporated, and had expended their capital, Government determined on adopting such precautionary measures in regard to future railways as the nature of the case might require, and for the purpose of fully investigating all matters connected with railway legislation, the committee I have referred to was, at the instance of Government, appointed. This committee sat for the greater part of the session, and, after a thorough investigation of the subject in all its bearings, came to the conclusion that it was inexpedient at that time to make such an organic change in our system as the purchase of railways by the State would involve; but that it was desirable to adopt such measures as would enable the Legislature to carry such a purpose into effect if it so thought fit, at a future period, and an Act to that effect was passed.

Under these circumstances it is desirable that the public, whose attention has not been in any way directed to the subject since the year 1844, and then but very partially, should be enabled to form a judgment on the general merits of the two systems—the one founded on the possession and management of the railways by joint-stock companies for their own benefit; the other on their possession by the State, and their management entrusted by the Legislature to those whom it should consider best qualified to perform that office.

In 1844, when the expediency of the purchase of railways by the State was first mooted in Parliament, the subject was not only little understood, but there existed, almost universally, strong preconceived opinions, not only utterly erroneous in themselves, but of such a nature as in a great measure to stop *in limine* all investigation of the subject. Nor were these opinions confined to those who, from their position in society, might naturally be supposed to be without the means of acquiring due information, but nearly all classes, even those who undertook to enlighten the ignorant, shared with them alike in the popular errors.

There existed at this time two prevailing ideas in the public mind in regard to railways, that had a very unfortunate effect; one was, that the charges on a railway must bear a certain proportion to the cost of its construction; and as the cost of English railways was exceedingly heavy, so the charges by them under any system, according to popular opinion, must always be very great. The other idea was, that if railways were the property of the State, they must necessarily be managed by Government, when there would be a great addition to its patronage and power, and the management might be still worse than it had been by the companies.

The *Quarterly Review* had an article on Railway Legislation in its number for July that year; and in criticising a publication that advocated a reduction of fares in this country to the level of those charged in Belgium, thus attempted to prove the impossibility of such a reduction being effected, without great loss to the State:—

"Let us look," said the reviewer, "at the expense of making the respective lines, as stated in Mr. Laing's report:—

	Cost of Construction.
Average of the 71 railways of England	£34,360
Average of Belgium	17,120

Will any one pretend that a thing which costs £40,000 ought to be furnished in detail to the public as cheap as if it had cost only £17,000 ? But is it not curious to find that the average expense of the Belgium lines turns out to be so exactly the one-half of the average of the British lines, as are the fares on the railways ?"

Is it not more curious, it might in reply be asked, if, as a general rule, it will be found that the English railways on which the greatest amount of capital per mile has been expended, are precisely those on which the charges are the lowest? The Charing Cross Railway, for instance, cost a million and a half sterling per mile, and passengers are carried at a lower rate on it than on some railways that were constructed at *the hundredth part of that cost.* The reviewer, it will be seen, fell into the prevailing error of confounding the cost of the *machinery* by which the passengers were conveyed with the cost of the conveyance itself, and does not seem to have been aware that when the fares exceed the actual expense incurred in conveyance, it becomes a mere question of numbers as to what fares best pay.

The second error I have referred to was not less prevalent than the first. It was universally assumed, as a matter of course, that the possession of railways by the State necessarily involved their management by Government; and although this fallacy, as well as the previous one, is too transparent to be seriously discussed, there are still many who do not perceive the broad distinction that exists between ownership and management. It might with just as much truth be contended, that the purchaser of an estate must necessarily farm it himself, as that the owner of a railway should himself be obliged to manage it. In 1844 the whole force of opposition was directed against this imaginary necessity. It is scarcely necessary here to observe, that any scheme in regard to the possession of railways by the State that would involve their direct management by Government, or greatly increase its power and patronage, would never in this country receive the sanction of public opinion.

It is easy, under these circumstances, to understand how little the Government plan for the future purchase of railways was appreciated at the time it was introduced: "As railways cost in this country double or treble per mile more than they do on the Continent," it was said, "so the fares must always remain in the same proportion, and badly as the companies manage here, the Government management would be still worse." Further, the Act could not come into operation till after the expiration of twenty-one years, and then only contingently; therefore, its future results were of no immediate interest to any one.

In addition to these special reasons we must add the great dislike entertained in this country against Government interference in mercantile affairs even in cases that many might deem absolutely necessary, and the little distinction drawn between the possession and management of railways and that of other industrial works of a *quasi* public nature.

"The *laissez faire* system," says Mr. Porter, in his "Progress of the Nation," "which is pursued in this country to such an extent that it has become an axiom with the Government to undertake nothing and to interfere with nothing which can be accomplished by individual enterprise, or by the associated means of private parties, has been pregnant with great loss and inconvenience to the country in carrying forward the railway system. Perhaps there never was an occasion in which the Government could with equal propriety have interfered to reconcile the conflicting interests involved, and to prevent public injury arising from the false steps so likely to be made at first in bringing about a total revolution in the internal communication of the country. It is not meant by these remarks to infer that Government should have taken into its own hands the construction of all, or any, of the railroads called for by the wants of the community, but only to suggest the propriety and advantage that must have resulted from a preliminary inquiry made by competent and uninterested professional men, with a view to ascertain the comparative advantages and facilities offered by different lines for the accomplishment of the object in view. If this course had been adopted before any of the numerous projects were brought forward for the construction of lines of railway between all imaginable places, and if it had been laid down as a rule by the Legislature that no such projected line could be sanctioned by Parliament which was not in accordance with the reports and recommendations of the Government engineers, the saving of money would have been immense." *

Mr. Porter appears to have forgotten how little the Government of a free country can do when it attempts to initiate a

---

* Sec. iii. chap. 5.

policy, however wise in itself, that is opposed to the feelings and prejudices of the people.

From the time the Act was passed till the present, the subject has remained in abeyance; but, next year, in the ordinary course of events, it may again come before Parliament, as the twenty-one years of probation granted to the present system will have expired. All the facts, figures, and arguments bearing on the merits of the two systems ought to be fully investigated by a Parliamentary committee, and the twenty-one additional years of experience we have had of railway management be turned to profitable account. For the purpose of preparing the public mind in some degree for this subject, if the occasion arise, the following treatise has been written. As there are many, however, who would wish to have first, before entering on details, a general conception of its nature, to know the precise objects sought to be attained by the transfer of the railways from the companies to the State, and why those objects cannot be attained under the present system, a brief introduction will be desirable.

The distinctive policy that marked the accession to power of Sir Robert Peel in 1841, was the substitution to a considerable extent of direct taxation in the form of an income tax for indirect taxation on the principal necessaries of life. "Give me," said Sir Robert Peel in effect, " a direct payment of five millions per annum, and I shall be able to reduce your taxation on tea, coffee, sugar, and all the other necessaries of life to the amount of twenty millions per annum," and he redeemed the pledge he gave to the nation. He made a reduction in the indirect taxation of the country that would have reduced the revenue by that amount, had there been no increase in the consumption of those articles on which the reduction of duty had been made; but the natural elasticity of the country, relieved of such a burthen, made up by increased consumption three-fourths of the loss to the revenue, and the income tax paid the remaining fourth.

We shall find, in the course of our investigation, that on this principle—but with a very important difference in matters of detail—was founded the Railway Act of 1844. Locomotion is one of the great necessaries of life, and then, as now, the means of locomotion throughout the country was a monopoly in the hands of private individuals, whose charges for the conveyance of passengers and goods were enormously disproportioned to its cost. The proprietors of railways, with very few exceptions, found it was more to their advantage to carry the comparatively few at high fares than the multitude at low fares, and neither the Legislature nor the Government had any right to interfere with their charges, inasmuch as they were strictly legal. What Government, however, had a right to do and did do was this; it induced the Legislature to pass an Act by which, after a limited number of years, the right of purchase, on certain specified terms, should revert to the nation, when the same policy could be carried out in regard to the charges on railways as had already been pursued in reference to our postal rates, and to our customs and excise duty.

It is highly probable, however, that the success of the Post-Office Reform scheme, which had been then several years in operation, had no small influence in inducing the Government to follow the course it did in respect to railways; and as the objects to be attained were in some respects analogous, we shall briefly notice the principles on which the Post-Office Reform Bill was based.

The gross amount of the Post-Office revenue in 1839 was, in round numbers, 2,400,000*l*., the net revenue 1,400,000*l*., and the number of letters conveyed 75,000,000. The postage varied according to distance from twopence to two shillings for a single letter, and any inclosure, however small, had the effect of doubling the postage. There had been for many years

c

great complaints of these high rates, but till Mr. (now Sir) Rowland Hill took the matter up, no step was taken towards reducing them. Sir Rowland Hill directed special attention to three matters :—1st, that the conveyance of a letter from one end of the kingdom to the other cost less than half a farthing ; 2nd, the great disproportion that existed between the cost of conveyance and the charge to the public ; and 3rd, the enormous increase that might be expected to take place in the number of letters conveyed by post, if the average postage was reduced to *one-sixth* of the then existing rates. The nation adopted Sir Rowland Hill's scheme, the average postage of sixpence on each letter was reduced to the uniform rate of a penny ; and we all know with what result.

The same principles applied with equal force to the conveyance of passengers and goods by railway as to the conveyance of letters by mail coach : there were the same high charges to the public compared with the cost of conveyance, and a great increase of passengers and goods might be expected by making a material reduction in those charges. Government, however, found itself in 1844 comparatively powerless to act with immediate effect in the matter, further than by entering into an arrangement with the old companies for the establishment of Parliamentary trains, and thereby securing to the working population, what they much needed, a very considerable reduction in charge, and some degree of comfort in travelling. There was not then in the opinion of Government sufficient experience of the working of railways by joint-stock companies to justify Government in recommending the Legislature to pass a bill for the purchase of railways then made, nor did it desire to have constructed at the public cost those railways that might be considered necessary to complete our system ; the middle course was adopted of securing the right of purchase, with its exercise reserved till a distant time.

The amount paid by the public to railway companies is now

increasing at the rate of more than two millions sterling per annum: in 1862 twenty-nine millions were paid; last year the income of the railways was thirty-one millions; this year it will amount to nearly thirty-four millions; and next year it will, probably, equal in amount the one-half of all our taxation! There is virtually no legal control over the fares and charges the companies make to the public; in some localities they are double, treble, or quadruple what they are in others—the interest of each company being its only guide, and the interests of the public entirely subsidiary to those of the companies.

Mr. Gladstone, on introducing the Railway Bill,* stated the principal reasons which induced the Government to bring it forward: the first of which was the vast increase that might, in the course of twenty years, be expected to take place in the payments of the public to the companies, and the consequent necessity at the expiration of that term of revising our present system of management—at that time the receipts of the companies amounted only to five millions per annum,—"But I do not think," said Mr. Gladstone, "that it will be a very extravagant estimate for me to assume that, in fifteen or twenty years, the payment by the public will reach to *fifteen millions* a year." Now, inasmuch as the estimated receipts of the companies for next year amount to fully THIRTY-SIX MILLIONS; and it would appear that Mr. Gladstone thought it desirable that the right of purchase should revert to the State when the payments to the companies by the public would amount to FIFTEEN millions—it follows that, according to the opinion then entertained by Mr. Gladstone, the time has long since arrived when the expediency of exercising that right should be discussed, and, if found desirable, be claimed by the Legislature.

There is, in one respect, a very important difference

* Mr. Gladstone's speech on the second reading of the Railway Bill, and the Act itself, will be found in Appendix IV.

between the Post-Office reform and the Railway reform projected by the Act of 1844. The great, and indeed the only, objection that ever had been made to the adoption of Sir Rowland Hill's scheme was the heavy loss it would entail, for many years at least, on the revenue; nor was this point disputed by Sir Rowland Hill; for the first few consecutive years there was a loss of a million per annum to the revenue, nor was it till last year that the net revenue, under the new system, equalled that of the old.

It would be a very different matter, in a financial point of view, to carry into effect the Railway Act of 1844. What is called "the purchase of railways by Government" would, if carried out as I suggest, be in effect an operation by which railway stock would, in a certain sense, be converted into Government stock, and its market value thereby increased in the proportion of $3\frac{1}{2}$ to 5, the profits of the transaction being shared in equal proportions by the State and the companies. To the profit the State would have from the transaction would be added the great saving effected by the amalgamation of all the railways under one general management; that is, on the supposition that a simultaneous arrangement could be made by Government with the great bulk of the companies; otherwise, if no better plan could be adopted, the Government purchase could be carried out in detail, according to the Act, as each company came severally within its provisions.

The exceedingly low cost at which passengers can be conveyed on railways is the broad foundation on which Railway Reform rests. Every one will admit that a very low tariff would greatly increase the traffic, but we cannot tell beforehand precisely to what extent. Could we ascertain that, the whole question could be solved to a mathematical certainty. But we can only approximate to a solution of that problem. We shall find, in the course of our inquiry, that the difference of fares within certain limits makes but little difference in the profits, and that there is every reason to believe the possession of railways by the State would enable Government to effect such arrangements as to have passengers conveyed at *one-third* of the present average fares without any assistance from the Treasury, and a proportionate reduction made on freightage.

It may, at first sight, appear to many, taking into consideration the small dividends that some companies pay, impossible for Government to make such a reduction in the fares without incurring a heavy loss, but the case in that respect is entirely analogous to that of the Post Office—it is a mere question of numbers. The reduction made on the Post-Office charges amounted to 84 per cent., and the reduction proposed on railway charges amounts only to 66 per cent. And we have seen that the Post Office, after reducing its postage rates from an average charge of sixpence on each letter to a uniform rate of a penny, without any extraneous aid, by the mere increase of numbers, returns now to the exchequer the same amount of net revenue as it did previous to the change. But, in regard to any reduction of fares and charges on our railways that the Legislature, under the new system, might determine on, there would be a reserve fund that might be calculated at *five millions sterling* to make up the loss incurred by reduced rates.

I have assumed in this treatise that a reduction on our railways to *one-third* of the present average rates would fully meet the wants and wishes of the public, and that would appear, by the reference made by Mr. Gladstone in his speech to the fares in Belgium, to have been the reduction that he intended.

"I believe," said Mr. Gladstone, "that the charges on the Belgium railways are not more than *one-third* of our charges. We must look at this subject in all its vastness and in all its bearings. It may be said that England is the richest country; but because this country is rich, it is no sound reason why it should pay the railway companies more than necessary, or that cheap travelling should not be provided for the public. But there is no likelihood that *the great experiment of the greatest possible cheapness* to the public will be tried under the present system." The companies are, unfortunately, much more inclined to try the experiment of the greatest possible dearness than that of cheapness.

Another point, which Mr. Gladstone thought of great importance, was the great saving that would be effected in the management by the amalgamation of all the companies. He quoted the opinion of Captain Laws, a man of great experience in railway management, that through these means alone " a saving of 25 per cent. would be effected to the public." It is to be observed that no provision whatever is made in the Act in reference to the management of the companies in the event of the railways being purchased by the State: that was left an open question, not then necessary to be disposed of, or ripe for settlement.

When the subject is mooted for the first time of the possibility of effecting a great reduction in fares if railways were the property of the State, there are few who can believe in the possibility of a great reduction in charges being made without loss to the revenue; they very naturally say: " Railway proprietors receive, on an average, only four per cent. for their money—how would it be possible then for Government to carry passengers at *one-third* of the present rates without incurring an enormous loss? I can, perhaps, best explain how that can be done by means of an illustration. If, in some part of the country, we saw an omnibus passing daily backwards and forwards, carrying on an average not more than two persons each journey, and the fare a shilling for the trip, and perceived at the same time a great number of persons pursuing the same route on foot; we might feel inclined to ask the driver why the proprietor did not charge a lower fare rather than have his omnibus travelling comparatively empty? The inquirer might possibly be told in reply, that the proprietor had tried every variation in fares, and although the profits of the concern paid him only four per cent. on the money he had invested, yet he had found a shilling fare and carrying two passengers more profitable than a lower fare with an increased number of passengers. He had tried sixpenny fares; that certainly had doubled the number of his passengers and had not increased his expenditure, but he made nothing by it. He was told then he did not go low enough, and that fourpenny fares would pay best, as they would, if his omnibus would fill, on the journey of only two miles. Well, the proprietor had tried that for six months, and found it did not answer; he did not carry more than five on an average each trip, and he was put to some little extra expense: he lost by the change and got only three and a half per cent. interest for his money. Finally, he came back to his old charge of a shilling a head, his two passengers, and his four per cent. interest.

Now if we substitute one hundred millions of passengers by railway for the one passenger we have assumed that travels by the omnibus, we have a case exactly parallel. The omnibus travels with the one-tenth part of the number it is capable of conveying, and so do the trains; if the omnibus carried five persons instead of two, the increase in expense would be scarcely appreciable, and in like manner with the trains. The omnibus man finds that it is rather more to his advantage to charge a shilling than a fourpenny fare; the one pays him four per cent. on his money, the other not more than three and a half; in like manner, if railway directors would lower their fares to one-third of their present average charges, it is not probable that such a reduction would increase the number of travellers quite threefold, and even if it should have that effect why should the companies carry three persons when they can obtain as much for one? There would not only be a slight increase in the expense for additional wear and tear, but a considerable increase of work in the several establishments, for which they would obtain no remuneration whatever. This illustration will, I trust, render sufficiently clear the causes which render it impossible that the low fare system can as a rule ever be adopted by railway companies. Can any reasonable man expect that a company paying, for instance, five per cent. to their shareholders would reduce their charges one-half, with the certain knowledge that such a reduction in their fares would reduce their dividend from five to four and a half per cent. and the market price of their shares from par to ten per cent. discount?

Nearly every one believes, when he hears first of the purchase of railways by Government and a great reduction in fares, that this is to be brought about by some proposed change of management; but management in the ordinary sense of that term has nothing to do with the matter. The State is one thing, and the Government that administers the affairs of the State for the time being, well or ill as the case may be, is quite another. Whether the management of railways after being purchased by the State should be undertaken solely by Government, or be conducted essentially as it is at present, or a middle course be adopted, would be for the Legislature to settle in whatever way would seem most in accordance with the general feeling of the country. All this is a matter of detail, very important no doubt; but the essential *principle* of the Act of 1844 was the transfer of the railways to the Government. The fund which the Government would acquire by the substitution of public for private credit, would enable it to make a vast reduction in fares and freightage by the application of this fund to indemnify the revenue against the deficit that might be expected as the natural consequence of these low charges.

We shall see, in the course of our investigation, that a first-class passenger can be conveyed, in a railway train carrying a fair load, *sixteen miles for a penny*, a second-class passenger *twenty-five miles for a penny*, and a third-class passenger *forty miles for a penny*, and that these fares would include all expenses, direct and indirect, of conveyance. It is obvious, therefore, that carrying first-class passengers, even at a fare so low as a *farthing* per mile, and the other classes in proportion, *might* pay better than if the fares were ten times higher, and *would* pay better if a sufficient number travelled.

To carry by one operation the Act of 1844 into full effect, would require not only the assent but the cordial support of three parties: these are severally THE NATION, THE SHAREHOLDERS, and THE GOVERNMENT. Each party, to a certain extent, has separate interests and motives of action, and therefore requires separate consideration.

1st. The Nation generally, it may be safely predicated, would gladly accept any scheme by which the fares would be reduced to one-third of their present average rates, and made uniform throughout the country; which would effect a similar reduction in the carriage of merchandise, minerals, and parcels; and would secure to all classes in the kingdom, not only a very low tariff, but the adoption of such precautionary measures for the safety of the traveller as it is now vain to look for. In a word, which would substitute for the present system one that would give to the nation all the advantages to be derived from a very low rate of transit, combined with an improved management directly responsible to the Legislature for its administration of affairs.

2nd. The Shareholders, it may be supposed, would be very willing to concur in any arrangement that would largely increase the value of their property. Railway property has very much improved within the last few years, and this has been mainly owing to the conservative policy of the present Legislature in refusing its sanction to the construction of new lines which would inflict injury on the old companies. But what security have the shareholders for the continuance of such a line of policy? Who can foresee what influences may be brought to bear on the future House of Commons so soon to be elected, and what view the railway committees of that House may take of their duty to the public? Railway shareholders know well that nothing can be more undefined and precarious than the protection they receive from the Legislature, the uncertainty of its continuance, and the heavy losses they would incur if subjected to unrestricted competition. Nor can there be any reasonable doubt that the great bulk of railway proprietors would be willing to exchange a certainty for an uncertainty, and co-operate with the Government in any great financial change from which they would derive their fair share of profit and necessarily increase the value of their shares.

3rd. The Government, it is only reasonable to suppose, would be willing to give effect to an Act which would confer such benefits on the country. When Government introduced this measure in 1844, it laboured, as we have seen, under the great disadvantage of having to encounter the prejudice arising from the erroneous belief that, if railways were purchased by the State, they must necessarily be managed by Government, and free action was in consequence to a great extent paralyzed. The Act was considered by a very large class as a covert measure, on the part of Government, to increase its influence, patronage, and power. It will be seen, however, that the Act has in it no provision of the kind, nor that any essential change in the present management is necessary, further than making it more stringent, the directors more immediately responsible to the Legislature, the rights of the public more clear, and their claim for compensation in case of wrong doing more easily enforced, than is the case at present. There can be no doubt the country would hail with satisfaction the announcement that Government had determined to carry into practical effect the Railway Act of 1844.

The *Quarterly Review*, in the article I have already quoted, thus truly and forcibly alludes to the imperial dimensions the subject would one day assume. "It is impossible," said the reviewer, "not to see that the system is developing itself to such an extent, penetrating all districts, superseding all other communications, affecting every species of public and private interests, and acting as the life-blood arteries of the empire, as to render it probable, almost to certainty, that the time must come when this great public trust can no longer be left to the management of private companies scattered over the face of the country. In truth, it seems only a question of time; railways must be made subject to some unity of management, and through whatever intermediate process it may pass, that management must finally be vested in the Government of the country."

At the time this article was written for the *Quarterly*, the payments to the companies, as we have seen, little exceeded five millions sterling; but at the rate the system is now developing itself, in two or three years more, the payments to the companies, if no change takes place, will exceed the whole amount paid by the country in customs and excise duties, for they are still going on increasing year by year, to an extent not definable by any limits. It surely, then, is time for our statesmen to grapple with this huge question, and devise some scheme for the consideration of the country, by which this "*Imperium in Imperio*" that is now erecting itself in the kingdom shall be abolished, and the whole system brought under the immediate control of the Legislature.

The average fares on English railways may be taken at *twopence farthing* per mile for first class, *three halfpence* for second class, and *one penny* for third; and a reduction to *three farthings*, a *halfpenny*, and *one farthing* per mile for the several classes, and a proportionate reduction in the charges for general merchandise, minerals, cattle, &c., and a uniform rate for small parcels, would, I have no doubt, give great and general satisfaction to the public.

The practical question we have to consider is, Whether or not a reduction of fares and charges on railways to *one-third* of their present average rate, without any charge on the revenue, could be at once effected on the principle of Mr. Gladstone's Act?

Let us first assume, for the sake of argument, that such a change in public feeling had taken place on the subject of railway proprietorship and management as to render an alteration in our present system possible, and that it only remained for the Government to devise a scheme, and the Legislature to give it the power of law, by which railways would become national property, subject to the immediate control of the Legislature. It must be premised that, as the main object in carrying out such a project would be with the view of making a very large reduction in the charges for passengers and goods, a moderately low tariff would be adopted.

There are three different plans by which the assumed wishes of the country in this respect could be carried into effect. The best, most economical, and efficient one would be for the State itself to make such railways as the Legislature, after due inquiry, might deem necessary.

Whatever may have been the errors and shortcomings of the Legislature in regard to its dealings with railway companies, it took care to let the companies know that at all times and under all circumstances the PUBLIC GOOD alone should be the paramount object in view, and that it reserved to itself the right of granting, at a future time, as many competing lines as the necessity of the case might require; nor has the right of the Government to lay down competing lines been ever for a moment questioned. The subject was especially brought under the notice of some of the leading representatives of the railway interest by Mr. Gladstone, when presiding over the committee in 1844. Mr. Glyn, then chairman of the London and Birmingham Company, and who subsequently held, for many years, the same office in the London and North-Western Company, expressed his opinion very clearly and distinctly on this point, as the following short extract from his examination will show:—

"Mr. Gladstone.—It would be perfectly possible, would it not, that the Government itself might undertake to make a competing line, and work that line in such a way as to effect a reduction of charges upon the public, both upon the old line and the new one?—*Certainly; there would be nothing to prevent it.*

"Assuming that to be the case, and assuming that would be the proper remedy for excessive rates and charges, do you think that that would be the best plan that could be adopted under the circumstances?—*I would much rather see a competing line in the hands of Government than in the hands of a private company.*"

Exception may perhaps be taken to the form in which Mr. Gladstone put the question in reference to the contingency that would necessitate the construction of a new line—viz. "excessive rates and charges" on the old line—but these may surely be deemed excessive, inasmuch as they often exceed twentyfold the cost incurred, or what might be incurred under a proper system of management.

Let it be admitted, then, that the State, acting with the most perfect good faith towards railway proprietary, should determine on laying out, in the first instance, a comparatively small sum in the construction of four trunk lines radiating from the metropolis to the north-west as far as Liverpool, to the south as far as the present lines extend, to the west as far as Exeter, and to the north-east as far as Norwich, with branches from all the trunk lines to the principal towns on their respective routes, but the trunk lines in the first instance to be completed. The new railways would be constructed at about *one-third* of the cost of the old lines, and the engineers who laid out the new lines would no doubt be instructed to lay them out as distant as circumstances would permit from the old lines, for the double purpose of doing the least possible injury to the old companies, and providing additional railway accommodation, in those parts of the country not well supplied.

According to the testimony of Mr. Brydges Adams, an engineer of the greatest experience and authority, a railway could now be constructed from London to Liverpool—200 miles—for three millions sterling. The interest on that sum, if borrowed by Government, would be about £100,000 per annum. If Government would think it expedient to carry first-class passengers at a farthing a mile, and the other classes in due proportion, and goods, minerals, &c., at rates varying from a farthing to a penny per ton per mile, from London to Liverpool, and *vice versâ*, those charges would yield a very great profit on the cost of transit, including the wear and tear of the line and an ample allowance for the expense of management. Now, if a line was constructed by Government, and this—with reference to other lines—comparatively low tariff adopted, it would not only pay the interest on the capital, but possibly yield a large revenue.

Four thousand miles of railways judiciously laid out, and constructed at a cost of fifty millions, would afford accommodation to all the principal towns in the United Kingdom; the annual interest to be paid on the capital would be considerably less than two millions per annum; and there can be no doubt that, with the tariff I have named, a very large revenue, after the payment of interest, would accrue to the State, even divided as the traffic would be between the companies and the Government lines.

Now, so far as the general interests of the community are concerned, there could hardly be two opinions as to the best mode of providing the public with the means of cheap travelling, and, as a matter of course, a uniform tariff throughout the country at *a farthing* per mile, in the case we have supposed, for first-class passengers, and the others in due proportion, would give great and general satisfaction.

But let us carry the case a little further. The Chancellor of the Exchequer we will suppose, when he opens his budget a few months hence, will be able to make the agreeable announcement that he can reduce the taxation of the country a couple of millions, but that, instead of giving up twopence in the pound of the income tax, he will propose that fifty or sixty millions be laid out in the construction of a network of State railways, and that the charges on the lines shall amount only to the actual cost of conveyance, together with a sufficient percentage added to maintain the lines in working order and defray the general expenses. Under this arrangement, first-class passengers would be conveyed, from London to Edinburgh, 400 miles, for *two shillings and a penny*, instead of the present fare, three pounds ten shillings; second-class, *one shilling and sixpence*, instead of two pounds ten shillings; and third-class, *one shilling*, instead of one pound thirteen shillings and fourpence. Coals, minerals, and general merchandise would be carried at rates, not exceeding, on an average, one-tenth those at present. Packages that the companies now charge six shillings for carrying would be conveyed for half as many pence; and parcels seven pounds in weight, the carriage of which varies from sixpence to three shillings, according to distance, might be assimilated to the penny-postage rate, and a uniform charge of a penny made for each without reference to distance!

Several years would necessarily elapse before the works could be constructed; ten years, we will suppose, from the present time, when our railway payments, increasing as they are at the rate of two millions per annum, will amount to FIFTY MILLIONS STERLING, or some ten millions in excess of all customs and excise duties combined. But on the morning of the 1st of January, 1876, the Government lines would be completed and opened to the public at charges in which shillings would be substituted for pounds, so that what the public in 1875 paid fifty millions for, in 1876 would be procured for the one-twentieth part of that sum, and all this would be brought about by the direct payment, on the part of the nation, of two millions per annum!

We will not enter on any calculation as to the amount the country up to that time would have lost, or whether what has been recklessly squandered away would have been sufficient to pay off the national debt. Nations, as well as individuals, must pay for any eccentricities they may be pleased to indulge in, and if, from feelings of fancied independence, a nation thinks proper to abandon its legitimate duties, and permits the work to be done by proxy which should be done by itself alone in its corporate capacity, it cannot complain of being obliged to pay the heavy penalty which such a course of policy inevitably entails. In Belgium, where, it is well-known, an opposite system was pursued to that followed in this country, and the railways were constructed by the State, and managed under the direct responsibility of Government, the charges have not exceeded on an average *one-third* of those made with us, and not only that, but the debt the Government incurred by the construction of the railways has, from that time, been gradually reduced by the appropriation of the profits arising from the traffic for that purpose. In 1884, the railway debt will be completely paid off, and the Belgian people will be able, from that time forth, either to avail themselves of the excessively low rates when only the actual expenses of transit are charged, or be in a position to decrease largely the general taxation of the country by continuing the present charges on the railways.

We have to deal, however, with a different state of affairs in this country. Four hundred and fifty millions sterling, under our system, have been expended. A great part of this enormous sum has been squandered away in doing what might have been better done under a national system for, perhaps, *one-third* of the money; useless competing lines, under such a system, would never have been made, and the reckless cost incurred in carrying bills through Parliament avoided. Although the nation and the Legislature are free to act in regard to the construction of lines, that liberty will, nevertheless, be found to be more nominal than real; inasmuch as the course I have indicated, of the State constructing new lines, and carrying without profit, would be tantamount to confiscating all the existing railway property of the country. Mr. Glyn, as we have seen, gave an unqualified assent to the right of the State to construct competing lines, but, as a matter of course, he never assumed that the State would construct and work lines without, at least, securing such a return from the railways as would pay the interest on the capital invested. Mr. Hudson, however, was more cautious in giving an opinion as to the right of the State to construct competing lines. "I do not question," said Mr. Hudson, "the right of the State to make railways, but they must first buy up the old lines." Mr. Hudson, in my opinion, took the right view of the case. It would be exceedingly unjust to bring the resources of the State into competition with private individuals, without first giving the latter the option of retiring on liberal terms.

There are few men in modern times who have done more to advance the great truths of economic science than Mr. Edwin Chadwick; and in a paper he read some years since before the Statistical Society, he thus described " competition within " what he terms " the field of service ":—

"From 1838 to 1841, whilst examining the sanitary conditions of town populations, I found urban districts in England, where there are two or three sets of water-pipes carried through streets which might be as well or better supplied under one establishment, and competitions ending in strict monopolies, bad and deficient supplies at high charges to the public, with low dividends to the shareholders, and an almost impracticability of improvement in their separate condition without augmenting the already excessive charges of the ratepayers or further reducing the low returns to the capitalists. These competitions are what I then designated as competitions 'within the field of service.' As opposed to that form of competition, I proposed, as an administrative principle, competition '*for* the field,' that is to say, that the whole field of service should be put up on behalf of the public for competition,—on the only condition on which efficiency, as well as the utmost cheapness, was practicable, namely, the possession, by one capital or by one establishment, of the entire field, which could be most efficiently and economically administered by one, with full securities towards the public for the performance of the requisite service during a given period. The principle was, upon due consideration, extensively adopted and advocated by permanent public officers, commissioners and disinterested public investigators for the regulation of enterprises in railways, then at their commencement;* but the views chiefly advocated by speculators and persons who profit by multiplied conflicts—who gain whosoever else lose—were adopted by Parliament. The principle was, however, upon independent consideration, adopted by the continental administrators and legislators, and the results stand out in wide and undeniable contrast of legislative and administrative ability and integrity; —in France, for example, in a much more responsible and more regular service for the public at lower fares, with higher-priced materials, with dearer fuel, poorer, thinner, and less active population, and lower elements of traffic; and yet, with an average return of from seven to nine per cent. to the original shareholders of the lines worked by companies. In England we have a clashing, immensely more dangerous, unsatisfactory, and generally less responsible service to the public, fares, as contrasted with the continental fares, generally one-third higher, with fuel, iron, and machinery cheaper, and population and traffic more active; yet with only an average return of 3·06 per cent. to the original shareholders, with

* *Vide*, amongst other expositions, that contained in the admirable report of Messrs. Drummond and Barlow, Commissioners for Railways in Ireland.

extensive ruin to them—with gigantic fortunes to the promoters of conflicts. In France, the original shareholders have, moreover, the elements of security and further improvement to their property, whilst the French public have in reversion, on the termination of the present concessions, the prospect of further reductions of fares and increased facilities for intercommunication, or a new source of revenue, derivable from past economy in reduction of the general taxation of the country. In England, the greater mass of original shareholders have before them elements of further depreciation, and loss, and even ruin, by the bounty afforded by the practicability of cheaper constructions and by competitive extensions, that are not to be averted by the patchings of quarrels or by any combinations of their respective directories,—whilst the public have the main arteries of communication—which ought with sound legislation to be as cheap and free as any in the world—clogged with inconveniences and even with delays as well with high charges, amounting to between six and seven millions per annum in excess at the present time, of what a sound administrative principle would have insured. The maladministration which has incurred the excessive outlays—which maintains nearly a hundred separate chief and independent establishments, at the expense of the shareholders, and to the inconvenience and loss of the public in working—seeks to impose these excessive charges upon the public by high fares, and does so in defiance of the experience thus enunciated by an observer of railway administration, that 'There is hardly an exception to the rule, that a high fare produces a low amount of traffic and stunts its growth, while a low or moderate fare collects a larger amount of traffic and fosters growth.'" *

I have extended this preface beyond the limits usual in such cases, as I am desirous, before we enter on the subject to be discussed, that its nature and object should be clearly defined and understood. There are also many persons who would wish to understand the elementary principles of Railway Reform without any desire to examine in detail the facts on which it is founded and the arguments by which it may be supported, and with that class of readers I must here part company.

* Paper read before the Statistical Society of London, January 18, 1859, by Edwin Chadwick, Esq., C.B.

Railway statistics is not the most inviting subject for pleasant reading. I hope that I have said sufficient to convey a clear idea to their minds of what is sought to be attained by a change of system, and that such a change without loss to the revenue is at least possible.

To that other, and I hope larger class, whom I may be able to persuade to accompany me all the journey, they will remember that inasmuch as a man may travel from Dan to Beersheba and not find it altogether barren, so the traveller who sets out on a journey with a clearly defined object in view may, even in a little-trodden and uninteresting way, pick up some "waifs and strays" that, in the absence of more interesting objects, may serve at least to beguile the tediousness of the way. In a few months this country will be, or at least should be, called on to discuss and come to a decision on a subject involving the most important principles in social and political science; this subject I have endeavoured, to the best of my ability, to elucidate—how far I have been successful the reader must judge for himself.

I should do much injustice to my own feelings if I omitted to express my acknowledgments to Mr. Roebuck for the great assistance I have received from him during the last six months in my humble endeavour to promote the cause of Railway Reform. It is now more than twenty years since I first consulted him as to the desirability of a change being effected in our railway system: although he concurred then generally in my views on the subject, he thought, and I believe correctly, that in the existing state of public opinion nothing more could be done at that time than had been done.

Mr. Horsman was on the Railway Committee of 1844, and was, I believe, the only one of its members who was in favour of the *immediate* purchase of the railways by Government. During the sitting of that Committee, I was in frequent communication with him on the subject, and was indebted to him for much useful information previous to my examination before it. Mr. Horsman did not then succeed, but subsequently he had the satisfaction of having his views, to a great extent, carried out in India: he was the first whom I consulted last session of Parliament, in reference to the expediency of making an endeavour to recall the recollection of the country and the Legislature to the Act of 1844; and from the encouragement I received from him I was induced to make this attempt, with what success time only will show.

November, 1864.

CONTENTS.

PART I.—THE NATION.

CHAPTER I.

PAGE

Introduction—Development of the Railway System—Cost of Locomotion on Railways—High Charges compared with the Cost of Transit—The Cause of High Charges—Difficulty of Companies in fixing their Fares—The Ascending and Descending Scales—Effects of Competition on Dividends—The Right of Companies to charge the best paying Fares—The Effect of High Fares in preventing Travelling—A Hostile Tariff in England—In what Sense Railways are a Monopoly—Report of the Irish Commission—Financial Position of the Companies—Receipts for 1863—Taxation of the Public—Necessity of this Inquiry 1

CHAPTER II.

Jealousy of Government Interference in Commercial Undertakings—The Construction of Railways undertaken by Companies—Opposition they encountered in and out of Parliament—Compensation to Landowners—Expenses of Parliamentary Contests—Non-interference of Government—Parliamentary Committee of 1839—Their Report—Legislative Doubts—Continental Railways—Belgium—France—Germany—Russia—Italy—Spain 19

CHAPTER III.

Progress of Railway Mismanagement from 1840 to 1843—Treatment of Third-Class Passengers—Extract from the "Times," December, 1842—The Companies' Defence—Classification of the Charges against the Companies—Their Reply 31

CHAPTER IV.

Prosperous State of the Country in 1844—Stimulus to Railway Enterprise—Appointment of the Parliamentary Committee—Their Reports—Third-Class Passengers—Parliamentary Trains—Evidence of Mr. (now Sir) Rowland Hill—Opposition of Railway Companies to the Government Bill—Their Arrangement with Government—The Three Fundamental Reforms projected by Government—Sir Robert Peel and Mr. Gladstone 40

CHAPTER V.

Evidence before the Parliamentary Committee of 1844—Mr. Laing, of the Board of Trade—Mr. Saunders, Secretary to the Great Western Railway Company—Mr. G. Carr Glyn, Chairman of the London and Birmingham Company—Mr. Baxendale, Chairman of the South-Eastern Company—Mr. George Hudson—Captain Laws, General Manager of the Leeds and Manchester Railway—Establishment of Parliamentary Trains 50

CHAPTER VI.

Difference between Public and Private Credit—Cost of Mail and Stage Coaches per Mile—Cost of a Railway Train per Mile—The various Items of Expenditure—Expense of carrying Passengers 100 Miles—Fares on Forty-two of the principal Railways in the Kingdom—The Highest, the Medium, and the Lowest Fares contrasted—A Reduction not to be expected—Excursion Trains and Fares—Legitimate Monopolies, Patents and Copyright—Quarrels of Companies—The Working of extremely low Fares exemplified—Proposed Tariff—Much lower Fares in India—Passenger Traffic for 1863 70

CHAPTER VII.

Return for 1863 of "Goods Traffic"—The Charges take the form of indirect Taxation—Charges for the different Classes of Merchandise—Each Company has its own Tariff—Complaints of the Carriers—Cost to the Companies of the Conveyance of Merchandise—Conveyance of Coal to the Metropolis—Its Cost on the Great Eastern Railway—Parcels, Packages, and Hampers—Proposed Tariff for their Conveyance—Post Office—Military and Militia Stores 98

PART II.—THE SHAREHOLDERS.

CHAPTER I.

Advantages possessed by the early Railway Projectors—Their Success—Value of Railway Property in 1845—Amalgamation—The Results of Competition—Quarrels of the great Companies—Their Refusal to abide by the Board of Trade's Recommendations—The Effect on the Value of their Shares—The Benefit to the Public from Competition—Lowering of the Fares throughout the Country—Great Number of unnecessary Lines constructed—Government Plan defeated—Results to the Shareholders—What they have now to consider 116

CHAPTER II.

The Effect of Competition—Some Shareholders favourable to Free Trade—The Duty of Directors—Necessity of opposing Competing Lines—Complaints against Directors—Improved Position of Railway Promoters—New Class of Contractors—Low Rate of Contracts—Complaints of Shareholders—"A fair and reasonable Charge"—Under the present System Competition must continue—Dislike of the English People to Monopoly—Battles of the Companies—Extracts from the last Half-yearly Reports of the great Companies—Great Eastern Northern Junction before Parliament—Railway Affairs in 1844, 1845, and 1846—The Effects of great Prosperity may again be anticipated—Complaints against Parliament—False Position of Shareholders—Struggles to maintain the present System—Mr. Gladstone on the Introduction of the Bill of 1844—A Shareholder at the South-Eastern Meeting—Appeal to the Directors 130

CHAPTER III.

The Right of the Companies to promote the carrying into effect the Bill of 1844—Meaning of the Term "Purchase" of Railways by the State—Superior Value of Government Security over Private Security—Its Effect on the Market Value of Shares—Clause of the Bill relating to Purchase—Different Modes by which it could be effected—Amount of Bonus to Shareholders—The Capital, Revenue, and Dividends of the Thirteen Great Companies—The assumed Bonus that the Legislature might be induced to grant to each 157

PART III.—THE GOVERNMENT.

CHAPTER I.

The late Sir Robert Peel's Opposition to Government Interference in Commercial Affairs—Change of his Opinion in regard to Railways—Extract from his Speech on the Second Reading of the Bill—Improvement in Railway Legislation—Bills for Non-paying Lines at one time refused—Railways that would have been refused Legislative Sanction had the Truth been known—The Value of a Railway to its Shareholders no Criterion of its Value to the Country—The Manchester, Sheffield, and Lincoln Company—The Select Committee of the Two Houses of Parliament—Assistance from the State in constructing Railways that will no pay—Cheaply constructed Railways—Lord Campbell's Act—Comparatively small Loss to Companies by Accidents—Refreshment Rooms 170

CHAPTER II.

The Post Office as managed in former Days—Mr. Rowland Hill's Scheme—Evidence of Post-Office Officials before the Select Committee of the House of Commons—Evidence of Lord Overstone, Lord Ashburton, and Mr. Cobden—Cost of the Conveyance of a Letter—Calculated Increase—System by which the Revenue was defrauded—Free Trade in carrying Letters considered—A well-governed Monopoly in some cases better than Free Trade—Test of the Applicability of Free Trade Principles—The extreme Free Trade Principles applied to Railways—Our Commercial Policy since 1842—The Effect of direct Taxation—What a past President of the Board of Trade has done—What a future Chancellor of the Exchequer may do—The Post Office and Railways compared 193

CHAPTER III.

Mr. Mill on the Functions of Government—Grounds of Opposition to the Bill of 1844—The Right of a Nation to act in its corporate Capacity—Constitutional and practical Objections to increase of Government Power and Patronage—False Issue raised to the Bill by its Opponents—Sir Robert Peel and Mr. Gladstone opposed to the immediate Purchase of Railways—The Management when possessed by the State—Their direct Management by Government not advisable—Their being leased out to Companies considered—The present Management, with some Changes, preferred—A general Board of Management to be formed from the Railway Boards—Plan analogous to that of our India Government—The influence of Legislators in creating and forming Public Opinion 208

CHAPTER IV.

Classification of the Groundwork of Railway Reform—The two main Grounds—Different Charges in Fares on the London and Blackwall Railway—The last Change and its Results—The Glasgow and Greenock Line—The slight Difference in the Results between high and low Fares—Evidence before the Committee of 1844 on the Subject—Railways into London—Displacement of the Poor—Cheap Morning and Evening Trains—The Earl of Derby's Resolution in the House of Lords the most important since the Introduction of Parliamentary Trains—The Effect of Government Purchase on the Money Market 232

CHAPTER V.

The Act of 1844 the Assertion of a Principle—Two Modes of proceeding under it—A strong Case of Necessity required to be made out—Amount of Capital in Railways—Percentage paid on it—Preference Shareholders and Bondholders—Improbability of Shareholders being disinclined to sell to Government—Approaching Half-yearly Meetings—Continued War among the Companies—Extract from the *Westminster Review*—Mr. Watkin on Government Purchase of Railways—Favours Scheme as a Director and Shareholder—Opposes it as a Senator and Citizen—His Arguments—Probable Appointment of a Royal Commission considered 246

CHAPTER VI.

Construction of New Lines laid out by Government Engineers and constructed by Contract—Constructed nearly on the present Plan—Joint Parliamentary Committees of the two Houses preferable—The Reduction of Railway Charges a National Question—Objections against its being considered so—The proper way of discussing the Question—Reduction of Charges amounts to Twenty-four Millions Sterling—Centralization—When it is advantageous—Distinction between Local Duties and those of the State—The Post Office—Objections of the Railway Press considered—Reductions on the Blackwall and Brighton Companies—Future Value of Railways—Exchange of Shares for Stock—*Herapath's* Objections considered—Ireland a convenient Field for trial of Government Control 269

CHAPTER VII.

Railway Receipts in 1865—An Agreement with the Companies to Reduce their Charges—The Justice of a Payment to the Companies for that Purpose—The Extent of Railways throughout the Kingdom—All Classes should derive Benefit from a Reduction in Fares and Freightage—Arbitrary Charges in the Tariff for Merchandise—Adam Smith—Payment to the Companies compared to the Income Tax—The direct and indirect Advantages of a Reduction in Fares and Freightage—Extract from Mr. Mill's "Political Economy"—Committee of the House of Commons—Experiments Suggested—Conclusion—Resumé . 288

APPENDIX I.—THE RAILWAY SYSTEM.

CHAPTER I.

Thomas Gray the first Projector of Railways for the Conveyance of Passengers and Goods—His Scheme for a "General Iron Railway" for the Kingdom—His Endeavours to have it adopted—His Failure and Death—The celebrated Article in the *Quarterly Review* of 1825 on Railways—The Injustice done to the Reviewer—A *Resumé* of the Article . . 313

CHAPTER II.

The Construction of Railways—The Smooth Tracks in Northern Italy—First Tramroads in the Neighbourhood of Newcastle—Tramways at the Close of the Seventeenth Century—Roger North's Description of them to his Brother, Lord Guildford—Derivation of the word "Tram"—George Stephenson—The Narrow, the Medium, and the Broad Gauges—History of the Locomotive—The Marquis of Worcester—Watt—Trevithick . 323

CHAPTER III.

The Nineteenth Century—George Stephenson—Mr. Smiles' "Life of Stephenson"—Killingworth High Pit—The Stockton and Darlington Railway—The Liverpool and Manchester Railway—The great Difficulties to be overcome in its Construction—"Navvies"—Trial of Locomotives on the Liverpool and Manchester Line—Lord Brougham's Speech on its Opening—The Success of the Undertaking established 333

CHAPTER IV.

Progress of Railway Enterprise—The London and Birmingham Line—Great Difficulties in its Construction—The Kilsby Tunnel—Robert Stephenson —Brunel—The Electric Telegraph—Compensation for Land—Charges against Landowners—Their Answer—Mr. Pease—Robert Stephenson lectures before the Institute of Civil Engineers—The Grand Junction Railway—Contractors—Thomas Brassey—The various Developments of the Contract System—Sir Morton Peto 340

CHAPTER V.

Railway Taxation—Its Impolicy and Injustice—The Great Western—The London and South-Western—The London and Greenwich—The South-Eastern—The London and Croydon—Parliamentary Contest for the Brighton Line—The London and Woolwich—The London and Essex—The Eastern Counties 353

CHAPTER VI.

Railway Legislation—Mr. Morrison's Motion—The Session of 1836—The first of the two Railway Manias—The *Edinburgh Review*—How Schemes were got up—The Reaction—Committee of the House of Commons in 1837—Lord Seymour's Act—Mr. Gladstone's Act of 1842—The Clearing House—Railway Department of the Board of Trade—Accidents—The Act of 1844—The Mania of 1845 and its Results . . . 364

APPENDIX II.

Statistical and Financial Sketch of our Railways 371

APPENDIX III.

Clauses of the General Railway Bill of 1844 relating to the Purchase of Railways by Government 384

APPENDIX IV.

Mr. Gladstone's Speech, July 8, 1844, on the Second Reading of the Government Railway Bill 391

RAILWAY REFORM:

ITS IMPORTANCE AND PRACTICABILITY CONSIDERED.

PART I.—THE NATION.

CHAPTER I.

Introduction—Development of the Railway System—Cost of Locomotion on Railways—High Charges compared with the Cost of Transit—The Cause of High Charges—Difficulty of Companies in fixing their Fares—The Ascending and Descending Scales—Effects of Competition on Dividends—The Right of Companies to charge the best paying Fares—The Effect of High Fares in preventing Travelling—A Hostile Tariff in England—In what Sense Railways are a Monopoly—Report of the Irish Commission — Financial Position of the Companies—Receipts for 1863—Taxation of the Public—Necessity of this Inquiry.

I PURPOSE in the following pages to discuss the theory and practice of the railway system as established in this country; to analyze the principles on which it is founded, and develope their results; to consider how far its practical working has proved advantageous to the shareholders on the one hand and to the public on the other; and, lastly, to examine the possibility of effecting an organic change, by which the shareholders would obtain a more secure return for their invested capital, and the public derive a still greater benefit than they now enjoy from the existing organization.

The railway system, developed as it has been in this country, presents the most wonderful combination of professional skill and commercial enterprise that the world has ever witnessed, either in ancient or modern times. Little more than thirty years have elapsed since the extended construction of railways commenced, when the work accomplished by the locomotive, as first displayed on the Liverpool and Manchester line, gave assurance to the world that the new POWER come into existence would, in the conveyance of passengers and goods throughout the kingdom, supersede both the stage coach and the waggon, which may now be considered as the relics of a bygone age, when locomotion was in its infancy, and the power of steam comparatively unknown.

There are few subjects of more importance to us than that which relates to the facilities of transit—the conveyance of passengers and goods throughout the country at the *maximum* of speed and *minimum* of cost; and whilst we have gone on day by day extending, by those mighty instruments of civilization—the steam-engine and the railway—the means of accomplishing this good, we appear, by an acquiescence in the present system of management, to have assumed that no improvement is wanted nor any change required.

The practical application of steam to the useful purposes of life was a gigantic step in the progress of the arts and sciences, and may be justly said to have marked a new era in the history of mankind; few discoveries in physical truth have been attended with more important results, or promise in their future development to produce such mighty changes over the face of the civilized globe. Amongst the various purposes to which this power has been applied, that of locomotion in connection with railways is by far the most important. No application of any discovery in science has, within the same period, produced such astonishing results as those which we see daily and hourly in the conveyance of passengers and goods on railways. Effects are now witnessed, which, had they been narrated forty years since, would only have been admitted into the pages of fiction or volumes of romance. Who could have credited the possibility of a ponderous engine of iron, loaded with some hundreds of passengers, in a train of carriages of corresponding magnitude, and a large quantity of water and coke, taking flight from London and arriving at Liverpool, a distance of two hundred miles, in five or six hours? The rapidity of transport thus attained is not less wonderful than the weight transported. Its capabilities in this respect far transcend the exigencies even of the two greatest commercial marts in Great Britain; loads varying from 50 to 100 tons are transported at the rate of 40 or 50 miles an hour, and loads of 200 or 300 tons can be transported by the locomotive with equal ease, although at a reduced speed. The circumstances under which the steam-engine is worked on a railway are not favourable to the economy of fuel; nevertheless, a pound of coke burned in a locomotive engine will evaporate five pints of water; in this evaporation a mechanical force is developed sufficient to draw two tons weight on the railway a distance of one mile in two minutes! The same weight in a stage coach on a common road, would require four horses, and occupy six minutes.

The transport of a train of coaches weighing about 80 tons, and holding 240 passengers, from Liverpool to Birmingham and back again, a distance of somewhat less than 200 miles, the trip each way occupying about three hours and a half, is effected by the mechanical force produced by the combustion of four tons of coke, the value of which is about *five pounds*. To carry the same number of passengers daily between the same places by stage coaches on a common road would require twenty coaches and an establishment of 380 horses, whilst the journey in each direction would not be performed in less than twelve hours, stoppages included.* Such are the wonderful economical results of the application of steam as a motive power, in the transport of passengers and merchandise on railways.

But then comes this strange anomaly: although the cost of transport has been thus reduced to less than the *one twentieth*

---

* Dr. Lardner on the Steam Engine.

part of what it was by stage coaches in days gone by, the average fares by railways are more than the *one-half* of what they formerly were by coaches. The accommodation, the rapidity of motion, the ease and comfort of travelling, are incomparably increased, and any man who would attempt to depreciate these advantages would be unworthy to enjoy them. But we are speaking now of the financial part of the question; the violation of the laws of common sense, as well as of political economy: these prescribe that reduction in price should follow in due proportion to the reduction in cost, and these laws are grossly violated in the working of our railway system. A low rate of transit, so far as relates to the expenditure of railway companies, is established throughout the kingdom, from which the public, for causes we shall endeavour to investigate, derive but partial benefit. To the companies the expenditure per train per mile is nearly uniform; but the case is very different in regard to their charges to the public. Nothing, apparently, can be more capricious or less governed by any fixed principle than their several tariffs. For the highest class passengers the fares vary between *one halfpenny* and *threepence halfpenny* per mile; and for the lowest, between *one farthing* and *one penny* per mile; if the low tariff were universally, instead of partially and in very rare cases, adopted throughout the kingdom, there would not be much cause of complaint, or necessity for any change in our system. Occasionally, the companies, as it may suit their interests — not that the public have any right to demand it—give days of grace and holiday, and permit the populace, who 'rush in crowds, to avail themselves of the privilege, to travel at about *one-third* of the ordinary fares. The lowest fare for which any company is obliged to convey each passenger per mile is one penny, and that only once each way per day; but on these special occasions—and they happen frequently during the summer—the " excursion trains," as they are called, convey passengers at very low fares compared with the ordinary traffic fares—at the rate, for the lowest class, of three, four, or five miles for a penny, and the other classes at proportionate charges.

What, then, is the cause of the high fares charged on most lines?—the great expense incurred in their construction? It cannot be that; for, as a general rule, we shall find, when we come to look closely into the matter, that the cheapest carrying railways in the kingdom are precisely those which have the heaviest works and been constructed at an enormous expense. It might be supposed, however, that those lines whose construction has cost comparatively little would be those which would carry at the lowest fares. So far from this being the case, we shall find that those companies whose lines were most cheaply constructed charge, in many cases, double the fares of the most dearly constructed lines. Is it, then, the difference of gradients on the several lines, and the increased cost of conveyance on those lines whose gradients are bad? Nothing of the kind; the difference in expense is utterly inappreciable in reference to the fare of a passenger. From none of these causes does the difference in fares arise; it proceeds from a cause widely different, and that cause is expressed by the one word—MONOPOLY.

Our railways are in the sole possession of companies, that, with certain limitations, which are very wide, and exceptions, which are very few, have the complete control and management of our inland transport. They fought very hard to attain their present position, in and out of Parliament, with landowners and each other, till they obtained their respective bills, and they never have been on the best terms with the public. Thirteen large companies monopolize about three-fourths of the railway traffic of the kingdom, and above sixty smaller ones divide amongst them the remaining fourth. All these companies are managed by boards of directors, composed generally of men of high social and commercial position, and well qualified to fulfil the duties of their office. These gentlemen hold respectively those highways of the kingdom as a trust to be exercised, not for the benefit of the general community, but solely for the profit of the shareholders, to whom the railways exclusively belong, and by whom alone they are paid for their services. The companies are under no pecuniary obligations whatever to the State; they have received neither subvention from the Legislature, nor assistance or special protection from the Government; and if, in the early days of railway progress the projectors of our great trunk lines were received with open arms by the landed proprietors, and welcomed as public benefactors, ungratefully they record it not! The directors, therefore, of the companies manage the railways with one view, and one view only—to obtain the greatest profit for their shareholders, without any more regard to the interests of the public than is necessary for effecting that object.

We have already noticed the wide range of fares adopted by the several companies, commencing as low as one halfpenny per mile for first-class passengers, and increasing by small fractional additions, till the highest fare of threepence halfpenny per mile is reached, and in the same proportion with the other classes. Thus we shall find that in some cases the lowest fares produce a greater profit than the highest; but it is one of the most remarkable phenomena of railway statistics, and one we shall have occasion to illustrate at some length, that within the range of fares adopted by the companies, *the actual profit varies but comparatively little, whether a high, low, or medium fare be adopted.* Every one will readily enough understand the great increase of passengers that results from a considerable reduction in fares, and the reverse when an opposite policy is pursued; but few persons would believe, who have not directed their attention to the subject, what a comparatively small difference it makes in a financial point of view when, from some cause, there comes a sudden change in the policy of a company, and low fares are substituted for high fares, or the reverse; nevertheless, there is *a* difference, quite sufficient to govern the policy of a company.

It was at one time a matter of some nicety and considerable anxiety to a board of directors, when a line was opened, to fix the fares at the exact point that would best pay. The operation was performed somewhat in the same manner as an *habitué* of the Opera adjusts his opera-glass to his sight; by alternately extending and contracting it till his glass is at the exact focus. On the same principle directors ascertained the precise point in their sliding-scale at which their tariff would best pay, and that knowledge was only to be acquired by going through the process of alternately raising and lowering the fares until it was ascertained. When directors were well advised and exercised due care and judgment before they fixed their tariff, very few changes were necessary, and unless from the opening of a competing line, or some other extraneous cause, the fares remained with little or no alteration for many years. The scale of fares naturally depends on the character of the population whose wants the railway supplies. Their general social position and many other circumstances now enable the clear-headed manager to decide at once on the best paying fares, or, at all events, go very near the mark, and recommend them to his board accordingly, so that very few changes are afterwards required. It was very different, however, in the early history of railways, when managers had but little experience to guide them in fixing the fares, and thought the tariff that paid best in one locality should pay best in all others. With railways that paid fair dividends the changes in fares were not very great, seldom exceeding 10 or 20 per cent.; but it was very different with the unfortunate class that paid very low dividends; the directors, attributing their want of success to not having charged the best paying fares, made the most extreme and sudden changes, in order to find them out. The tariff would be reduced 30, 40, or 50 per cent., or tried the other way, and raised 50 or, in some cases, 100 per cent. We shall find, when we go into these cases, this curious result, from all these changes—that let the directors alter their fares as they would—make them high, low, or moderate—change them from threepence per mile for first class to three farthings, or one penny per mile to one farthing for third class, the difference in dividend to the shareholders was comparatively small, seldom exceeding a half per cent. per annum. That difference, however small in itself, was of considerable consequence to the shareholder, not merely as regards the income, but its effect on the market price of shares, every pound of income representing about twenty pounds of capital.

Some boards commenced with low fares, and gradually increased them till the highest paying point was attained. Let us suppose a case in which the directors think that the first-class fare should not exceed one penny per mile, and the other classes in due proportion; but find that such a tariff pays only 4 per cent. per annum. Not being satisfied, they double their fares, and find that pays $4\frac{3}{4}$ per cent.; they hope still better to improve their position, and add 50 per cent. more to their fares, but the increase reduces their dividend to $4\frac{1}{2}$ per cent.; by a few more trials they soon ascertain the best paying point, which, perhaps, turns out to be an addition of 20 per cent. instead of 50 per cent. to the second tariff trial. Let us take now the descending scale. The directors of another company, we will suppose, believing that high fares would pay best, charge threepence per mile for first class, and the others in proportion; these fares they find pay them at the rate of 5 per cent. per annum, with which, however, they are not satisfied. They reduce their fares 33 per cent., and they find that reduction raises their dividend to $5\frac{1}{4}$ per cent.; thus encouraged, they make another reduction, and reduce these last fares 50 per cent.: this actually raises their dividend to $5\frac{3}{4}$ per cent. They go on and reduce another 50 per cent., but they find now they have gone beyond the mark, for their dividend is reduced to $5\frac{1}{4}$ per cent., so they come to the right conclusion—being somewhere between the present and the last charged fares, the exact point they soon discover,—and slightly raise their fares till they find that three farthings per mile for first class, and one halfpenny for second class, for the whole length of their line, return tickets at a fare and a half, and slightly increased charges for shorter distances, pay them 6 per cent. These are the fares now charged, 6 per cent. being the dividend paid, on the North London line. There are, however, very few railways in the kingdom but would lose considerably as compared with their present earnings, by carrying their ordinary first-class passengers at three farthings per mile, instead of twopence or twopence halfpenny, the usual charge; their second class at a halfpenny per mile instead of three halfpence; and their third, at one farthing per mile instead of one penny.

We all have known of violent contests extending over a considerable length of time, having taken place between different companies, and the fares being suddenly reduced to one-third or one-fourth of their ordinary rates. Some of us may possibly have lived in districts where the public have derived the advantages arising from such contests. What rejoicing it caused for the time being! The two companies, like desperate opponents, appeared only intent on each other's ruin, and the people rushed in crowds to avail themselves of the short-lived opportunity of cheap travelling the contest afforded them. The companies appeared to differ only from the old opposition coaches, in not giving their passengers a dinner and a bottle of wine gratis, after conveying them for almost nothing! Few persons who have seen or heard of this ever troubled themselves to inquire what was the result, as it affected the companies financially. Such an extreme and sudden change in the policy of a company either by raising or lowering its fares is always attended with bad results to the shareholders, because it may be safely assumed that the several companies have settled down to their most profitable scale of fares, and that either to raise or lower those fares to any great extent would produce a serious loss. The London and North-Western Company, for instance, in 1863 paid £5 2s. 6d. per cent. to their proprietors, but if the fares were reduced to *one-third* of what they now charge, their annual dividend might at first be reduced to £4 per cent. per annum, a large reduction, representing a loss in the market value on each £100 share of £22 10s. The greatest loss, however, that I have been able to trace to any company by a change of policy was that caused by a sudden reduction of *four-fifths* in their fares: the loss in that case amounted to one per cent. dividend per annum on their capital. To ascertain the loss companies would incur in their dividends by any assumed reduction in their fares, when all the data are furnished, would be a matter of little difficulty to any well-skilled manager of a railway.

There is, however, another party who have some interest in the matter, not only in the fares of the London and North-Western Company, but in the fares of all the railways in the kingdom, and that very large party is the PUBLIC; who have no voice or influence, either direct or indirect, in the matter, by themselves individually, or their representatives, nor, under the present system, have a right to require any reduction in the fares on a railway more than they have a right to require their grocer or baker to reduce the price of their tea and their loaf. It is a part of our recognized policy to grant to private individuals the possession of these great arteries of communication which monopolize the conveyance of passengers and goods throughout the country, and they who exercise the trust on behalf of the shareholders find themselves obliged, in the exercise of their duty, to exclude at least *three-fourths* of those who have occasion to travel. It is universally acknowledged that the first step from barbarism towards civilization is shown by the construction of public roads, and that in proportion as the facilities for intercourse throughout a country is extended its happiness and prosperity are increased. In no country in the world has such an enormous expenditure been incurred as in Great Britain within the last thirty-five years, in making public highways of the best construction, and with all the modern improvements. Mountains have been bored through with incredible labour and expense; viaducts have been carried over deep valleys and wide rivers; the treacherous moss that scarcely a sheep could venture to cross, now bears in safety the ponderous train, drawn by the swift flying locomotive. But that train, ponderous as it may appear, is comparatively empty; it conveys but fifty or sixty passengers; whilst, without any diminution in its speed or increase in its expense, three or four times that number might be seated in its carriages. There is the merchant who has business to transact; there is the trader who would fain go and personally select his own goods at the best market; there are the mechanic and the labourer with whom work is dull at home, but who know where it is brisk abroad; there is the invalid who would seek health, and the man of the world who only travels for recreation or pleasure: all are stopped by a HOSTILE TARIFF.

Yet it sounds very odd—a hostile tariff in free England! If there is any country on the face of the earth where one might suppose every facility would be given to promote the utmost freedom of transit—where there would be no endurance of any artificial hindrance to the extension of trade and commerce—where a people would be the most determined to abolish any laws that trammelled their free intercourse with the most remote districts—that country we should certainly suppose to be England. It has been said, and with great truth, that England hates monopoly, and what we have to consider in these pages is, whether under the specious disguise of free trade a monopoly has not established itself among us of the most pernicious nature, which has had the effect of greatly enhancing the cost of transit, and depriving the country of the manifold advantages that under a sound system of management it would otherwise enjoy.

We are told that the most elaborate and *recherché* mode of dressing a cucumber should only be made use of as a preliminary to throwing it out of the window; and on the same principle may our railways be said to have been constructed, and afterwards left unused. There was nothing that genius could invent, or capital and labour supply, that has been spared in their construction ; but who planned them—made them—and undertook to manage them ? Not the representatives of the State, but the commercial class of speculators and capitalists.

Public opinion in this country declared at the outset, when the necessity of constructing railways was established, that it was of paramount necessity that no time should be lost; and without the importance of the step being duly considered, or the vast difference that existed between the high roads of a country and all other works of a *quasi* public nature being taken into account, the construction of our railways was, not undertaken by the State, but left open to any party who might be able to get up a company and succeed in obtaining their bill. The agreement between the Legislature and the companies might be thus summarily stated : The companies were not to receive any subvention or assistance of any kind from the State, either directly in money, or indirectly by assistance in obtaining land or by any protection from opposing lines, or by any reduction in the heavy Parliamentary charges to be incurred in obtaining their respective bills ; on the other hand, the companies selected what districts they thought best for their operations, and fought their way as they best could, till they obtained their bills. They were allowed, in order to indemnify themselves for the enormous expenses they were thus put to, to charge the public more than *twenty times* what it cost themselves, for the conveyance of passengers and merchandise ; they were not obliged to adopt a uniform tariff: each company chose its own, according to its peculiar circumstances. The results we have already described. The old channels of communication throughout the country were thus superseded, and to the companies was granted a monopoly of the new—a monopoly the most extensive, as it stretched out on every side over the whole face of the land, and the most injurious that could be conceived to the public good, as it placed the community in the power of irresponsible parties to tax them *ad libitum*, without any possibility of appeal.

Although we use the term "monopoly," as applied to railway companies, it must be remembered that they have none by law; their monopoly only arises from the superior excellence of their conveyance, by which every opponent is driven from the common road. The commission appointed many years since, before railways were introduced into Ireland, for the purpose of inquiring into the expediency of their being constructed by the State in that country, drew out a long and able report on the subject, which was presented to both Houses of Parliament. After describing the manifold blessings which the full development of the resources of a country bestows on all classes, the report points out, in forcible language, the jarring interests of private monopoly and public good where companies and not the State are the holders of railway property. " So great are the powers," says the Report, "so vast the capabilities of a railway, that it must, wherever established, at once supersede the common road; and not only will all the public conveyances now in use disappear, but even the means of posting will, in all probability, rapidly decline, and eventually, perhaps, cease to be found along its line. Its superiority is too manifest and decided to admit of rivalry, it possessing almost unlimited means of accommodation. No amount of traffic exists on any road, or is likely to exist, which a single railway is not capable of conveying; no concourse of passengers which it cannot promptly dispose of. The velocity of the locomotive, when impelled even at a very considerable reduction of its full power, surpasses the greatest speed which the best appointed coach, on the best made road, can attain. The monopoly of the railway is complete from the moment of the railway's opening. The salutary dread of competition can never stir the activity or ruffle the repose of the railway monopolist, who finds himself in a moment invested with despotic power, to which the best interests of society must succumb. Private enterprise, of course, selects for the field of exertion those portions of the kingdom where the most extensive intercourse promises the largest profit. The main avenues throughout the country cease to be the property of the State, and are handed over to the absolute possession of monopolists, placed beyond the reach of rivalry or control. They are enabled to establish a monopoly in the most extensive sense, and to keep the intercourse of the country entirely at their command. The rate of speed, the choice of hours for departing, the number of journeys in a day, rest at their discretion; and, as they have the unlimited right for fixing the charges for the conveyance of both passengers and goods, then they have an opportunity of repaying themselves not only for the legitimate cost of constructing and maintaining the railway, but for all the heavy expenditure incurred either through their own extravagance or in consequence of the various impositions practised upon them. Thus every item of unnecessary expense falls eventually on the public."

It is just twenty-five years since the report, of which the above is an extract, was presented to Parliament, but it was not followed by any beneficial results. It is no easy matter to change, or even to essentially modify, the traditional policy of a country, and the policy of this country was, and is, to leave, without exception, our great industrial undertakings to private enterprise. Nevertheless, the laws of England are not like those of the Medes and Persians. We shall find, in the course of our inquiries, that many of our statesmen and legislators are far in advance of the public mind on this subject. We shall discover, also, many reasons which have prevented the attention of the people generally being directed to this subject; and, if it can be made clear to those who possess their confidence that the management of our railways should be an exceptional case to our general commercial policy, and that a change may be effected, by which increased security would be given to the shareholder, and the Legislature enabled to reduce the fares to *less than a third* of their present average rates, the support of able and influential men may be calculated on in furthering any project that would produce such a result.

When we remember that it is the recognized policy of this country to allow the companies to choose whatever scale of fares pays them best, it can be no just matter of complaint against them, that they exercise that right to the fullest extent. There may be reason for complaint against some of the companies in other matters, but not in that relating to fares. When the directors lower their fares or raise them, it is from the same motive —to increase their profits; and as they have received no favour either from the State or the public, they consequently look to no interests but their own. Take an ordinary case in travelling: you have been accustomed, we shall say, to use, on some particular line, a second-class carriage; the accommodation was pretty good, and the fare reasonable. But a change occurs: the fare is raised, the accommodation is worse, and you write indignantly to the newspapers. But why should you complain? The directors have no wish to inconvenience the public. They only intend the changes in the second class as a civil hint for you to travel by the first. You are not obliged to travel at all on the line if you don't like. You say you are; you have no other means of getting to your destination. That may be a very good reason for your asking the Legislature to effect, if possible, an arrangement with the companies, by which you will acquire a right to complain; but so long as railways are, in one sense, private property, and the directors, in endeavouring to make the greatest profit by them, do not violate the law, there can be no just cause of complaint.

But have the companies, armed with the great powers they possess, holding the public completely within their grasp, regulating at will, by their tariffs, the vast traffic that daily ebbs and flows to and from the extremities of the kingdom—have they, in the undisturbed possession, for more than thirty years, of the most gigantic monopoly the world ever saw, been very successful? Far from it. Within the last few years their affairs, from exceptional causes, have considerably improved. The average dividends of all the companies, for the year ending the 31st Dec., 1863, was considerably less than four per cent., and I think we shall find, in the course of this inquiry, that they may have reason to fear that their position is not by any means secure, and their future dividends liable to be considerably decreased by the encouragement given by the public to the formation of new companies. It is, therefore, not at all unlikely that, as a body, they would be willing to come to equitable terms with Government, and, for the sake of a secure dividend under Government guarantee, accept a much less dividend than that which they now receive, so that from the saving thereby effected a low and uniform rate of fares could be established throughout the kingdom.

Let us consider for a moment the load of railway taxation under which this country labours. Last year it amounted to the enormous sum of THIRTY-ONE MILLIONS ONE HUNDRED AND FIFTY-SIX THOUSAND THREE HUNDRED AND NINETY-SEVEN POUNDS STERLING, fully six millions in excess of the sum required to pay the interest on the whole of our national debt, or more than five millions in excess of our customs duty, and, excluding the income tax, just equal to the half of all our other taxation combined. Twenty years ago our railway taxation amounted only to about five millions sterling; ten years ago it had increased to more than treble that sum; and since that time the average increase per annum has been about a million and a half. The number of miles open for traffic at the close of 1863 was 12,322, and the annual increase varies generally from 300 to 500 miles. But so far from there being any tendency towards a decline in the construction of railways, we find that they go on continually increasing; and in 1863 bills were passed for the construction of 790 miles, not to speak of a still greater number rejected. It is impossible, therefore, to form any estimate as to what amount our railway taxation will ultimately reach. It is very possible that, long before we have reached the end of the present century, our railway taxation will have fully equalled all our other taxation combined. Under these circumstances, it will be fully admitted that it is impossible to over-estimate the importance of a thorough investigation into this subject in all its bearings.

Objection may, perhaps, be taken to the term "taxation," as applied to the payments made to railway companies, on the ground of such payments being voluntary, but the same argument might be applied to all Government taxes. We paid, last year, in postage £3,600,000; but that was all in "voluntary" payments. No one obliged us, in the first instance, to write letters; and if we chose to write them, we were not compelled to send them by post, we might have forwarded them by special messenger. The absolute necessaries of life are untaxed; but tea, coffee, sugar, malt, tobacco, spirits, and wine, however much they may add to our comfort and enjoyment, do not come strictly within this category; the bulk of our indirect taxation is derived from the revenue produced by their consumption, and the payment, therefore, by us of that revenue is altogether "voluntary." So, in regard to railway companies, it may be said, and quite truly, that our payments to them are voluntary. That cannot be denied. If we require to travel, we can either walk, hire a carriage, or go by railway, and we take our choice accordingly; but as we agree to use the term "taxation" in the payments we make to Government, we may, in the same sense, use it in those we make to railway companies. There is, however, a wide difference in the principles on which State taxation and railway taxation are founded, and their respective payments enforced, which we have already noticed, but shall have occasion to consider, in some detail, in these pages.

I have, in the Preface and in this preliminary chapter, sufficiently indicated the general purport of this inquiry, to enable the reader to form a judgment of its importance and the desirability of some change. So far from there being anything novel in the suggestion of the purchase of our railways by the State, we shall find, as I have intimated in the Preface, that it has been strongly recommended to the Legislature by men of the greatest experience and ability; that the most important evidence has been given on the subject before Parliamentary Committees; and that, during the administration of the late Sir Robert Peel, an Act was passed in 1844 enabling the Government, if they thought fit, after the expiration of 21 years, to purchase the railway property of the kingdom on certain terms therein specified. As the period when the Legislature would be free to act, has now almost arrived, it is in every way desirable that the subject should be thoroughly ventilated—the facts, figures, and arguments bearing on the case gone into—and the thirty years' experience we have had in the working of our railways turned to profitable account.

CHAPTER II.

Jealousy of Government Interference in Commercial Undertakings—The Construction of Railways undertaken by Companies—Opposition they encountered in and out of Parliament—Compensation to Landowners—Expenses of Parliamentary Contests—Non-interference of Government—Parliamentary Committee of 1839—Their Report—Legislative Doubts—Continental Railways—Belgium—France—Germany—Russia—Italy—Spain.

HAVING in the foregoing chapter given some idea of the evils complained of in the working of our railways, and endeavoured to show that from their nature they were inherent in the system we have adopted, we shall now proceed to notice the difficulties that the early promoters had to contend with, and the obstacles to overcome, before they obtained their respective Acts: thence we shall trace the progress of our legislation to the parliamentary session of 1844, when the abuse of power, together with the increasing strength and contemplated amalgamation of the companies, rendered the interference of the Legislature necessary.

There is no class of the community to whom the public are more indebted than to that enterprising class of speculators and capitalists who first undertook the construction of our railways. Our own system—if such it could be called—grew up without either order or method from within, or control or guidance from without. The commercial policy of this country, ever jealous of the interference of Government in matters of trade, having considered these great industrial works merely in that light, forbade any attempt on the part of the executive either to render any assistance to, or exercise any but the slightest supervision over, the new schemes as they started into existence. It was left entirely to enterprising speculators and wealthy capitalists to take up what districts they thought proper, to employ surveyors and engineers, in laying out lines, who ran the risk of being treated as trespassers in taking hurried surveys on lands, to which their owners denied them access; and many amusing stories are told of the adventures of these knight-errants. These impediments, however, were but the preliminary difficulties which the early projectors of railways had to encounter. The Government and Legislature declined to give assistance, direct or indirect, in support of any line; and as the opposition of any considerable landed proprietor, whose property would be affected by the railway, would be fatal, success could only be secured by paying such enormous fines, under the name of compensation, as the owners of the land thought proper to demand, or the project had to be abandoned. The Eastern Counties Company had to pay, in one instance, above £120,000 for lands not worth £5,000; and this company, in consequence of this and similar acts of imposition, to which it was obliged to submit before obtaining its Act, is scarcely able to pay now 2 per cent. per annum to its shareholders. This is but an instance of what happened, in a greater or less degree, to all other companies in the early days of railway construction.

But the projectors of a railway almost invariably found, on their first introduction to a parliamentary committee, after the lords of the soil and other interested parties had been settled with on their own terms, that they generally had to meet several competitors for the same prize: there were one or more rival lines proposed between the same towns, and enormous expenses were incurred in the contest for victory. From London to Brighton no less than four lines were proposed. Their parliamentary expenses for one year alone amounted to upwards of £100,000: how they were incurred is graphically described by one who took part in it. "There were about twenty counsel engaged, headed by six king's serjeants and kings' counsel; there was a regiment of twenty eminent solicitors flanked by a whole brigade of parliamentary agents, and a whole army of surveyors and engineers, whose chief business appeared to be to contradict each other, the lawyers aiding and assisting and chuckling with delight." That is but a counterpart of what took place almost before every committee.

For the first ten years of railway progress—say from 1829 to 1839—the policy of the Government was to hold itself aloof from all contests, leaving the several parties, without any regard to the merits of the rival schemes, to fight their own battles; and to such an extent was this abstinence from intervention carried, that, on great occasions, when a railway bill of more than usual importance was to come on, not for discussion, but division, after the President of the Board of Control perhaps had delivered a long speech to empty benches on the affairs of India, the rush of members plainly announced that something of real interest was about to take place: it was a railway bill, and the adherents of the rival lines had been busily engaged for the last week or two in canvassing the House of Commons for votes. The important night has arrived, and the contending parties are assembled, when the Prime Minister rises from his seat, and, followed by the other ministers, leaves the House, to prevent the suspicion that even their presence may influence a single vote. That was the way we managed business in the early days of railway legislation.

The increasing power and extension of the companies, and the abuse, as might naturally be expected, of that power, rendered interference on the part of the legislature necessary; and in 1839, a select committee was appointed by the House of Commons to inquire into the state of our railway communication. It was composed of some of the leading members of the House, including Sir Robert Peel, Lord Stanley, Sir James Graham, Mr. Poulett Thompson, and Mr. Shaw Lefevre.

Their attention was specially directed to two points:—

1st. The financial position of railways ;

2nd. The power given to them by the legislature ;

and the probable exercise of that power upon the general convenience of the public and intercourse of the country.

"It does not appear," the committee state in their report to the House of Commons, "to have been the intention of Parliament to give to a railway a complete monopoly of the means of communication on their line of road ; on the contrary, provision was made in all or most of the Acts of Incorporation to enable other persons to place and run engines and carriages on the road upon payment of certain tolls to the company. The intention, however, of Parliament cannot be carried into effect in the way contemplated by legislation ; for it is obvious that the payment of legal tolls is only a very small part of the arrangement which is necessary to open the railways to public competition. Any person with mere authority to place an engine and carriage on the railway would be practically unable to supply his engine with water, or to take up and set down his passengers at any convenient station or terminus, and, indeed, would be placed in such a disadvantageous situation, that all competition with the company would be rendered impossible." So completely, indeed, had the legislative enactment referred to become a dead letter, that probably few persons at the time were aware that it had ever existed.

Even at this early period the legislature began to suspect they had committed a mistake in adopting a system which left to private enterprise the task of supplying a public want, and that already appeared to confer something very like a monopoly on those who undertook and accomplished the task. The attempt to carry out the analogy between promoting competition on an ordinary high road and a railway, by permitting parties, on paying a fixed price, to compete with the proprietors of railways on their own line, as they might do with the trustees of a turnpike road, was a proposition in itself so preposterous and absurd, that it is difficult to believe it ever could have been supposed effectual.

A new era in railway legislation was, however, now to be inaugurated. The attempt to carry out competition by promoting opposition to shareholders on their own lines had failed owing to the directors of the company not considering the subject in precisely the same light as the legislature, and declining to provide their opponents in trade with the means of carrying on the proposed rivalry. It was now, therefore, proclaimed from high places that the only remedy for the public lay in promoting opposition lines to those already constructed, in order that the fares of the old lines might be forced down and all other grievances complained of remedied. Such were the palmy days that "free trade" in railways were to bring with them.

But there were two or three matters connected with the subject not then duly considered. First,—That to construct a railway where one already existed sufficient to supply the public wants was a mere waste of national wealth. Second,—That as but a small proportion of the railways necessary for the country were then constructed, there was little likelihood of promoters seeking to make opposition lines, when the greater part of the country lay before them unoccupied. And Third,—That whenever the time should arrive when it would be the interest of parties to construct a rival line, the same interest would induce them, as soon as possible after attaining their object, to come to terms with their opponents. But competition of this kind at the time we speak of was a long way off; it is true there was great competition before Parliament for obtaining an Act by the various competitors, but none after it was obtained. The Parliament, therefore, of 1839 did little or nothing towards effecting any important change, and the companies, becoming stronger from year to year, seemed alike independent both of Parliament and people.

We shall now briefly direct attention to our continental neighbours, for the purpose of contrasting their mode of proceeding with ours, and illustrating the comparative merits of the two systems of railway management, one, as we have seen, under the control of the companies, the other that we have to consider under that of the State.

Belgium was the first of the continental kingdoms to recognize, in a practical manner, the good results to be derived from a well-established system of railway communication throughout the country; lines were accordingly laid out by eminent engineers, through the most populous districts, constructed at the expense of the State, and subject to the complete control of the Legislature. The end aimed at was not the gain of the speculator, but the extension of the traffic and communication of the country to the utmost limits of the public capability, at the lowest rate of charge at which the original outlay could be reimbursed; the project undertaken by Government was an establishment which was intended should neither be a burden nor a source of revenue, and required merely that it should cover its own expenses, consisting of the charge for maintenance and repairs, with a further sum for the interest and gradual redemption of the invested capital. Such were the terms in which the Minister of Finance in 1836 reported on the system established in Belgium. The fares were fixed very low, less than a penny per mile for first class, and the others in proportion. A small, but well-laid-out network of railways was amply sufficient at that time for the population: the whole extent of the lines did not exceed 500 miles. There were constructed two great trunk railways forming a cross, the intersection of which took place at Malines. The length of the cross was extended from Ostend to Liège, and continued through the Prussian territory by Aix-la-Chapelle, to

Cologne; the transverse line was carried at right angles to this from north to south, extending from Antwerp, through Brussels by Mons, to the French territory; there were many other subsidiary lines, not necessary to notice.

That, however, which requires our special attention is the difference in the mode of treating the same subject in the two countries—England and Belgium. When the project which afterwards became law, was first introduced into the Belgian Chambers in 1834 there were not wanting advocates to recommend the course we were pursuing in England, and leave the whole business to " competition." " No," said M. Rogier, the Minister of Finance, " the state of affairs in which competition corrects the evil, does not apply here; whoever holds the railways holds a monopoly, and that should only be allowed to exist in the possession of the State, subject to the responsible advisers of the Crown." We cannot dispute the fact that the owners of railways hold in their hands the monopoly of the means of transit throughout the country. Do we, then, agree with or dissent from M. Rogier, when he asserts that a monopoly should be only held by the State, and administered under the immediate control of the legislature?

It was not till 1835, five years after the opening of the Liverpool and Manchester line, that a railway movement was made in France, and an Act passed authorizing the construction of a line between Paris and St. Germain, which was opened in 1837. In that year a commission was authorized to prepare a project of law on the subject of national railways, the general opinion being in their favour, which was submitted to the Chambers the following session; but the majority had in the meantime changed their opinion, and were now opposed to the principle of the State assuming the direction and management of these enterprises. The majority was composed of two parties—one the political party, distrustful and jealous of the influence which the possession of such vast patronage would invest the Government with; and the other, a most large and influential party, representing the financial and commercial interests, which looked forward to reaping great profits from the operations of the Bourse, resulting from the traffic in shares, if the railways were executed, as in England, by joint-stock companies. The combination of these parties prevailed, and the project of Government was rejected. These events took place in 1838, and during the next four years but little progress was made by companies; but in 1842, M. Teste, being then the Minister for Public Works, presented a project to the Chamber for the execution of a system of railways in which the Government should co-operate with private companies, and this, with some modification, was adopted. The conditions were, that the Government should purchase the land, buildings, and other property necessary for the construction of the lines, that two-thirds of the expenses were to be repaid by the communes through which the railways would pass, and that companies were to have leases. These terms, however, failed to produce any considerable extension of railways in France; and when the present Emperor ascended the throne, scarcely twelve years since, the entire length of the French lines did not exceed thirteen hundred miles. He made surprising changes in the whole system; and, under the fostering protection of Government, the mileage of railways in France is rapidly increasing every year. At the expiration of ninety-nine years from 1852, all railways revert to the State. In order to indemnify the original holders of shares, sinking-funds have been established for the reduction of the capital. Every year so many shares are drawn by lot, and paid off at par. The fares are about 25 per cent. less than in England. The French lines pay well—much higher than the English; and some of the larger lines pay a very high dividend. It is not at all impossible but that the Emperor may revert to the original policy intended, and make all the railways Government property, and reduce the fares to one-third of their present amount. They understand these matters and manage them better in France than with us; and the full development of the vast resources of that magnificent country could not be promoted by any other means so well as by extending the means of communication to all classes of her people.

Within the last few months the French Government have published their annual review of the state of the country, and in it is contained an elaborate report of their railway system. The entire length of railways in France open on the 31st December, 1863, was 7352 miles, and the gross receipts for the year £19,546,416. The railways have cost £200,000,000 sterling, and the Government has contributed about one-eighth of that sum. It has now divested itself of all separate property in railways. In the words of the Report, it was the duty of Government — which was legally authorized to construct most of the railways at the expense of the public revenue—to escape, as soon as possible, from a position which was onerous to the Treasury, and necessarily temporary. The great companies were willing to relieve the State of its engagements; but they required, as a consideration, that certain guarantees which they had obtained in 1859 should be revised and augmented. The guarantees had been founded on statements furnished by the companies themselves; and it is worthy of remark and satisfactory to Englishmen to know that in almost every case the estimates were found utterly insufficient. The Western Railway, especially, satisfied the Government it would be utterly ruined if it were held to its contract four years ago. The Lyons and Mediterranean, and Orleans companies were unwilling to spend money on branches; and the Lyons company insisted on the concession of a disputed line from Cette to Marseilles. The Government having no disposable capital, and more than 200 miles of railway which it was bound to make, complied with the demands of this company by increasing its guarantees, and by adjudging the Cette line to the Lyons and Mediterranean Company. Stipulations were inserted in the tariffs for the protection of travellers and freighters; and it is especially stated that coal was to be carried at a rate of from ¾d. to 1¼d. per ton per mile, according to distance.

The enormous railway business of France is committed to six great arterial lines projected by the State:—

1st. The Northern line, from Paris to Calais, Boulogne, Dunkerque, and the Belgian frontier.

2nd. The Western line, from Paris to Havre and Dieppe, &c.

3rd. The Orleans or Central line, from Paris to Orleans, Bourdeaux, Nantes, &c.

4th. The Southern line, from Bourdeaux to Cette, Bayonne, Toulouse, &c.

5th. The Paris, Lyons, and Mediterranean, from Paris to Marseilles, with branches to Cette, Bayonne, Toulouse, &c.

6th. The Eastern line, from Paris to Strasbourg, Châlons-sur-Marne, &c.

Some companies pay 20 per cent. dividend, and the average is about 7 per cent.

In Spain considerable progress has been made within the last few years in the construction of railways, and about 2100 miles are now open. In Italy the number of miles open is about 3400. In Russia the progress has been slow, owing to political and financial causes; but, last year, a concession was made to an English company for the construction of a line from St. Petersburg to Sebastopol, passing through some of the richest provinces of Russia, which will tend greatly to develope the resources of the country.

Germany is well supplied with railways; in some cases constructed by the State, and in others by companies. Those of the Grand Duchy of Baden, the kingdoms of Würtemburg, Bavaria, and Hanover, the empire of Austria, the Duchy of Brunswick, and the Principalities of Hesse, have been, with a few exceptions, constructed and worked by the States. In cases where the construction of particular lines was confided to companies, the Governments have generally redeemed them. In Prussia the State has in most cases abstained from any direct interference with the construction or working of the railways; but has given encouragement to the present companies, by whom the extensive system of lines which cover its territory has been executed. In cases where the traffic did not offer sufficient encouragement to stimulate private enterprise, the Government has extended its aid either in the shape of subscription or by taking certain shares in the line, or in guaranteeing a minimum rate of interest on capital. The Government, however, reserves a power of redemption at the end of thirty years, on the condition of paying to the railway proprietors a capital equal to twenty-five times the average amount of dividend enjoyed by the proprietors for the preceding five years. The State, in that case, would assume the responsibility and debts of the company, but it would, at the same time, take possession of their entire assets as well as their reserve fund.

Travelling on the Continent is much slower than in England: it is not, on an average, more than twenty miles an hour. There is but a small weight of luggage allowed to each passenger; and every package, on most railways, is weighed with the greatest exactness, and not a pound extra allowed. The formalities, delays, and countless stoppages are, to English travellers, very annoying. Let it not, however be supposed that I am setting up the Continental management of railways, under Government, as a model for imitation in this country: on the contrary, I should be inclined to say that, with a few exceptions, railway management in this country is preferred by the English people to that on the Continent. What we have to consider here is, not the management of Continental railways, but the extent to which our own system can be improved. The accommodation, however, in second-class carriages on the Continent is much better than with us; they are all well cushioned and made nearly as comfortable as first-class carriages here; and by far the larger proportion of that class which, in England, travel only in first-class carriages, make use of the second-class on the Continent; a remarkable fact when we compare their respective fares; but so far does this practice prevail abroad, that they have a common saying to the effect that "None but princes, fools, and Englishmen travel in first-class carriages." The *cuisine* is also far superior on the Continent to what we find at any English station. With these exceptions, the English system of management is, in many respects, better than the Continental.

The following table shows the average fares charged in the several Kingdoms and States on the Continent as compared with those of the United Kingdom:—

	Average Fares for 100 Miles.			
	1st Class.	2nd Class.	3rd Class.	4th Class.
	s. d.	s. d.	s. d.	s. d.
Belgium	6 6	5 6	3 0	
Spain	11 9	8 10	5 9	
Italy	10 6	7 11	4 0	
France	13 4	10 0	7 0	
Prussia	13 0	10 0	6 6	4 0
Switzerland	13 6	9 4	6 9	
Denmark	13 0	8 6	6 0	
Austria	13 0	7 6	5 9	
Norway	13 4	9 0	4 6	
Holland	14 0	11 2	7 0	
Portugal	14 2	11 0	6 9	
Russia	14 5	10 10	6 6	
The United Kingdom	18 9	12 6	8 4	

On some of the Belgian lines the first-class fare is so low as one halfpenny per mile, and the other classes in proportion. The fares on the French Northern Railway are from 10 to 20 per cent. lower than in other parts of the empire. In most of the continental countries the scale of fares in each class is tolerably uniform.

CHAPTER III.

Progress of Railway Mismanagement from 1840 to 1843—Treatment of Third-Class Passengers—Extract from the "Times," December, 1842—The Companies' Defence—Classification of the Charges against the Companies—Their Reply.

WE have already noticed that the legislative measures of 1839 had but little influence on the management of railways. The Legislature had discovered the mistake they had committed, and acknowledged it, but did not see their way clearly how to rectify the error. The boards of directors possessed all but absolute power over the traffic throughout the principal parts of the kingdom; for although the length of our railways at that time scarcely exceeded 1000 miles, they were the great trunk lines over which then, as now, the greatest amount of traffic naturally passed. The directors soon began to make their power painfully felt by the manner in which they exercised it; they would first lower the fares, in order to drive opposition from the road, then suddenly raise them when they had succeeded, and frequently change them, to discover the best paying tariff. The arrangements of the companies to force passengers to travel by first-class carriages, and the surveillance alleged to be exercised over third-class passengers, in order to deter a higher class from travelling in third-class carriages, gave great dissatisfaction to the public. In regard to the goods traffic, the constant quarrels and lawsuits they had with carriers, were carried on for the purpose of driving them from the line. The greatest cause, however, of complaint against railway directors was their treatment of third-class passengers. The *Times*, in a leading article, in December, 1842, thus alludes to the general feeling entertained towards railway companies in general, and more especially in regard to their treatment of the poorer class of passengers.

"We have received communications," said the *Times*, "from several correspondents, imploring us to maintain an advocacy for the poorer class of railway travellers, who have to avail themselves of the stinted accommodation afforded by the leading lines, and desire us to urge the necessity of more comfort and facility in their transit than they at present enjoy. It would appear from the facts stated in the several letters received, that little choice exists in one more than another, and that all the great lines are as parsimonious as they possibly can be in providing comfort or convenience for those having the misfortune to travel in third-class conveyances. The manner in which the Great-Western Company treat this class of passengers is described as worse than any other pursued, the only trains by which they forward them being those used for the transit of coals, cattle, and merchandise of all descriptions. For instance, it is stated that a third-class passenger leaves Paddington in an open carriage, no difference being made to counteract wind or weather, at half-past 4 A.M. When he arrives at Swindon he is detained upwards of an hour, and at last gets to Bristol, if the train keeps its time, in nine and a half hours, while the first and second class carriages make the same journey in less than half the time. If a third-class passenger wish to go on to Taunton from any place east of Bristol, it is alleged to be still more inconvenient, since he is detained from four to five hours in Bristol, and is kept on the road, at a moderate calculation, from fourteen to sixteen hours; whereas, on the other hand, first and second class passengers arrive at the same destination in six and a half hours. These are strong statements, and unless satisfactorily explained away, must, sooner or later, bring these undertakings within the managerial scope of the Board of Trade, the authorities of which bodies would do well to see that fair and adequate provision is made by all the railway companies for the conveyance of the poorer classes during seasonable hours of the day. Railway directors have at present the exercise of too much irresponsible power, and therefore imagine they can deal with the public as they choose. They, however, must be mindful not to carry it beyond proper bounds; for though much good may have been achieved by the construction and successful completion of intercourse by means of this system of communication, it remains to be seen what will be the actual results of this description of management, should it, without some superintending control, be left entirely to the judgment of the persons who have the sole exercise of this power. It may possibly prove a useful hint to have said thus much on the subject, without pressing more severely on the attention of the several railway boards the necessity existing for some amelioration of the plan at present adopted in the conveyance of third-class passengers; for, regarding them in the light of national improvements, raised on the foundation of the nation's wealth, they must be considered as intended to furnish a comparative convenience to one class of the public as well as the other. The French, who are now following out the system of railways extensively, are provided against these deficiencies, should they arise, in a much better manner than we are at home, because the Government of that country, having identified itself in close alliance with these undertakings, by affording assistance in a pecuniary point of view, have the superior right of interfering, without encountering the condemnation of that part of the public who may be interested in the maintenance of the superiority of railway directorates against such supervision. It is a barrier to expression among our railway interests, and one that certainly once or twice occasioned strong opposition against the inspection of the Board of Trade in these matters, viz.,—that the Government having, in the first instance, refused all responsibility, and allowed private capitalists to surmount the difficulties which these undertakings presented, ought not now to provoke or desire an immediate connection with their management. But the great answer to all this is, that when the safety or convenience of the public is concerned, then the Government have the power of inspection, and will exercise it for their benefit."

The above judgment, from the principal organ of public opinion in this country, shows how strong the general feeling on the subject ran. Nevertheless, the companies were not without advocates; not that they required any, for they could very well defend themselves. "We are willing," said their directors, "to accommodate the poor as far as we possibly can without injury to ourselves. We carry them now at less than half the price we are authorized to charge. The working classes and those of moderate means can travel, at all events, more comfortably and cheaper than they could a few years since outside a coach; if they are made as comfortable as they would be inside, the result will be that second-class passengers will take third-class carriages, and so there will be a large falling off in our revenue; but if Government will make us compensation, we are willing to entertain the question." Now, it must be remembered that, at the time we speak of, Government had made no proposition to the companies on the subject; it was not till some years subsequently that any proposition was made which, after some demur, was accepted by the companies.

I shall briefly notice a few of the principal causes that, from 1840 till Parliament found it necessary to interfere in 1844, operated in making the companies so unpopular with the public:—

1st. A traveller about to proceed over more than one line, and having started in a second-class carriage, when he arrived at the terminus of the first line would be obliged to take a first-class carriage over the next line, or to discontinue his journey, perhaps, for several hours, or the day, as it might happen. If a passenger, for instance, left London for Liverpool, by the first train in the morning, he would arrive at Birmingham about ten o'clock, and a train would then be ready to start on the Grand Junction for the North of England; but as this train carried none but first-class passengers, second-class passengers would be detained eight hours before they had an opportunity of continuing their journey. This is a specimen of the arrangements that then existed generally between the companies.

2nd. The method adopted by the companies to drive opposition from the road was very effectual, by lowering the fares till all opposition was crushed, and then suddenly raising them. Sometimes a feeble attempt would be made to compete for the traffic by a speculative coach proprietor, but in the course of a few months, he generally found himself in the *Gazette;* so it was no very difficult matter with the companies to secure an effectual monopoly of the passenger traffic.

3rd. The frequent and unceremonious manner in which the companies changed their fares, raising them and lowering them as they thought proper, gave cause for great dissatisfaction, more especially with those companies that paid well, and added but very little to their dividends by the higher fares, although by such changes they laid a heavy impost on the public. The Grand Junction, for instance—now that section of the London and North-Western that runs from Birmingham to Warrington—when they were paying 10 per cent. dividend raised their fares 27 per cent., and thereby increased their dividend only a half per cent. There was in this proceeding no legitimate cause of complaint, and all other companies naturally did the same when they thought they could profit by it, whatever their dividends might be, but the public were much dissatisfied when they contrasted the little gain the companies made by these changes with the heavy loss to themselves.

4th. A great abuse in the railway system was the injury and annoyance one company had the power to inflict on another and the public; they possessed the right, and frequently exercised it, of buying up a small company, whose line might give a command of several other companies, so as to form, as it were, a key to them, and thus enable them to charge what fare they thought proper over the short line.

5th. The agreements that were entered into between the companies, not intended to be published, but which occasionally came to light in consequence of some disagreement between the contracting parties, took the public by surprise, and furnished a very disagreeable proof of the extent to which the companies had not merely the passenger but also the goods traffic in their hands. One of these cases attracted considerable notice:—a paper war having broken out between two companies, then called the Manchester and Leeds, and the Manchester and Birmingham, it appeared that one of these companies paid the other a large annual sum not to compete with them in a particular district, although to carry on the competition it would be necessary to bring the merchandise an additional forty miles. Yet there was nothing particularly objectionable in this; on the contrary, it is the usual practice of traders, when they find it to be their interest, to make an agreement of this kind; but it proved, nevertheless, that, by the organization of the several companies, their control over the goods traffic was as complete as it was over the passenger traffic.

I should not have thought it necessary to enter into these details of the differences that existed between the public and the companies, more than twenty years ago, were it not that I consider any treatise professing to narrate the progress of our early railway legislation, would be incomplete without such notice; and, further, these events serve as a key to the legislative measure that shortly followed. It must be acknowledged that the directors of the companies were placed in an entirely false position; their shareholders had invested their capital in railways as they would in any other speculation, and elected the directors to manage their property and protect their interests. But it was alleged that the directors, in exercise of a public trust, were bound to protect the public as much as their shareholders in directing the affairs of the companies. Having said so much in reference to the charges made against the companies, it is only fair to hear, in reply, what was then said in their defence. "Let the rights," said one of their advocates, " of railway property be considered, its duties being already so well understood. And, first let us inquire who these great railway proprietors are, and what they have done for the public. Are they not the authors of one of the greatest boons ever conferred by enterprise and skill, upon commerce, industry, and social advancement? Have they not carried through to a happy issue one of the greatest inventions of modern times, and carried it through in the face of difficulty, discouragement, and vast unpopularity?

"Let us see what has been the general expression of public feeling towards railways. The inventor of a new art was despised by the Greeks and Romans. Are we to advocate an apotheosis of the great projectors and constructors of railways? There seems little fear in the present temper of public opinion of our perpetrating that folly. Never, perhaps, were there such great enterprises achieved with so little aid from public opinion.

"While the experiment was doubtful the attempt was denied by all who were indifferent, and denounced by all who were prejudiced. Its objects were assailed by selfish interests, and its resources devoured by rapacious claims from those whose aid was required, or whose neutrality had to be purchased. From the first survey to the final completion of the line, difficulties of all kinds met the projectors,—local hostility, corporate opposition. The public looked on, and if it took part it was with their opponents;—the Legislature, the Government afforded no effectual aid. The promoters fought their way, step by step, and were received as if, instead of preparing for the country the greatest boon it has received in modern times, they had been conspiring to deface and impoverish it. Such, in general—for the instances of better judgment were mere exceptions—was the temper with which the railway projects were met in the first stage of their national existence. Lamentable enough; but not unnatural. It is the price which those must be ready to pay who attempt anything at once great and new. But surely it entitles them to enjoy their reward when, in spite of these obstacles, their energy and perseverance have conquered success.

"Their efforts had indeed been successful; the invention was found to surpass belief, and the country saw itself enriched by benefits which the most sanguine of the projectors had not dared to promise. A rapidity of transit almost miraculous; a reduction of expenses quite unexampled; system and uniform tariffs substituted for irregularity and vulgar extortion, and with all this a safety, which only the silliest panic could dispute, hitherto unknown in public travelling. These were benefits, vast, incalculable, notorious, experienced by every one every day. Under any circumstances, they surely demand a large reward, a larger if the real difficulty of the task had been troubled by needless hindrances. And how was this reward bestowed? By an universal outcry, so loud and general that one might have thought it had been raised to denounce some great national enormity. The directors, the engineers, the proprietors, the managers of railways, were questioned, and lectured, and worried on every side. Mortified men, who wanted courage to share in the work while it was full of risk—men of habit averse to new ways—men of rank and wealth, accustomed to command wherever they travelled, and impatient of all regulations—superseded rivals, who covered their anger with pretences of public care—liberals whose wisdom lay in repeating the phrases of 'monopoly,' 'competition,' and similar words without ideas—the weak of all classes whom the hubbub alarmed—inventors eager to have their nostrums tried, or at least purchased—busy men anxious to regulate—idle men wanting to be employed—all joined in the cry, while Parliament became suddenly full of zeal, and the Government itself, stepping in to meddle when it had not learned to mend, after standing aloof when it might have done good, seemed to sanction the general excitement."

It is not necessary now to discuss which of the two parties, the public or the railway directors, were more in fault or had more to complain of. The latter felt that they had nothing to thank either the public or the Legislature for, and showed a determination, somewhat impolitic perhaps, to maintain their strict legal rights, with but little regard to the wants, wishes, and feelings of the general community. They considered that they had been, to use the conventional phrase, unmercifully plundered by landowners and others, whose goodwill to obtain their bills was indispensable; and as they received no special protection or assistance from the State, they considered they had a right to make the most of their position, and so long as an opportunity was afforded them to turn it to the best account.

CHAPTER IV.

Prosperous State of the Country in 1844—Stimulus to Railway Enterprise—Appointment of the Parliamentary Committee—Their Reports—Third-Class Passengers—Parliamentary Trains—Evidence of Mr. (now Sir) Rowland Hill—Opposition of Railway Companies to the Government Bill—Their Arrangement with Government—The Three Fundamental Reforms projected by Government—Sir Robert Peel and Mr. Gladstone.

DURING the year 1844 the country enjoyed an unusual degree of prosperity; an abundant harvest the preceding year, and a flourishing home and foreign trade, had added largely to the material wealth of the kingdom; the operation of free-trade measures had begun to develope itself, and the Three per Cents., for the first time in the present century, reached par. In the previous year twenty-four railway Acts were passed: the number was not more than the public service required, but the present year brought with it a great number of new projects, and was destined to mark a new era in railway legislation.

The public discontent with the general management of railways, together with the great number of new schemes projected for the session, convinced Government of the necessity of a thorough investigation, not merely into the working of the system, as it then existed, but also into the soundness of the principles on which the system itself was based. The question had been recently mooted, whether or not it was desirable to follow the example of Belgium and other continental countries, where railways were the property of the State, and although few were inclined to go that length, there existed, nevertheless, a very strong feeling that such precautionary measures should be taken by the Legislature as would leave the whole subject open to be dealt with at a future day, as circumstances might require.

On the 5th February, immediately after the opening of Parliament, a select committee was appointed by the House of Commons, to consider whether any or what new provisions ought to be introduced in such railway bills as would come before the House, during that or any future session, for the advantage of the public and the improvement of the railway system. The committee was presided over by Mr. Gladstone, then President of the Board of Trade, and was composed of some of the leading political men of the House, and of those most prominent as representatives of the railway interest. The Committee, shortly after their appointment, proceeded to hear evidence on the various subjects which required their attention. Amongst others, the powers to be given to the Board of Trade, the standing orders, loan notes, the rating of railways, and the vexed question between the carriers and the companies occupied no small portion of their time. But into the consideration of these several matters; however important at the time, we do not intend to enter.

The first Report of the Committee recommended that all bills that should pass during that session of Parliament should not be exempt from any general Act passed during the session.

The second Report contained a recommendation as to the manner in which railway committees should be formed.

" From the number of bills for the formation of new lines," say the Committee in their third Report, " now before Parliament; from the appearance of many new schemes likely to come under consideration in the next session; from the greatly increased favour and support which, as compared with the projects of former years, these undertakings now receive from the owners of landed property through which they are to pass; from the reduced amount of estimates of cost, and the comparative economy with which they can be made, and from the improvement of trade and redundancy of capital in the country, combined with the prevailing indisposition to run the risks which have rendered some kinds of foreign investments so disastrous, the committee anticipate a very great extension of the railway system within the next few years.

"It appears, therefore, to your committee, that the present moment, while Parliament still retains in its own hands an entire and unimpaired discretion, with regard both to the inauguration of new companies and the enlargement of the powers of old ones, affords an opportunity more favourable than any that can be expected hereafter to occur for attaching beforehand to the legislative sanction which is sought by those parties on their own behalf, the conditions which may be deemed necessary for the public good, and which may realize and apply such conclusions as our experience of the new system up to the present time may be deemed to have sufficiently established."

The committee, after noticing the great augmentation that might, in the course of a few years, be expected in the receipts of railways, and the desirability of establishing a more direct connection between the interests of the public and those of railway proprietors, go on to say:—"The committee deem it clear that, although the practical monopoly of railway companies has been acquired in the main by the superior manner in which they have accommodated the traffic of the country, it is nevertheless regarded, even in the present day, with considerable jealousy by the public at large, that questions of an embarrassing nature, founded on the original views with which Parliament granted Acts of Incorporation to new companies, might be raised, which it would be far better to obviate, and that on those accounts it is time to reserve on the part of the State the right of intervention at a date sufficiently remote in the convenience of these companies, and of a reconsideration of their powers and privileges.

"Again, great as have been the benefits of railways to the public, that circumstance does not afford any good reason against seeking by any just and reasonable means to enlarge their advantages. Now, it is material to observe, that in this country what is called the High Fare System ordinarily prevails, that the average charge of railway communication—a charge falling in no inconsiderable degree on trade and commerce—is very much higher than in other countries where railways have been established, and that there is no clear or early prospect of a general reduction of the rate of charges under the present system of independent companies, even although it might be advantageous in particular cases.

"The committee are aware that Parliament will regard with a just jealousy whatever even appears to tend towards the discouragement of competition, or to impose restraints upon the application of capital to domestic enterprise; but the committee also consider that this subject should be approached with the recollection that the matter now under discussion is not the expenditure of capital by mere individuals, or even by companies associated under ordinary liabilities, and with ordinary powers, but by permanent incorporations exempted from the very material check the general principle of unlimited liability imposes, and armed for given periods with compulsory powers, under which they are authorized to set aside private rights, to affect seriously by new works the existing communications of the country, and especially the local communications of rural districts, and contingently on their abandonment to entail, according to the common law, a considerable amount of permanent liability upon the districts which they traverse for the repair of bridges and other works which they may have constructed."

The committee having thus stated the case, proceeded to lay down the rules by which, in their opinion, it ought to be governed. It is the established practice, they say, of Parliament to regulate or altogether prevent the expenditure of capital without certain conditions being attached, as the public good may require, "and the committee conceive that the grounds of this policy are to be found first in a regard to the interest of the public in the widest sense, but also in regard to the interests of those whose rights such companies are to control and supersede, of those with whom they are to deal and to contract, with those private dealers with whom they are to compete in carrying on their business, and of those extensive classes of persons who, not being capitalists, or possessed of commercial knowledge, are induced to invest their small means in enterprises of this kind, and in doing so are encouraged to a great extent by the idea that they are under legislative regulation, and that Parliament has made every just and practicable provision for the protection of the subject. Further, in the case of railways the number of possible competitors is of necessity so restrained as to give to any project the aspect and operation of a substantial monopoly, and in such cases it is the practice of Parliament to impose special conditions for the benefit of the public; the rule and measure of which condition the committee conceive to be this: that all such limitations on projections are legitimate as leave to them sufficient and ample inducement to carry into effect beneficial speculations. The committee trusts that Parliament will be on its guard against the superficial reasonings by which it is attempted to apply popular maxims, sound in their ordinary operation, to cases more or less removed by their peculiarities from the reach of such maxims, and will keep steadily in view, as a paramount consideration, the attainment, whether by ordinary maxims or by such modifications of them as circumstances may justify and require, of the greatest amount of ultimate public advantage. The willingness of parties to expend capital in making a new railway is not to be at once taken as a sufficient ground for granting the necessary powers; *there is no public advantage in the construction of a work which cannot afford remuneration*, as there can be no security for the working of a railway except its yielding a profit.

"New railway companies may, as is quite conceivable, be formed, and may come before Parliament with the specious promise of combating monopoly, and of carrying, at lower rates, the traffic now carried at higher ones, and under these pretexts powers might be obtained in proportion to the engagements contracted before Parliament, and it might, notwithstanding, prove, when the Acts of Incorporation had been passed, that on the one hand there were no adequate means of enforcing the engagement, and that the guarantees taken on the part of the public for their fulfilment were barren and valueless, but that on the other hand the powers had been improperly used as efficient instruments of extension against the subsisting companies, to whom might be offered only the alternative of losing their traffic or of buying off opposition."

The committee recommended that railway bills should be submitted to the Board of Trade previous to their coming under the notice of Parliament—the committee conceiving that the Board, or such other public department as might be entrusted with the care of railway matters, could advantageously examine these bills and also the schemes themselves before they had assumed the forms of bills—and that the reports from the Board of Trade should on no account be regarded in any other light than as intended to afford to Parliament additional aid in the elucidation of the facts by the testimony of witnesses, competent by official knowledge, habit, and opportunity, and officially responsible for the advice they might offer.

This recommendation of the committee was subsequently adopted by Parliament, but worked very unsatisfactorily; the reports received but little attention from the committees, their recommendations were as frequently set aside as adopted, and the duties of the Board of Trade in regard to these preliminary investigations and reports were in the course of a few years formally abolished by law.

A great deal of evidence was taken by the committee in regard to the treatment of third-class passengers, and the effect that the establishment of what are now well known as "Parliamentary" trains might be expected to have on the general traffic. A compulsory measure to convey passengers in enclosed carriages at one penny per mile was received with great alarm by the railway interest; it was contended that the necessary consequence of such a measure would be the reduction of first and second class fares, and a decrease in dividends.

Among the many witnesses examined on this subject was Mr. (now Sir) Rowland Hill, the author of "Post Office Reform," and then chairman of the London and Brighton Company. Mr. Rowland Hill bore testimony to the great benefit his company had derived from a large reduction they had made in their fares, namely, from 14s., 10s., and 7s., for the several classes, to 12s., 8s., and 5s.; and that the gross receipts had been considerably increased without any addition whatever to the expenditure. Mr. Hill was, however, altogether opposed to the establishment of "parliamentary" trains; he thought passengers could be carried more cheaply in open than in covered carriages, and if companies were left to their own management, the probability would be that passengers would be carried in open carriages at less than one penny per mile, but if companies were required to enclose their carriages, he doubted whether they would charge less than the maximum penny per mile. He was therefore opposed to any compulsory measure on the subject. Mr. Rowland Hill entered into considerable detail to prove the lowness of the fares charged by railways compared with those charged formerly by coach. "You have compared," said Mr. Horsman, one of the members of the committee, who, after Mr. Gladstone, took the most prominent part in conducting its proceedings, "the fare which is paid by first class by railway with that which is paid by coach. Have you made an estimate of the different costs of transporting passengers by the two modes of conveyance?" "The cost of transport," replied Mr. Rowland Hill, "leaving out of consideration the cost of the road, is incomparably less upon a railway than by a coach, *but the great cost consists in the interest of capital expended on the road."*

In the concluding part of Mr. Rowland Hill's reply to Mr. Horsman, which I have marked in italics, it will be seen that he fell into the common error of assuming that the high cost of a railway acts as a preventive against low fares; and his falling into such an error is the more remarkable, as it is one he carefully avoided when giving evidence on his own project some years previous of post-office reform. Mr. Rowland Hill then proved, before the committee appointed to investigate his plan, that the cost of conveying a letter from London to Edinburgh was only the thirty-sixth part of a penny; but that expenditure had nothing to do with the capital invested in the road, and coaches and horses, on and by which the letters were conveyed.

There were, at this time, three great fundamental reforms projected in the railway system by Government, which they were determined, if possible, to carry. The first we have noticed with regard to the compulsory conveyance of third-class passengers; the second was the right of revising the fares, under certain contingencies; and the third was the concession to the State of the absolute right to purchase the railways, on certain specified terms, at the expiration of a fixed time.

It must be remembered that, in 1844, the main trunk lines were paying 10 per cent. and upwards; and with the protective system Government proposed to adopt for existing railways by discountenancing the construction of competing lines, it was generally supposed that the ordinary increase of the trade and commerce of the country would add largely to the dividends of the companies. Government shared this opinion; and lengthened negotiations were carried on between the Board of Trade and the representatives of the railway interest, for a considerable time, in vain endeavours to come to an amicable arrangement with regard to conceding to Government the right to revise the fares, and other knotty points; and at one time a total rupture between the two high contracting parties was threatened. A meeting took place, at which nearly all the great companies were represented. Mr. Hudson, at that time high on his iron throne, took the chair, and denounced the bill introduced to Parliament as injurious to railway property and prejudicial to public welfare. Mr. Saunders, on behalf of the Great Western, followed, declaring his belief that the provisions affecting future lines would be brought to bear on the old as well as the new, avowing that his directors were, to a man, opposed to it; while others, in the depth of their despair, saw only ruin before them. It is quite impossible to describe the stormy feelings which then pervaded the railway world. Mutual distrust and mutual dissensions were forgotten. Opposing chairmen met in the same room, discussing the same interest, and denouncing the same Government. It was the great question of the day—the absorbing topic of the time. Men magnified its dangers, drew pictures of its consequences, and trembled at the distresses they had evoked.*

One of the main points of dispute between the Government and the companies, on which a vast deal of evidence was given before the committee, was in reference to the period that should elapse, after the new companies were paying ten per cent. dividends, before Government should have the right to revise the fares. It is quite unnecessary to take any notice either of the evidence or the details of the dispute on this section of the Railway Act; it became virtually a dead letter. Very few of the railways, new or old, pay much beyond five per cent.; and I need hardly add, that there is not the least probability of any of them ever paying ten per cent.

The third projected reform in the railway system, proposed by

* Francis.

Government on the recommendation of the committee, and which ultimately passed the Legislature, was that which forms the more immediate subject of this treatise, viz. the absolute right of the Government to purchase all railways that obtained their Acts of Incorporation in 1844, or any subsequent date, the terms, should the parties not otherwise agree, to be settled by arbitration. I may as well state here that the details of the General Railway Act of 1844 were ultimately arranged to the satisfaction of the railway body, and that all opposition was withdrawn on its third reading.

It may well be imagined that nothing but a strong conviction on the part of Sir Robert Peel, Mr. Gladstone, and the other members of Government, of the importance of the case, and the necessity of providing remedial measures, although they should not come into operation till a long distant day, would have induced them to depart so widely from that traditional policy of the country which excludes Government, so wisely and so well, from all management of, and control over, our great industrial works. Yet even Sir Robert Peel, strong as he was in the esteem and affections of his countrymen—with his well-known liberal tendencies, high constitutional character, and it may be added, large parliamentary majority—would not venture, even in an exceptional case like the present, to run counter to the prejudices of the English people. Parliament, under his guidance, enacted that a period of twenty-one years should elapse before the Legislature would be in a position to resume those rights and privileges, which, for the intervening period, they considered necessary to delegate to the railway companies.

It must, however, be remembered that at this time it was assumed as a matter of course that the direct management of railways by the Government would be the necessary consequence of their purchase by the State. No one disputed this absurd proposition, nor was it till many years afterwards that it was entirely exploded.

CHAPTER V.

Evidence before the Parliamentary Committee of 1844—Mr. Laing, of the Board of Trade—Mr. Saunders, Secretary to the Great Western Railway Company—Mr. G. Carr Glyn, Chairman of the London and Birmingham Company—Mr. Baxendale, Chairman of the South-Eastern Company — Mr. George Hudson — Captain Laws, General Manager of the Leeds and Manchester Railway — Establishment of Parliamentary Trains.

THE time occupied in the examination of witnesses before the committee extended over three months, and embraced every subject connected with railway management. The witnesses were principally directors, managers, and others connected with railways, and Government was represented by Mr. Laing, of the Board of Trade. An extract from the evidence of this gentleman will sufficiently explain the views of Government in regard to the deferred right of purchase on the part of the State :—

Q. You stated, said (Mr. Gladstone,) that part of the scheme which you proposed was to give the power to the Government at the expiration of twenty years under certain circumstances of buying up the whole of any given railway, and taking it into their hands ?—Yes; that was part of the scheme.

Q. Was that part of the scheme assented to by railway companies ?—Yes; certainly it was; that part of the scheme was rather favourably received by them. It was proposed that at the end of twenty years from the next following 1st January, after the passing of this Act, it shall be in the option of the Government to take the line at twenty-five years' purchase of the annual divisible profits calculated upon the average of the three last preceding years.

Q. You would propose the alternative of the Government purchasing the railway at the end of this period of twenty years, in case you could not make an arrangement as to the rate of fares?—Either in case you could not make an arrangement as to fares, or if Government should think it consistent with policy to do so.

Q. Then for twenty years from the present time, whatever inconveniences might arise from the want of adaptation of the different connecting lines, would be permitted to go on?—We propose to take the control over one train for the poorer classes; as regards the others, I do not see how you can remedy that, unless you are prepared at once to interfere with their charges.

Q. The proposal is to leave the railway companies alone for twenty years—you adjourn the consideration of the question for that time?—No; Parliament has always the power to interfere.

Q. Are not you proposing a scheme which is not to take effect unless there is something advantageous to call for it?—I look upon it in this way: that whereas now you have granted this power to railway companies in perpetuity, you are going to reserve the right of interfering at the end of a limited period.

Q. Do you propose that the Government should take the railways into their hands?—The Government would take them into their hands only in the event of exercising the option of purchasing.

Q. In the proposals which you submitted to the railway companies, have these various points which have been alluded to been included and discussed?—Yes; I think they are understood fully by most of those with whom I have communicated on the subject.

From the foregoing extracts from Mr. Laing's evidence, it will appear that the assent of the railway body had been obtained to this proposal on the part of Government, and this is confirmed by the fact that the bill was read a third time in the House of Commons without opposition, and passed through the House of Lords, unopposed at every stage.

Mr. George Carr Glyn, chairman of the London and Birmingham Company, was not opposed to the Government making, in case of necessity, competing lines, and in the Preface I have given a brief extract from this gentleman's evidence; but Mr. Glyn did not define what, according to his ideas, constituted a case of necessity, nor did Mr. Gladstone, in examining Mr. Glyn and using the term "excesssive rates and charges," say what was the standard by which their moderation or excess should be tested, and without some such standard I do not well see the possibility of applying a test. At that time the great object of companies was to drive competition off the road, and thus secure a monopoly, and having done this, immediately raise the charges to the highest paying point. It is not likely that Mr. Glyn meant more than that, in some extreme and exceptional cases, the Government would be justified in constructing competing lines.

It is not at all likely that the extreme case supposed will ever occur; — we have enough, and to spare, of legitimate opposition, and however high the charges and bad the management of a company might be, it would never be tolerated that the resources of the State should be brought to bear on private individuals, to have their profits reduced by Government opposition when that remedy was wanting in the ordinary and fair way of trade.

Mr. Glyn had great apprehension that competing lines, without effecting any great good for the public, would place railway property in general in great danger; he was strongly in favour of yielding many privileges to the public for the sake of protection against competition.

There was no company so determined as the Great Western in their opposition to Government in every project they brought forward; they would receive no protection from the Board of Trade, nor grant any privileges: all they desired was to be let alone; they had a strong objection to be in any way interfered with; and their great dread was, that by some piece of clever legerdemain on the part of the Board of Trade, the Government should acquire the right to purchase, at the expiration of twenty years, the old lines as well as the new, the effect of which would have been to limit the price of their shares, now selling for £67, to £250! really four times their present price. It is rather odd that the company that eventually suffered most from competing lines was the very one, above all others, to offer the most determined opposition to any offer of protection, come from what quarter it might. Mr. Russell, the chairman of the board, was on the committee, and its able secretary, Mr. Saunders, was its representative, and a very difficult task he had to perform, to prove the manifold benefits the country would derive from railway monopoly, and the evil consequences that would result from competition; and not only that, but to satisfy the committee that this monopoly could be maintained without some such protective system as was proposed by the Board of Trade. Let Mr. Saunders, however, under the guidance of the chairman of the committee, explain his own ideas on the subject.

Q. Do you (said Mr. Gladstone) think it possible, under any circumstances, absolutely to prevent competition between railways, or to prevent the creation of new lines, which, though intended for other purposes, may collaterally and indirectly have the effect of competition?—I do not think you can—that is the difficulty I have always felt with respect to it. I do not see how you can, in the interest of the public, take that course.

Q. Supposing it were possible to protect them against indirect competition; do you think it also hopeless to endeavour to obtain any protection against direct competition under any circumstances?—I am afraid that it is so, to endure any great length of time.

Q. Then is the committee to understand that you do not think it worth while, under all the difficulties of the case, to make any attempt to get protection against competition?—I am afraid you cannot do it; I should be very glad to see it done, but I should be afraid of anything that is apparently affording protection, which you either cannot give, or if you apparently give you cannot maintain.

Q. If there were now before Parliament a body of persons willing to make a new railway from London to Birmingham, and offer to place themselves under restrictions to carry passengers at two-thirds the present prices, should they obtain this bill? —No; I reject it on this principle, that you have made a bargain with the London and Birmingham Railway Company; if you show that they offer impediments to trade, or if they used their powers unfairly as regards the public, if their rates of charges are a discouragement to traffic, you retain in your hands the power of remedying it.

Q. Where do you find a bargain between Parliament and the railway companies, except in the Acts under which these companies are constituted?—These are the bargains which I speak of.

Q. Is there any bargain, express or implied, in those Acts of Parliament to discourage the formation of competing lines?—On the contrary, I say competition is not the bargain. I say you hold the power of competition in your hands. If, instead of moderate fares and remunerating rates, they charge their maximum rates; if there is any misapplication of the power you have granted them, you reserve to yourself the power of granting a competing line; that is what I say you ought to retain. I do not think you ought to fetter it.

Q. You ought to retain it, but not to use it?—You ought to use it, I think, when there is a misapplication of the powers given to the company.

Q. In case the powers granted by Parliament are not exceeded, should a competing line be granted?—Not if the work is properly done. We all see and know the result when twice the capital is expended; the two parties at last come to terms, and then must draw from the public, as a remuneration for the capital that has been so expended, a larger sum than would have been required for the smaller expenditure; for I do always maintain that it is essential in this country that the Government itself shall either employ the national funds as the means of carrying on these improvements, or that you must encourage the accumulating wealth of this country to be employed in them, for the purpose of getting such improvements made, and at the same time enable the parties to obtain a remuneration for the capital so employed.

Q. Your mode of encouraging parties to employ the accumulating wealth of the country would be, that when parties came forward to make a second line, you would reject their bill?—Yes; if that line is to be made for the mere purpose of lowering the profits of an undertaking in which you have already encouraged the accumulated wealth of the country to be applied.

Q. Would it be fair to say to a company, "We will give you your choice; if you make a reduction in your terms we will reject the bill for a new line, but if you will not we sanction it?"—I think it would be a very unfair thing to do; it is very much a piece with the highwayman who says, "Your money or your life!" I think it would be considered as ungracious, and so unfair that it would recoil immediately on the public.

Q. You think that Parliament would reject those parties and refuse the bill, although they would offer to carry the public at two-thirds of the present charge?—I hold that they should. I am confident they would.

Q. Assume that Parliament would act on the opposite principle, and grant bills whenever they find parties willing to carry on better terms?—Then the policy of Parliament would, in fact, be to enforce new competition without regard to necessity, unless you should choose to reduce your charges below those at which you can afford to carry the traffic.

Q. Please to assume that Parliament would, if you so please to call it, force on you competition when you refused to carry as low as other companies would offer to do. Under this assumption, I ask, would it be wise on the part of the company to make some sacrifice in order to get an arrangement from Parliament which would prevent this competition?—You hint a hypothetical case for an opinion on it; still I should be very much disposed to take my chance rather than encounter the certain sacrifice you have proposed.

Q. The London and Birmingham charge 30s. for a first class, and 20s. for a second class to Birmingham; if a body of persons competent in respect to capital were to offer to carry first-class passengers at 20s., and second class at 15s., should they get their bill?—Most undoubtedly not; you will be introducing this destructive principle, and authorizing a competition whether necessary or not.

Q. Do you think railways ought to be invested with a patent right of carrying passengers between two places?—Subject to certain conditions, I do; and I must contend that you would be doing the greatest possible injustice to this country, if, when it can be shown that a company by economy and proper management, and not by under charges, had been successful, you were to break down their success by competition.

It would appear from the foregoing evidence that the prevailing idea in Mr. Saunders' mind—and he represented one of our greatest companies—was, that the public were made for the railways, and not the railways for the public. In his opinion, railways were almost too sacred to be in any way disturbed by competition, and however largely the public, according to ordinary ideas, would benefit from a reduction in fares, if such reduction was the result of competition, it would be a fraud on the first company in possession; the Government that would even intimate to a railway company the possibility of a rival scheme being countenanced by the Legislature, Mr. Saunders compared "to a highwayman that demands your money or your life."

Notwithstanding Mr. Saunders' denunciation of the absolute fraud that any company would be guilty of in competing with the London and Birmingham Company for their traffic, only a few years from that time elapsed till another company, utterly regardless of the high moral principles laid down by that gentleman as those on which companies should act, but under the guidance of a secretary as clever as himself, succeeded in establishing a rival line to the London and Birmingham. It will, therefore, be seen that Mr. Saunders had formed far too high an opinion of the Legislature, for they did, after all, "a very unfair thing, much of a piece with the highwayman," when they granted this competing line. Curiously enough, this second company has been the means of reducing the fares from thirty shillings and twenty shillings, to twenty shillings and fifteen shillings, the exact reduction Mr. Gladstone indicated as likely to result from a rival line. "The recoil on the public" that has produced such a great reduction in fares, has been anything but "unsatisfactory;" and to complete this strange coincidence, the rival company—" the highwayman that said your money or your life"—happens to be the Great Western, and the bill was carried through Parliament under the management of Mr. Saunders himself!

It is twenty years since Mr. Saunders gave his evidence before the committee; and in conformity with it, the Great Western directors have consistently acted; their shares, which at one time were selling at £170, have been reduced by competition and guarantees to little more than the third of that value.

One of the principal witnesses on behalf of the railway interest was Mr. Baxendale, head of the great carrying firm of Pickford and Co., and chairman of the South-Eastern Railway. This gentleman was undoubtedly the highest authority in the kingdom in all matters relating to traffic, and the best manner in which the public should be served. He was asked:—

Q. Do you anticipate great injury to railway property without some change of policy?—Certainly. One feeling I have as to railway property is its insecurity. I would much rather have a more moderate income with a certainty than the uncertainty which at present prevails in my mind.

Q. Do you think that an effectual provision could be made for the interests of the public by the multiplication of competing lines?—Competing railways have, in effect, not been competing railways; matters become worse than if there never had been a competing line, for the parties soon coalesce. I have very strong feelings on this subject. I have always considered that the commerce of this country has always prospered to the extent it has done in consequence of the great freedom of communication; I have always considered that the roads of the country belonged altogether to the people, just as much as the light of heaven. I have therefore invariably said that leaving the whole of the roads of Great Britain, as they would ultimately become, in the hands of irresponsible parties, did not appear to me to be sound. At the time I took upon myself the management of the London and Birmingham Railway, I then considered the whole of the proceedings which they were adopting were very unsound, very stringent, and very unwise for themselves and injurious to the public. I am sure that the millions will never rest if a few thousands are to have these great powers.

Mr. Baxendale entered into considerable detail in regard to the charges and profits of the passenger traffic. The charge for third class on his line was seven-eighths of a penny per mile, and he calculated the expense at three-eighths of a penny per mile, but there were a great number of vacant seats in the carriages, which, consequently, considerably increased the cost of those which were carried. "Whenever there was a great multitude of third-class passengers," he said, "if you could carry them by tens of thousands where you now carry them by hundreds, no doubt the third class would pay well." It will be seen that Mr. Baxendale calculated the *cost* of the conveyance of each third-class passenger at three shillings and one penny for each hundred miles. Liberal as his views undoubtedly were, I think he hardly anticipated that before twenty years had elapsed from the time he was speaking, third-class passengers would be carried in excursion trains on his line at half the price of what he then stated to be the cost of conveyance. But to proceed with his evidence.

Q. Your opinion is, that it is impossible to prevent the combination of two companies against the public?—Having had to do with public bodies all my life (more, perhaps, than any other man), I know they are never to be depended upon, and therefore I would never leave in the power of public bodies more than I could help.

Q. Do you think that new lines should be undertaken by Government?—Certainly, because there would be no possible reason for the Government adopting a course that was hostile to the public. If the question were now a blank sheet of paper, I should let the Government take the matter entirely in hand.

Q. Does there exist at this moment among railway companies a great apprehension as to the effect of what are called competing lines?—There does in my mind, as a railway man.

Q. Would not the best way be to purchase the existing railways, if Government were disposed to lay out their capital for such a purpose?—*I think the country at large would probably hail a measure of that kind, because they would get out of our trammels.*

Q. Take the South Eastern—has your line been threatened with competition?—No; but in the present state of the public mind, there are so many schemers looking round for jobs, and so many people who are induced to enter into these undertakings, that I feel no security at its not being carried out. If one short piece of railway is commenced at one end, and another piece at the other end, by-and-by they get another piece attached to it, and so they would ultimately get another line of railway that would compete.

Mr. Baxendale appeared even then to have some forebodings of the future London, Chatham, and Dover, and was not disposed to be very complimentary in his language to those who would be the promoters of the line. Mr. Baxendale's evidence on the increase of goods traffic was important.

Q. Can you give the Committee an idea of the aggregate increase of the traffic of the country as respects goods?—The fact is, that every day thousands and tens of thousands of tons that formerly were left upon the ground, and not removed from one point to another, are now removed, and brought an immense distance into the country. I do not know to what extent it is likely to increase, nor can I say what the extent has been, but most assuredly the low rates of freight have increased to an enormous extent the traffic.

Q. You were asked your idea as to the Government purchasing up the railways—do you think that a practicable one ?—I am not sufficiently acquainted with the finances of the country to give an answer to that question.

Q. Do you see any difficulties in carrying that scheme into execution besides financial ones ?—I think the question is one that might be very well grappled with. If two or three railway companies can make arrangements for working, I think it is within the grasp of Government to manage the subject.—Pp. 234-256.

The most important witness examined before the Committee was Captain Laws, manager of the Leeds and Manchester Railway—a gentleman of great experience in his particular department. It was on the line of which he was manager that, on his recommendation, third-class carriages were first introduced in England. I have given his evidence in reference to the purchase of the railways by Government *in extenso*, not only for the purpose of throwing all possible light on the subject, but because the plan of purchase proposed by him was recommended by the Committee and adopted by the Legislature.

I may observe here generally that if ever a change takes place in the public feeling of this country in regard to our railway system, it must be mainly, if not entirely, brought about by the conviction that men of high character and great practical experience, such as Mr. Glyn, Mr. Baxendale, and Captain Laws—naturally attached as we may suppose them to have been to a system indigenous to the soil—would never have proposed or recommended such a change as that involved in the transfer of railways to the State, or the construction of competing lines by the Government, unless they were strongly convinced of its necessity, and the great benefit the country would derive from a change in our present mode of railway management. The English are, *par excellence*, a practical people, and the most plausible theory can have but little weight with them unless supported by the testimony of those best qualified to form an opinion how that theory would operate in practice. The evidence given before the Select Committee in 1844 was by those who, not only from their position and experience, could best judge of the merits of the two systems, but who had also an interest in maintaining the present one. Mr. Hudson, at that time the chairman of six railway companies, in his evidence admitted that great reductions might be made in the scale of charges if the railways were purchased by the State. Nor had he a word to say against the policy of Government constructing competing lines; he fully admitted that Parliament never intended to give companies a monopoly, and all he contended for was, that if Government constructed competing lines, they were bound to buy up the old ones.

The Committee was appointed on the 5th February, and made their first Report on the 18th May. They entered on their inquiry, they said, with a strong prepossession against any general interference by the Government in the management and working of railways, and left off with a recommendation that the Legislature should pass a general Act whereby the whole system should undergo revision in 1865. The number of witnesses examined was 27; the examination of one alone— Mr. Laing—occupied seven days; and the aggregate evidence and reports formed a bulky quarto volume of some six hundred pages. Important as a great portion of this evidence is, in regard to railway economy and management, we must necessarily confine our extracts to the most salient points, principally relating to the purchase of the railways by the State; and as Captain Laws' is, in that respect, the most important, we shall conclude our extracts with that gentleman's evidence. He was asked by Mr. Gladstone:—

Q. Do you think it desirable that Government should become purchasers of all the railway property now existing in the country?—Yes, I do.

Q. Can you state in what way you think the purchase of the railway interests could be carried out beneficially to the public?—I think a simple and equitable mode of purchasing the existing lines, as well as promoting the formation of such as ought to be made in addition to the existing lines, might be adopted in the following manner:—That from the date of the passing of any Act to authorize Government to make such purchase, or ten years from the time any railway was completed and in full operation under their parliamentary powers, they should be subject to purchase under the following conditions: the amount of compensation to be estimated entirely by the amount of benefit on an average of the last three years; and, to prevent the companies dividing a larger dividend than their earnings would have authorized had no such purchase been in contemplation, by allowing working stock of engines (locomotive or stationary), rails, turnplates, buildings, tools or machinery, carriages, waggons, furniture or stores, &c., to become in disrepair or disused from improvements, I should deduct from the net profits, after paying the working expenses, 15 per cent., which forms about the average portion of railway capital devoted to that particular part of their plant; that is about the average proportion of capital of railways generally for furnishing that part of their property.

Q. You mean that 15 per cent. is about the proportion of their gross capital which is employed in that way?—Yes, but I have an addition to make to that. The stock should then be valued. I first say, here is £300,000 net profit for the last three years. I deduct £45,000 from the £300,000, and that leaves £255,000. But the £45,000 is a matter to be inquired into. That is to be done by a valuation of all the articles included in this.

Q. What are the advantages which you propose the public should derive from making the purchase?—I look upon it that the advantage the public must derive would be, either by greater accommodation, by means of the railway communications, or an advantage in having a very considerable revenue to devote to the public expenditure from this source.

Q. Then you contemplate that the Government should either make this a means of revenue, or should, in fact, reduce the charges very materially to the public?—I think there are two modes of the Government making all the railways, merely speaking in a financial point of view, with very great advantage to the public. One would be to work it something on the penny post system, and that the rates would be very little more than sufficient to cover the working expenses and the interest of the money—that would give very great facilities and greatly promote every description of domestic industry, whether of manufacture or agriculture. On the other hand, if they were to work it as private companies do—exact the most they could from the public, so as to get the largest profit—if they work it upon that principle, of course, whatever there is over the working expenses and the interest of money, would be available for the public expenses of the nation.

Q. What you contemplate is that they should either use railways as the Post Office is now used, or that they should use them as the Post Office was previously used, as a means of revenue?—Those are the extremes of the case; I should recommend an intermediate course.

Q. At what rate do you suppose that Government would borrow money in order to purchase up the railways?—Three per cent., or a shade above it.

Q. What do you consider to be the present number of years' purchase at which the public is willing to buy railway property? taking the established railways of the kingdom, what number of years' purchase would the public be willing to give?—It is very difficult to say; the confidence in one would be so very different to that in another. I could go and purchase some railway stock now that would pay 8 per cent. on the purchase; but I should be sorry to hold that stock. In fact, on the good lines—the London and Birmingham, the Great Western, the South-Western, and any of the well-established lines—we have no difficulty in getting money at $3\frac{1}{2}$ per cent.

Q. Do you mean that the shares on these established lines sell at such a price that they will only pay $3\frac{1}{2}$ per cent. to a purchaser?—The Manchester and Leeds shares were selling yesterday at £118 for an annuity of £4 18s.; that is about $4\frac{1}{2}$ per cent., but this is a line which has not yet developed itself; in fact, its connection with Liverpool is not yet open; but I apprehend you could not get an annuity in the London and Birmingham now of £3, much under £100.

Q. Then the credit of the railway is now as good as the credit of the Government?—It is approaching it very rapidly.

Q. Then the Government would not get any advantage in the purchase; they would not buy a property which, with the present changes and the present incomes, would pay them a much larger interest than the interest which they would have to pay over to the persons from whom they purchased the property?—Yes, they would, because there is not one-tenth part of the railway property that stands in the description I have described.

Q. But by purchasing the good lines, in point of fact, the Government would obtain no surplus?—I have no doubt they would purchase the good lines for perhaps one-half per cent. better terms than any individual would give for shares in the market; but that, of course, is very much dependent upon the state of the market. The money market is now in a position that has brought the better railways into great repute as to credit and stability.

Q. Does it not follow from your view that any surplus revenue which the Government may obtain, even under the present charges, must be derived from some improvement in the management?—A great deal of saving, no doubt, would be derived from an uniform and far less costly management; and generally taking the whole of railway stock, *I should think there would be one or one and a quarter per cent. in favour of the Government purchasing against the public now.*

Q. What would you estimate the railway stock at?—It is so mixed a question, that it is difficult to say. I can now buy railway stock varying from a promissory dividend of 8 per cent. to one of about 3, $3\frac{1}{4}$, or $3\frac{1}{2}$. Whenever you find it is $3\frac{1}{2}$, there is some notion of the issue of new stock, by which you participate in all the prospective advantages.

Q. Can you state any definite sums as to the amount for which the Government might purchase the railways, the amount of interest they would have to pay, the amount of profits of the railways at present, so as to make a comparison of the sum the Government would receive with the sum which the Government would pay?—I think I could solve that question in a very simple shape. I would say, let the Government take the best of the lines. Suppose the Government has made up its mind to begin the purchase, I should by no means suggest they should run headlong into it, and give every railway company notice, "We intend to buy you on such a day;" but they should begin and introduce themselves gradually into the system and into the management by giving notice to one of the great lines. I would give notice to those lines which are completed. Take the London and Birmingham and the Grand Junction, which are completed over a distance of 200 and odd miles. The value of those lines I hold to be as simple a question as the value of the Three per Cents. to-day. I divide a profit of so many hundred thousands a year; I take that and deduct 15 per cent. from it, to set against the working stock, including rails and the plant. Now, value this stock. Their engines are as good as anybody's; but still the Government would have a great advantage in this respect, that there has been a reduction in the price of that stock within the last four years of full 50 per cent., and the probability is, that when you come to value that stock at its present market price, instead of paying back £45,000, which would be the amount of 15 per cent. upon the present income of those three lines, the value of that stock is not above £35,000, and I say that would be as fair a purchase to all parties as anything could be.

Q. Does the consideration that the railway companies possess, in many respects, something in the character of a monopoly, enter materially into the grounds of your opinion?—Yes, it does, and not only monopoly now, but every extension is calculated to increase immensely that monopoly and a continuation of monopolies.

Q. Do you anticipate that there will be a tendency among the railway companies to amalgamate to a considerable extent?—From what I have seen I can state that there is a much more extensive combination than probably the committee have any idea of.

On being further questioned by the committee, Captain Laws proceeded to detail the various combinations and amalgamations projected by the several companies, nearly all of which were subsequently carried out. He further noticed the way in which companies used their power of purchase, and instanced the York and North Midland having bought up the Leeds and Selby, not for the purpose of using it, but for closing it up and taking passengers and goods by a circuitous route on their own line, charging what fares and rates they thought proper. Captain Laws then went into considerable detail as to the inconvenience and losses inflicted on traders by the capricious and unfair manner in which they were treated by several companies, from whom there was no appeal so long as they kept within the letter of the law. The purchase of the railways by Government was again referred to. Captain Laws was asked:—

Q. Do you think that very great economy would result in the management of railways from the consolidation in the hands of Government which you propose to effect by means of purchase?—I have not the smallest doubt of it. If there is any advantage in amalgamation, of course the extension of that principle would be of advantage. Uniformity of practice and a reduction of the large staff which every railway company has would, of itself, be a considerable item in reduction of expense.

Q. Would you regard a great reduction in the present average of railway fares as a very great advantage to the trade and commerce of the country?—I think there can be no doubt about it.

Q. Do you think that advantage bears directly, to a very great extent, upon cheapening production in all the great branches of the industry of the country?—I think so.

Q. Do you think that if your plan were acted on, it might be possible for the Government, without risk to the Treasury, to try the experiment of cheaper communication?—I think they might; I think it depends upon the nature of the lines. In the case of a line like the London and York, I do not think it would be of any great advantage to have a cheap rate upon it. That line would hardly touch any town. The traffic would principally consist of gentlemen going backward and forward to London occasionally; but when you come into a densely populated district, or when you come into a district one part of which is agricultural and the other manufacturing, then the more intimate and cheap you can make the connection, the benefit will be the greater.

Q. Where the communication is connected with business and trade, then you think low fares are advantages; where it is connected in a great measure with the private comfort of the rich, then you see no particular advantage in low fares?— To a less extent, certainly.

Q. May it not be argued that if that be the case, it will, under the present system, be to the interest of the proprietors to adopt low fares where they are desirable?—It is very possible; but I think there is this objection to any private interest being so powerful an instrument as a combination of railways, that it may be to their interest to shut out one section of country from the advantages which are enjoyed by another.

Q. Is it your opinion that if the railways were in the hands of Government, and if the Government were disposed at some future time to make a great effort for the purpose of giving the advantages of cheap communication, that that effect ought to be confined to certain parts of the railway system, and not extended to the whole?—The more extended it is the better. It would be expedient to begin with certain sections, and to feel your way thoroughly. Though my own conviction is, there would be no great difficulty in establishing the whole thing under complete Government control in a few months; still I would say, feel your way, and you will soon discover that there is no great difficulty in working the thing most beneficially to the public.

Q. You would suggest that the railways ought to be taken not simultaneously, but one after another, for the convenience of making the experiment in the best way; but looking at the ultimate result, do you think it would be desirable to attempt the experiment of cheap fares all over the kingdom?—I do not think any evil could arise from it, and much good might.

Q. Do you think there would be a great benefit, looking at the communications of the country as a whole with a view to the development of its traffic, from establishing universally low prices?—I think there can be little doubt about it.

Q. You draw a distinction between railways that carry trading traffic and railways that carry wealthy persons travelling for convenience or pleasure; but are there not a great number of railways that have a mixed traffic; and can you always draw a line of distinction between those two classes?—I apprehend that every railway has power; but when I spoke of high fares I was speaking of the thing now in public, then in private hands. If I was a director of the London and Birmingham Railway, I should adopt the plan of high fares, because I could command a traffic at those fares that is very profitable, and it would be a dangerous experiment to give up a certainty for an uncertainty; though as a private individual conducting the Birmingham railway, I should adopt the course they have. On the other hand, as a private individual conducting a railway of a very different character, which depends very largely on the profits for goods of a lower description of traffic altogether, such as third-class passengers, we can hardly go too low to arrive at a remunerating price, and that is in consequence of the short distances more than anything else.

Q. Looking at the Liverpool and Manchester traffic, and the traffic upon your railway, *is it a traffic a great portion of which enters directly into the cost of production of goods;* that is to say, is it almost all carried on by persons in business going from Liverpool to Manchester, connected either with the purchase of raw material, or the manufacture or export of goods?—That is the case.

Q. Therefore the establishment of low fares, even upon that railway, would be very beneficial to the commerce of the country?—No doubt of it.

Q. When you recommend the purchase of existing railways by Government, do you contemplate that all new railways should be constructed by the Government?—No; I should adopt the opposite course to that pursued on the Continent; I should say let private speculators make any new railway that appeared calculated to serve the public purpose, because I believe they would do it cheaper than the Government.

Q. First of all with regard to allowing them to make any railway that seemed well calculated to serve the public purpose, you would not be willing to take the readiness of parties to expend their capital in the construction of a certain railway as a sufficient test that it would serve the public purpose?—No, certainly not; the public should have the choice whether they would have it made.

Q. Would you recommend that all lines to be made should be subject to the control of Government?—Certainly; the position of those lines.

Q. Do you think that Government should purchase all existing railways, or only those they thought desirable?—The whole of the existing ones; but giving to private enterprise which had brought out those railways fair scope to develope what it contemplated.

Q. What is the length of time you would consider it equitable to allow private speculators to have before the Government became the purchasers?—I stated ten years before; I think that would be a fair time.

Q. You consider the advantages of cheap travelling as much for one class as another?—Certainly.

Q. Then practically, supposing your scheme was carried out, and that the Government acquired all the railways, would you expect that the Government could safely make a large reduction in the present fares of passengers?—I think they might on some lines with advantage.

Q. Can you state to what extent that reduction should take place?—It is a mere matter of opinion. If I had to decide the thing, I should not hesitate about making a reduction of 25 per cent. on all the then heavy fares.

Q. Do you think that would be sufficient to give a great stimulus to the traffic of the country?—I would try it; I think a fourth is a large reduction.

Q. Do you know to what extent railway proprietors might be willing to come into a general arrangement of sale to Government?—Those whose opinions I am more intimately acquainted with view it as a fair proposition, I think; they have well considered the matter, both as to the question of check to private enterprise and the equitable arrangement of the right of those who hold this property as investments; and they think that a proposition founded on the Third Report of the Committee might be fairly entertained.

Q. Have you considered how far it might be equitable to take the price of the day as a foundation on which Government should buy up railways?—I think it would be a very dangerous thing to deal with, because, let there be the slightest intimation that a purchase was to be made, and of course those shares would rise so high that you could hardly fix a day to form the price.

Q. But you must fix a day that had already occurred?—You might fix a day retrospectively, but I do not think that would give satisfaction.

Q. In order to carry out your object you must have a classification of railways; the one class you would subject to purchase by the Government on so many years' purchase on the average of the last three years' divisible profits; the other class having had no divisible profits, or the traffic not having been firmly developed, you must deal with in some other manner?—Yes, if there was no intent I would give them as much time as they asked for, say five years; I would say, we will leave you to yourselves for five years, and see what you may have developed.

Q. Is it your opinion that placing any limit by Parliament on the profits of a railway, so that in no case they would be able to divide more than that limit, would only lead them to lay out money unnecessarily?—It must be quite so, and I hold it to be impossible that Parliament should completely limit the dividend.

Q. Do you think it unreasonable to ask that there should be limited accommodation provided for the poorer classes in carriages protected from the weather?—There are great difficulties in the way of it; on some lines one-half of the passengers would go that way.

Nearly all the witnesses connected with railways expressed great apprehension that the adoption of Parliamentary trains would have a most serious effect on the dividends. Captain Laws was not an exception to the number; how far subsequent events proved that their fears were groundless, is a matter of dispute; the increase in numbers caused by the establishment of the Parliamentary trains was very great, but it is doubtful if it was sufficient to make up the difference in the reduced numbers by second-class trains. It is, however, quite certain that, without the pressure brought to bear on the railway body by Government, such a measure would never otherwise have been adopted. It is very true the old companies were not included in the Act which gave the Government the right of purchase, but they were "invited" by the President of the Board of Trade to accede to certain arrangements—the establishment of Parliamentary trains among others—for which certain privileges in return were granted. There is great potency in a Government "invitation" on the other side of the Channel, and perhaps it is not less powerful here when, as in cases like the present, it is backed by popular favour. In this evidence we have seen that Captain Laws suggested a mode of purchasing the railways.

There was also another mode proposed to the Committee, viz., making the market price the criterion of value. We shall subsequently have to discuss the relative merits of the two plans. Captain Laws did not recommend, as we have seen, any very low scale of charges to be adopted; he thought first-class fares, then at $3d.$ per mile, should be reduced to $2\frac{1}{4}d.$, but did not recommend a low and uniform scale of charges throughout the country for the several classes. The fare that he suggested of $2\frac{1}{4}d.$ for first-class passengers may be taken as the average fare now charged for that class of passengers.

Captain Laws appears to have somewhat misunderstood Mr. Gladstone's questions in reference to the number of years' purchase at which the public were willing to invest in railway property, or, in other words, what percentage they would require for their money; he appeared to think the question referred to the rate at which first-class companies could *borrow* money. When Captain Laws was examined in April, 1844, Consols were at par, and shares in the best paying railways in the kingdom, such as the London and Birmingham, Liverpool and Manchester, Stockton and Darlington, Grand Junction, and other first-class companies, would pay the investor, at the then existing state of the market, at an average rate of £4 7s. 6d. per cent.

Captain Laws' evidence, taken in conjunction with that of Mr. Baxendale, threw a flood of light on the whole subject of railway management, and incontestably proved the false position in which a country is placed which abandons to private speculation the possession, management, and control of her great highways.

CHAPTER VI.

Difference between Public and Private Credit—Cost of Mail and Stage Coaches per Mile—Cost of a Railway Train per Mile—The various Items of Expenditure—Expense of carrying Passengers 100 Miles —Fares on Forty-two of the principal Railways in the Kingdom— The Highest, the Medium, and the Lowest Fares contrasted—A Reduction not to be expected—Excursion Trains and Fares— Legitimate Monopolies, Patents and Copyright—Quarrels of Companies—The Working of extremely low Fares exemplified—Proposed Tariff—Much lower Fares in India—Passenger Traffic for 1863.

I HAVE thought it desirable to give the *ipsissima verba* before the Select Committee of some of the most eminent men of the railway world, in reference to the purchase of our railways by the State. The evidence of these witnesses, from their position and experience, was of great value in affirming a principle; but they did not enter into any detailed explanation as to how their views in reference to Government possession should be carried out. Captain Laws, however, in one of his answers to the Committee, which I have *italicised*, directed their attention to a very important fact, viz. : That the superior credit of Government would enable it to borrow money at such a low rate as would yield a profit on the purchase of the railways of 1¼ per cent.; or, according to another witness, 1*l*. 7*s*. per cent.; and that, by the use of this surplus, Government could make a great reduction in the fares without incurring any loss; other witnesses, of a minor class to those whom we have noted, also entered into elaborate statistical details as to railway receipts and expenditure, and on every point connected with the subject, the Committee had the most ample information. This evidence I shall incidentally make use of, as occasion may require.

Let us now go back to the old accustomed way of travelling

before the introduction of railways, for the purpose of contrasting the expenditure then incurred by coach proprietors in the conveyance of passengers compared with that of railway proprietors in the present day for the same purpose.

Thirty-five years ago, mail and stage coaches were the only mode of conveyance for the better class of passengers throughout the country; the general average fares by the former might be taken at fivepence inside and threepence outside per mile, and by the latter, threepence and twopence per mile. The working expenses of a four-horse mail coach, travelling at the rate of ten miles per hour, which might be compared to an express train, and carrying eight passengers, was calculated to cost the proprietors one shilling and eightpence per mile; and a stage-coach, travelling at the rate of six miles per hour, and carrying four inside and twelve outside passengers, which might be compared to an ordinary train, cost its proprietors, for working expenses, one shilling and fourpence per mile. These charges were exclusive of tolls, but they included all legitimate charges and current expenses in keeping up the establishment, feeding the horses, and replacing them when worn out; keeping the coaches in repair and replacing them; payment of servants, and other incidental expenses. Thus, when the mail and stage coaches carried their maximum loads, the cost to the proprietors of the coaches for the conveyance of each passenger per mile was respectively twopence halfpenny and one penny; if they only had half the number of passengers they could carry, the conveyance of each consequently cost double these sums, and so in proportion, more or less as the case might be, each journey. All that the proprietors of the mail and stage coaches received beyond their expenses—the former having the advantage of being paid a considerable sum in addition for the conveyance of mails—made, of course, the dividend which they received for their invested capital.

Now, the cost of the conveyance of each passenger by railway can be calculated with much greater exactness even than that of the conveyance of a passenger by coach; for we have all the several items of expenditure in the companies' accounts, together with detailed reports and statistical tables, published annually by the Board of Trade, giving the fullest information on all matters connected with railways and railway management. The working expenses of railways are generally classed under the following heads:—1st, Maintenance and renewal of way and works; 2nd, Locomotive power; 3rd, Repairs and renewals of carriages and conveyances; 4th, General charges; 5th, Rates and taxes; 6th, Government duty; 7th, Compensation for personal injury, &c.; 8th, Compensation for damages and loss of goods; 9th, Legal and parliamentary expenses; 10th, Miscellaneous working expenditure, not included in the foregoing. All these items of expenditure are so easily understood that they scarcely require any explanation. They are calculated on this principle: not only are all the ordinary current expenses of the establishment paid, but the railway is kept in a state of efficient repair by the substitution of new rails and sleepers for old ones, and all other works of a similar kind that may be necessary; the same principle is acted on with regard to what is called, in railway phraseology, the "rolling stock"—engines, carriages, waggons, and trucks. All are kept in efficient working order; and, when worn out, are replaced by new stock. All this outlay is comprised in "working expenses."

We have seen what the expenditure is, or rather was, per mile, for the conveyance of a passenger by mail and stage coaches when they carried their full loads; how do we arrive at the same result in regard to a passenger by railway? No process can be more simple or easy. We have only to ascertain the expense per mile on any given line which the company incurs for the conveyance of a train, and the number of passengers that can be conveyed by an engine on it; and divide the one by the other. The expense on the English lines per train mile varies from half a crown to three shillings; on the Irish and Scotch lines it is somewhat less. The average expenditure per train mile, taking all the railways in the United Kingdom, has, according to the Reports of the Board of Trade for the year 1862, been two shillings and sevenpence halfpenny, and for 1863, two shillings and sevenpence. But it is necessary to note the different items which go to form the whole, and this we are able to calculate from the data furnished by the companies, and reproduced by the Board of Trade. It is to be observed, that this average expenditure per train mile includes goods, coal, and other mineral trains conveying two or three hundred tons each.

Average cost of conveying a train per mile:—

	s.	d.
Maintenance of way and works	0	5¼
Locomotive power	0	9
Repairs and renewals of carriages and waggons	0	2¼
General traffic charges	0	9
Rates and taxes	0	1¼
Government duty	0	1
Compensation for personal injury and damage and loss of goods	0	0½
Legal and Parliamentary expenses	0	0¼
Miscellaneous working expenditure not included in the above	0	2
Total	2	7

We now know the exact average charge for which trains, passengers, and goods, are conveyed on our railways. The expenditure may be classed under two heads—direct and indirect. The first three items are direct: they are the actual expenses incurred in the conveyance of each train, and amount to one shilling and fourpence three farthings; the others embrace the general expenditure of the establishments, and by dividing the sum to which that amounts by the number of miles travelled by trains, we are enabled to allot to each train mile its exact proportion of expense; the indirect expenditure on each train per mile, we find, is one shilling and twopence farthing.

In regard to the traction power of a locomotive, there are few persons in this country who have not seen, at some time or other, a monster excursion train of thirty carriages, with forty or fifty excursionists in each, dragged along by an engine, at a steady pace of some twenty miles or so an hour. A train of that size, however, is inconveniently large. Consequently we may take a train of twenty-five carriages, with an average number of forty passengers in each, making in all 1000, as a fair maximum load on the majority of our railways. Our travellers are carried in three separate classes—so far, at least, as a distinction in charge can divide them—and the expense of conveying a second-class passenger, when properly accommodated, is considered to be about one-half more than that of the third class; the greater space allowed for first class, and the expensive accommodation they enjoy, make their conveyance cost rather more than double the expense of third-class passengers. Let us take, then, a train containing 1000 passengers, such as we constantly see on most of our lines during the excursion season, and supposing it to contain the proportionate number of first, second, and third class passengers who travelled in 1862, the result would be 128 first class, 287 second class, and 585 third class. If this train had travelled 100 miles—say as far as from London to Brighton and back again—the cost of the train for the 100 miles would be 13*l.* 2*s.* 6*d.*, and the expense incurred for the conveyance of each first-class passenger for the trip would have been *sixpence;* for the second class, *fourpence;* and for the third class, *twopence halfpenny*. The lowest wholesale price, if I may so use the term, for which passengers can be conveyed in bulk —that is, the engine carrying a full load—would be for each passenger, per 100 miles, an average cost of something less than *threepence farthing*.

The traction power of the locomotive is so great that it is only on comparatively rare occasions it is brought into full use in the conveyance of passengers. The average number of passengers conveyed by each train in the kingdom is 71, exclusive of season-ticket holders, and this class may raise the number probably to 74; but, on the other hand, there is included in this average all the summer excursion traffic, the trains containing from 500 to 1500 excursionists, and if these be excluded from the general average, the number of passengers in the regular trains cannot exceed 50, scarcely the *one-twentieth part* of what we have considered as the fair *maximum* load of an engine on a railway that has good gradients. An ordinary passenger train may thus be compared to a four-horse stage-coach, carrying *one* passenger on an average each journey. The cost of conveyance that was divided in our former calculation among 1000 passengers is now reduced to 50, and the passengers that were conveyed among the multitude, as we have seen, 100 miles, at an average cost of less than $3\frac{1}{4}d.$, cannot be conveyed the same distance by the company amongst the select few of an ordinary train, at a less cost than five shillings and fivepence!—that is, *three farthings* per mile, on an average for each, or one penny for first class, three farthings for second, and one halfpenny for third class per mile.

In all these calculations in reference to the expense incurred in the conveyance of passengers by railway, it must be borne in mind that we have allowed no margin for profit—nothing but the bare current expenditure, and that which is sufficient to keep the road and stock in an efficient state of repair; carrying first-class passengers from London to Liverpool for one shilling, second-class for eightpence, and third-class for fivepence, would not yield any profit to the shareholders, although there should be 1000 passengers in each train. In fact, should there be a less number, they would be carried at those fares at an actual loss. Now, in the ordinary trains, *one-*

fourth of that number could never be calculated on, except at much lower rates than are ever likely to be adopted in this country, and therefore the *data* applicable to excursion trains are totally inapplicable to the ordinary traffic. If the State should become the possessor of the railways, and adopt a very low tariff, *there would be no necessity, unless in some special cases, to run an additional train;* there would be an enormous increase in the number of passengers, and, I think, we might safely estimate that the ordinary existing traffic would be *trebled,* and that the average number by the trains that we now assume amount only to 50, would be increased at once to 150, and might be expected to go on steadily increasing. Taking the average number of passengers by an ordinary train at that number, and the different classes in the usual proportion, there would be twenty first-class, forty-three second-class, and eighty-seven third-class, and the expense, direct and indirect, for the conveyance of the first-class passenger would be, for each 100 miles, two shillings and eightpence; the second-class, two shillings; and the third, one shilling and threepence.

We have now before us:—1st, The expense of conveying each passenger by excursion trains, with a maximum load; 2nd, By ordinary trains, as at present, with an average load; and 3rd, The reduced expense that would be incurred if a low tariff was adopted.

Although the difference in the intrinsic cost in the conveyance of a passenger by the several railways is utterly inappreciable, any one who has never studied the subject must be surprised at the wide range fares take in the several companies, according to the peculiar interest of each, whether it be a low, moderate, or high tariff. We shall best illustrate this phase of railway management by giving the fares on our principal railways, together with some others of lesser note, so as to have a fair view of the average fares throughout the kingdom, commencing with those few railways whose managers have discovered very low charges to be the most profitable.

Name of Railway.	Average Fares per Mile.				
	Express.		Ordinary.		
	1st Class *d.*	2nd Class *d.*	1st Class *d.*	2nd Class *d.*	3rd Class *d.*
North and South Western.........	...	...	0·6	0·5	0·3
North London.........................	...	...	0·7	0·4	
Stirling and Dunfermline	...	...	0·9	0·4	
London, Tilbury, and Southend .	...	...	0·9	0·7	
London, Crystal Palace, and Victoria	...	...	0·8	0·6	0·4
Caledonian	...	...	1·2	1·1	0·7
Belfast and County Down.........	...	...	1·2	0·9	0·5
Leeds, Bradford, and Halifax ...	...	...	1·3	1·0	0·7
Limerick and Castleconnell	...	...	1·4	1·1	0·7
Lancashire and Yorkshire.........	...	...	1·6	1·3	0·7
Dublin and Drogheda...............	...	...	1·6	1·2	0·7
South Eastern.........................	2·1	1·6	1·7	1·2	0·7
Glasgow and South-Western......	...	...	1·7	1·3	0·8
Great North of Scotland............	...	...	1·7	0·9	
Belfast and Northern Counties...	...	...	1·8	1·3	0·8
London and North-Western	2·4	1·9	1·9	1·4	0·9
North British	...	...	1·9	1·5	0·9
Edinburgh and Glasgow............	...	...	1·9	1·2	0·9
Ulster	...	...	2·0	1·5	0·9
London, Brighton, and South Coast....................................	2·6	1·9	2·0	1·4	0·8
Great Western.........................	2·4	1·7	2·0	1·5	0·9
Dublin and Kingstown	...	...	2·1	1·6	0·9
London, Chatham, and Dover ...	2·4	1·7	2·1	1·5	0·9
Great Northern	...	...	2·1	1·6	0·9
North-Eastern.........................	...	...	2·2	1·3	0·8
Great Southern and Western ...	...	...	2·2	1·6	0·9
Bristol and Exeter	2·6	1·9	2·2	1·7	0·9
Midland Great Western............	...	...	2·3	1·7	1·0
Midland	...	...	2·3	1·7	0·9
Dublin and Belfast Junction......	...	...	2·3	1·8	1·0
London and South Western	2·7	1·9	2·4	1·7	0·9
Great Eastern	2·8	2·0	2·5	2·0	1·0
Manchester, Sheffield and Lincoln	...	...	2·5	1·8	0·9
North Stafford.........................	...	...	2·5	1·5	1·0
Cornwall	...	...	2·6	1·7	0·9
Leven and East Fife	...	...	2·7	1·7	0·9
West Midland	...	...	2·7	1·8	0·9
Wellington and Severn	...	...	2·7	1·7	0·9
Colne Valley and Halstead	...	...	2·8	1·9	1·0
Bideford and North Devon	...	...	3·0	2·0	1·0
Stamford and Rouline	...	...	3·0	2·0	1·0
Carmarthen and Cardigan.........	...	...	3·5	2·0	1·0

Thus the fares vary "from grave to gay, from lively to severe," from the lowest charge compatible with a fair interest on invested capital, on the one hand, to the highest rate that monopoly can enforce on the other. Let us examine in detail the fares of some of the companies, and the result as it affects their dividends. The North and South Western Company occupy the post of honour, and head the list. This company, as we see, carry passengers lower than any other in the kingdom; they are quite satisfied with an inappreciable fraction over a halfpenny per mile for first-class passengers, or 100 miles for five shillings, a halfpenny per mile for second, and three miles a penny for third-class, and on these low fares now return a dividend at the rate of *six per cent.* per annum to their shareholders. The North London charge a little more—nearly three farthings per mile for first-class, and less than a halfpenny for second, and likewise pay a dividend of *six per cent.* to their shareholders. Some people imagine that where a railway costs a great deal of money, the fares must, in order to pay, be proportionately high. Now, this line, for its length, is about one of the most expensive in the kingdom, its construction having cost as much for one mile as would pay for ten miles of an ordinary line. Nevertheless, with the low fares this company charge, they pay about the largest dividend in the kingdom. Let us take next the London, Crystal Palace, and Victoria line. The company charge for the entire length of the line— sixteen miles—first class, one shilling; second class, ninepence; and third class, sixpence. All the companies carrying passengers at very low fares, give return tickets at the usual charge—a fare and half to all classes.

It will be remembered that, in 1844, Mr. Gladstone experienced the greatest difficulty in overcoming the opposition of the railway interest to the establishment of Parliamentary trains; and it was only through his very pressing "invitations," accompanied by the promise of certain benefits in return, that he was eventually able to succeed. Such men even as Mr. Rowland Hill and Captain Laws, representing the railway interest, were by no means favourable to the measure, and, perhaps, with reason. By the Parliamentary trains there are no return tickets given. Whether the journey be long or short, the full fare—a penny a mile—is charged each way, and the charge is fully enforced by the great majority of companies; but by some of these cheap carrying lines passengers are constantly being conveyed during the day in second or third class carriages, at a half, a third, or a fourth, as the case may be, of the established Parliamentary fare of one penny per mile, and, as I have before noted, some of these lines pay the best in the kingdom.

But is there any likelihood of any great trunk line, such as the London and North-Western, making any reduction in their Parliamentary fares? There appears none whatever. All the great companies, since they were established, charge the full fare allowed by law, and I have no doubt that any diminution in the Parliamentary fare would, for a considerable time at least, be followed by a loss; therefore, it is not to be supposed that these companies will ever make such reduction.

It may be objected, on the other hand, that the reduction in fares that I propose is not sufficient. It might be said, for instance, that twenty years ago, the fare of a third-class passenger from London to Liverpool was one pound five shillings, and the charge for a telegram was exactly the same; but the charge for the telegram has been gradually reduced, and now it seems is fixed at *one shilling*. Why then, it might be asked, should not the charge for a third-class passenger to Liverpool from London be reduced to the same rate? The cases, however, are not parallel; the actual cost of the conveyance of a message must be very trifling—the wear of the machinery and the time of the manager, the clerk, and the messenger, would probably not cost sixpence, whilst the conveyance of a third-class passenger from London to Liverpool would cost, under ordinary circumstances, by railway fully one shilling. The same reduction in charge could not therefore be made.

But to return to the average fares charged, and the wide range they take throughout the kingdom. Of the companies whose low fares we have quoted, there are only *five* whose first-class fares do not exceed one penny per mile. Of those whose first-class fares exceed one penny per mile, but do not exceed three halfpence, there are *six;* of those whose fares exceed three halfpence, but do not exceed twopence, there are *ten;* between twopence and twopence halfpenny, inclusive, there are *thirteen;* and from twopence halfpenny to threepence halfpenny, the highest fare, there are *eight;* of the three companies at the bottom of the list, and which charge the highest fares in the kingdom, two pay no dividend whatever to their shareholders.

From the foregoing table we deduce the following general results:—

	1st Class. £ s. d.	2nd Class. s. d.	3rd Class. s. d.
The cheapest travelling in the United Kingdom is represented by the North and South Western Railway; their charge for 100 miles is . .	0 5 0	4 2	2 6
The average charge, as represented by the Great Western Railway, is .	0 16 8	12 0	7 6
The highest charge, as represented by the Carmarthen and Cardigan Railway, is	1 9 2	16 8	8 4

Whence, then, does this great difference of charge arise? How does it come to pass that an Englishman, travelling in one part of the country, must pay three, four, or five times as much, as the case may be, for the same distance and mode of travelling, and with no greater degree of speed or comfort, than he is called on to pay in another part of the country? Is this extra charge, this tripling, quadrupling, or quintupling the fares, the natural result of the increased cost of conveyance on those dear lines? Increased cost of conveyance! Why, a first-class passenger, as we have seen, can be conveyed 100 miles on any line in the kingdom, and all the expense, direct and indirect, can be brought within the small sum of *six-*

pence! Does this extra charge arise, then, from the heavy cost incurred in the construction of the line? So far from that being the case, we generally find, as we have already noticed, that those lines which have been constructed at the greatest cost, carry at the lowest charges. Does it arise from the means of conveyance on some of the railways being physically overtaxed, and the inability of their managers to provide accommodation for all who wish to travel? Nothing of the kind. The trains on all the railways do not carry, on an average, *one-tenth* the number of passengers they are capable of carrying, and could, with scarcely an appreciable increase in the expense, convey three or four times the number they actually do. From none of these causes is the difference of fares to be accounted for. Why does the Stirling and Dunfermline Company charge the traveller 50 per cent. more than the North and South Western Company? Why does the Caledonian Company charge 33 per cent. more than the Stirling and Dunfermline Company? Why does the Lancashire and Yorkshire charge 30 per cent. more than the Caledonian; and the London and North-Western 20 per cent. more than the Lancashire and Yorkshire; and the Midland 20 per cent. more than the London and North-Western; and the Great Eastern and the Manchester, Sheffield and Lincoln, 10 per cent. more than the Midland; and the Colne Valley 10 per cent. more than the Great Eastern; whilst our old friends, of the Carmarthen and Cardigan, pour the last drop of bitterness into the traveller's cup by adding a final 12 per cent. to the fare charged on the Colne Valley line; thus the last fare our traveller pays per mile in the imaginary route we have traced out for him, after passing through a gradually ascending scale, exceeds the first by 450 per cent. We want to know "the reason why."

Had we lived 1000 years ago, and England been then portioned out among the Danes, Saxons, and Normans, we could pretty well have understood how the unhappy Englishman, in travelling through a country in the possession of foreigners and enemies, should be unmercifully plundered as he passed along; or, had we even lived 500 years later, in the time of the Norman barons, we should probably have found them by no means backward in exacting whatever they might have been able to extort from the unprotected traveller in the way of toll. The old barons on the Rhine were said to have been famous hands at this kind of business; and our modern directorates in England, with due respect, be it said, are by no means bad imitators of the German barons, not less in the sagacity by which they are enabled to test the ability of the traveller to pay than in the determination with which they enforce their claims. Here, however, the comparison must end. What the directors do is perfectly legal and justifiable; they are not acting, it is true, in the spirit of the constitution, but they are conforming to the letter of the law in disregarding the most vital interests of the country, when it interferes in the slightest degree with their profits as traders. A Committee of the House of Commons has declared "that the roads of a country are public concerns, and necessary to the people as the air they breathe;" but we ignore these sentiments; and the State, acting on the erroneous supposition that its possession of the railways would increase the power and patronage of the Government, delegates to private individuals the charge of these highways, which should belong to the Queen, and be managed under the direct control of the Legislature alone. These private individuals are empowered to make the most of their position, and all their differential fares we have noted arise from mere statistical accident, as it is developed in the working of this great monopoly. It so happens that although the London, Tilbury, and Southend Company charge their first-class passengers less than a penny per mile, their fares are 50 per cent. more than the North and South Western; and the London and North-Western Company charge 100 per cent. more than the London, Tilbury, and Southend, and so on to the end of the list. All the fares on the different railways throughout the kingdom are settled by the mere chapter of accidents. From some local cause a very low, a moderate, or a very high fare is found to pay best, as the case may be, and accordingly adopted. The difference in the result to the shareholders, as we shall subsequently show, between a very high and a very low tariff, is very small; but, however insignificant it may be, it is quite sufficient to turn the scale in favour of the particular tariff that gives the greatest profit.

Thirteen great companies possess and manage three-fourths of the traffic of the United Kingdom. Of these, the lowest tariff is that charged by the Caledonian; the medium tariff by the London and Brighton; and the highest by the Great Eastern, and the Manchester, Sheffield and Lincoln Companies. As a general rule, the worst paying companies charge the most.

On many of the great lines there are, strictly speaking, no third-class, but only Parliamentary, trains. The Great Eastern charge third-class passengers over the greater part of their line three halfpence per mile. The lowest, the medium, and the highest charges on the thirteen great lines are as follow:—

	1st Class. £ s. d.	2nd Class. s. d.	3rd Class. s. d.
The Caledonian Company charge per 100 miles	0 10 0	9 2	5 10
The London and Brighton charge per 100 miles	0 17 6	13 0	8 4
The Great Eastern charge per 100 miles	1 0 10	16 8	12 6

I have excluded express fares from these calculations. As travelling by express trains is quite exceptional in its character, and, as it is attended with great expense, the fares must always be comparatively high. The number of passengers is limited, and the wear and tear, both of railway and rolling stock, in consequence of the rapid speed of travelling, is very great. Those whose time is valuable can afford the extra expense. The trains, however, might travel at a greater speed on some of the lines, and the fares at twopence for first and three-halfpence for second class passengers would be sufficient. The lowest express fares are those charged on the South Eastern; the medium fares are those charged by the Great Western; and the highest by the Great Eastern.

	Express.	
	1st Class. £ s. d.	2nd Class. s. d.
South-Eastern Company, per 100 miles . .	0 17 6	13 4
Great Western ,, ,, ,, . .	1 0 0	14 2
Great Eastern ,, ,, ,, . .	1 3 4	16 8

We are now enabled to form a pretty accurate judgment on the different degrees of expense incurred by railway travelling in all parts of the kingdom. From the specimens afforded by the forty-two companies whose fares I have given, the two extremes for first-class travelling per mile are one halfpenny and threepence halfpenny; for second-class, one halfpenny and twopence per mile; for third-class, one farthing and three halfpence per mile.

There are two kinds of passenger traffic, which, from their nature, must be dealt with in very different ways—business and pleasure traffic. In conducting the former, trains must be despatched regularly at certain fixed intervals all the year round, varying only according to the requirements of business, and without regard to the number of passengers that at any time may be conveyed in each train. For this branch of traffic we have given the fares on all the principal railways in the kingdom; but most of the companies carry on during the summer and autumn months a large excursion traffic, and as such trains are well filled, and they can calculate on their being so filled, the excursionists are carried at comparatively low fares. This branch of business is considered one of the most profitable the companies possess. The great advantage consists in having the choice of their own time for departure, so as not to interfere with the general traffic; and the large number who are induced by what they consider low fares to take these trips, and the very low cost, as we have seen, at which the companies are able to carry passengers, render the trains very profitable.

A large excursion traffic is carried on between London and the several watering places and seaports within a hundred miles of the metropolis, especially to Gravesend, Southend, Dover, Margate, and Ramsgate; there is also a considerable traffic of the same kind carried on by the great lines north of the Thames to the principal towns of the kingdom. Passengers can be conveyed at a low sum by excursion trains, or, in fact, by any trains where there is a full load, as we have seen—one hundred miles, first class, for *sixpence;* second class, *fourpence;* third class, *twopence halfpenny.* All beyond those fares obtained from the passengers is clear profit. Each company, therefore, regulates its own tariff according to its views of what will pay best, and there is about the same difference in the several fares charged by the companies for excursion as we have already noticed for the ordinary traffic. A few instances will suffice in showing the extremes between the charges of the companies out of London:—

EXCURSION TRAINS.—Fares per 100 miles.

	1st Class.	Enclosed Carriages.
	s. d.	s. d.
South Eastern, to and from Ramsgate	3 8	1 8
London and Brighton, to and from Portsmouth	4 0	2 0
London and North Western, to and from Liverpool	5 0	3 0
Great Western, to and from Plymouth	6 3	4 2

And the same difference in fares prevails throughout the kingdom.

The South-Eastern Company, we thus find, charges lower than any other company out of London for excursion traffic, and the Great Western the highest; but the average excursion fares may be taken at about *one-third* of the ordinary traffic fares.

It happens, however, occasionally, that we have a violent contest continued over many months between some of the companies, when the public are carried at what may be really termed moderate fares—so low, indeed, that I should never venture to propose them for general adoption. We shall, however, be enabled, by examining these tariffs, to get a glimpse of the practical every-day working of a low fare system. Let us take three contests, memorable in railway history—the first between the London and North-Western and the Great Northern Companies in 1857; the second between the South-Eastern and Great Western in 1852 and 1853; and the third between the Edinburgh and Glasgow and the Caledonian Companies in 1854.

The first two companies I have named, having quarrelled, made a sudden reduction in their fares at those points on their respective lines at which they came in contact. The reduction was to an extent altogether unprecedented, at least on long lines. The Art Exhibition was then being held at Manchester, and during the summer months, for two or three days in the week, the companies gave excursion tickets between London and Manchester, allowing the traveller to remain four days at the latter town; the distance travelled over was about four hundred miles, and the fares for first class were seven shillings and sixpence, and, for second class, five shillings. They ran not only fast trains on both lines, but the second-class carriages were comfortably cushioned, as they always are on the Continent, and rarely with us. These trains must have interfered, to a great extent, with the general passenger traffic of both the companies with all the large towns in the north of England. As the companies allowed four days for the traveller in Manchester, it gave him ample time to extend his journey to other districts, and get back in time for his return journey. The loss to each company was calculated at about *a half per cent.* in their dividends—a considerable loss, no doubt, to them, and not wisely incurred; but what a benefit to the hundreds of thousands who for once in their lives were enabled to travel at a moderate rate of charge and get a fair value for their money!

Let us stop now for a moment to inquire into the particulars of the profit and loss account of this quarrel. These trains were well filled, and carried, I have been told, on an average, about six hundred passengers—say two hundred first class, and four hundred second class, the fares for the double trip amounting in all to one hundred and seventy-five pounds. The cost of a train per mile is two shillings and sevenpence, and taking the double distance at four hundred miles—it is rather more by the Great Northern and less by the London and North-Western Company—the whole expense of each train (both the direct expense and its proportionate expense for management) comes to fifty guineas, and the receipts, as we have seen, to one hundred and seventy-four pounds, leaving a profit of nearly two hundred and fifty per cent. on the conveyance of passengers by each train. The fares of the passengers, be it remembered, were, for first class, each 100 miles, one shilling and ninepence, or less than a farthing per mile; and for second class, in carriages comfortably cushioned, one shilling and twopence, or a penny for seven miles!

The contest of the South-Eastern with the Great Western for the London and Reading traffic lasted about a year and a half. The distance on the South-Eastern line is 67 miles, and the company conveyed passengers the double distance by every train for three shillings, first class, and two shillings, second class; being at the rate, per hundred miles, first class, two shillings and threepence, and second class, one shilling and sixpence. In this case the chairman of the company stated at the half-yearly meetings of the company that the company lost nothing by the change in fares; they paid the same dividends, and they were very well satisfied to go on. Nevertheless, the South-Eastern and Great Western were charging on one part of their lines about *ten times* as much as they were charging on other parts, and on those parts where they were carrying lowest their profits amounted to about 250 per cent. in the cost of conveyance by each train!

The most remarkable case, however, that ever happened in this kingdom, as confirmatory of the truth of the principles on which the Act of 1844 was founded, occurred ten years ago on the Edinburgh and Glasgow line; when, in consequence of a dispute with the Caledonian Company, the fares were reduced to about *one-eighth* of the ordinary charges. The Edinburgh and Glasgow line is forty-six miles in lengths, and the regular fares for the three classes were respectively eight shillings, six shillings, and four shillings; these were suddenly reduced to *one shilling, ninepence,* and *sixpence;* the Caledonian, of course, following suit, and carrying likewise at the same fares. For a year and a half this contest continued, to the great satisfaction, comfort, and benefit, no doubt, of those two great Scotch cities, but to the serious injury of the shareholders. The Edinburgh and Glasgow Company paid *one* per cent. per annum less to their shareholders, and the loss to the Caledonian was calculated at something less than a *half* per cent. per annum to theirs. It is to be remembered that these were the fares by *all* trains, and not confined to a few on certain days of the week. The sum charged per hundred miles for first class was two shillings and threepence; second class, one shilling and ninepence; and third class, one shilling and twopence.

If we put into a tabular form the original fares charged by the companies for the three classes, the reduced fares, the distance, and the loss of profits they incurred by the reduction, shown by their dividends, it will stand thus:—

Original Fares. Return Tickets.			Miles.		Reduced Fares. Return Tickets.			Loss in Dividends per cent. per annum.
s. d.	*s. d.*	*s. d.*			*s. d.*	*s. d.*	*s. d.*	*s. d.*
60 0	40 0	—	380	London and North-Western.	7 6	5 0	—	10 0
60 0	40 0	—	410	Great Northern .	7 6	5 0	—	10 0
10 0	7 6	—	134	South-Eastern .	3 0	2 0	—	—
8 0	6 0	4 0	46	Edinburgh and Glasgow	1 0	0 9	0 6	20 0
8 0	6 0	4 0	55	Caledonian . .	1 0	0 9	0 6	10 0

We have now before us the result, in a financial point of view as affecting the companies, of what are termed relatively very high, moderate, low, and extremely low fares; and we find that it makes comparatively little difference in the annual dividends, not exceeding in any case one per cent., whether they charge one farthing per mile for first-class passengers or fourteen farthings—the two extremes—and the other classes in the same proportion. It, however, happens that, although the difference in profit would not be great, fourteen farthings would invariably pay better than one, and, as the companies have no obligation, legal or moral, to consider anything but their own interest, they would always adopt the fourteen if they had no other choice; but they have a free choice from one farthing up to twelve or fourteen farthings for first class per mile; and, accordingly, we find that their ordinary scale of fares commences at two farthings and ends with fourteen farthings, but, as a general rule, that nine farthings, or twopence farthing, for first class, and the other fares in due proportion, pay best. Never, except in cases of violent competition, do they go as low as a farthing per mile for first class, and although, as we have seen, carrying at that fare yields in a moderately filled train a profit of 250 per cent., it nevertheless tells on the dividends to the shareholders. We shall find, however, that there is nothing peculiar in this wide range of charges in railway fares; that it is inherent in all monopolies; and that the monopolist, having no fear of competition, has only to consider whether the charge of a shilling, a pound, or an intermediate price pays him best, and adopt that price accordingly.

It is necessary for those unacquainted with commercial affairs to understand clearly the distinction to be drawn between the profits on a business and the interest or dividends those profits will pay on the capital invested in it. One shopkeeper may sell his goods at cent. per cent. profit, and not be able to realize more than pays his current expenditure, whilst another charges only five or ten per cent. profit and will gain twenty per cent. or upwards per annum on his capital. In regard to the railways of the United Kingdom, their average earnings per train mile is five shillings and sixpence, and the expenses as we have seen, amount to two shillings and sevenpence. The expenditure is forty-eight per cent. on the receipts, or, to put it in another form, the average returns on the working of railways yield a profit of rather more than one hundred per cent., and these profits paid on the invested capital last year a dividend of nearly four per cent. per annum to the shareholders. A railway company might receive from each passenger ten times as much as his conveyance costs, and yet pay no dividend to the original shareholders. The number of trains might be so few, and the business done so insignificant, that the profits would be absorbed by the bondholders or preferential shareholders.

There are two kinds of monopoly—one is produced from artificial, and the other from natural, causes; and to these a third may be added that arises from a combination of the first two. An artificial monopoly is created simply by a law forbidding competition; a natural monopoly arises from an invention being so excellent that whoever uses it can set competition at defiance; the third kind of monopoly is exemplified in our railway system, where, from the circumstances of the case, the invention can either be only used by one party, or at most by two or three, who combine instead of compete, and divide the monopoly which it was intended they should destroy. No presumed increase in the number of railways can alter their character as a monopoly.

We have, however, in this country monopolies that are perfectly legitimate and duly recognized by law. Those granted for limited periods to patentees and authors, who are allowed for a certain time to derive as much profit as they can from the productions of their brains—what do these monopolists do? The same as all other monopolists; they make the best of their opportunity, and charge five, ten, or twenty times as much for their works as those works could be sold for if no monopoly existed. A work, for instance, is published in London at a guinea and a half, and immediately afterwards the same work is published on the Continent for four or five shillings; but the cheap republication is not confined to the Continent: as the period approaches for the expiration of the copyright in England, the price of the work is gradually reduced, till at last we find that our most popular novels, published originally at a guinea and a half, end their "monopolist" career by being published at two shillings! And these two prices represent the respective tariffs of free trade and monopoly, and the two extremes of fares on our railways represent the two principles when for a short time free trade flourishes.

In some cases, however, the author considers it to be more profitable to publish his work in the first instance at a low price, at half a crown, in preference either to half a sovereign or a still higher price—and calculates on the large sale compensating for the low price. Occasionally this calculation may prove correct, but in the vast majority of cases a high tariff pays somewhat better, and is accordingly adopted. The same principle holds good in regard to railways and all other monopolies. The monopoly enjoyed by a patentee or an author is the only equitable arrangement devised by which this class of persons can derive a profit from their inventions or their works. Without such protection we should have neither inventors nor authors, and I refer to them merely as an illustration of the injury a monopoly inflicts on the public compared with the little advantage to the monopolist, even in cases where the justice of its being granted cannot be disputed.

But these monopolies differ in two very important respects from railway monopoly; their time is limited, and their sphere of operation circumscribed. In a few years, comparatively speaking, the most useful and important invention or discovery can be used and enjoyed by the public without any fiscal restriction whatever, and till that time arrives, if the price does not suit the public, they are neither compelled to use the invention nor read the work. But I need hardly observe that the case is quite different with railways; the public must use them and pay the monopolist charge, not for a limited time, but in perpetuity, or, at all events, so long as our present system is permitted to continue.

The sketch I have given in the foregoing pages shows the practical working of our railway system as regards the conveyance of passengers, and how the delegated authority of the State is carried out by the companies. The Government, in effect, said to the companies when they entered into a new contract with them in 1844, "You can carry first-class passengers four miles, second-class passengers six miles, or third-class passengers ten miles, for *one farthing each*, that sum covering all expense, direct and indirect, of their conveyance; all beyond that sum being necessarily profit, we give you the power practically to charge the public what you please, but at the end of twenty-one years we reserve the right to revise the system and take the railways into our own hands should we think such a course advisable." Well, twenty years have passed away, and 1865 has arrived, and we shall enter its parliamentary session under circumstances in regard to railway projects similar to those under which we entered the session of 1844. Let us assume for the present that the working of our system since that period may not have proved altogether satisfactory to the Legislature; that they may come to the opinion that the State should possess the railways; and that a low tariff, universal in its application throughout the country, should supersede the present tariffs of the companies. We have now to consider what that tariff should be.

It has been assumed throughout these pages that it is the desire of the Legislature that the fullest development should be given to the traffic of the country and to that department of it especially relating to passengers. What the fares ought to be for ordinary traffic we have already noticed; business people *must* travel, more or less, and this, to a great extent, they regulate, by choice or necessity, according to their ability or inclination to pay the fares charged. Excursionists, however, have no absolute necessity to travel, and there if were not a very great reduction in the regular fares there would be no business whatever for excursion trains. The companies, as we have seen, differ very much in their charges, according to circumstances or the policy of their respective boards, the fares ranging from two to five miles for a penny for the lowest class. These low fares attract a large number of excursionists, and it is only reasonable to suppose that the companies have settled their fares at that point which gives the greatest profit. If the railways become the property of the State, the Legislature will, I apprehend, fully carry out what the companies do but partially, and will afford an opportunity to all classes, the poorest especially, to have some relaxation at convenient times by a short change of scene and air. The Legislature would be in a position to consider the matter in a very different light, and in a much more liberal spirit, than that of the companies. They would, no doubt, consider it to be their duty to place excursion trips within the humble means of those who are sunk far below the respectable artizan class, and who form such a large proportion of every great city. Now, we have seen that the South-Eastern carry a great proportion of their lowest-class excursionists at the rate of five miles for a penny; but that rate, low as it may appear, is far too high for the classes of whom I am now writing. I think ten miles a penny for third class, six miles a penny for second, and four miles a penny for first, would fairly meet the general wants; and although these fares for a considerable time would not probably yield so large a profit as the present excursion fares, nevertheless, considering the object in view, the Legislature might deem a profit of 300 or 400 per cent. on the conveyance of this class of passengers sufficient.

The last class of travellers whose mode of travelling and payment to the companies we have to consider are those who hold periodical tickets and live generally at distances varying from two to twenty miles from large towns, to which they come daily to transact their business, and, when the distance is very short, frequently several times in the day. Companies charge generally about £2 10s. first class, and £1 10s. second class, per mile per annum up to five miles. From that distance the fare per mile gradually decreases in proportion to the distance; at ten miles the fares are about £1 10s. and £1 per mile; at twenty-five miles they decrease to about £1 and 15s. per mile; after that they decrease to about 15s. and 10s. per mile. Very few take periodical tickets at a distance beyond twenty-five miles from their place of business, unless for a few months whilst at Brighton or some other watering place. The holders of periodical tickets are generally a well-to-do class, and travel in fast trains for long distances. *One-half* the present rates would meet the necessities of the case, except third-class passengers, whose case requires separate consideration.

The scale of fares I have through the foregoing pages suggested may be classified as follows:—

EXPRESS.

1st Class, twopence; 2nd Class, three halfpence per mile.

FAST TRAINS, calling only at first-class stations.

1st Class, one penny farthing per mile.
2nd   ,,   three farthings   ,,
3rd   ,,   one halfpenny   ,,

ORDINARY TRAINS, calling at all stations.

1st Class, three farthings per mile.
2nd   ,,   one halfpenny   ,,
3rd   ,,   one farthing   ,,

Return tickets for all classes at a fare and a half. Second-class carriages cushioned.

EXCURSION TRAINS.

1st Class, four miles for one penny.
2nd   ,,   six miles   ,,
3rd   ,,   ten miles   ,,

Annual and Season Ticket-holders, one half the present average rates.

The lowest payment, one penny.

I have not much to add to what has already been said in

regard to the proposed fares; those by express trains cannot be much reduced from their present rates, but their speed on many of the lines on which they now run may be considerably accelerated, and this has been done within the last few years by the London and North-Western Company. There are scarcely a dozen lines in the kingdom on which express trains run; their expense being great, and the number of passengers for a very high speed being necessarily limited, the fares by these trains must always be high.

For first class by fast trains I have proposed one penny farthing per mile, which is about the half of the present fare by express trains on most of our great lines; many may think even this too high, and no doubt it is if we are to take as our standard the fares charged by companies running at opposition fares, such as we have already noticed. The return fares for first and second class between London and Manchester are at present respectively £2 12s. 6d. and £1 17s. 6d., and on the London and North-Western line the distance is 188 miles. By the scale I propose, the fares would be reduced to £1 9s. 4d. and 17s. 7d. for the respective classes. What a paltry reduction this appears with what the company made themselves! They reduced their fares by a stroke of the pen from their normal rate of £3—to 7s. 6d.! and the result we have seen. However, it must be remembered that this reduction did not extend over all the company's lines, and therefore the experiment was only partial.

It is, however, by the ordinary trains the multitude would be carried, not requiring a great speed, and stopping at all stations, like our Parliamentary trains, with accommodation suited to every class according to their inclination or ability to pay. The public would thus be amply provided for at such moderate fares as would leave no fair ground of complaint. Continuing the comparison of return fares between London and Manchester under the proposed tariff and the present fares which we have given above, by this train a return ticket for the three classes would be severally 17s. 7d., 13s. 5d., and

6*s.* 9*d.*; which would be about *one-third* of the present fares charged for first and second class, and *one-fifth* of the fare by a Parliamentary train, as by the latter there are no return tickets. The lowest fare there and back is £1 11*s.* 4*d.*, with which the payment of 6*s.* 9*d.* would contrast pleasantly.

Although the foregoing tariff may to some appear low, it is very high compared with that on some railways elsewhere. Mr. Danvers, in his last report to the Secretary of India, says that on the Bombay and Baroda line there is one element of working which does not belong to other Indian lines. The gradients are unusually favourable, the line is very level, and one engine can thus draw heavy weights, thereby rendering frequent and light trains unnecessary. The average weight, he says, of our English goods trains is about 60 tons, and of our coal and other mineral trains about 200 tons, and an average passenger train, with seventy passengers in six carriages, about 100 tons; but a Bombay and Baroda train is composed of seventy-two carriages and trucks, with a gross load of 720 tons, at an average rate of speed of twenty miles an hour; and the average rate of fares for all classes is two shillings per 100 miles, or about *one-sixth* of our average fares in England!

Such, as I have endeavoured to trace out in this chapter, is the working of the railway system in this country in regard to the conveyance of passengers, with all its anomalies, absurdities, and abuses, the natural results produced by the working of an overgrown and but little checked monopoly. If these high charges were made from unavoidable circumstances, if they were the natural results of a sound system of management, they should be submitted to in silence; nay, more—if they even were the result of an unsound system, but one still in accordance with the general policy of the country, there would be no special cause of complaint; but the contrary is the case. Within the last twenty-five years the abolition of monopolies began, and has been continued without interruption up to the present time, or, at least, so long as in popular opinion there remained any to be abolished; but our railway system so far has escaped the general doom. Yet it is one of the most gigantic monopolies that ever existed in the British Empire, and how it is working among us I have endeavoured faintly to describe. That the carrying into full effect the Act of 1844 would remedy all the evils complained of in our railway system can hardly, I should imagine, be a matter of doubt, although there may be much difference of opinion as to the tariffs that in such case should be adopted.

The Board of Trade railway returns for the year 1863 have been lately published, and show an increase of mileage over the preceding year of 771 miles, and in receipts of £2,027,839. The earnings of the passenger trains amounted to £14,521,528, and of the goods trains to £16,634,689. The number of passengers carried was 204,635,075, exceeding by twenty-four millions the number carried the preceding year.

It will be seen from these returns how the trade of the country is yearly increasing, and it is satisfactory to know that in 1863 railway proprietors shared in the general prosperity, and that for 1864 the dividend will be still further increased.

CHAPTER VII.

Return for 1863 of "Goods Traffic"—The Charges take the form of indirect Taxation—Charges for the different Classes of Merchandise—Each Company has its own Tariff—Complaints of the Carriers—Cost to the Companies of the Conveyance of Merchandise—Conveyance of Coal to the Metropolis—Its Cost on the Great Eastern Railway—Parcels, Packages, and Hampers—Proposed Tariff for their Conveyance—Post Office—Military and Militia Stores.

IN the returns by the companies, the traffic, as we have seen, is classed under two general heads—"Passenger" and "Goods." The latter include all other kinds not carried by passenger trains, viz., coal and other minerals, live stock and general merchandise. The sum paid by the public to the companies during the year 1863 under this head amounts, as we have seen, to £16,634,689, viz.:—

For the carriage of sixty-eight million tons of coal and other minerals	£5,419,667
For the carriage of live stock, viz.:— 3,200,000 cattle, 8,250,000 sheep, 2,100,000 pigs,	636,773
For the conveyance of general merchandise...	10,578,249
	£16,634,689

Although the sum paid annually for the conveyance of minerals and merchandise by that portion of the public who are merchants and tradespeople considerably exceeds that paid by the general public as travellers, the complaints against the companies, in the matter of goods traffic, with the exception of those made by the carriers, and some other isolated cases, have never at any time been very great, and this absence of ill-feeling may, to a great extent, be accounted for by the fact that the payments in the one case take the form of direct, and in the other of indirect taxation. Without entering into the merits or demerits of the two systems, it cannot be denied that direct taxation, as the name implies, comes more immediately home to the tax-payer than indirect taxation. He is much more sensitive in the one case than in the other to any injustice in its operation, and more determined, when an opportunity presents itself, in his opposition to the enforcement of payment. If the Chancellor of the Exchequer abolished the duties on tea, sugar, coffee, malt, spirits, and tobacco, and sent in his little bill at the end of the year to each household, claiming by a direct payment the remitted duties, how many items in the account would be criticized, discussed, cavilled at, or denied, before the unhappy tax collector would be enabled to remit to the Treasury that which now, by indirect taxation, is collected so easily and securely, and comparatively with so little grumbling!

Nothing, however, can be more certain than that the sixteen and a half millions sterling paid by merchants, traders, carriers, and other freighters to the railway companies in 1863, and what has been paid every preceding year, is an indirect tax levied continually on the public; as much so as our customs and excise duties, and in many articles of merchandise the expense of carriage forms no inconsiderable component part of its price. It will be found, when we examine into the charges by the railway companies, that they are as disproportioned to the cost of conveyance as we have seen to be the case in that of passengers. The tariff of the "goods" department varies, as may be supposed, very much, according to the value of the multifarious kinds of merchandise carried; these are generally divided into four classes, with the annexed charges permitted by Parliament. They vary somewhat on different lines, but the following may be taken as the average rates allowed :—

1st class.—Lime, limestone, manure, and stone for the repairing of roads, three halfpence per ton per mile, or 100 tons one mile for 12s. 6d.

2nd class.—Coal, coke, charcoal, stones for building, brick, tiles, iron ore, and bar iron, twopence halfpenny per ton, or 100 tons one mile for £1 0s. 10d.

3rd class.—Sugar, grain, flour, meal, potatoes, linen, cotton, yarn, earthenware, timber, deals, threepence halfpenny per ton per mile, or for 100 tons one mile, £1 9s. 2d.

4th class.—Cotton and other wools, drugs, fish, manufactured goods, and all other merchandise, fourpence halfpenny per ton per mile, or 100 tons one mile for £1 17s. 6d.

Let us now see what is the cost of conveyance of one hundred tons of general merchandise one mile. A full load on our railways may be taken at 200 tons, although frequently the load is much heavier, exclusive of engine, tender, and trucks, and the average cost of all the trains per mile in the kingdom amounts, as we have seen, to two shillings and sevenpence per mile; consequently one hundred tons of merchandise is carried a mile for *one shilling and fourpence,* or one ton one hundred miles at the same cost; whilst the authorized charges for the same weights for different classes of merchandise vary for the carriage of one hundred tons a mile from twelve shillings and sixpence up to one pound seventeen shillings and sixpence!

The average load of a goods train may be taken at about seventy tons. The high price the companies receive for the carriage of goods compared with the cost of transit makes it with them a matter of little account whether the load be weighty or light; but coal and other mineral trains, the rates for which are low, form an exception to the rule in this class of traffic, as excursion trains do to that of passenger traffic.

It is not my intention, and would, indeed, be quite beyond my power, to enter into any analysis of the different charges on the various kinds of merchandise, or to offer an opinion as to what extent they should be reduced. The same variation exists throughout the kingdom in charges on merchandise, as on fares to passengers, the policy of each company being governed by what it may consider its peculiar interests. A state of warfare generally exists between the carriers and the companies, and great complaints are frequently made of alleged arbitrary increase of charges, but these complaints seldom come before or interest the public. The practical right is conceded to the companies to make what charges they think proper, and, unless in some extreme case, the public never hear of any complaint. Should the railways ever become the property of the State, a searching inquiry no doubt would be instituted by a Parliamentary committee into the charges for carriage of each description of merchandise in the different classes, and a reduction be made, according to the necessity of each case. Those cases where the reduction in the carriage would materially lower the price of the commodity, so as to increase its consumption, and be sensibly felt as a relief by the general community, would no doubt receive the special attention of the committee.

There are many kinds of merchandise that fall within this description. Coal is the only one I shall notice; its consumption enters largely into every family, and forms no small item in the household account. In severe winters the want of a sufficient supply, arising from its high price, is severely felt by the poorer classes. In the northern counties of England, whence nearly all our supply comes, it is sold at the pit's mouth at six or seven shillings per ton, and the selling price when delivered to the consumer should not exceed the original cost, the carriage and other incidental charges, together with a fair profit to the trader. Within the last dozen years a large and continually increasing trade has been carried on by the London and North-Western, Great Western, Midland, Great Northern, and other companies, in supplying the London and other markets, and it is a matter of some interest to know the expense per ton in the conveyance of coal by the several companies from the pit's mouth to the London market. It should be no very difficult matter by calculations to come close enough, for all practical purposes, to the cost of carrying a ton of coal per mile, and so work out the result; but, unfortunately, curious people in this sort of calculation derive but little information from the reports of railway meetings, or the returns made by railway officials, or the speeches of railway chairmen. What could be more interesting, for instance, to the public of the outer world than to hear from the address of the chairman of the London and North-Western Company to his shareholders that, the cost of coal at the pit's mouth being seven shillings, and the carriage to London being so much per ton, they would be able to deliver it to the public at such a price, which would leave them a good profit of so much per cent.? Now, the chairmen of our railway companies not only never give these interesting details, but seem totally unable to comprehend any question put for the purpose of eliciting such information by an independent shareholder. There are secrets in every trade, and railway directorates naturally wish to keep all information from the public that might have the effect of raising a popular clamour against them, and nothing would be more likely to produce such a result, so far as regards ignorant and prejudiced people, than a comparison of what coal costs the companies in London with the price at which they sell it; yet they charge no more than the market price, and only act as all other traders do in realizing as much profit as they can.

Although the directors of companies are not in any way called on—as it appears they think it contrary to the interests of their shareholders—to direct the attention of the public to the great difference between their charges for the work they perform and the expenditure they incur in performing it, I am, nevertheless, fully persuaded that no class in the community have such a deep interest as the shareholders have in making every individual in the kingdom fully cognisant of the fact. That they are in possession of a great monopoly is no fault of theirs; that they turn any advantage they have to the best account they can, without regard to the interests of the public, is a failing, if it be one, shared in common with all classes and conditions of men, whether in their individual or their corporate capacity; that they derive but a very moderate percentage on their invested capital is patent to the world; but what is not patent is the enormous loss the nation sustains so long as the present system continues. No change can be effected without the concurrence of the shareholders, and, as a necessary consequence, they must be liberally dealt with by the nation; so no class in the community has so deep an interest in making the facts of the case fully known as the directors themselves.

But to proceed. We have, however, one case, and one case only, on record in which the chairman of a railway company entered fully into the matter, giving the most minute details of expenditure, thereby showing the actual cost of the conveyance of coal per ton to the metropolis, and incidentally to any other place. The circumstances were these; some years ago a popular outcry arose amongst the shareholders of the then Eastern Counties Railway against their chairman, and one of the principal charges against him was for the conveyance of coal for certain contractors at rates which his opponents termed "unremunerative," and "didn't pay." These terms, I may observe in passing, are frequently used by railway writers and speakers without their attaching any clear and distinct idea to them; and they may be understood in several ways—first, charges on a railway that will not pay five per cent. interest on the invested capital may be termed "unremunerative," as that percentage on investment is only a moderate return, and a lower percentage would reduce shares to a discount, but in that sense double the present charges on some railways would be still less "remunerative," because with those charges they would pay still less dividend; second, charges may be termed "unremunerative," and are so, comparatively, when a higher rate would pay better; and third, they may be "unremunerative," and are so absolutely, when they don't pay more than the actual expense of carriage. In this last sense the shareholders considered the chairman's tariff unremunerative. The chairman of the Eastern Counties, in answer to the charge, gave the following minute detail of expenditure, signed by the traffic manager:—

"Mr. Gooch's Report on Working Expenses of Coal Traffic. Cost of Working the Coal Traffic on the Eastern Counties Railway.

"This traffic is worked in full trains, excepting when required to make up to full loads the ordinary goods trains. Each train contains not less than thirty waggons, including break vans, at $6\frac{1}{2}$ tons each—190 tons net load; for which the sum paid by the contractor is eight shillings and sevenpence per train per mile, or about one halfpenny per ton per mile.

"The cost to the company is as follows:— *d.*

1st. Locomotive power	9·68
2nd. Guards	·50
3rd. Green lamps, oil	1·
4th. Permanent way	1·
5th. Management and office expenses...	1·
Total cost per mile per train of working expenses	13·18

"But as these trains return empty, only earning money in one direction, this account must be doubled, and would give a total sum of two shillings and twopence farthing to earn eight shillings and sevenpence, showing a profit of nearly 300 per cent."

Mr. Gooch enters into considerable detail on other matters, which we need not follow.

The contractors in the above contract found the waggons, which might be calculated at $3\frac{3}{4}d.$ per mile, bringing up the entire expenditure—say, to two shillings and sixpence per mile for the double journey. The cost, therefore, of conveying each ton of coal on the Eastern Counties line is one shilling and fourpence for a hundred miles, or from the pit's mouth to London less than two shillings per ton.

It is to be observed that there is a considerable difference between Mr. Gooch's mode of calculation and that of the Board of Trade; the difference, however, is more apparent than real. Mr. Gooch goes little beyond the actual expenditure incurred in the conveyance of coal, whilst the Board of Trade distributes the general expenditure over all the trains, and, by dividing that sum by their number, apportions to each its share. The case in question, however, was an exception to the general rule. The charge against the chairman of the company was that he carried coal at "unremunerative" rates; the answer, in effect, was that the general expenditure of the establishment was scarcely affected by the carriage of the coal, which would have been incurred whether they were carried or not, and that the company, for every shilling of actual expenditure incurred, received back in return nearly four shillings.

Now, here is one of the great necessaries of life which, if railways were in the possession of the State, we could have delivered at our very doors, exclusive of cartage, at the rate of seven or eight shillings per ton, or, adding a large percentage profit on the railway carriage, at eleven shillings per ton. Such a fact requires no comment.

In the parliamentary session of 1863 a committee of the House of Lords was appointed to consider the best means of providing London with railways, more especially with connecting lines north and south of the Thames. In the evidence taken on the subject the manager of the Midland Company stated that after they had brought coal from Derbyshire and Nottinghamshire at a charge of six shillings per ton, a demand of two shillings per ton was made for passing over the lines to Kensington basin, which practically had the effect of stopping the passage, and doing its part towards keeping up the price.

It would be impossible, I think, to give a stronger instance than this of the evil results that follow from entrusting a monopoly of such magnitude as the traffic on our railways to private, irresponsible parties. There is no want more severely felt, nor any commodity in a hard winter so soon run up in price, as coal. We can buy it, as we know, at the pit's mouth, and transport it to the metropolis, for seven or eight shillings per ton, but as a general rule we pay four times that price in London. The price the poor pay for the small quantity they are able to purchase at a time during a severe winter, the extent to which they are cheated, and the sufferings they in consequence endure, are matters every one is well acquainted with. Monopoly charges them three or four hundred per cent. in ordinary times, and in extraordinary times as much more as it can lay on to bring the coal not into the heart of London, but to its extremities; another monopoly meets it then, and stops the way, unless a charge equal to two thousand per cent. profit on the work done is paid before the coal is taken to its destination! And yet no blame can be attached to the managers of these monopolies; they do nothing in ill-will against the public. What they do is for the benefit of the shareholders, and so long as the country permits monopoly to mask itself, and assume the garb of free trade, and carry on such a system as we have in this case illustrated, the less we boast of our advance in the knowledge and practice of social economy will be the more to our credit.

The quantity of coal conveyed to London by the railways has largely increased within the last few years, and has become an important source of revenue to many of the companies.

The following is the number of tons conveyed by each company to London in 1863:—

	Tons.
London and North-Western	759,763
Great Northern	550,908
Midland	165,984
Great Eastern	160,323
Great Western	110,440
South-Western	19,902
London, Chatham, and Dover	7,569
London, Tilbury, and Southend	598
	1,775,487

Clay Cross pits, near Chesterfield, supply of the above quantity about 200,000 tons, and the Silkstone coal from various pits in south-west Yorkshire nearly the same quantity; the remaining quantity comes from the widely scattered coal districts of the North.

The returns of the coal trade for the year 1864 show a very remarkable increase; they have risen to 2,342,720 tons, being an increase of upwards of 30 per cent., and "these figures," says the writer of the City article in the *Times*, "very inadequately indicate the progress that might, under perfectly favourable circumstances, be witnessed in the consumptive capacities of the Metropolis. Had facilities existed in the shape of additional lines of railway having direct and independent access to the northern coalfields, it is apparently beyond doubt that the public would have been benefited from one shilling and sixpence to three shillings per ton, since, during that period, and especially at the present moment (December 30), in consequence of the prevalence of easterly winds and gales on the north-eastern coast, the ordinary sailing ships have been prevented, though laden, from putting to sea, and the two principal railways, notwithstanding their extra efforts, have been unable sufficiently to meet the demand."

It will be remembered, and I shall have to refer to the case in some detail hereafter, that a committee of the House of

Commons refused permission to the Great Eastern to construct a line that would connect them with the coalfields of the north. But the Great Eastern, apparently not at all discouraged, renews its application to Parliament during the coming session.

Before a proper tariff could be drawn up, regulating the charges for conveyance of all classes of merchandise, &c., throughout the kingdom, evidence representing all the several interests affected would be required, so that justice might be done to all. When it is remembered that a ton of merchandise can be conveyed one hundred miles for little more than a shilling, that the companies are authorized in the majority of cases to charge that sum twenty times over, that they do charge it, that the public have not the slightest power or control in regulating these charges, and that the amount paid in 1863 for the conveyance of general merchandise, minerals, and live stock amounted to upwards of SIXTEEN MILLIONS AND A HALF sterling, it must, I think, be admitted by every one who will consider the question in all its bearings, and the vast interests at stake, that the expiration of the twenty-one years shadowed forth by Mr. Gladstone in 1844 as the proper term when our railway management should undergo revision, and the comparative merits of the two systems be investigated, will not arrive too soon.

Many persons might perhaps be inclined to suppose that, in accordance with a very common but very erroneous saying, "the interests of the companies and those of the public are identical," and that the rates of carriage have now a downward tendency. The following extract from an article in *Herapath's Railway Journal*, of the 14th of May, 1864, will show the fallacy of such an opinion :—"London and North-Western and Great Western Railways. — Two small advertisements in another column, one from each of the two companies, make important announcements, both to the public and to the shareholders. They are to the effect that, from the first of next month, the rates for goods traffic will be revised and increased, and that a very host of new through rates for goods traffic will be made for the conveyance of goods to and from the principal stations of the two great companies, and also of other leading railways of the kingdom.

" Both announcements are most important to the interests of railway proprietors, and the second to the interest of the public."

The increase of rates here announced varies from twenty to thirty per cent., and a similar increase may be expected on most of the other great lines.

Great dissatisfaction has been generally expressed in the northern counties at the high rate of freightage. " At a meeting of the Liverpool Chamber of Commerce," says the *Daily News* of the 8th Nov., " held yesterday, Mr. Grainger presiding, the question of the excessive rates of carriage charged by the various railway companies to and from Liverpool was discussed. On the motion of Mr. R. A. Macfie it was resolved to refer the matter to their committee on railways."

In no part of the kingdom does the working of the system appear to give satisfaction.

It would be almost impossible to over estimate the value of the boon that would be conferred on the mercantile community by the establishment of a low and, to some extent, uniform tariff for parcels and packages throughout the kingdom.

The annual charge to the public for the conveyance of parcels is very small in amount compared with that paid for general merchandise, and does not probably exceed three hundred thousand pounds, but the return is mixed up with that of others. Great, however, as the difference is between the two sums, I am almost inclined to believe that a low, and, to some extent, uniform tariff for parcels, packages, hampers, &c., throughout the kingdom would even be a more popular measure than a general reduction in the charges for merchandise. It would come more home to each household; it would partake more of the nature of an abatement in direct taxation than almost any reduction would be in the charges on general merchandise, coal only excepted. A low tariff for the carriage of parcels and packages would be a great boon to most families; it would enable them to procure direct at a moderate charge, from any district throughout the country, the produce for which it might be most celebrated. The Yorkshire hams, the Devonshire cream, the Norfolk turkeys, the Yarmouth bloaters, the Cork butter, the Coleraine whisky, and all other local dainties throughout the kingdom, would contribute their regular supplies direct to the consumer when they could be procured at a low charge for carriage.

Let us first note the present charges for parcels and packages on the principal lines out of London. Small parcels are carried for much less by the Post Office than by the railway companies—in some cases less than a fourth. The Post Office pays between five and six hundred thousand pounds sterling per annum to the companies, and beats them out of the field in competing for the carriage of small parcels; or perhaps it would be more correct to say the companies do not think it worth the trouble of giving the necessary accommodation to the public. We can send by the Post Office to the remotest part of the kingdom a parcel weighing 1 lb., and have it delivered at the same time with our letters, for fourpence. If we send it by a railway company it will cost in some cases half a crown, and probably take double the time before it is delivered. This illustrates the difference between monopoly under strict control and directed only for the public good, and monopoly run wild, guided by private interests, whim, or caprice, and doing exactly as it likes. On the London and North-Western line the lowest charge is 6d.; for this sum a parcel is carried 20 miles; 40 miles, 8d.; and so on increasing up to 220 miles, when the charge is 2s. 6d. That is the maximum for one pound weight on this line. The Great Western minimum charge is 6d., and maximum 2s. 8d., for the same weight.

In considering a new tariff under a national system it is not necessary to take a lower weight than 3 lbs. The following table will show the scale of charges for such a parcel on three of the principal railways out of London:—

	London and North Western.		Great Western.		Great Northern.	
	s.	d.	s.	d.	s.	d.
Not exceeding 20 miles	0	6	0	6	0	6
,, 40 ,,	0	8	0	8	0	6
,, 80 ,,	0	10	0	10	0	8
,, 120 ,,	1	0	1	0	1	0
,, 160 ,,	1	3	1	3	1	3
,, 220 ,,	2	0	2	0	1	6
Exceeding that distance	2	6	2	8	1	6

On all lines there is a most unreasonable charge of 2*d.*, in addition to the rates I have quoted, for booking, however small the parcel may be.

It is only justice to the companies to state that they will carry a much greater weight than 3 lbs. for the charges I have affixed to their names, but if a person require to send a parcel of only 3 lbs. he gains little by being informed he can send five times that weight for the same price. It is to be observed also that the above scale of charges is only in reference to each line. When a parcel passes over several lines the charge in many cases is considerably increased. It will be seen, however, that, at the present rates, charges for small parcels of little value are almost prohibitory, and that a low and uniform rate for which they would be conveyed to every part of the kingdom would confer a great benefit on the community. I think that the following scale, uniform for all distances throughout the kingdom, would not only be generally acceptable to the public, but probably, in a few years, produce a larger revenue than what is derived at present from their carriage. Proposed scale, by passenger trains:—

Parcels not exceeding 3 lbs. ... ... 4*d.*
,, ,, 7 lbs. ... ... 6*d.*
,, ,, 10 lbs. ... .. 9*d.*
,, ,, 14 lbs. ... ... 1*s.*

and for every additional 7 lbs., or fraction of 7 lbs., 6*d.*

No charge to be made for booking; and all to be paid in advance by stamps, as the delivery would be as quick as the post.

The rates for long distances for packages and hampers are very high. The charge, for instance, on a package between London and Dublin, not exceeding 56 lbs., is 5*s.* 6*d.* It is unnecessary to go over the different rates charged by the companies, but they may be said to be almost prohibitory in reference to the transport of merchandise or other commodities of no great intrinsic value. When the distance is not great the charges are comparatively moderate. The carriage of a hamper, for instance, weighing 28 lbs., on the Great Western for 40 miles, is 1*s.* 2*d.*, but when it is conveyed 220 miles or upwards it is 4*s.* 8*d.* Now, the principal expense is the terminal charge—the expense of collecting and delivering—and that expense is equally incurred when a package is carried 20 miles or 200. When it is remembered that a ton of goods can be conveyed 100 miles for one shilling and fourpence, it will be seen that the difference in expenditure is scarcely appreciable, whether the distance a package has to be conveyed is 20 miles or 200; assuming even that the conveyance of packages, hampers, and heavy parcels costs 5*s.* per ton per 100 miles, that would only be at the rate of threepence per hundredweight. I think, therefore, a *maximum* charge for the greatest distances for packages, &c., by goods trains at the following scale might be adopted with great advantage to the public:—Maximum charges for parcels by goods trains, not exceeding 28 lbs., 1*s.*; not exceeding 56 lbs., 1*s.* 6*d.*; not exceeding 1 cwt., 2*s.*

Now, this scale could not be universally adopted, inasmuch as for short distances it would in some cases exceed the present charges. For any distance, therefore, not exceeding 50 miles I should propose half-rates, viz.:—for parcels not exceeding 28 lbs., 6*d.*; 56 lbs., 9*d.*; 112 lbs., 1*s.*; and threepence for every additional quarter of a hundredweight. This tariff would bring the *minimum* scale considerably under the lowest charges on any railway.

It will be generally admitted that a low scale of charges

for heavy packages, &c., would open up a new trade between many parts of the kingdom where none now exists, prove a great convenience to many private families, especially those residing for a part of the year in London with a residence in the country, and facilitate communication and an interchange of goods with the most distant and isolated districts, which hitherto have been all but excluded from the benefits to be derived from railway communication.

There are many other advantages the public would derive from the possession of the railways by the State. I shall briefly notice but two; one is the increased facilities the Post Office would derive from the conveyance of the mails. The annual payments by the Post Office to the companies exceed half a million sterling, and the heavy charges the companies make for conveyance of the mails diminish considerably the accommodation the public would otherwise receive. The expense would be so great of carrying into full effect in the rural districts the forwarding of mails by railways, that the Post-Office authorities, in many cases, are obliged to avail themselves of the old modes of conveyance. The subject was brought before the House of Commons on the 4th of April, 1864, when Mr. Long moved for the appointment of "A Select Committee on the Post Office, with an especial view to the improvement of existing arrangements for the transmission of mails in the provincial districts." In many districts, where railway communication exists, according to the statement of the hon. member, it had not been taken advantage of, and mails were still sent by horse and cart, and even by messengers on foot. In some cases it took three days to get an answer to a letter sent ten or twenty miles into the country, just as it did thirty years ago. Although there had been for many years a railway between the important towns of Hereford, Ross, and Gloucester, the mails were still conveyed by a horse and cart, as they had been fifty years ago. It was the same in South Wales; Newport, Cardiff, Merthyr, and other towns were similarly situated. Between Shrewsbury and

Liverpool letters were still sent by a mail cart; they were twenty-four hours in passing between the two towns, whilst passengers by train went in three hours. In Kent and Sussex the postal communication was very imperfect; in some places not more than nine miles apart, it required four days to receive an answer to a letter.

Mr. Long proposed that the chief and central Post Office should be removed from St. Martin's-le-Grand to Charing Cross, that there should be letter-boxes at each railway station, and mails sent by trains to all stations along the lines.

In Cornwall and Devonshire, Mr. Wyld stated there was great cause of complaint in regard to the conveyance of letters, and that the First Lord of the Treasury and the Postmaster General would soon be compelled to find a remedy for the evil complained of.

Mr. Bentinck suggested that, as the railway companies enjoyed a certain monopoly, it should be rendered obligatory on railways to carry mail-bags at a reasonable rate; and in cases where the correspondence was not sufficient to pay for increased accommodation, the Post Office might be empowered to charge additional rates.

Mr. Baillie complained that revenue was too much looked to by the Post-Office authorities, and that the right principle was being departed from on which the establishment should be conducted. When a district asked the Post Office for increased accommodation, the usual answer was—Would it pay, or was it likely to pay? He had presented petitions at various times from the Isle of Skye, which, with a population of nearly twenty thousand, had postal communication only three times a week between Fort William and Inverness, and the answer of the Post Office to a request for increased accommodation was, that there was no certainty of its paying.

It was contended throughout the discussion that, to make the necessary Post-Office accommodation throughout the country a fiscal question, was altogether opposed to the principle on which its management should be conducted; and as there was a million and a half of revenue now derived from its working, that sum, if necessary, should be applied to the full development of the system.

The Chancellor of the Exchequer, whilst acknowledging that the principle on which the Post Office was conducted was fairly stated by Mr. Baillie, said, if the suggestion was acceded to, that a million and a half should be laid out in providing additional accommodation, the result would be that there would be a gap to that extent which should be stopped by the laying on of a new tax, or the augmentation of some tax already in existence.

It is not necessary to pursue this question further at present than to remark, that to carry out fully Sir Rowland Hill's postal reform, as required by the country, and as advocated in the House of Commons, would involve the sacrifice of no small part of the million and a half of revenue the Post Office now yields; whilst, if the railways were in the possession of the State, the expense of conveyance of *all* the mails in the kingdom would be almost nominal, with the exception of those few special cases where great speed is required, or the trains despatched at hours not suited for the general traffic.

The other advantage I have referred to would be the facilities which the possession of the railways would place at the disposal of the Government for the transport of our regular troops, militia, volunteers, and military stores to all parts of the kingdom, whenever or wherever occasion might require. Government pay for soldiers a penny per mile, and the same fiscal causes that operate so much to the disadvantage of the complete working of the Post Office have an equally injurious effect on the public service in the military department.

PART II.—THE SHAREHOLDERS.

CHAPTER I.

Advantages possessed by the early Railway Projectors—Their Success—Value of Railway Property in 1845—Amalgamation—The Results of Competition—Quarrels of the great Companies—Their Refusal to abide by the Board of Trade's Recommendations—The Effect on the Value of their Shares—The Benefit to the Public from Competition—Lowering of the Fares throughout the Country—Great Number of unnecessary Lines constructed—Government Plan defeated—Results to the Shareholders—What they have now to consider.

WE now enter on another phase of this inquiry—To discuss the past, present, and, so far as we can form an opinion, the future financial position of our railway shareholders; to examine into the causes which have produced such a great depreciation in the value of their property, once classed among the best investments in the country; to consider whether or not the causes which have produced such an unfortunate result are from their nature likely to be permanent in their operation; and, lastly—the more especial subject—to inquire, whether or not it would be for the interest of shareholders to avail themselves, so far as is in their power, of Mr. Gladstone's Act of 1844, and support any movement for carrying it into effect.

Although the early projectors of railways encountered great opposition, and were in consequence put to heavy expense before they obtained their Acts, yet the practical monopoly that seemed to lie within their reach, the undisturbed possession of the public highways, promised at one time to yield a most ample and permanent return for their large outlay. There was but little interference, either on the part of the Legislature or the executive, and it only required union among themselves to extend to a much later period than eventually happened, that undivided monopoly which cost them so much to acquire.

Thirty-six years ago, after the success of the Liverpool and Manchester line had been established, the construction of railways throughout the country became general. The fear of future competing lines never appears to have been entertained by the promoters; they were, in fact, too much occupied in overcoming the obstacles they had then to meet, to waste idle speculations on those which might never exist. They had to conciliate or circumvent the hostile landowners, to obtain their Acts from a jealous Legislature, to surmount the physical difficulties encountered in the construction of their works, and to find the pecuniary means for carrying them on, many of them being of the most expensive nature, and on a gigantic scale. At the time we speak of, such a contingency as the construction of a competing line does not appear to have occurred to the mind of any one. The whole country was, so to speak, unoccupied. A vast field had been opened for British skill and capital, and nothing could have appeared more unlikely than that those who had money to invest would voluntarily enter into speculation on ground already occupied, when the attempt to obtain possession would be so violently resisted, and, in the event of success, the traffic would necessarily be divided. The Parliamentary concession to make a railway, for instance, that, when constructed, would pay its shareholders a ten per cent. dividend, was, no doubt, violently contested for; but when once the successful projectors obtained their Act, all rivalry was considered at an end, and future opposition was never dreamt of. The traffic that would pay ten per cent. to one railway would not pay four per cent. to two, as the traffic would be divided, and the expenses but little decreased. It was further considered that, in any case, Parliament would never permit an unnecessary, and consequently wasteful, expenditure of capital. From these causes future opposition lines entered not into the calculations of our early railway projectors.

Whatever might have been the calculations or expectations of railway projectors or shareholders, the Legislature took care to keep itself clear from all engagements, either expressed or implied, in reference to withholding its sanction for the construction of competing lines; indeed, from a very early period in our railway history, the construction of competing lines was held out by the Legislature as the main remedy the public should rely on as a guard against excessive charges, or any other unfair conduct on the part of directors of companies.

For many years the companies, as they succeeded each other in extending the great trunk lines through the kingdom, prospered with each extension; the more continuous and uninterrupted the lines, the greater the traffic, and, of course, the greater the profit to the shareholders; and so the companies went on increasing in prosperity, and confining their operations to the wealthiest or most densely populated districts of the country, avoiding all competition or intrusion into each other's "territories," and finally proceeded to consolidate their power by the process of amalgamation, whereby several were united together for a common interest, and formed into one large company.

The measures taken by the companies towards amalgamation were received at first with considerable distrust both by the country and the Legislature. It was contended, on the one hand, that it would provide that necessary accommodation at their terminal stations and their general establishments which many of the companies could not afford—that it would enable small companies, whose lines were worked at great expense, to obtain the benefit of cheapness and general arrangement which were enjoyed by lines of greater extent, and that in the more populous districts of the country the formation of numerous lines under different management tended to create expense, obstruction, confusion, and damage to life and property. These facts could not be disputed; but the opposition relied more on the application of general principles than of special reasons to defeat the companies in carrying out their projects; it was asserted that amalgamation was but another name for centralization, and that it was in the highest degree unconstitutional to extend and consolidate the powers of the companies in the manner proposed. The arguments, however, founded on these principles failed to convince the Legislature, and the amalgamations of the several companies that applied to Parliament were, after due investigation, permitted to take place.

When the process of amalgamation commenced, the companies had reached their highest state of prosperity. This was in the autumn of 1845. From the share list of September in that year we quote the market price of all the principal railways in the kingdom:—

Name of Railway.	Amount paid.	Price per Share.
	£	£
Birmingham and Derby	100	128
Birmingham and Gloucester	100	131
Bristol and Exeter	70	90
Eastern Counties	25	21
Edinburgh and Glasgow	50	76
Great North of England	100	217
Great Western	80	165
Grand Junction	100	242
Hull and Selby	50	106
Liverpool and Manchester	100	217
London and Birmingham	100	222
London and Brighton	50	75
London and Croydon	13	25
London and South Western	50	80
Manchester and Leeds	76	215
Manchester and Birmingham	40	90
Midland	100	160
Newcastle and Darlington	25	64
Newcastle and Carlisle	100	113
Northern and Eastern	50	67
North Union	100	225
South-Eastern and Dover	50	45
Sheffield and Manchester	95	148
Stockton and Darlington	100	275
York and North Midland	50	118
	£1,774	£3,324

Thus we find that when the railways were at their culminating point, the shares could be sold at an average profit of nearly cent. per cent. on the outlay. The best-paying railway, the Stockton and Darlington, paid fifteen per cent., the Grand Junction eleven per cent., and many from seven to ten per cent. These were happy days for the shareholders. Many, foreseeing the coming change in affairs, sold out, and placed their capital in safer investments. Of the above railways the Liverpool and Manchester, the Grand Junction, the London and Birmingham, and the Manchester and Birmingham, form part of the London and North-Western line; the Birmingham and Derby, Birmingham and Gloucester, and York and North Midland, form part of the Midland line; the Great North of England, Hull and Selby, and Stockton and Darlington, form part of the North-Eastern line; and the Northern and Eastern and Eastern Counties form part of the Great Eastern line. A few of the companies in the foregoing list are leased at a high guaranteed rate. The shares of all the others are greatly reduced in value, in many cases to the half, and in some cases to the one-third, of their former value.

To what cause, then, or combination of causes is to be attributed such a ruinous depreciation in the value of railway property? Is it a falling off in the trade and commerce of the country, and a consequent decrease in our national prosperity? So far from that being the case, our trade and commerce have for a long series of years been rapidly increasing, and probably at no former period did there exist such a degree of national prosperity as there does at present. Do the public travel less than formerly, or are railways superseded by some new mode of transit? The number of travellers in the year 1863 was unprecedented, and, as we have seen, amounted to more than two hundred millions! Nor is there any probability that the present mode of transit will be ever superseded by any other. Well, then, is it to the falling off in the carriage of goods and minerals, as compared with passengers? The direct contrary is the case. In the year 1845 the amount received for the carriage of goods and minerals did not amount to one-third of that received for passengers; whilst for the year 1863, as we have seen, the amount received for the earnings of the "goods" trains considerably exceed that received for the earnings of the passenger trains. So far as regards railway legislation, there may be some cause of complaint as to unequal parochial rates, and other causes of a comparatively trifling nature, all of which have either been remedied, or are of too trifling a nature to affect the general results. What, then, has caused this great deterioration in the value of railway property, and reduced an interest that promised at one time to be the most flourishing and permanent in the kingdom to little more than half its former value, its directorates struggling to overcome difficulties apparently insurmountable, and without a prospect of any *permanent* revival? I answer, the cause of all these accumulated evils to the railway interest may be summed up in two words—COMPETITION and GUARANTEES.

So long as the companies' operations were confined to thickly populated districts, "all went merry as a marriage bell;" the best-paying districts were naturally the first selected, and the close of the session of 1844 saw all the best parts of the country in possession of the companies which up to that period had been formed. From that time forward competition may be fairly said to have set in. The battle of the gauges almost equalled in its way the Wars of the Roses; all the great companies, grown powerful by amalgamation, carried on a fierce internecine war for possession of the districts between their several trunk lines. An ineffectual attempt had been made (as we have had occasion to notice) by the Legislature in 1844 to put some check on this warfare, by requiring the Board of Trade to make a preliminary report to the Parliamentary Committees; these reports, however, were soon discontinued. It was considered unfair by the railway interest generally that the Board of Trade should use its influence in favour of either of the contending parties—and that they should be left to fight it out themselves before the Parliamentary Committee. The Committees soon ceased to pay any attention to the Board's reports, and so they became discontinued. If the companies, in carrying on this warfare, had, when defeated before a Committee, retired from the field, it would have been happy both for them and their opponents; but there were too many interested —lawyers, engineers, contractors, and jobbers of all kinds— to let the good work so happily begun die easily out. New schemes were soon brought forward, and carried through Parliament, that competed, directly or indirectly, as the case might be, with those that but a year or two previously were thought quite sufficient to afford ample accommodation for the districts in that part of the country.

Thus commenced the war between Monopoly on the one hand and Free Trade on the other which, from that time to the present, has been continued in each successive session of Parliament. The great amalgamated companies were not only intent on securing, in railway phraseology, within their own extensive domains all their legitimate traffic, but, by extending branches and feeders from their trunk lines into the neighbouring territories, to abstract from " the lawful owners" whatever they could lay their hands on. This naturally produced retaliation, and so the war went on.

It is a favourite dogma of the railway faith that the public derive no permanent benefit from the construction of opposition lines; that, after a short-lived opposition, the two or more companies come to terms, the opposition is abandoned, and higher charges are agreed on and enforced, to make up for the loss incurred by the opposition. This, however, is not by any means a correct representation of the general effect produced by the construction of opposition lines. In most cases the public derive considerable benefit by a large and permanent reduction in the fares.

The traffic between the metropolis and our large towns is, in a certain sense, competed for; that between London and Liverpool, for instance, once in the sole possession of the London and North-Western, is now shared by the Great Western and the Great Northern Companies; to these will be shortly added the Midland, as they have carried their bill for the continuation of their line into London. And so throughout the kingdom is there competition in a greater or less degree; there can scarcely be named a district of any importance for which the traffic is not competed for by two or more companies; they agree as to the fares to be charged, and in a limited sense compete for the traffic. Trade, no doubt, has vastly increased within the last twenty years; but what increase can compensate for the loss caused by duplicate and triplicate lines, and fares and charges reduced in many cases to less than one-half of what they originally were? From London to Liverpool, twenty years ago, a passenger could not make a continuous journey in the same day for less than £2 7s. 6d., viz. by second class on the London and Birmingham, and first class by the Grand Junction to Liverpool; now, he can go through by first class express for £1 12s. 6d., or second class £1 5s. Then he required *two* days by a third-class open carriage, at a cost of £1 7s.; now he can go down twice a day, either morning or afternoon, in an enclosed carriage, for 16s. 9d. We have seen what it was to travel by third class on the Great Western; all that is now changed. The fares by this line, that were formerly to Bristol, first class, £1 10s., and second class £1, are now £1 and 15s. respectively. Twenty years ago you paid from London to Birmingham, first class, 32s. 6d., and second, 25s.; now you can travel there by express in one-third less time than you could do then, and the fares have been reduced to 20s. and 15s. From Birmingham to Liverpool you paid by the Grand Junction 26s. first class, and 18s. second class; now you pay by the same classes 15s. and 10s. 6d. The same high rate of charges prevailed in all parts of the kingdom, and within a much nearer period than twenty years the fares between London and York, and the other great towns in Yorkshire, where the Midland had a monopoly, were very high. Of the route to York the fares were respectively, for first and second class, £2 10s. and £1 15s.; now they are £1 15s. and £1 5s. It is only two or three years since the South-Eastern charged from London to Dover, by express, 22s., and all other classes in proportion throughout the line; now, since the construction of the London, Chatham, and Dover, the express fare has been reduced to 19s., and all other fares in the same proportion.

It is a common error to suppose that when companies waste money they are able to extract this extra expenditure from the public by an increased charge, and so recoup themselves for their previous loss. This is not so; the companies charge in *every* case, whether the speculation be good or bad, the highest *paying* price, whether that be high or low, and as they cannot exceed that, and would make exactly the same charges, whether any particular loss had been incurred or not, whatever losses they incur fall on themselves, and they suffer by a decreased dividend. The public, therefore, can never lose by competition, and always gain more or less.

It cannot, then, be a matter of surprise that opposition lines should receive such encouragement from the public and the Legislature. They are the only means by which charges on the old lines can be reduced. It is contended for by railway writers that competition does not effect this end, and that after two competing lines have "run opposition" for a few months, they both find it to be their interest to settle their differences, and raise their charges to the old level, and so the public are no better off than they had been previously. The last case, they say, in point, is that of the South-Eastern and London, Chatham, and Dover. There was for a time a strong rivalry between the two companies; afterwards they became friends, and mutually agreed to a scale of charges; but, as we have seen, the present fares are much below the original fares, and it is only necessary to compare the present charges on those lines where there is competition with their previous charges, when they had a monopoly of the traffic, to satisfy the most incredulous of the great benefits that have resulted to the public from even a partial competition. But it is not alone by the reduction of fares that the public gain by competing lines. Large districts, previously without railways, or but partially supplied, receive increased accommodation, and thus by degrees, as the system is extended, the network of railways is thrown over the whole country, till the most distant village as well as the populous town will share equally in the benefits of railway communication.

So far, therefore, as the general community is concerned, it has, in many respects, but little to complain of in the general working of the present system compared with the shareholders, and if it be continued, the more it is extended, and railways are multiplied and competition increases, so will the causes of complaint decrease, although by carrying on such a system the shareholders must sustain a heavy loss.

The main object of the Legislature in passing the General Railway Act of 1844 was to avoid the waste of national wealth by preventing the construction of direct competing and therefore unnecessary lines. Whether the machinery for that purpose was the best that could be devised might be a matter for discussion, but it would be impossible to conceive any object more calculated to promote the interests of the shareholders than that Act of 1844. What did it do? It gave the whole weight and influence of Government to carrying out a policy strictly conservative in its character, by the appointment of a Board for promoting useful, and preventing the construction of unnecessary, lines. Although the bill passed, the railway directors of that day refused to co-operate with the Board of Trade, to submit to its recommendations, or acquiesce in the line of demarcation the Board drew between the respective "territories" of the rival companies; they preferred fighting out their battles before Parliamentary Committees, and, as a necessary consequence, the functions of the Board in this department were soon abolished.

Let any one take up a railway map of England, and cast an eye over that entangled mass of lines running here, there, and everywhere in wild confusion, twisting and twining about, sometimes in duplicate, and not unfrequently in triplicate, and forming all sorts of odd complications—that is what we call our railway system. What untold scores of millions sterling has this "system" cost the unhappy shareholders who have been its victims!—how the money has been squandered away in fruitless Parliamentary contests, in the construction or purchase of worthless lines, or the guarantee of high dividends here, carrying the war into the enemy's camp there, or "protecting the rights and privileges of the shareholders from unjustifiable aggression" somewhere else! So has the game gone on for twenty years—a profitable and pleasant one, no doubt, for many parties, but it is not unreasonable to suppose that the shareholders may be pretty well tired of it; and the question is, will they now endeavour to abolish it?

Let us examine for a moment the Government project for discouraging the construction of competing lines, and endeavour to form some opinion as to its result, if the Government had succeeded in its plan, and prevented that frightful waste of capital which it was one of the main objects of the Act to effect.

There have been made clear, I hope, in the first part of this work three important facts in connection with railway management:—1st. That one railway between any two places is quite sufficient for the ordinary purposes of traffic; 2nd. That the cost of conveyance on it is exceedingly low; and 3rd. That, as fares and charges decrease, in nearly the same proportion does the traffic increase. We have seen that within certain limits (viz., from three farthings to threepence per mile for first-class passengers, and for the other classes in proportion), it made but comparatively little difference in the companies' profits; in few cases, perhaps, more than one per cent. per annum less dividend on their capital; but if a rival line were constructed, the loss in dividend would far exceed that percentage. "Would it be fair," said Mr. Gladstone to one of the witnesses before the Select Committee, "to say to a company, 'We will give you your choice; if you make a reduction in your terms, we will reject the bill for a new line, but if you will not, we will sanction it?'" Judging from this and similar questions put to other witnesses, the policy, apparently, of the Government, if they had succeeded in carrying out their plan, would have been, in each case where a rival line was projected, not to sanction its construction, if the old company consented to make what Government might consider a reasonable reduction in its tariff, according to the circumstances of the case; and, failing to make a bargain with the old company, to enter into terms of arrangement with the new, and by these means secure a very low rate of transit both for goods and passengers throughout the country. How would this scheme have worked for the then existing companies? Their interests would have been fairly protected, there would have been no unnecessary lines made, and they would have been saved from the ruinous results of that constant warfare they have had to struggle against from that time to the present. Parliament found it absolutely necessary, at the opening of the session of 1864, to appoint a committee for the purpose of laying down a distinct and definite plan for protecting London from the vast number of railways that threatened invasion on a gigantic scale; and from all these different projects the Committee have settled on a perfect plan by which London is to be amply supplied with railways. If the same principle that is now applied to the metropolis had been applied twenty years ago to the whole nation, what a vast amount of capital would have been saved! lines better adapted to serve the public would have been planned and executed, unnecessary competing lines would never have been constructed, the shareholders would have been fairly remunerated for the outlay of their capital, and the public would now be deriving all those advantages produced by a low rate of railway charges throughout the country, of which they are unfortunately deprived by the failure of that part of the Government scheme that referred to the construction of railways.

It remains now for the shareholders of the present day, and more especially the directors of the companies, to consider whether or not it would be for their interest to support a movement towards the carrying out of that part of the General Act of 1844 which refers to the purchase of railways by the State. It is true that Government in the coming session may have a Committee appointed to investigate the subject, but as attention has not been directed to it for twenty years, a great deal of information must be given to the public before the matter can be thoroughly understood. In forming an opinion on the subject there are three topics which would naturally suggest themselves to the mind :—1st. How would such a proposal as the purchase of the railways by the State be received and entertained by the public? The answer would depend in no small degree on the position of the party from whom the proposal would proceed, and on their opinion as to the general soundness of the theory and correctness of the facts that could be advanced in support of it. It might, I think, be safely predicated that the public would offer no opposition to a scheme, if pronounced sound and feasible by those best qualified to judge, that would enable them to travel at a uniform rate through the country at fares varying from a half to a fifth of what they now pay, and with similar reductions on goods, parcels, &c. 2nd. The shareholders, in considering the proposal, would naturally direct their attention to their present position and future prospects. Is the former secure, and the latter hopeful? Are the causes which have produced such a depression in the value of railway property temporary in their nature, and likely soon to pass away? Is the source of all evil to shareholders—competition—on the decline? and may shareholders indulge in a reasonable anticipation that the Legislature will refuse its sanction in future to competing lines, and otherwise discourage such projects by throwing the expense of defending existing interests brought before Parliament on hostile projectors? 3rd, and this is the main, consideration with shareholders—the others I have noticed being only of consequence so far as they bear on this—what bonus would the Legislature probably give for the shares, in addition to their market value? For if liberal, the shareholders would naturally support such a movement. The whole affair is a question of price. Into the sale of houses, land, or other property there are many considerations enter besides that of actual value; there is the inconvenience or loss to the owner, which he naturally estimates from a different point of view to that of the proposed purchaser; but with joint-stock property, constantly changing hands in the market, it is a different affair altogether. A shareholder has no sentimental attachment to "North-Westerns," "Brightons," "South-Easterns," or "Great Northerns;" even its "A Stock" he would just as soon sell out if he considered the price of the day a pound or two beyond its value, and buy in the worst description of non-dividend-paying shares in the market if the latter were in his opinion selling a pound or two below their value. But as each shareholder can at any time get the market price for his shares, he would have no inducement to trouble himself about the matter unless he was offered a liberal bonus by the Legislature. We have now, therefore, to direct attention to two branches of our subject—the future prospects of shareholders, and the probable bonus in addition to the price that the Legislature might be induced to give them for their shares.

CHAPTER II.

The Effect of Competition—Some Shareholders favourable to Free Trade—The Duty of Directors—Necessity of opposing Competing Lines—Complaints against Directors—Improved Position of Railway Promoters—New Class of Contractors—Low Rate of Contracts—Complaints of Shareholders—" A fair and reasonable Charge"—Under the present System Competition must continue—Dislike of the English People to Monopoly—Battles of the Companies—Extracts from the last Half-yearly Reports of the great Companies—Great Eastern Northern Junction before Parliament—Railway Affairs in 1844, 1845, and 1846—The Effects of great Prosperity may again be anticipated—Complaints against Parliament—False Position of Shareholders—Struggles to maintain the present System—Mr. Gladstone on the Introduction of the Bill of 1844—A Shareholder at the South-Eastern Meeting—Appeal to the Directors.

IT is important for shareholders, and those especially who have the direction of their affairs, to ponder well the impossibility of adopting any means under our present system to put an end to competition among railway companies. Its effect, as we have seen, has been to reduce railway property, within the last eighteen or twenty years, to less than half its original value, and, although the severe pressure only recurs at intermittent periods, it is not the less disastrous in its results.

There are, however, some shareholders who contend that a free trade in railways would have been profitable to both parties—the public and themselves; that if the directors had abstained from all opposition to rival lines, the shareholders in the old companies would now have been much better off, and been receiving large dividends. They further contend that this bad policy was further aggravated by the directors, when defeated in the first instance, purchasing up at extravagant prices, or guaranteeing exorbitant dividends to, successful rival lines. In condemnation of this policy they instance the enormous sums spent in fruitless Parliamentary contests, and the heavy burdens entailed on the old lines by such purchases and guarantees. I think, however, when all the circumstances of the case are duly considered, it will be admitted that the directors could not, in these respects, have acted better for the interests of their shareholders than they have done.

Before going into this matter, we must endeavour to see clearly what was the duty of the directors in reference to the shareholders on the one hand and the public on the other. Up to a certain point their interests were identical, but at that point they diverged, and became antagonistic. Whose interests, then, should the directors promote? No one, I think, can for a moment doubt that they were bound to use every fair and lawful means to protect and promote the interests of the shareholders in preference to those of the public.

To do justice to the directors, their position must be fairly stated. They represented a body of men who had rendered no small service to the State in the creation of public works— works which had been undertaken, carried on, and completed under great difficulties, without ever having received, as in other countries, either subvention, assistance, or special protection from the Legislature. The men who executed these works made no pretensions to philanthropy. They were working undoubtedly for their country's good, but that was a mere incident; they were shrewd, hard-headed men of business, who laid out vast sums of money to attain a certain object—that object being the possession, working, and monopoly of the great high roads of the country. All this was done as a matter of profitable speculation. The Legislature was under no obligation to the shareholders, nor the shareholders to the Legislature. So far as regards the general public, there was the same absence of obligation on either side. The public wanted to travel as cheap as they could; they cared nothing about the shareholders, or what return they would have for their invested capital, or whether they should have any return—that was the shareholders' business; they made the railways on speculation, and must abide by the consequences. So far as the general public were concerned, their feeling was decidedly hostile to the directors. It is clear, therefore, that when the interests of the shareholders and the public clashed, the directors had but one course to pursue, viz. to use their best endeavours to advance the interests of the shareholders.

Let us now examine the policy pursued by the directors in opposing competing lines. There are some persons, no doubt, who contend that competition is good alike for all parties, but I do not think that that theory can stand a moment's investigation. When a man can sell his wares or his services at his own price, his estimation of their value is, in general, somewhat higher than that of the public; and when he can enforce that valuation his situation is decidedly pleasant, and may be made very profitable. Competition is all very well for the public, but no sane man would give up a monopoly so long as he could possibly retain it. The directors, therefore, in upholding the interests of their shareholders, could only do battle with all comers who would venture to intrude into their territories, and offer to every project, come from whatever quarter it might, that would threaten to interfere with their monopoly, the most determined opposition. This the directors have always done, and on that head I do not think the shareholders have any fair ground of complaint. I do not see how they could have done better to promote their interests.

The second matter of complaint against the directors, viz., buying up or guaranteeing high dividends to successful opposition lines, is certainly more feasible than the first complaint. It was said, and no doubt with truth, that such purchases only gave encouragement to hostile projectors to proceed to new aggressions; but of the two evils the lesser one undoubtedly was to buy the rival line up, or adopt any other means by which they could secure their monopoly, and prevent the public being carried at the exceeding low rate at which they otherwise would on the new line, to the great disadvantage of the old line.

A great change has of late years taken place in the position of railway promoters. The almost fabulous prices paid for land in the early days of railway progress, and the opposition encountered from landowners and others, rendered the success of a bill a matter of the greatest difficulty, and the inexperience and necessary ignorance of contractors added heavily to the expenses. Up to 1844 the average cost of railways was £35,000 per mile; but times have changed wonderfully since then. Landowners, traders, and all other classes now fully appreciate the benefit to be derived from railways. The value of land is increased in the same proportion as they are made available for traffic, and traders would be shut out from their markets were they not within their immediate reach. Into whatever districts promoters now go, they are welcomed as friends, where, thirty years since, they would have been treated literally as enemies. The landowner sells his land at a fair price, sometimes takes the amount in shares, or in many cases gives it free, and all other classes locally interested support the undertaking; and, last of all, the public eagerly take up the shares. This is not all, nor the worst so far as regards the position of shareholders in the old lines. The general demand for railways has called into existence a new class of speculators, who unite in their own persons the several functions of promoters, contractors, shareholders in the first instance, and lessees when necessary—men of great wealth, enterprise, experience, and energy, in every way fully competent to carry out whatever they undertake, always on the look out for business wherever they can see there is work to be done, and the likelihood of a profitable investment. This class is the scourge of the railway interest; in former times they were unknown. Railway companies then only contended with each other; now, two or three individuals form a company, and run up an opposition line with or without assistance from others, as the case may be; and when the line is finished they sell it, lease it, or work it in opposition to an old line till they can get their own price, and having cleared a small fortune by the transaction, they are off to " fresh fields and pastures new " in search of some other enterprise.

This class, it may be well imagined, stand in very bad favour with railway shareholders. They are generally designated as speculating jobbers, shameless intruders into other men's domains, interlopers, and pirates! But, whatever names be applied to them, the gentlemen who follow this profession take the matter very coolly, and realize large fortunes; and well they may, as the average cost of railways is now £12,000 per mile, or about *one-third* of what they formerly cost. Every year the expense appears to be decreasing. Last year a railway, constructed by Mr. John Bower, one of our most able and successful Irish engineers, called the Finn Valley Line, in the county Donegal, was completed at the low cost of £5160 per mile, being the cheapest of any constructed in the kingdom. There are many concurrent causes which operate now, in enabling contractors to make lines at a very low rate, compared with former times. In addition to the favourable terms granted by landowners, then unknown, there is the greater experience in laying out the best lines, and the increased facility in constructing works, by having a well-trained body of men kept in constant employment at the skilled and unskilled labour incident to their calling—an advantage not possessed, of course, by contractors in the early days of railway construction.

It is thought a hard case by most shareholders that their property should be subject to what they term constant and unjustifiable attacks, when, in their opinion, they are giving every accommodation to the public, making only fair and reasonable charges, and receiving but a very moderate return for their capital; further, that Parliament does not give them sufficient protection, nor lay down a line of policy with sufficient clearness to enable them to draw a line of demarcation between those schemes that should and should not be opposed in Parliament. These complaints are not entirely without foundation, but there is great difficulty in dealing with the subject.

What, for instance, is "a fair and reasonable charge" on railways, how is it to be tested, and what should be the standard? The London and North-Western and Great Northern charged, as we have seen, at one time, on their respective lines, one farthing per mile for first class. The North and South Western charge now one halfpenny per mile, the North London three farthings, the London and Tilbury one penny, the Lancashire and Yorkshire three halfpence, the London and Brighton twopence, the Great Eastern twopence halfpenny, the North Devon threepence, and the Cardigan threepence halfpenny. There is a wide range!—from *one* farthing to *fourteen* farthings, that at three farthings paying the highest dividend. And which of these fares is to be adopted as the standard of a "fair and reasonable charge?" Even on the same railway, on different days of the week, there are different charges. I might refer again, as it affords a familiar illustration, to the different prices of a book, first published at a guinea and a half, again at six shillings, and lastly at two shillings. Which of these prices is "fair and moderate?" The first is the monopoly, and the last is the free-trade price; but which of the three prices is "the true Simon Pure," and which the counterfeit? When we see that the ordinary every-day working fares on some railways are three, five, and even seven times as much as on others, and the companies charging the lowest pay six per cent. dividends, there may, under these circumstances, be some difference between the public and the shareholders as to what constitutes "a fair and reasonable charge." Let us suppose that the price of tea, of the same quality, varied, owing to local causes, over the kingdom from one shilling per pound to seven shillings; would it not be obvious to every one that, if such a state of things existed in regard to tea or any other necessary of life, there would be a constant action going on to reduce those inequalities, and bring competition to bear for that purpose on those markets at which the highest charges prevailed.

So long, then, as our present railway system lasts, so long must railway proprietors make up their minds to a continuance of that warfare which has proved so ruinous to their interests; and in proportion as the public find the fares decrease through competition, so will increase the desire to encourage competing lines. There is, in this country, a great dislike to monopoly, or anything that appears to strengthen monopoly. In the early part of the last session, a bill promoted by the Caledonian, Edinburgh, and Glasgow, and Scottish Central Railway Companies, for their amalgamation, was thrown out on the second reading, and the same bill had been thrown out several times before, although the projectors had great Parliamentary influence, and proposed a reduction of 35 per cent. on their second-class, and 25 per cent. on their third-class fares. These and similar proposals to Parliament to make great reductions in fares on certain conditions are, unfortunately for railway shareholders, highly suggestive, both to the public and to Parliament, of gross overcharges being made; and, coupled with this, the extremely low fares on some lines and their high dividends, confirm the popular opinion that nothing but increased and unlimited opposition can effectually bring down the fares.

We have seen that landowners now find that railway communication is a necessity of civilization; that those parts of the country unprovided with such means of transport are not, in the present state of society, fit places for habitation; that new promoters rush in where old ones feared to tread; and, what with internecine wars between old companies not grown wiser by experience, and between new companies without either experience or wisdom—and what with the wars between engineers, lawyers, contractors, and jobbers of all sorts, whose experience has been most pleasant—the poor shareholders may well look forward with anxiety to that happy millennium when their troubles shall cease—when their ruinous Parliamentary warfares shall be at an end, when a new competing line shall be a thing unknown, and when they shall be able to enjoy their present dividends, such as they are, without any fear of further reduction, or molestation from angry opponents. How far that prospect, under the present system, is likely to be realized, we have now to consider.

This future time, so anxiously looked for by shareholders, is to be marked by the "completion of our railway system," when the nation and the Legislature, it is assumed, will agree in opinion with them as to the impolicy of permitting the construction of competing lines. I am greatly afraid, when we come to examine the foundation on which this rests, it will be found altogether imaginary; and a little consideration, probably, will satisfy the most sanguine shareholder that it is utterly futile to suppose, under the present system, such a "completion" can ever come to pass.

We have, in the United Kingdom, about 120,000 miles of common roads, and about the one-tenth of that distance of railways. I am very far from supposing that, under any assumed circumstances, our railways will reach the one-fourth of that extent during the present generation. But as there are many different causes in operation that have a direct tendency to promote the construction of cheap opposition lines, they must still continue to operate so long as these causes exist. Although the completion of our leading lines may take place in the course of a comparatively few years, our railway system will go on extending itself for many years to come. As the population increases, and villages become large towns, so does the necessity for a continual extension go on, and we generally add, in ordinary times, from 300 to 500 miles per annum to the existing lines. But it is not from this moderate extension the railway proprietors so severely suffer. What they have to dread is that vast influx of new schemes into Parliament which periodically occurs after two or three consecutive years of great prosperity. When the coffers of the Bank of England are filled to overflowing, when the rate of interest is down to $1\frac{1}{2}$ or 2 per cent., when there is a vast amount of unemployed capital lying idle for want of a profitable investment, the general community anticipate increased happiness and prosperity, but to railway shareholders these signs of the times are only the forerunners of disastrous speculation and unlimited competition. They have had the bitter lesson of 1844-5, and it is not likely that that lesson will be soon forgotten.

These two years were remarkable for their good harvests, their prosperity at home and abroad, the consequent easy state of the money market, and the increasing supply of bullion in the Bank—for a large average circulation, and for discounts varying from $2\frac{1}{2}$ to $3\frac{1}{2}$ per cent. In 1842 the bullion in the Bank coffers had been as low as £5,629,000; in January, 1844, it had increased to upwards of £14,000,000; in January, 1842, the circulation was £16,923,000; in January, 1844, it had grown up to £20,301,000; and during the whole of 1844 it averaged about the same amount. Money was very abundant; the great discount houses were full. The Bank discounted at $2\frac{1}{2}$ per cent.; Consols reached par, a similar event not having taken place in the present century; the Chancellor of the Exchequer effected a saving of £1,200,000 per annum by the reduction of the $3\frac{1}{2}$ per Cents. to 3. Four of the principal railways in the kingdom—the London and Birmingham, the Grand Junction, the Liverpool and Manchester, and the York and North Midland—paid from 10 to 12 per cent., and the Stockton and Darlington, 15 per cent. per annum; everything, in fact, promised a continuance of the golden age.

Up to 1844 railway enterprise might be regarded as the natural effort of capital to procure a fair and proper interest; but the superabundant capital in the market, seeking for investment, brought about a widely different state of affairs. The leading railway companies, willing enough of course to remain quiet, found it impossible to do so; opposition lines were proposed, which it was necessary to fight at great expense; and small branch railways being projected, the old companies were forced to take and guarantee dividends from 4 to 6 per cent., and in some cases as high as 10 per cent., many of these lines having only been projected for the purpose of extortion. *"Parliament gave almost unrestricted scope to competition; little regard was paid to the claims and interests of railway companies.* Their proprietors saw, with terror and dismay, the reckless encouragement to competing lines, by which all their calculations were so disastrously interfered with. So determined were the proprietors of new lines to succeed in their projects, that no price for the purchase of land seemed too great to arrest opposition. Sums varying from £5,000 to £20,000 were given, ostensibly for slips of land, but really to avert opposition."

I have drawn freely, in the foregoing sketch of Parliamentary legislation in 1844, 1845, and 1846, from Mr. Francis' interesting "History of English Railways;" and the lesson there conveyed should not be without its use to the directors of the present day. It is for them to watch the signs of the times, and, by a wise foresight, secure themselves and their constituents against the coming evil day. Nothing can be more certain than that, sooner or later, this country will be visited by one of these periodical returns of extraordinary prosperity, and similar results, in regard to railway property, may fairly be anticipated. What reason is there to think otherwise? The Chairman of the London and South-Western recently complained that ten "attacks," in Parliament, had been made on their line in 1863. The London and Brighton came successfully out of their Committee in the same year, but their dividend was reduced in consequence one per cent. What are we to expect again, when the money market will be in the same state as that which we have just noticed, when £20,000,000 will be lying at the Bank of England; when our discounts will be again at $2\frac{1}{2}$ per cent.; some 70 or 80 millions sterling of deposit lying in our joint-stock banks, paying $1\frac{1}{2}$ or 2 per cent. interest, and the depositors anxiously looking out for some more profitable investment? With the encouragement which railway projectors now receive from landowners—with the great facilities which exist for constructing lines, and the comparatively low price at which they can now be constructed—with the activity, wealth, and energy of the great contractors, who project and carry out their lines, and the wider field for operations which still exists in the vicinity of good paying lines—these combined causes must, I think, satisfy any reasonable man that, when that season of great prosperity comes again, the railway interest will be the first, the greatest, and perhaps the only sufferer? When the flood-gates are again opened, and the unchecked torrent of speculation rushes in, neither Parliament nor shareholders can stop its course.

History, it is said, runs in cycles, and railway history is no exception to the general rule. Since the railway mania, twenty years ago, there has not been so great a number of railway bills brought before Parliament as in the last session; yet the times are very different; we have not had a succession of good harvests, there is not, as in 1844, that vast accumulation of gold at the Bank of England; money is not going a-begging at 2 or 3 per cent.; and, although too many companies for general purposes have been formed, there is not that wild and reckless spirit of speculation abroad, as in 1845, that alarmed all interests and brought such numbers to ruin; nevertheless, there is a determination on the part of the public to convert their surplus capital into new lines; and there is no lack of companies, both old and new, to avail themselves of that desire, and turn it to profitable account. 336 Bills, claiming sanction for the construction of upwards of 3000 miles, were introduced into Parliament, attacking, without exception, all existing interests, and threatening ruin to many of the companies. Let, however, the reports of some of the principal companies, at their half-yearly meeting in February, 1864, speak for themselves. It is true that a great number of these bills have been either thrown out or withdrawn, but only to reappear the next or some succeeding session, with hundreds of others.

"The directors of the London and North-Western Company regret to say that the bills introduced into the present session bearing on the interests of this company, and requiring the watchful attention of the board, are, as on former occasions, too numerous to be described in the Report." They waited, they state, on the President of the Board of Trade, and urged that the proprietors of existing railways, as the owners of nearly four hundred millions of capital, might reasonably expect that Parliament will not allow their property to be sacrificed, as is now too frequently the case, for the sole benefit of speculators, who, under the guise of public advantage, claim to use works already established at great cost, and, having acquired such rights, seek only to dispose of them to the highest bidder. The directors further urged that, under existing circumstances, they, as trustees, have little or no option but to appear in committee on any bill by which their interests may be affected, well knowing, from experience, that a lodgment made by a speculating scheme in one session is too often made a stepping-stone to a serious invasion of their property, and to a costly contest in a future session. At one time these contests might have had their origin in an expectation, based on the apparent policy of Parliament, that monopoly might be maintained; yet, for some time past, that expectation has been very generally abandoned. At the half-yearly meeting, the chairman, in reference to the general policy of Parliament, said: "We had the North London, when we got 3 and 4 per cent.; and now, when we have brought it into play, and your capital makes something of it, Parliament steps in to rob you of your labour."

Here now is a corporation, with a capital of some forty millions sterling, and an annual revenue equal to many of the second-rate European powers, with a "territory" extending over 1200 miles, and possessing all that power and influence which such an elevated position commands, obliged to live in a state of chronic warfare, and to seek the special protection of the

Board of Trade against the numberless schemes with which they were threatened, "in the hope that Parliament will not allow their property to be sacrificed, as is now too frequently the case, for the sole benefit of speculators," &c.

The question that naturally suggests itself, on reading this report, is, Why should the owners of private property be placed in such an anomalous situation, that the interference that Parliament may deem necessary for the public good is injurious to their interests? Parliament, they say, has too frequently sacrificed their property for the sole benefit of speculators. Well! If "speculators" promote a good bill, why should they not obtain it? In other words the Legislature has granted bills for lines that compete with the London and North-Western, which the directors think wholly unnecessary; but we have seen that these competing lines, from London to Liverpool and elsewhere, have greatly reduced the fares and charges, no doubt at a ruinous loss to the company. Parliament has to judge between parties altogether antagonistic so far as regards the principle of competition, and railway companies occupy a false position in standing between the public and the public good. Look what competition has done for the London and North-Western Company—it reduced their dividends from 10 per cent. down to $3\frac{1}{2}$ per cent. For the last few years they have been slowly recovering, and have now attained a tolerably fair position, having paid £5 2s. 6d. per cent. dividend in 1863, and 1864 will probably produce £6 per cent.; but it needs no prophet to foretell the results, as affects the company, if one half the projects continually being launched against them receive eventually the sanction of Parliament.

The chairman of the Great Western Railway, at their half-yearly meeting, said that, looking at the enormous mass of merely speculative schemes that were brought forward, and which involved great expense in opposing them, he thought the leading companies were somewhat hardly used. There was no substantial guarantee against new projects having little or no local support, or any real substantive basis. A speculative engineer, a speculative lawyer, and a financial discount company at their back, set them up. It was not like 1844 and 1845, when there was a great rush of capital into railways, when there were railway shareholders and railway directors; but in the great mass of schemes which were now being promoted, there were neither shareholders nor directors, and there was no substantial local demand for those schemes. When authorized, these schemes were merely made use of for exciting jealousy and discord between neighbouring companies. They were made for sale, and sale only.

All the great companies, in their reports to their shareholders, spoke much in the same terms as the London and North-Western and Great Western companies. The Lancashire and Yorkshire directors said that it was a source of extreme regret to them that they must again, in Parliament, resist encroachments upon districts both in Lancashire and Yorkshire. They felt bound to protect the shareholders' property, as much as possible, from injurious legislation; and they requested the authority of shareholders to authorize the board to take all necessary proceedings for that purpose. The term " injurious legislation " is a relative term; and it must be remembered that the directors are speaking from the directors' point of view, as affecting the interests of the shareholders, and totally ignore those of the public.

The chairman of the London and South-Western Company, at their half-yearly meeting, said the directors had been unwillingly obliged, by the action of others, to introduce a line for affording accommodation to Richmond from Kensington, which the company had been driven to promote in order to protect themselves from the attacks of others. No less than four lines had been projected, to rob them of their Richmond traffic, three of which were still before the public. "They had offered terms to the promoters of those schemes, and to the Great Western and North-Western companies, which, he trusted, would satisfy the

House of Commons that there was no public necessity for these hostile and useless lines."

The directors of this company were placed in a bad position: "they had given up all ambitious schemes, had abandoned all incursions into their neighbours' territories, and wished to live at peace with all men; but they were dragged unwillingly into the fray." "No less than four lines had been projected to rob them of their Richmond traffic," and, *nolens volens*, they must enter into the strife. Last session they had been attacked at "ten different points."

The Chairman of the Great Northern, at the half-yearly meeting, said that the directors had to regret that the Eastern Counties had thought it right to invade, in the most unwarrantable manner, the country occupied by the Great Northern Company, by promoting a bill for the construction of a new line from a point a few miles north of Cambridge to Askerne and Doncaster. He (the chairman), acting as a member of the Legislature, thought the case so bad a one, that he had endeavoured to throw out their bill on the second reading, and had the House entirely with him; but the Chairman of Committees, Mr. Massey, thought the proceedings to defeat a bill on its second reading so unusual, that he recommended the House to allow the bill to go before a select committee; and, in deference to the opinion of that gentleman, which carried great weight and authority in the House, he (the chairman) withdrew his opposition; and the company were now, at great expense, compelled and driven to oppose that line before a Parliamentary Committee. It would pass between the main and loop lines of the Great Northern Company, and would not be farther than three to four miles from any of them; and the honourable gentleman went on to prove, of course, that the line was quite unnecessary.

The Great Northern is now one of the best-paying companies in the kingdom, originally promoted under the name of the London and York, in direct opposition to the Midland. It eventually succeeded in making its way to Liverpool, in opposition to the London and North-Western, and extending its branches in all directions. What the predecessors of the present directors did twenty years ago—not, it is to be presumed, as speculators, or with a view to profitable investment, but solely for the public good—the present directors denounce as a most unwarrantable invasion on Great Northern territory by the Great Eastern Company, and have succeeded in convincing a Parliamentary Committee that such is the fact.

The Chairman of the Midland said, as to their position, "It was a most difficult matter to know how to deal with such new complications as might arise in railway affairs. The new lines and new projects springing up would require careful judgment; it would be impossible to apply any particular principle; every circumstance must be carefully weighed, and each project discussed on its own merits. It had been said that something like the French system ought to be applied; and Lord Dalhousie's report recommended a sort of restricted monopoly; but that was upset by Parliament, which kept things, as it were, at haphazard. Many years ago, he gave evidence in favour of a line from Derby to Leeds; since that time a second line to that town had been obtained by the London and North-Western, and a third by the Great Northern, and now a fourth was threatened; this showed the absence of any fixed principle. The public feeling varied; and whenever a disposition was manifested to make a new line, Parliament was too apt to give power, highly injurious to other interests. Of the new projects before Parliament, about *one hundred* proposed to do something or other with the Midland."

This company, like the Great Northern, is one of the most prosperous in the kingdom; but that very prosperity is, in one sense, to this class of companies, the cause of their greatest anxiety and trouble. It very naturally attracts great numbers of competitors, who are desirous of sharing in their prosperity by relieving them of their traffic, involving them in enormous Parliamentary expenditure, forcing on them the construction of new lines, which may really be quite unnecessary and productive of no benefit to the public, as they are not competing lines.

At the meeting of the Great Eastern, Mr. Bidder (a director) said, "He was responsible for recommending the Great Eastern Northern Junction line. It was said that it would bring them into antagonism with the Great Northern Company; but he asked them whether the latter company had not invaded their territory at several points? They had invaded the Great Eastern district at Hertford, Cambridge, and Lynn, and they were now endeavouring to get into Norfolk."

The Great Eastern is one of those companies that never enjoyed the smiles of Fortune. Once on a time an attempt was made "to make things pleasant" for the shareholders by paying them dividends the line never earned; but it ended, as we all know, in a most disastrous failure. They endeavoured in the session of 1864 to better their fortunes, in what they considered a legitimate manner, by promoting a line to the North by a junction with their main line near Cambridge. The length, with branches, was 134 miles, and the estimated cost £1,500,000. The gradients were exceedingly favourable; and they looked to the carriage of coals as one of the principal sources of revenue. They proved to the Committee that a locomotive of ordinary power on such a line would be able to drag 400 tons; so they would be able to bring coals in any quantity at *a shilling* per ton to London. They encountered, however, the most determined opposition from the Great Northern and Midland Companies, and the Committee rejected their bill!

It is not, I apprehend, necessary to go into any further details in regard to the position and prospects of railway proprietors. Nearly all the reports of the several companies partake, more or less, of the same character as those we have quoted. The bill for constructing a new line between London and Brighton has been defeated in the two last sessions of Parliament by the Brighton Company, but at a fearful expense; and, sooner or later, it is pretty sure to be carried. The established companies passed through the Parliamentary ordeal of the last session without suffering much damage from "territorial invasion," but their expenditure must have been exceedingly heavy.

What is it that the railway shareholders of this country, above all other things, desire in regard to their property? They desire *peace* and *security*, and, under the present system, it is impossible they can have either. No man can believe that the causes are temporary, that have a direct tendency to depreciate railway property. The directors of companies claim from the Legislature protection against competition, and hitherto, to a considerable extent, that protection has been afforded them. The present Parliament, especially, has given but little support to competing lines, and (unless where a very strong case has been made out for intervention) has supported existing interests. Under its fostering influence, railway property has increased considerably in value within the last few years, and most of the great lines are now at a fair premium; but it is for the shareholders to consider how long that prosperity will last, when the principle on which it is based is not that on which is founded the general commercial policy of the country; the one is based on MONOPOLY, and the other on FREE TRADE. The next Parliament may regard railway competition *in* quite a different light from that of the present Parliament, and it is for the shareholders themselves to consider—How long the exceptional policy of protection now afforded to them, contrary to the general policy of the country, is likely to be continued? In the somewhat strong conventional language of the railway world, it is called "a robbery to intrude into your neighbour's territory." It is assumed that a railway company ought to have an exclusive right of conveyance in its own particular district. It is true this assumed right has never been claimed, in express terms, by the railway interest; they qualify it to the extent of admitting the right of Parliament to sanction all lines it may deem necessary for the public benefit, but they complain most bitterly of the manner in which that right has been often exercised.

In regard to the conveyance of coal to London, the Great Northern, whilst admitting the fact that the Great Eastern could carry coal on the proposed line from the North of England to London at a shilling per ton, and that it would cost themselves a few pence more, contended that the difference in the cost of conveyance was so slight, compared with the price of coal in London, or the reduction that the Great Eastern might think proper to make, that it would not justify Parliament in permitting the construction of a competing line; the arguments of the Great Northern eventually prevailed, and the Great Eastern, for the time, at least, will not be able to bring up coal from the North of England at any price whatever.

Let any one but think of the densely populated district of the east of London, with its half million of inhabitants, the great majority of whom are poor hard-working people, in connection with the fact that coal can be brought to their door from the pit's mouth at an expenditure, say, of half a crown per ton; let it be remembered that during the winter months their greatest deprivation is the want of sufficient fuel; that frequently during the season the most exorbitant prices are charged for it; that its cost at the pit's mouth is but six or seven shillings per ton; when we remember all this, we can form some idea of the benefit that would be conferred on that section of the London population if they could get their coal from the pit's mouth with only an additional charge of some two hundred per cent. profit on the carriage. The main contest of the session of 1864 was the one we have referred to, between the Great Northern and Great Eastern Companies. It was, in many respects, a most remarkable contest, and the result is a good illustration of the principles on which Parliamentary decisions are generally founded. It also affords a full confirmation of the evidence given before the Select Committee of 1844, as to the great benefit the public would derive from the railways being transferred from the companies to the State.

The Great Eastern Company, as we have seen, projected a line that would give them direct communication, not only with the great coal-fields of the North, but also with the Lancashire and Yorkshire, the North Eastern, the Midland, the Manchester and Sheffield, and all the other lines in the northern and north-eastern parts of the kingdom, and notwithstanding its length, and consequently the great number of landowners who were affected by them, none practically opposed it. One of the main features of the case was the engineering superiority of the line to any system of similar length yet constructed, and the effect of such construction was, practically, nearly to double the load which an engine could carry, as compared with the load actually carried on the existing line of the Great Northern; the latter is 240 tons, whilst on the former line a load of 400 tons would be conveyed at the same cost. The cost per train mile of working the traffic, including every expense, was found not to exceed one shilling and sixpence, and taking the total distance at 176 miles, the cost of carriage of each ton from the pit's mouth to Shoreditch would scarcely amount to *a shilling!* The bill was rejected by the committee, apparently on the grounds, 1st—that as the Great Northern line was not so good, it would subject the company to an unfair competition; and 2nd—that the public would derive but little benefit from the construction of the new line, as the Great Eastern required permission to charge a profit of between 400 and 500 per cent. on the cost of transit.

Now, as to the first ground, the reasoning on behalf of the Great Northern is the old economical fallacy of protection, as applied to railway traffic, and if it were well founded it should have operated to prevent railways themselves from superseding the capital invested in canals and turnpike trusts; they, too, are tied down to "their inherent imperfections." Yet it was not thought necessary to deny the public the benefit of an improved method of locomotion, simply because the old roads and canals would suffer by the improvement. Suppose some inventor were to discover a new and cheaper fuel, which would entirely supersede coal and gas, and would supply heat and light at a far cheaper rate than any at present in use, what would be thought of the Attorney-General who refused a patent for such an invention, or the Parliament which refused to sanction the means of carrying it into effect, because the capital expended by the gas companies and in coal mines was not to be superseded, but consideration was to be shown for the great services they had in past times rendered to the country.

Such were the arguments addressed to the committee by the advocates of the Great Eastern Company, but which, unfortunately for them, failed in producing any effect, and so their bill was rejected.

The position of railway shareholders is altogether anomalous; they are the supporters of a system not an absolute monopoly, but still less one of free trade; it is a system which combines the worst qualities of both, without any of the redeeming qualities of either. At the present day, it is simply an anachronism. The landed, the shipping, and all the other interests, great and small, of the country, that, twenty years ago, were monopolies, more or less close, have gradually undergone a change, and the railway direction alone is making a desperate struggle to maintain its position against the innumerable assailants who are attacking it on every side. It is for the directors themselves to judge, from the signs of the times, which party, in the end, is likely to succeed, or if the successful defence in one session will prevent the renewed attack in another, and then to calculate the costs. Is there any director or shareholder who will assert that railway property is on a sound and satisfactory footing, or say there is any likelihood of less encouragement being given to railway extension, or fewer speculators ready to throw competing lines over the face of the country, than at present? Or can the railway directors point out any remedy that has the most remote likelihood of being adopted by the country or the Legislature which will reverse the present order of things, and give what they consider due protection to their interests—a protection, however it may be qualified, that is not granted to any other class in the community? I may confidently answer that no hope exists, even amongst the most sanguine of shareholders or determined of directors, of such protection ever being given to the railway interest.

This is not all. There is a large, influential, and increasing class in this country, who contend that every facility should be granted by the Legislature for the extension of railways—that competition is the only means by which charges can be reduced —that when landowners are willing to give their land, and capitalists contribute their money, the duty of the Legislature is to promote the benefit of the public in preference to that of the shareholders, and that the latter have no claim to special protection more than any other class of traders. If these principles should ultimately prevail—and that is a matter on which every one will form his own opinion—there are much worse times in store for railway proprietors than they have ever yet experienced.

The Railway Bill of 1844 was intended for the mutual benefit of the nation and the shareholders. It was supposed that at the expiration of twenty-one years both parties would be in a position to form an opinion of the working of our railway system as then established, and the Government desired to be in a position to have it changed if the future Legislature should so desire it. "The question," said Mr. Gladstone, "of the whole bill, is the purchase or option on the part of the Government. If we agree about that, we shall not quarrel about the rest. On the other hand, if we differ about that, it will be a question for our consideration, whether we will take the rest, or postpone the whole till a future period. With railways the Legislature are dealing with a new system, producing new results, and likely to produce unforeseen effects. Is it not wise, then, to make provision for the future? Is it wise to trust ourselves to all the changes which the next ten or fifteen years may produce with regard to public communication by railway, without a thought for providing for the difficulties that might arise? Is it wise to place ourselves in a position in which, whatever might be the exigency, we shall be debarred from any interference, because now, before these new companies have obtained their powers, it has been neglected to obtain proper powers, to enable the question to be entertained. With respect to the *purchase of railways at the present moment*, gentlemen of great experience and intelligence had recommended that it should be so. I do not think the committee were prepared to concur in that view; and I say I would, at the present moment, vote against a plan for the purchase of railroads. I would do so because, in the present state of the system, there are not grounds for coming to that conclusion. But it is a very different question whether I shall reserve a free agency for either the purchase or revision at any future time, in case such a measure should appear advisable, to enable the State, after a term of years, to purchase the railways, if the judgment of the Legislature should be such as to render such a measure politic and expedient. In the present state of the question, the elements which enter into it are rude and unformed, and the evidence, I admit, is not complete."

The time provided by the Act, when the Legislature should take the working of our system into consideration, has now nearly arrived, and there are ample materials to enable the nation and the Legislature to form a perfect judgment of the comparative merits of the two systems. The Legislature of this as of every other free country, is but the reflex of its public opinion, and only a knowledge of the facts of the case is required to create and form that public opinion in this country to support the Act of 1844. To say that the public are opposed to the purchase of the railways would convey a very inaccurate idea on the subject. The question has been but little more than mooted, and the relative merits of the two systems never discussed. A proposition at the present time from the Government to buy up the railways, before the matter is fully discussed, and the public enlightened on the subject, would be just as appropriate or successful as a proposition to buy up the land. It remains, therefore, for the directors of our great companies to consider whether or not it is for the interest of themselves and their constituents to let matters go on in their present course, or to bring the provisions of the Act of 1844 under the consideration of the public and the Legislature, and express their willingness, so far as they are concerned, to give every facility to their being carried out.

The policy hitherto acted upon by railway directors—and, considered as traders, not an unfair one—has been to keep the public in complete ignorance of the internal working of our railway system, so far as regards the extremely low rate at which passengers and goods can be conveyed on railways. " How does it happen," said a simple-minded shareholder in the South-Eastern Company, to the chairman at the last half-yearly meeting, " that we carry passengers at such a low tariff ? The fares must be unremunerative. In 1855, I see by your report that we carried between seven and eight millions of passengers, for which we received 635,000*l.*; but last year we carried between thirteen and fourteen millions, and only received 755,000*l.* That will not pay." " I cannot undertake," said the chairman in reply, "to discuss these delicate matters in public (hear, hear) ; but I would say, look to your dividend, and rest and be thankful." The dividend for 1855 was 3*l.* 1*s.* 8*d.*, and for 1863, 4*l.* 15*s.*

But the chairman might have said, " The fact is that we and all the other companies can carry passengers at exceedingly low rates. A first-class passenger we can carry four miles for a farthing, a second-class six miles for a farthing, and a third-class ten miles for a farthing ; and all beyond that, with fairly loaded trains, is profit. You may remember several years ago, when we carried on the opposition for the Reading traffic, charging about a farthing per mile to first-class passengers, and, as I told you then, we lost nothing by the business. We have latterly been obliged, by the opposition of the London and Chatham, to reduce our fares ; it has done us no injury. We have come to terms with our opponent, and agreed to divide the monopoly, and now we can pay you a better dividend than ever we paid you before. We may soon be able to restore the fares to what the honourable proprietor terms 'remunerative rates.' That must not be done too suddenly, nor till we have fully arranged our plans with the Chatham and Dover." Now the chairman might have said all this with perfect truth —but what would Mrs. Grundy of the railway world have said?

So long as the railway monopoly remained secure, this policy on the part of the directors appears to have been the best that, under the circumstances, could have been adopted. To share a monopoly with one or even more companies does not absolutely destroy it, however much it may impair its value; but when there appears an influx of companies so great in number, promoted under such favourable circumstances as we have described, so determined to carry out their projects and with every probability of their number increasing from year to year, the possibility must be kept in view of the monopoly being entirely broken up owing to so many companies obtaining their Acts that combination would practically be impossible. Light will, sooner or later, break in on our present system; with light comes knowledge, and with knowledge comes action. The public look only to one remedy—more lines, more competition. The directors must know, as practical men of the world, that, sooner or later, all matters relating to railway statistics will be fully known; and when the public come to know that a passenger can be conveyed one hundred miles for *twopence halfpenny*, for which he is charged *eight shillings and fourpence*, and that a ton of coals can be brought from the extreme north of England for about *a shilling*, the cost being there six or seven shillings, and the price here four or five times that sum, it requires no prophet to foretell that the days of railway monopoly in private hands will in this country soon be numbered.

But the remedy the public will seek, if not better advised,

will not only greatly reduce the value of existing railways, but will afford a very insufficient remedy for the evils complained of; the cry of the public will be for very cheap travelling, and new companies will be promoted solely for that object. Last session there were applications to Parliament for as many miles of railway as, if properly laid out, should be sufficient for the next ten years. Would it not, then, be for the interest of the shareholders that the directors should say to the Country, the Legislature, and the Government, "Here is a property on which nearly four hundred millions sterling has been expended, and which, with some comparatively trifling exceptions, affords railway communication to every part of the country. You have two courses before you, either to allow our property to be greatly depreciated, the capital of the country to be wasted, and very insufficient and partial remedies provided for the evils of which you complain,—or to take this property off our hands. Give us, in addition to the market price of the day, a liberal bonus as provided for by the Act of 1844, and we on our part will render every assistance to the Government in carrying out the views of the Legislature, in enabling the public to travel at such low fares as you may determine."

I have now detailed as clearly as I can the grounds of my belief that it would be for the interest of the shareholders that the directors of our great companies should themselves take the initiative or support any movement of others in bringing this matter before the country. Their predecessors in office twenty years ago made a sad mistake in rejecting the advice of such men as Mr. Glyn and Mr. Baxendale, and refusing to co-operate with the Government of the day in protecting the companies from competing lines, and giving in return certain benefits to the public. Their successors have to deal with the second crisis that has occurred in the railway history of this country now, when a speculating mania for railway extension has set in not equalled since that of 1845. It is for them to judge whether or not the policy of the past shall be the policy of the future. If they can stop the progress of current events; if they can roll back that torrent of speculation that threatens to sweep them along in its course; if they can eradicate from the minds of the British people that hatred of unchecked monopoly which may now be said to form part and parcel of their very being; if they can persuade the public at large, when the day of reckoning comes, that a system is sound which gives a practical monopoly to the vendor of a necessity of life, and enables him in many cases to charge the public *fifty times* over the sum he pays; if they believe all this, any argument I could use would be quite unavailing to convince them to the contrary. We have a system based on a principle, of which they are the administrators, not to be justified on any enlightened principle of legislation—a system of forced taxation under which this country, last year, paid upwards of THIRTY-ONE MILLIONS sterling. If, then, the directors of our great companies, men, almost without exception, of wealth and influence, and many of very high position, both social and political, maintain the affirmative of these propositions, it would be merely a waste of time to discuss the question further. It is a matter that, for the present, apparently, must rest solely with them; they have only to consider what line of policy will most benefit their shareholders, and they may very possibly think that of inaction the best, but I hope it may be otherwise. In the first crisis, in 1844, Government took the initiative in a movement intended for the benefit of the shareholders and the public, but partially failed. The second crisis in the affairs of the shareholders has now arrived, and it remains with themselves alone to consider what is best to be done, whether to proffer their willingness, so far as they are concerned, to carry out the Act of 1844, or follow the old course of opposition to competing lines in a vain struggle to maintain and perpetuate their monopoly.

CHAPTER III.

The Right of the Companies to promote the carrying into effect the Bill of 1844—Meaning of the Term " Purchase" of Railways by the State—Superior Value of Government Security over Private Security—Its Effect on the Market Value of Shares—Clause of the Bill relating to Purchase—Different Modes by which it could be effected.—Amount of Bonus to Shareholders—The Capital, Revenue, and Dividends of the Thirteen Great Companies—The assumed Bonus that the Legislature might be induced to grant to each.

ALTHOUGH the Act of 1844 left it optional with the Legislature to exercise, on certain prescribed terms, the right to purchase the railways, it is nevertheless quite open to the companies, as one of the parties to the bargain, to bring the subject before the country and Parliament, to state the grievances under which they labour, and suggest any remedy they may consider will meet the justice or necessities of their case. What we have now to consider is, would the carrying out of the Act of 1844, so far as it relates to the purchase of the railways by the State, be a measure calculated to promote the interests of the shareholders?

In regard to the term "purchase," as applied to Government and the railways, it is used more in a conventional than in an absolute sense. Properly speaking, purchase implies payment, or a promise of a money payment; and should the State claim to exercise the right of purchase, and insist on that exercise against the will of the shareholders, the latter could—and no doubt would—claim a money payment, and therefore a purchase on the part of the State of all the railway property in the kingdom would be simply an impossibility. In the conventional sense, however, it means the exchange of their shares for a certain amount of Government stock, the shareholders giving up their property, from which they receive a fluctuating dividend, and receiving in exchange a fixed annuity for a lesser amount in perpetuity. With the great bulk of people the rate of interest is a secondary consideration, compared with the security of the principal; and as no security in this country is considered equal to that guaranteed by the State, a certain rate of interest from it represents a much larger capital than the same rate of interest from any ordinary mercantile investment. All shareholders would willingly accept a much lower rate than they now receive if it was secured by a Government guarantee; not merely by reason of the certainty of always getting that interest, but from the still more important consideration of the security of capital and the higher price that stock would realize when sold. It follows, then, that the income arising from any particular kind of property is not to be taken solely as the test of its value. If a capitalist invest in French, Russian, or Colonial Government securities, or railway shares, he will not give a higher price than will pay him $4\frac{1}{2}$ to 5 per cent. on his outlay; although he would lend his money to the English Government and be satisfied with one or one and a half per cent. less interest than he would receive from any of those investments, he would consider his money safer, and, when he required his capital, receive back a larger sum.

The consideration, therefore, of a proposal by Government to purchase the railways, looking at it from the shareholders' point of view, would be mainly—if not entirely—in reference to the effect it would have on the market price of their shares. They know how much they can sell for now; how much more could they obtain if they sold their shares to Government? Or, to put the question in another form,—What bonus would the Government give to induce them to sell?

The extreme supporters, however, of the application of free-trade principles to railways, are either entirely opposed to their being purchased by the State; or, at least, think that such purchase should be deferred to a distant period, when, as they contend, the value of railways will be greatly lowered by being subjected to unchecked competition by the construction of a vast number of new lines.

It must be admitted that from the commencement of the railway system in this country, no principle could have been more clearly and distinctly laid down by the Legislature, and more constantly acted on with more or less stringency, than that of competition. Each company, in obtaining its Act, had it granted on the clear understanding that the Legislature could and would permit whatever competing lines in the same district they might think necessary. This right has never for a moment been disputed by the railway body, although complaints have been continually made of Acts being granted for which, in the opinion of the objectors, there existed no necessity.

It is contended by many that, as the Legislature has the power, so should they exercise it in giving full scope to railway extension and competition—the more the better, they say, for the public—and railway proprietors, in their opinion, have no right to claim protection more than any other class of the community; they had, they say, their day of prosperity, their high dividends and premiums, and these should not be maintained at the expense of the country. Railways, they contend, can be made at one-third of the price they formerly cost, and let the public have the full benefit of them; their competition with the old lines will pull down the present fares and charges, and their number will render combination impossible, their market value will become proportionally depreciated, and if the State at a future time desire to purchase the railways, it can do so for a moderate sum. Such was the general purport of a well-written article in the *Westminster Review*, that appeared about two years since.

To follow out, however, this course for the purpose of first depreciating the value of railway property and then purchasing it, although not contrary to the letter of the law, would certainly be opposed to its spirit. There always has been a degree of protection given to existing railway interests—very uncertain and undefined, it is true, sometimes loose and at other times stringent, depending entirely on the judgment or bias of railway committees, the state of the money market, or the public pressure on Parliament, one committee passing a line in one session of Parliament that had been refused by another Committee in the previous session. Nevertheless, there always has been given some degree of protection, and to depart from that principle for the avowed purpose of enabling the State to acquire the railways at a price below the market value, could hardly be considered a fair mode of procedure.

But without any intention on the part of the Legislature to depreciate the value of railway property, the effect of constructing competing lines, as affecting the present shareholders, is just the same. If a committee think that a new line would be for the public good, that is sufficient to justify them in passing the bill, and the opinion of Parliament is to a greater or less degree modified by the opinion out of doors. Nothing, therefore, can be more uncertain and precarious than the position of railway shareholders; it is the only class in the country that have any protection; that protection they have no legal claim to, and it may at any moment be entirely abolished.

We shall now proceed to notice how the Parliament of 1844 proposed to deal with the companies in regard to purchase.

There were two different modes of procedure recommended to the committee for adoption. One was to take the average dividends paid by the companies respectively for three years previous to the purchase by Government, as the standard of value, the other to take the current market price as the basis on which the purchase should be made. The committee recommended Parliament to reserve the right of either mode of purchase; and accordingly the Legislature enacted that, "Whatever be the rate of divisible profits in any such railway, it shall be lawful for the said Lords Commissioners, if they think fit at any time after the expiration of the said term of twenty-one years, to purchase any such railway, with all its hereditaments, stock, and appurtenances, in the

name and on behalf of her Majesty upon giving to the said company three calendar months' notice, in writing, of their intention, and upon payment of a sum equal to twenty-five years' purchase of the said annual divisible profits, estimated on an average of the three then next preceding years." The Act goes on to provide for the case of companies which do not pay ten per cent., and as that proviso extends to all the companies in the kingdom, it is the only part requiring notice. It says:—
" If they [the companies] shall be of opinion that the said rate of twenty-five years' purchase of the said average profits is an inadequate rate of purchase of such railway, reference being had to the prospects thereof, to require that the rate of purchase, instead of being calculated on such average rate of profit, shall be taken *at a valuation* to be determined in case of difference by arbitration."

A little consideration will, I think, satisfy any one that the first mode proposed of ascertaining the value of any particular railway, would for many reasons entirely fail.

1. The money value of railways. Like any other property, this value cannot be tested merely by the dividend produced; the price of shares rises and falls from other causes, political or commercial, as the case may be, quite independent of annual dividends; there is no property in the country the value of which is more fixed than our Government securities; yet in times of peace and war, prosperity and adversity, good harvests and bad harvests, abundant trade and commercial panic, these extremes —when you come to realize—will make a difference of ten or fifteen per cent., although the income remains exactly the same. In 1844, when this Act was passed, the Three per Cents. stood at par; ten years afterwards—when we were at war with Russia— they were down to eighty-six. As the variation in railway stock from commercial and other causes is much greater than in Government stock, it follows that the test would be altogether fallacious that would make the income alone the rule by which the value of a railway could be determined at a future period.

2. Assuming, however, that dividends alone should be taken

as the measure to determine the value of a railway, the system of averages enacted by the bill would entirely alter its character; the average dividends " for the three next preceding years," are to be taken as the test of value : a railway, for instance, that for the three preceding years was increasing in value and had paid each year respectively three, four, and five per cent., and next year might be expected to pay a still higher dividend, would be valued in the market according to the prospective increase ; but by the Act its value would be calculated as paying only four per cent., and a railway that was decreasing in value whose dividends for the last three years had been five, four, and three per cent. respectively, with a gloomy prospect for the future, would be considered of the same value. Thus the shareholders in one company with a bright prospect before them, and receiving five per cent. interest on their money, would obtain no more than the shareholders of another company receiving only three per cent. interest for their money, with perhaps a likelihood of a still smaller dividend. The market value of the shares of the first company would be nearly double the value of those of the second company ; but by that mode of calculation would be paid for at the same rate.

3. But even assuming that an average of three years of the dividend was correct so far as it went in determining the value of a railway, there are other matters besides the actual dividend that form the component parts which determine the market price. These are the hopes and fears that exist as to the future prospects of a company. If the trade of a district is likely to increase, if there is no fear of " aggression," no danger of the line being "tapped," and if the " territory may be considered safe from invasion," these considerations greatly increase the market value of the shares, and, it need hardly be added, that a contrary state of affairs produces just the contrary effect.

4. But there is one class of companies that, after paying their interest on loans and their preference shareholders, have very

little for their original shareholders; and another class have absolutely nothing. What would be done with them? The former class can always obtain a much higher price in the market than they would obtain by receiving the twenty-five years' purchase on their dividends from Government; and, as to the latter, the carrying out of such a plan would be simply confiscation, and therefore impossible. To carry out, then, the first clause of the Act, in its precise terms, would give to one class too much, a second too little, and to the third nothing whatever, as they could make no claim where they received no dividends, and in that case their property would revert to the State without any compensation whatever. The value of railway property is determined by a variety of circumstances, the abundance or scarcity of money, the political and commercial state of the country, the actual dividends paid, and the future prospects of the company; all these go through, as it were, the crucible of public opinion, and the result is, that buyers and sellers agree on a certain price, and that price we find recorded daily in the Stock Exchange list.

Let Acts of Parliament enact what they may, there is no royal road to be devised for the purchase of railways more than for the purchase of any other article of merchandise; and should the Legislature ever authorize the Government to purchase them, the Chancellor of the Exchequer will have to make the best bargain he can with the companies, independent of all Acts of Parliament. The clause, nevertheless, in the Act relating to the purchase is not without its value in showing, to a considerable extent, the terms which the Legislature considered fair, and these were agreed to by those members who represented the railway interest in the House of Commons. It must be remembered that at the time this Act was passed 3 per cent. Consols were at par.

From the evidence laid before the Committee, it appears that investments in railway property at that time paid to purchasers on an average 4*l*. 7*s*. per cent., and if railways had then been purchased by the State at twenty-five years' purchase on the dividends and paid for in 3 per cent. Government stock at the current price of the day, it would have given a bonus of about eight per cent. to the shareholder on the amount of his shares. It was evidently, therefore, the intention of the Legislature, if Government should at any time exercise the right of purchase, that the shareholders would receive a bonus in addition to the market value of their shares. It is true no mention of this is made in express terms in the latter part of the clause where arbitration is provided for; but from the premises of the bill it is evidently intended that, should the State at any time require possession of the railways, the shareholders should be dealt with in a liberal spirit, as twenty-five years' purchase on their dividends at that time would have given them a considerable bonus.

Whether or not the Legislature intended the Stock Exchange list to be taken as the great arbitrator on the value of railway property does not appear quite clear, but it certainly is the best we could have. When there is an open market, and you can either buy or sell, whichever may suit your purpose, a number of shares in any railway with only a fractional difference in the price between the two operations, you may fairly conclude that the shares are as closely valued as can possibly be done, and that both parties, unless in very exceptional cases, are fairly dealt with.

I am quite certain, however, that a bonus of eight per cent. on the market value of their shares would not induce the great bulk of shareholders to part with them; and it might be contended on the part of the companies that no reference is made in the Act to the fluctuations of the market, and that therefore it was the intention of the Legislature, in the event of purchase, whatever should be the state of the market, that the shareholders should have all the benefit they could derive from the credit of the nation in being paid in Government stock equal to twenty-five years' purchase on their annual dividends; that on the other hand would, I think, give them more than they would be entitled to, or than the Legislature would be willing to grant. It is very possible, under all the circumstances of the case, and with the prospect of unlimited competition before them, the great bulk of shareholders would be willing to accept an amount in Government stock equal to a bonus of 15 per cent. There are very few shareholders, I imagine, in any railway that would refuse such an offer from a private individual. Let us put the matter in a practical way: we will take the London and North-Western Company. The quotation for their shares, 30th June, 1864, was 114*l.*; and a bonus of 15 per cent. would have raised their price to 131*l.* Looking, then, at the probabilities of the case, and still from the shareholders' point of view, would it be prudent in them to reject such an offer, and is it likely they would do so if it were made? We can only judge in this as we would in any other analogous case. A man seldom refuses any advantageous offer that may be made him to part with property he has no particular interest to retain, and a railway share is only valued as the representative of so much money. Real property, such as houses, lands, or demesnes, may have a value in the eyes of their owner far above their intrinsic value, but it is totally different with shares in public companies; all the holder wants is a good investment for his money, and he will change from Brightons to North-Westerns, and from North-Westerns to Midlands, or sell out his Midlands and purchase Government stock, as the case may be, if he think he can make anything by it. Capital, it is said, like water, will always find its level, and this is especially true in a country like this, where there is such a facility for its transfer, or, to keep up the similitude, when it can flow unimpeded from one investment into another. The holders of shares in the Sheffield, Manchester, and Lincoln Company, or the London, Chatham, and Dover Company, who receive such a small return for their investments, know or may know as much of the affairs of the London and Brighton Company as the shareholders of the latter company themselves; and if the London and Brighton shares were thought below their value by the shareholders in these or any other companies, they would immediately sell out their own shares and purchase those of the London and Brighton Company. There is no peculiar advantage, therefore, in one investment over another; one man chooses this company, and another man that; and a third, under the advice of his broker perhaps, divides his money among half a dozen different companies, and various kinds of Government stock.

If the Government, then, were to propose to the London and North-Western Company a price tantamount to a bonus of 17*l*. per share, in addition to their premium of 14*l*., I cannot conceive the likelihood of the shareholders refusing such an offer, except on the supposition that by holding out they could get still better terms. That is a point we shall not discuss at present; but, in the absence of any such motive, and comparing the present position and prospects of the shareholders with what it would be by accepting the offer of the Government, it is very possible that the offer would be unanimously accepted. Is there any shareholder in the London and North-Western that would refuse 131*l*. per share at the present time from a private individual, on the sole condition that he should not purchase back again into the company? I should think hardly one; and this appears to me the fair way of testing the liberality of such an offer.

It might, however, be contended on the part of the companies that it was the intention of the Legislature that their shares, taking them at their market value, should be converted virtually into a 4 per cent. stock without any reference to the state of the market. I have endeavoured to show that it would be impossible to ascertain the value of a company's shares by mere calculation on the dividends they have paid. That, however, is now a matter of comparatively little consequence, as the Act never can be carried out, in the manner I propose, by compulsory means, and therefore, if carried out at all, must be by voluntary agreement between the respective parties. It is very certain that if the Legislature were satisfied that the purchase of the railways was a desirable project, they would act liberally with the companies. If they would give a bonus of 15 per cent. on the market value of shares, our railway companies might consider themselves liberally dealt with.

Let us, by way of illustration, take the quotations from the Stock Exchange list of June 30, 1864, of the selling price of shares in the thirteen great companies. To that we shall add the amount of capital expended in each, their receipts for 1863, their dividends, the premium or discount at which they then stood, and the assumed bonus the Legislature might be induced to give. The shares of all the companies are 100*l.* paid.

Capital expended.	Name of the Company.	Receipts for 1863.	Dividend paid.	Prem.	Dis.	Government Bonus.
£		£	£ s. d.			
9,947,494	Caledonian	871,677	5 15 0	19	...	18
20,960,200	Great Eastern ...	1,539,751	1 17 6	...	53	7
15,825,395	Great Northern ...	1,523,252	6 10 0	34	...	20
43,972,630	Great Western ...	3,067,613	2 10 0	...	33	10
19,960,007	Lancashire and Yorkshire	1,813,700	4 10 0	15	...	17
48,995,114	London and North Western	4,912,846	5 2 6	14	...	17
11,797,181	London and Brighton	976,463	5 0 0	4	...	16
14,658,647	London and South-Western	1,143,219	5 0 0	...	3	15
12,743,981	Manchester and Sheffield	806,321	0 15 0	...	40	9
23,187,222	Midland	2,177,705	6 7 6	32	...	20
10,448,170	North British......	655,201	1 10 0	...	46	8
31,109,980	North-Eastern ...	2,524,409	4 19 0	4	...	16
15,063,243	South-Eastern ...	1,142,628	5 3 4	...	8	14
278,669,264		23,154,785				

It will be seen from the foregoing list that the shares of seven of the great companies were, on June 30, 1864, at an average premium of 17*l.*, and the assumed Government bonus would be 18*l.* per share. The shares of six companies were at an average discount of 29*l.*, and the assumed Government bonus would be 11*l.* per share.

After deducting from the gross receipts forty-eight per cent. for expenditure—that being the proportionate expenditure on the receipts of the year 1863—the net revenue has yielded a return of 4*l.* 8*s.* per cent. on the invested capital. In that average is of course included the interest on loans and preference shares. The length of these railways is 7360 miles.

In addition to the thirteen great companies, there are fourteen lesser companies; their united length is 1640 miles. These are the Bristol and Exeter, the Edinburgh and Glasgow, the Furness, the Glasgow and South-Western, the Great Southern and Western, the London, Chatham and Dover, the Metropolitan, the Midland Great Western, the North Staffordshire, the North London, the Scottish Central, the Scottish North-Eastern, the South Devon, and the Taff Vale.

The shares of six of these companies are at an average premium of 33*l.*, and the remaining eight at an average discount of 28*l.*

These twenty-seven companies, whose lines extend over 9,000 miles, absorb seven-eighths of the entire traffic of the kingdom. The remaining eighth is shared by about fifty small companies, many of them, however, being of considerable importance, and the extent of their lines somewhat exceeding 3,000 miles.

The general reader who may have but a slight knowledge of railway matters, will find in the Appendix the railway history of the country given in some detail.

There are few who know so well as the directors of our companies the soundness of the principle on which the Government Act is based, or could bring a greater variety of interesting statistical information to illustrate and confirm the arguments that have been used in its support.

If the present system is unsound, sooner or later it must come to an end; and, if such is the case, it surely would be for the advantage of the shareholders that the initiative in creating and forming a public opinion on the subject should be taken by the railway body itself, by those who have a deep interest at stake and are in every way best qualified to undertake the task. It should not be deferred to an indefinite period, when railway property may again be subjected to hostile influences; when a succession of good harvests and other favourable causes produce a glut of money in the market, and when speculation will again take the same turn and with the same result as it did in the memorable years of 1844 and 1845, will not be the time for railway shareholders to appeal to the Legislature for protection or assistance. It should not be forgotten by them that their position as traders is altogether exceptional, that they enjoy at the present time both privileges and protection to which they have no legal claim, and which at any time they may be deprived of. What would be the value of railway property if all protection were withdrawn from it, and what security will they have from session to session that such may not be the case after the present Parliament has passed away? There is every prospect of the dividends for 1864 being much better than they have been for many previous years; the returns for the half-year ending the 30th June show a large increase on the corresponding last half-year. The traffic is much increasing, and railway property within the last year has greatly improved. Shares are, consequently, rising in the market, and so far as we can judge from present appearances, the prosperity of railways for the present will be uninterrupted. Although the railway interest is too strong to fear any attack, come from what quarter it may, it would, nevertheless, be in many respects desirable that, whenever the Act of 1844 becomes the subject of discussion, with a view to its provisions being carried out, those who are most deeply interested in its success should take the initiative in its settlement; for if such a change as we have been discussing shall ever be effected, it must be by the cordial co-operation of the two parties to the bargain—the public on one side, and the great bulk of railway companies on the other.

PART III.—THE GOVERNMENT.

CHAPTER I.

The late Sir Robert Peel's Opposition to Government Interference in Commercial Affairs—Change of his Opinion in regard to Railways—Extract from his Speech on the Second Reading of the Bill—Improvement in Railway Legislation—Bills for Non-paying Lines at one time refused—Railways that would have been refused legislative Sanction had the Truth been known—The Value of a Railway to its Shareholders no criterion of its Value to the Country—The Manchester, Sheffield, and Lincoln Company—The Select Committee of the Two Houses of Parliament—Assistance from the State in constructing Railways that will not pay—Cheaply constructed Railways—Lord Campbell's Act—Comparatively small Loss to Companies by Accidents—Refreshment Rooms.

IF there ever existed an English statesman, the leading characteristic of whose mind was to keep the Government of this country clear from all management of, or connection with, commercial companies, that statesman was the late Sir Robert Peel. Whenever an occasion presented itself in the House of Commons for contrasting the policy of this country in such respect with that of most foreign countries, no one was more prominent than he in dilating on the advantages we had derived from pursuing such a line of policy, and pointing out how much it had contributed to promote that spirit of independence, enterprise, and self-reliance so characteristic of the English people. Many will remember with what unction he used to tell the House the story of the Caledonian Canal: how the Government, in an evil hour, conceived the idea of executing a great industrial work which, if necessary at all, ought to have been left to private enterprise, but having been undertaken by Government was necessarily a failure; how it became a concern utterly bankrupt, supported by the public purse; and that the Government would be only too happy to get rid of it, and make a present of it to any joint-stock company who would accept it and undertake to carry out the purposes for which it was formed. The undertaking, he would say, had, however, one useful result; it served as a warning to that and every succeeding Government not to undertake the management of such affairs, opposed, as such a proceeding was, to all the political traditions of the country.

Sir Robert Peel, in the early part of our railway progress, had great dependence on competition, and, perhaps, did more than any other man then living to promote in this country railway extension. In 1839, however, he, with the present Earl of Derby, then Lord Stanley, were members of the Select Committee appointed by the House of Commons to inquire into the state of the railway communication of the country, and from that period his views appear to have undergone a change, or at least considerable modification, in reference to the benefits the country would derive from competing lines. Sir Robert Peel returned to power in 1841, and in 1842 commenced that series of commercial reform measures, with which his name will be for ever associated, and one of these was the Railway Act of 1844. He must at that time have had great doubts as to the soundness of our system, and contemplated the possibility at some future day, of our national policy being reversed, and that the Legislature should desire to be in a position to claim from the companies the possession of the railways — not in the exercise of an abstract right, but in the ordinary course of carrying out a duly settled contract. Sir Robert Peel appeared then to have some forebodings not only of the vast waste of capital that would be incurred in constructing unnecessary lines, but the inefficient remedy it would afford for the many evils complained of; he knew, on the one hand, that to make competition in all respects effectual, there must be a sufficient number of competitors to prevent combination, and, on the other, that every unnecessary line laid down would be, in many respects, not only a wanton waste of the national wealth, but a great injury to the shareholders in the old lines. At this time, however, there were many difficulties in the way of the Government taking more direct and immediate measures to bring about the transfer of railways from the companies to the State. Mr. Gladstone, as we have seen, stated in the House that "gentlemen of great experience and intelligence had advised the immediate purchase of the railways; but, in the present state of the system, he could not advise such a course." At that time there were scarcely 2000 miles of railway in the kingdom, not the one-sixth of their present extent, and as it never was contemplated that Government should make the lines, Sir Robert Peel and Mr. Gladstone appear to have concurred in opinion that it would require about twenty-one years to complete our railway system, or at least so far to complete it that the subject could be properly dealt with by Parliament. "The question," said Sir Robert Peel on the second reading of the bill, "is, whether they have not arrived now at that period of legislation, with respect to railways, when it was advisable that Parliament should take some precaution for the furtherance of the public interests respecting them. The hon. gentleman who had preceded him wanted to see another railway between Manchester and Liverpool. Was the hon. gentleman sure he could guarantee to the public any advantage from that competition? He did not call the railways monopolies in an invidious sense; but surely in one sense they were. The parties who enjoyed the existing monopolies had the power of exercising their influence in Parliament, and of even successfully preventing competition. He was not prepared to advise the immediate purchase of railways, nor did he wish to see the Government, or part of the Government, the directors of railway concerns; that was not the object of the bill; but seeing that there was a vast number of new railway projects that were about to receive the sanction of the Legislature, seeing that there was a power of taking land, and a monopoly with respect to conveyance and communication, the Legislature should have the power of purchasing, after a certain period, after giving due notice thereof to the parties concerned. They were about to say to the railway companies, '*You shall not have a permanent monopoly against the public,* but, after a limited number of years, we give you notice we shall have the option of purchasing your property.' It had been said that this was a hasty legislative effort on the part of Government. Why, the whole of the Third Report of the Railway Committee, which was printed in the early part of the session, was one continuous notice of the measures the Government had now brought forward." It is pretty clear from the foregoing extract what were the opinions of Sir Robert Peel on the subject, viz. :—That the possession of the railways by the companies should be only probational; that the system should undergo revision at a future time, that time being fixed at twenty-one years from that date; that the Legislature would by that time have sufficient data on which to form a sound judgment, and then, but not till then, could the nation come to a definite conclusion as to which of the two systems was the better. The Legislature of 1844 admitted the truth of the facts and soundness of the arguments adduced by Sir Robert Peel and Mr. Gladstone in support of their views, and passed the bill, thus leaving to the Legislature of 1865 the task of completing that investigation which they had so well commenced. The doubts and difficulties which existed twenty years ago, when so little, comparatively, was known about the management of railways, ought now no longer to exist. Aided by the light which such a long experience has given us of the working of our own system, the Legislature should now be able to form a judgment whether or not it is the best that could be adopted to meet the wants and wishes of the community, and to develop the resources of the nation to the greatest practicable extent.

Great improvement has taken place of late in railway legislation. Some years ago, before a company could obtain their Act, they were obliged "to prove their traffic;" and the great test of the necessity of a railway was whether or not it would "pay." If it were a beneficial investment for the proprietors, it must be so for the public; but if it would not give the proprietors a fair return, then its construction could be only a public loss: these were the grounds on which the promoters of a bill claimed the assent of Parliament, and that was one of the tests. Now, if this principle was sound, it followed that any line that did not pay should never have been constructed —an axiom quite true, no doubt, so far as the interests of the shareholders were concerned, but quite a different matter as regards those of the public. Where would have been our original Great Western and its eight hundred and odd miles of tributary lines, and all our communication throughout the West of England? Where our South-Eastern and its 250 miles, securing communication between the metropolis and the Continent? Where our Great Eastern, with its 600 miles of railway, and all our communication with the eastern counties and the eastern coast? Nay, more, take our London and North-Western and its 1200 miles, and our communication with Liverpool, Manchester, Birmingham, &c. The shares are now above par, but a few years since they were considerably below par, and if the test then adopted were true the line should never have been constructed. It may be said that some of these lines originally paid well, but their dividends fell off in consequence of loss of traffic through competing lines; but the Legislature first declared that the test of the necessity of a line, of its being required by the public, depended on the proof of its being a profitable investment for its shareholders, and by a parity of reasoning, some might argue, when it ceased to be a good investment, it must likewise cease to be a benefit to the public.

Parliament next granted competing lines, which reduced many of the old lines to a non-paying point. This, according to the legislative opinion of that day, destroyed all their public usefulness; but to be in any way consistent, the Legislature should have required all such non-paying lines to be closed.

But there was not the slightest truth in this now defunct legislative principle, nor any connection whatever between the dividends to the shareholders and the advantage to the public? Could we dispense better with the services the Great Western renders to the public, because it only pays 3 per cent. to their shareholders, than with the Stockton and Darlington, which pays 7 per cent.? Would the population of the eastern counties have any reason to rejoice over the abolition of the Great Eastern, as it only pays 2 per cent. to its shareholders, whereas the Midland pays 6 per cent.; or have the inhabitants of Dover, and all the towns in the south-eastern district of England, gained the less, because the London, Chatham, and Dover, which, as yet, pays but a mere trifle to their shareholders, was made, in addition to the South-Eastern, which pays $4\frac{1}{2}$ per cent. to their shareholders, whilst the public have not the less gained by increased accommodation and reduction of charges?

The soundness of the principle on which the Legislature, for a long time, acted in refusing to permit the construction of a line unless there was a traffic "proved to be remunerative," will not stand the test of examination. It was assumed, as we have seen, that if the traffic was not sufficient to be profitable to the shareholders, the line could not be wanted by the public. Now, whatever plausible grounds there might have been for this assumption if railways were constructed at the same cost throughout the kingdom, it is reduced to nothing when we consider that the physical difficulties in the construction of some lines are so great, and those lines of the greatest commercial consequence, not merely to their respective localities, but the kingdom at large, that they never would have been constructed had their cost of construction been foreseen. Take, for instance, the group of railways amalgamated under the title of the Manchester, Sheffield, and Lincoln, running through the most populous of the manufacturing districts, having an invested capital amounting to nearly twelve millions, and a revenue of upwards of 750,000*l.* per annum. The traffic per mile exceeds that of four-fifths of any one of all the other lines in the kingdom, and nearly equals some of our greatest trunk lines; but the expenditure incurred by this company was enormous. There is one tunnel alone between Manchester and Sheffield three and a quarter miles long, double in length to that of any other in the kingdom. The works were of a very expensive nature, so that scarcely any traffic could repay such an expenditure as has been here incurred, and the company scarcely pays 1 per cent. to their shareholders; but is there less necessity, so far as the public interests are concerned, for railway communication throughout these densely populated districts, or between such great manufacturing towns as Manchester and Sheffield, because the railway by which the traffic is maintained pays little or nothing to the shareholders? This line would never have received Parliamentary sanction had a correct estimate of the traffic and cost of the railway been made, nor would it have ever come before Parliament.

It may be asked how did these non-paying companies ever succeed in obtaining their Acts? The reply is, that the projectors in most cases made erroneous estimates of the necessary outlay, that the capital "proved before the committee as sufficient" had in the execution of the works to be far exceeded; and the extravagant estimate of traffic fell considerably short of the mark. So far, then, as the public are concerned, it will hardly be contended that the most unprofitable railway to the shareholders may not be the most useful; and, in fact, indispensable to the public. This principle is now acknowledged in the Legislature, and no proof of "remunerative traffic" is required.

The greatest advance in railway legislation of late years, is that which took place in the last session of Parliament, by the appointment of a joint committee from both Houses, to stop the influx of railways into London, and lay down a general plan by which London and its suburbs should be sufficiently supplied with railway accommodation on the one hand, and duly protected from hostile invasion, as it may well be termed, on the other; it is much to be hoped that the same principle that is acted on in regard to the metropolis will be applied equally to all the other parts of the kingdom; it would confer a great benefit on all parties concerned, by preventing useless contests, stopping *in limine* wild projects, and saving both to old and new companies vast sums of money that will otherwise be squandered away in contests before Parliamentary Committees. Without any reference whatever to the scheme of the Government purchase of the railways, it would undoubtedly be most desirable that some general plan should be sketched out of what is wanting for the country at large, as was done in the session of 1863 by a Committee of the House of Lords, in reference to the projected railways for the metropolis; a joint committee, composed of members from both Houses, sitting for a few weeks and having heard the best evidence to be adduced on such a subject, would be perfectly competent to define what lines they considered necessary to complete our system for the present; and there would be enough of competitors to carry out all that such a committee would deem necessary.

Our actual want at the present time is the completion of our railway system, the links to be let in, in the unfinished network, thrown over the country, and the attention of promoters, as in the case of the metropolitan lines, to be directed to what railways the country yet requires. It is only necessary to glance at a railway map of the United Kingdom, to see that many parts of the country are totally unprovided with railways; many districts are so mountainous, and so thinly populated, that, during the present generation, there is little likelihood of that want being supplied; but there are many populous districts totally without railway accommodation, in consequence of the heavy cost that would attend their construction. As we have already noted, some of the most important and useful lines in the country would never have been made, had the shareholders foreseen the results of their several speculations, unless they had received from the State substantial assistance in their construction. It is not to be supposed, in such cases, the Legislature would have allowed the country to be without railways; but, considering them in the light of great industrial works necessary for the development of the resources of the nation, would have given such support, in some form or other, such as would have ensured their construction. The State has already done so in some instances in Ireland, and the same principle would, I presume, be acted on in England, if such a course should be considered conducive to the national welfare. The Legislature, as we have seen at one time, considered, that if a railway would be a loss to its shareholders, it would also be a loss to the country, and would not allow it to be made. That opinion has been so far modified, that they consider it quite a secondary matter, whether a railway pays the shareholders or not. It is not clear, however, that the Legislature is prepared to go beyond this point, and consider it a positive benefit to the nation to construct lines that would not pay the shareholders, and it is doubtful if it is prepared to take a step still further in advance of what has been yet done, and be willing to give some assistance, direct or indirect, as the case may be—in most cases, a Government loan would be sufficient for the construction of such lines as a joint committee of both Houses should define as necessary to complete our railway system. But I cannot help thinking that, in so doing, the Legislature would confer a great benefit on the nation.

A very prevalent opinion prevails, that in process of time, as the cost of constructing railways decreases, and Parliamentary and other expenses are lessened to the companies, the public will derive a proportional advantage by the reduction in fares and charges; the companies, they say, can then afford to carry for less: but all companies charge as much in every case as they can, just as private individuals do. The New River Company, whose 100*l.* share sells for 18,000*l.*, paying off their original capital each year five times over, cannot "afford" to sell their water for less to the public than another company not paying their expenses; if the public on the one hand lose nothing by any expense a company may be put to, so, on the other, they gain nothing by any saving the company can effect; all is reduced to one dead level, without the prospect of beneficial change to either one party or the other.

One of the most serious evils inherent in our present system, and altogether inseparable from it, is the number of frightful accidents that happen during the summer months, which, in the great majority of cases, can be traced to the deficient arrangements of directors and managers; and this happens more especially to those companies which pay very small dividends, and whose directors are naturally anxious to increase them: the result is an inefficient, badly paid, and overworked staff of officers and men, a road kept in bad repair, and the rolling-stock in many cases quite unfit for use. When accidents happen from causes of this nature, the sufferers, or their representatives, can recover damages against the offending company. But last year a bill was introduced into Parliament, and only rejected by a small majority, to change the common law of England in favour of railway proprietors! The allegation was, that they suffer a heavy loss from the operation of Lord Campbell's Act, by which they were compelled to compensate, so far as money could compensate, widows and orphans, for the loss sustained by the deaths of their husbands or fathers, when caused by negligence. The companies thought it unjust, that when a valuable life was lost through the criminal negligence of their servants, they should be bound to make up in a pecuniary point of view the loss to his family. They contended, that beyond a certain sum, a traveller should be bound to value his life when starting on a journey, and pay a premium accordingly, to enable his relations to recover damages in case of death. Putting aside the arguments *pro* and *con* in this matter, it must be pretty obvious, that, looking at the practical effects of this bill on railway finances, the companies can have but little to complain of. We know that the average expenses of the companies amount to 2*s.* 7*d.* per train mile; and all the losses that they sustain, not only by compensating parties for personal injuries, but also for loss and damage to goods, amount to one halfpenny out of the 2*s.* 7*d.*; they do not object to paying for loss and damage to goods, nor to a fixed sum, where lives are lost by the culpable negligence of their servants. All they would gain, then, by the abolition of Lord Campbell's bill, and substituting their own, could not reduce their expenditure more than *half a farthing* per train mile!

The popular belief has been, that the heavy damages awarded against companies form so large an item in their expenditure, as to be no small protection to the public, by increasing the vigilance and caution of the companies against accidents. But how do these accidents occur? Not so much from gross negligence in the ordinary sense of that term, as from a systematic cheese-paring economy, either in the number of officers or men being insufficient or overworked, or ill-paid and negligent, or from undue saving being attempted in some other way; take, for instance, the serious accident on a large scale that occurred some time since on the Great Eastern Railway, when six persons were killed, and a great number seriously injured. The immediate cause was a bullock straying on the line; but the proximate causes were the want of sufficient superintendence to have the line properly protected, and the rottenness of the third-class carriages in which the unfortunate passengers were killed; there is a great saving in the expenditure, when the carriages are in that state; they may serve their purpose so long as nothing occurs to test their strength, but when that is once tested, a catastrophe is the result. Had there not been undue economy in another department, that should have provided for the proper superintendence of the line, and the hands necessary to execute needful works, and had the fences been in proper order, the accident in question could not have happened. Again, on the 13th July last, another frightful accident happened on this line, within half a mile of the Bradford Station; the engine lurched over and dashed down a steep embankment, dragging all the train after it. The stoker was killed on the spot, and a great many dreadfully injured. "The permanent way," says the report in the papers, "was in too weak a condition to support the weight of the train, and this weakness resulted simply from the rotten condition of the sleepers, many of which were broken and the metals torn up."

So in regard to accidents on other lines. Sometimes they result from the employment of servants totally unfit for their situation, but engaged at low wages; at other times, there are not sufficient to do the work; take, for instance, the following paragraph that went the round of the papers last autumn without contradiction:—

"RAILWAY SERVANTS.—At the Oxford City Court yesterday, before Mr. J. R. Carr and a full bench of magistrates, Philip Tuttey, an engine-driver, and Elijah Weatley, a fireman in the employ of the Great Western Railway Company, were brought up in custody, charged, on the information of Mr. Wright, the superintendent of the locomotive department between Oxford and Reading, with being drunk while on duty. The evidence showed that early yesterday morning the defendants were in charge of an empty luggage train, proceeding from Paddington to Oxford. When they arrived at the Culham station they were detained four hours, in consequence of a pointsman having neglected his duty, and caused two trucks to be thrown off the line. The defendants partook somewhat freely of ale and rum in the interim, and on their arrival at Oxford, at about half-past five A.M., Weatley was found lying drunk on the foot-plate of the engine. Tuttey was too much intoxicated to render it prudent for him to be allowed to take further charge of the train. Tuttey had been in the company's service fifteen years, and until this happened his conduct had been irreproachable. Weatley had only acted as a fireman for a fortnight. Both defendants alleged that *during the past week they had been so hardly worked as to be only able to obtain sixteen hours' repose,* which so exhausted them that the drink they had taken produced the effect above alluded to. In answer to the Bench, they said that the average working hours of engine-drivers and firemen on the line were *fourteen hours daily*. These statements, *which were uncontradicted*, drew forth strong observations from some of the magistrates. The defendants were fined 15s., including costs, with the alternative of fourteen days' imprisonment."

Now if a company—like the Great Western, and other companies similarly situated—are obliged to resort to such means to eke out the miserable dividends they pay to their proprietors, it more strongly proves the utterly false position in which directors are placed between the public and their shareholders. The amount the companies pay per annum per train mile for loss of life and personal injury to their passengers, caused by the neglect of their servants, amounts, as we have seen, only to *one farthing* out of the 2s. 7d.; but the traffic charges and maintenance of ways and works amount to *one shilling and threepence* per mile, and these are the items affected in keeping up an efficient staff and the line in working order. It is easy, therefore, to imagine that, looking at it in a monetary point of view, the fear of the penalty in case of accident can have little or no effect. In reality, however, the directors—even on the worst-managed lines—never anticipate an accident; they fear it as little as the man who never insures fears that, some night, his house will be burned; and the trains may run nine hundred and ninety-nine times in perfect safety; but the thousandth time, the catastrophe occurs: the result to the public is DEATH, and to the saving railway companies—who are, in effect, their own insurers —that penalty which, in the aggregate of their several expenses, is represented completely by *one farthing* loss per train mile.

It is to be observed that if a passenger is either killed or injured on a railway, not owing either to any fault of his or the company, but to some unforeseen accident, the company pays nothing. If the State, however, at some future time undertake the charge of the conveyance of passengers, it would be desirable to provide, as far as possible, against unavoidable accidents, and that the payment of the fare should be considered, at the same time, an insurance against death or accident. Suppose each farthing paid per mile by the several classes to represent an insurance for 100*l.* in case of death, or a reasonable allowance for personal injury. This, I consider, would be sufficient to meet the necessities of the case.

The refreshment department at our railway stations is by far the worst of any in Europe. On many lines, it is absolutely a national disgrace; squabs of pork lie offered without the slightest reference to the season, old three-cornered jam puffs, fossil sandwiches, sausages concealed in heavy pastry, are humorously but very truly described by a writer in the *Saturday Review*, as the staple food provided for railway travellers in England. Nor is the drink better; there is a curious brown dilution of chicory—or imitation of chicory—sold as coffee; but it is not even good chicory. As for drinkable tea, it is a beverage altogether unknown at our railway stations.

"If it is asked," says the *Saturday Review*, "what it is that is wanted, we can only reply that we want, at the best English stations, something like what we get at a bad *buffet* in France. Nothing could be easier than to furnish coffee made of foreign berries—not of roots and beans—plenty of good fresh milk, fresh rolls, and pats of cool, clean butter. The more aspiring stations might go as high as tea, made recently of an honest black foreign leaf; but this, we know, is going too far. The coffee, and rolls and butter, are what we must ask for, because then there would always be something on which we could rely; and if other people wanted to eat their puffs, and pies, and concealed sausages, they might. But if the reform were to be sweeping and universal, the whole style of thing might be changed, and there might be the variety, the quickness, and the cleanliness of such *buffets* as those of Macon and Lyons. There is, indeed, a long way from where we are to where we should be then, and we do not expect such a wide interval to be passed over very quickly. It seems as if there were some inherent incapacity in Englishmen to keep *buffets*. We remember to have heard of a traveller who went along the whole length of the Grand Trunk Railway of Canada. He wished to eat and drink with decency and comfort. Time after time he was disappointed. Everywhere there was the usual English management—the old original pork pie and imitation chicory. At last, and as it happened, on a Saturday evening, he got to a station where there was a refreshment-room after a very different pattern. All was neatness and order. The things to eat were eatable, and the things to drink were drinkable. The enchanted traveller descended, established himself in the refreshment-room, and determined to pass the Sunday there. He knew that if he went farther, he would be sure to fare worse; and a very pleasant, though rather quiet, Sunday he passed with his host, who was, of course, a Frenchman. How sincerely every Englishman must wish that such a being could come to this country, to preside over an exceptional refreshment-room! English managers of these places know no better, and, unfortunately, they find their own villanous arrangements highly profitable. They have a monopoly, and the *dura Anglorum ilia* are found to endure, and even to desire, the squabs and the concealed sausages. So the money comes in, and the administrators not only make money for themselves, but are able to pay a good rent to the railway company. This satisfies the directors, who do not conceive themselves to be under any further responsibility, and who would never think of making any objection, even if things were worse managed than they are."

These refreshment-rooms are leased out to contractors at enormous rents, and they make proportionate charges to the traveller—the quality of their viands and the prices charged every one knows. The directors of our railways, the bad-paying lines especially, endeavour to screw something out of everything under their control, down, it is said, on some lines, even to the shoe-blacks, towards a dividend; and although, under all the circumstances of the case, it is hard to blame them, such a state of things could never be permitted under a national system.

There is, perhaps, no neglect on the part of railway companies that has caused a stronger feeling of indignation than their refusal to provide means of communication between the passengers and the guard, and the frightful murder on the North London line last year has very much increased that feeling.

Our carriage accommodation requires complete revision ; by providing open compartments, as well as separate sleeping compartments for those who can afford to pay for them — some carriages being made in this fashion and others in that — all parties would be satisfied.

It would be quite out of place here to enter on any discussion in regard to the benefits that would be derived by the country from the adoption of a liberal and enlightened policy in the management of our railways; with us it has never been made a party question, and those who have most widely differed in politics, have from time to time joined cordially together in an endeavour to effect beneficial changes in the system we have now to consider.

How should railways be managed were they in the hands of the State?

1st. Should they be leased out to companies?

2nd. Should their management be entrusted to the Government?

3rd. If not, should Government have a limited control over the management of affairs?

4th. If none of these three courses should be thought expedient, to whom should their management be entrusted?

These are questions of the greatest importance, but before entering on their consideration, it is desirable to notice what Parliament has done of late years in regard to a reduction of taxation, which largely affects the present subject.

The whole course of our commercial policy for the last twenty-two years has been to reduce, as far as possible, taxation on the necessaries of life. This policy was inaugurated by the late Sir Robert Peel when at the head of the Government, and has been continued by his successors in office down to the present time.

This policy is now clearly understood, and consistently carried out; if the thirty millions and upwards sterling per annum that we pay in the ordinary way of business to railway companies were paid by us to Government in the form of direct taxation, as we pay postage, the tariff for passengers and merchandise would undergo the strictest scrutiny; and, unless I have greatly deceived myself, it would appear beyond controversy that the principle on which that tariff was founded, although perfectly sound as regards the principle of commerce as carried on by private individuals, was utterly opposed to our modern principles of taxation, and would accordingly undergo the strictest revision.

I have no doubt it would be found on trial, that a great reduction in the charges would have the same financial result, as affects the receipts on railways, as similar measures had on the duty derived from tea, sugar, coffee, and other articles of daily consumption, and on the postage on letters.

How, then, might we imagine the Chancellor of the Exchequer would deal with railways? It would be impossible to suppose any department in which a great reduction in charges could be more called for, whether in regard to the enormous amount paid by the public, or the universal relief it would afford to all, and especially the commercial and the poorer classes. On the other hand, there would be with the present charges a branch of the revenue conducted on sound commercial principles, and to make a large reduction in these charges, analogous to that made in the Post Office, would involve the revenue for many years in a heavy loss. By Sir Rowland Hill's measure, postage was reduced on letters to *one-sixth* on an average of their former rates, and the immediate effect on net revenue was a reduction to *one-third* of its previous amount, viz.: from a million and a half to half a million. The net revenue from the railways last year, after paying working expenses, which amounted to forty-eight per cent. on the gross receipts, was sixteen millions; and, assuming the Chancellor of the Exchequer would reduce the fares and charges to one-third of their present average amount, instead of the one-sixth that Sir Rowland Hill carried out in the Post Office, the deficiency in the railway revenue for some years could not be calculated at a less rate than five millions per annum; and how would this deficiency be made up? It would, no doubt, be a very wise policy on the part of the country to submit to an addition to the income tax to have such a reform carried out. The carriage of letters is surely not more important than that of the whole population, and of all on or by which that population lives. But would the country submit to an addition of five millions to the income tax for any object whatever? I think that may be greatly doubted. We have a great dislike to direct taxation, people generally prefer paying double or treble the amount in indirect taxation. In the hypothetical case I am assuming, if the traffic were no more than doubled, the nation would be a great gainer by the change, although the five millions would still be paid by the nation in the aggregate—one part of the nation that previously paid the whole of the tax, would now pay only the half for the same service rendered by the railways, and the other half would be paid by a new class who previously had been unable to use them. This shows the benefit of direct taxation to a limited extent when judiciously applied.

If the public opinion of this country undergoes a change—and a change it must assuredly undergo, sooner or later, if the principles in the Act are sound—some future Chancellor of the Exchequer will be in a position to deal with this important question. Let us, for the present, assume this to be so; how will that future Chancellor of the Exchequer deal with the subject? He will be able to tell how, in times long gone by, a President of the Board of

Trade designed a total reorganization of our railway system, and for the purpose of carrying that design into effect he succeeded, after encountering the most formidable opposition, in making a commencement of this great work; that he laid the foundations broad and deep, but had been obliged to leave to other hands in more favourable times the task of raising the superstructure and completing the work.

That Chancellor of the Exchequer's task will be a very easy one, when the public mind is prepared for such a change; but many years may possibly elapse, and hundreds of millions be paid in railway charges, before the attention of the public is directed to this subject from any influential quarter; but it will one day be known that in 1865 an Act of Parliament came into force, by the operation of which the fares and freightage on all railways throughout the country might have been reduced two-thirds without any charge whatever to the public, and the difference to the shareholders made up by the substitution of national for private credit; the sure and comparatively unfluctuating credit of the State for the uncertain and ever changing credit of commercial undertakings.

It may be said that to reduce the fares to one-third of their present amount instead of one-sixth, as in the case of postage, would only effect a compromise of the question, and that the public, with the successful example of the working of the Post-Office reform before their eyes, the number of letters increased ninefold, and both gross and net revenue greater than under the old system, would be dissatisfied till they had a similar measure of reform, viz., a reduction to one-sixth of the present charges. The cases of the Post Office and the railways are, in some respects, however, not analogous, and one point of difference, I apprehend, would be in regard to numbers. I doubt very much, if passengers were even carried free, that their number would increase ninefold. It is a very different matter sending a letter by post and taking a journey per train; and if the fares were fixed at the respective rates of three farthings, a halfpenny, and a farthing per mile, with return tickets, and a liberal allowance for time, I think comparatively few persons having business to transact would be prevented from travelling, but the increase would not, probably, be more than threefold for some years to come.

In considering this part of the project, it must be clearly kept in view that, although the public accommodation should be the first consideration, its financial success should be undoubtedly the second, and that it would be a mere wanton sacrifice of revenue to make large reductions in charges not appreciated by the public, and which they did not require. If, for instance, it was proposed to reduce the penny postage to a halfpenny postage, so far from such a reduction being hailed as a boon, it would, I believe, be denounced as a very foolish measure, throwing away a million and a half of revenue, perhaps, without any appreciable good to any one. The present postage rates but rarely prevent any person from writing that has a wish to do so; and, with the exception of circulars, the increase would be very slight. It has been suggested, however, that the transmission by post of printed circulars, not exceeding a quarter of an ounce each, with halfpenny stamps, would pay better than with penny stamps, and so far the change might be an improvement.

It must be remembered that the fare is not the only expense in travelling; there are many other expenses, and, what is often to some persons more valuable, the loss of time—which is money; consequently, if travelling for long distances were perfectly free to business men, the loss of time and, to all, the expenses of hotels, would act as a considerable preventive. The first-class fare, for instance, from London to Edinburgh, 400 miles, is at present £3 10s., and although that might be reduced by two thirds, which would of course cause a great increase of travellers, yet the hotel expenses and loss of time would always be effective in preventing an increase in ordinary travelling in anything approaching to the same ratio as the increase of letters under the reformed system. There would be a very great increase in the number of third-class passengers by the Parliamentary trains; there are no return tickets given at present, so that travellers by that class who would use a return ticket, would travel at about *one-fifth* of the present fare; their time not being very valuable, and their expenses for lodging, &c., but light, it would be difficult to estimate the vast increase that would take place with that class of travellers.

If the regular, safe, and cheap conveyance of our letters and papers is to us a matter of such importance, of how much more importance to us is the whole of our inland traffic as carried on by the railways of the country? The one is represented in a money point of view by three millions and a half sterling, and the other by ten times that sum: to the one we entrust merely our correspondence, to the other our lives and property. The charges, regulations, and management of the one is absolutely under the control of the nation through its Legislature, and its working devoted solely to the public good: the charges, regulations, and management of the other are independent of the nation, the Legislature, and the executive, and are under the sole control of the directors, and all considerations for the public are sacrificed in order to obtain the largest dividend for their shareholders. In a word, both systems are monopolies carried on for purposes somewhat analogous, but conducted on principles widely different, and the public should now be able to form an opinion as to whether the Post-Office system should be assimilated to the railways, or the railway system to that of the Post Office.

The superiority of the Post-Office system is obvious: the Legislature settle at once, distinctly and definitely, the proper charges, which cannot, under any circumstances, be altered without its assent. The object of competition is to effect by a very roundabout and imperfect process the same result. Were it possible to enact and carry out a law by which a fair price should be fixed for everything that is sold, there would be no occasion for competition, for all that competition aims at is to keep down prices to that rate; but as it would be impossible to carry out such a law, we do the best we can under the circumstances— we promote competition and, so far as we can, extend free trade. So long as we do not make the mistake of attempting to apply free-trade principles as a complete remedy where they are not applicable, we do well, and no test can be more simple than that of their applicability. Is there a likelihood of a sufficient number of competitors coming into the field to prevent the possibility of combination? If that question cannot be answered in the affirmative, there is not a free-trader in this country but will admit that to attempt to carry out his principles in such a case is perfectly hopeless. In the case of railways we have long attempted to accomplish that purpose. We have succeeded, no doubt, in multiplying railways and dividing the monopoly, and to that extent have done good.

It is contended, however, by no inconsiderable section of free-traders, whose views are represented in the *Westminster Review*, that it is owing to the fault of the Legislature that there is not perfect free trade in the construction of railways. Every year, they say, there is a vast number of projects rejected, and if every bill were permitted to pass the monopoly would soon be destroyed. I admit the truth of that proposition, and that carrying it out would, in a certain sense, be in accordance with free-trade principles; but what would political economists say to the waste of capital it would involve? Look at many parts of England—Birmingham, for instance; there are three lines laid down between that town and Wolverhampton, closely parallel, the distance between them, at any point, scarcely exceeding a mile, and consequently affording no increased accommodation to the public by passing through widely separated districts; the monopoly is divided, but not destroyed, and the fares are moderate, little more than twopence per mile for first class, and the others in proportion. But how much better would it be, both for the public and the shareholders, to have only one line, an absolute recognized monopoly, supposing even a company had it, with first-class fares limited to a halfpenny per mile, and the others in proportion? We know that two companies with these fares are each paying six per cent. to their shareholders, and with the traffic existing in that part of the country confined to one line, the dividend would be very high indeed.

Let us now look at the railway question from another point of view, viz., in reference to the general taxation of the country. We will suppose that the railways had been constructed by the State, that they were under Government control, and the fares and charges the same as they are now; would the common sense of the country permit them to be continued? Would it be permitted, in the present day of advanced legislation, that Government should charge the public fourfold a fair price because it happened to pay a little better? The main cause that has prevented public attention from being directed to this subject arises from the fact, that, as railways are private property, and their proprietors have a right to make what charges they think proper, speculative inquiries of such a nature are considered of no practical use. Let us, however, assume that, like the Post Office, they were the property of the State, and let us examine closely into the working of that institution before and after its management had undergone reform in 1839. We shall thus be enabled to form an opinion of the benefit to the public from a change somewhat analogous in the management of our railways.

CHAPTER II.

The Post Office as managed in former days — Mr. Rowland Hill's Scheme—Evidence of Post-Office Officials before the Select Committee of the House of Commons—Evidence of Lord Overstone, Lord Ashburton, and Mr. Cobden—Cost of the Conveyance of a Letter—Calculated Increase—System by which the Revenue was defrauded—Free-trade in carrying Letters considered—A well-governed Monopoly in some cases better than Free-trade—Test of the Applicability of Free-trade Principles — The extreme Free-trade Principles applied to Railways—Our Commercial Policy since 1842—The Effect of direct Taxation—What a past President of the Board of Trade has done — What a Future Chancellor of the Exchequer may do — The Post Office and Railways compared.

That part of the present generation who are under middle age have very little idea of what the public suffered in regard to postal rates, before Mr. Rowland Hill introduced his celebrated scheme of a low and uniform rate of postage throughout the kingdom. The conveyance of letters was then, as it is now, a Government monopoly; but at that time it was considered merely as a source of revenue, and conducted as the railways, or any other private commercial monopoly is conducted, viz.:—without any more regard to the general convenience than was necessary to extract the greatest amount of money from the public. In this respect, the unreformed Post Office was not a whit behind the most obnoxious of its compeers; it laid on the most exorbitant rates, it guarded with the utmost jealousy any attempt to infringe on its patent right to carry letters, and prosecuted with the utmost rigour trespassers on its domain. In those days writing a letter, or rather sending it by post, was a serious matter; not to be undertaken rashly, but only on due consideration, and when the circumstances of the case warranted it. Although the cost of conveying a letter from one end of the kingdom to the other did not amount to half a farthing, the Post Office charged half-a-crown; the monopoly was most stringent, even a friend taking charge of a letter was liable to fine or imprisonment; the phrase single, double, or treble letter is now happily obsolete, but in those days it had a very unpleasant signification; it meant, that the postmaster, holding up the letter to the light, and prying between its folds, either saw or fancied he saw one or two slips of paper within, and the postage in consequence was doubled or trebled. The poorer classes were deprived almost entirely of the use of the Post Office, and the middle classes used it only when they could not help it.

Application had been made at various times to the Post Office, or rather to successive administrations, for some reduction in the rates of postage, and a general feeling existed, that they were much higher than they should be; still, there was no movement of the nation, there was no pressure brought to bear on Government, and the stereotyped answer in this, as in all similar cases, was, "The revenue cannot afford it." It was in 1837 that Mr. Rowland Hill's pamphlet appeared, and its effect throughout the country was electrical; it took people's breath away! That a very considerable reduction was desirable in the charges for postage, no one doubted; but such a revolutionary measure, one that struck so completely at the root of all heretofore recognized principles on which a commercial establishment had been conducted, had certainly never been dreamt of: "How," it was said, " can a treble letter be conveyed from Edinburgh to London for a penny ? Great as the profits of the Post Office are, the expenses amount to one-fourth of the gross receipts; the postage on a treble letter is three shillings, and therefore the actual cost to the Post Office for the conveyance of the letter is ninepence, and there would be an actual loss of eightpence by the transaction; the scheme is impracticable."

The Post Office was, as we have noticed, then conducted like any other mercantile monopoly, the average postage paid on each letter was sixpence, which Mr. Rowland Hill proposed to reduce to a penny; the Post-Office officials were strongly opposed to the project, and from their point of view, looking at it as a branch of the revenue from which all the money should be drawn that it was possible to extract, were quite right. There was a great number of witnesses examined before the Parliamentary Committee appointed to inquire into the subject, some of whose evidence we shall briefly notice.

We shall first take that of Lieutenant-Colonel Maberly, Secretary to the General Post Office. He was asked—

Q. Are you of opinion that the high rates of postage prohibit the middling and humbler classes the use of the Post Office?—Of course, the very high rates prohibit them when they wish to write; but my feeling is, they do not wish to write in the manner that people imagine, that they are not disposed to write.

Q. Is it your opinion no one is prevented corresponding by the present high rates of postage?—Of course, those persons who have no money to pay the postage are prohibited corresponding; but that would apply equally to the penny charge; if a person had not a penny, he could not write.

Q. How could the illicit correspondence be suppressed?— If the Government were to take it in hand, a great deal might be done; but it would be a question of policy whether you would institute a right of search, and whether you should as a Government employ informers very extensively, to lay informations against merchants, who evade the present rates of postage.

Q. What is your opinion of Mr. Hill's plan of reform?— It appears to me a most preposterous plan, utterly unsupported by facts, resting entirely on assumption.

Q. You are of the opinion that every reduction will tend to a loss of revenue?—Certainly, that is my opinion; that with a small reduction the revenue will recover itself; but if it were reduced to one penny, it would not recover itself for forty or fifty years.

Q. Do you think persons have an objection to a high rate of postage?—I think they have an objection to any postage, if they can avoid it.

Let us hear what Mr. Godby, Secretary to the Irish Post Office, says:—

Q. Would Mr. Hill's plan much affect the revenue?—Mr. Hill's plan would cause a very great decrease in the revenue. I do not think any human being living would ever see such an increase of letters as would make up the loss.

Q. Have you formed any opinion as to the extent to which the Post-Office regulations are evaded?—I was always aware they were evaded by every one who could evade them; but, I confess, I was never even suspicious of the astounding facts revealed by this inquiry—I must say mortifying facts that are disclosed in the volume of evidence I have gone through; I never had the most distant suspicion of it.

In answer to further questions, Mr. Godby said:—

‘ "The time has come to adopt some means, either by a severity of punishment against the commission of crime or the other alternative of a reduction of postage, to meet the smugglers.

"I see by the evidence that the increase, in the opinion of some people, would not be immediate. I am of the opposite opinion; I think at first there would be an immense revenue, but a declining after."

The Earl of Lichfield, then Postmaster-General, gave evidence to the same purport; and, so far as the immediate effect on the revenue was concerned, these gentlemen were quite correct in their prognostications, for the first five years after the change the loss to the revenue averaged about a million sterling per annum.

A writer of some note thus expressed his opinion of the scheme some years after it had been in operation:—

"In looking back at this extraordinary scheme, suggested only at the distance of six years, it is really surprising how sensible men could be deluded to such an excess upon points which scarcely required the experience of twelve months to bring them back to a sober estimate of what was proposed. To raise revenue by means of a Board is one thing, to accommodate the public, and all the individuals which compose it, equally and at all places, and upon an abstract principle, is another. To a philosopher who assumes to regulate a department by a theory of his own, the argument for uniformity in the case put by Mr. Hill is specious enough, but, to a Minister who wishes to derive revenue from it, it is totally unreasonable and inconsistent with common sense.

"But it must be borne in mind that the Post Office is *not under any obligation* to convey the correspondence of the public. The Post Office is as much intended to bring its quota to the service of the State, as the Excise or Customs. In arguing, therefore, upon the fairness of uniformity, it should have proceeded further than by showing its abstract equity.

"But what has Mr. Hill's plan effected? It has prostrated the public revenue; instead of being an auxiliary to safety, it has so impaired the former security of transmission, that a money letter sent by the post since Mr. Hill's plan might as well, says the Postmaster-General, 'be cast down on the pavement in the street;' it has changed the whole character of the department, it has pretty nearly converted it into a Parcel and Conveyance Delivery Company, a public general carrier, a kind of flying bazaar, instead of maintaining its former and permanently honourable position as a Board of Revenue, and a safe and effective instrument of conducting the correspondence of a great commercial empire. When mesmerism and other attractive novelties of the day have had their hour and are passing away, the quackery of penny postage ought surely now to follow the same course. Mr. Hill has fixed the nation with a penny postage, and what statesman is likely hereafter to come forward and retrieve us? Like the Sphynx in the palace of Thebes, the Post Office may only deem itself too happy if some future Treasury Œdipus were to redeem it from this intolerable plague."

The last witness put forward by the Post-Office authorities, whose testimony I shall quote against Mr. Hill's scheme, was a gentleman who had been in the service nearly forty years, whose evidence was a curiosity in its way, and as it was brief, we shall allow him to tell without curtailment the grounds of his opposition.

In answer to questions from the committee, this gentleman said, "he thought Mr. Hill's plan would be well received by the public; but he thought the reduction *too great*, so long as the establishment was made a branch of the revenue, he must always look to *that*. As to payment in advance, he thought it would be objected to by many persons; he would mention one description, viz., letters applying for the payment of debts; the creditor writes to the debtor, and very often his having been obliged to pay the postage produces the payment of the debt, lest he should have another dunning letter; but in case of the payment in advance being compulsory, the writer would have to add that additional charge to his former debt [that is, one penny] without being able to recover it of his debtor!"

If there had been no other question at issue beyond that relating to the immediate effect on the Post-Office revenue, the inquiry would have been totally unnecessary, as Mr. Rowland Hill, from the very outset of the inquiry, protested against considering its immediate fiscal effects as the criterion of success.

The Post-Office officials of that day, from the Postmaster-General down to the humblest postman, were naturally opposed to a scheme that, in their opinion, would not only reduce their establishment to insolvency and ruin, but would also degrade it into "a Parcel and Conveyance Delivery Company—a Public General Carrier—a kind of flying bazaar, instead of maintaining an honourable position as a Board of Revenue." It does not seem to have occurred to any of these gentlemen, that if the Post Office lost a million a year of its revenue, the nation paid so much less, and was, consequently, to that amount a gainer; and if the Chancellor of the Exchequer required that million, or part of it, or twice that amount, he would take care to have it back again from the nation through some other channel; so far, therefore, as the revenue was concerned, it had the same result; nor did these gentlemen remember, that the Public was the paymaster, and consequently entitled to choose the mode of payment.

I turn now to another class of witnesses, and shall confine myself to some extracts from the evidence of Lord Ashburton, Lord Overstone (then Mr. Jones Loyd), and Mr. Cobden, who, together with a host of others, supported Mr. Rowland Hill's scheme. I shall first give some short extracts from the evidence of Mr. Jones Loyd, banker: he was asked—

Q. Have you formed any opinion as to the justice of the proposed plan of an uniform rate of postage for all distances? —It seems to me the justice of the plan is perfectly obvious, except on the ground that the cost of conveyance differs. It is clear that the present rate of postage does, in point of fact, produce a prohibition of the use of the Post Office to all classes that may be below the higher classes.

Q. Is it a just mode of reasoning to maintain that persons do not feel the oppression of a tax, because they were prohibited from using the taxed article?—No: it appears to me so absurd, that I can hardly suppose anybody uses such reasoning. They may not know the loss they sustain, but that does not alter the fact that they sustain a great loss, and it would be highly criminal and cruel voluntarily to inflict such a loss on a person, merely upon the ground he does not know it. A child that is born blind, does not know the advantages of sight, but still it would be a very extraordinary thing to inflict blindness on a child, merely upon the ground, if you do it in time, he will not know the loss he has sustained. As to other modes of conveyance, last night we received thirty-six parcels containing 3500 documents; the total value of those documents was 95,000*l*.; a letter, weighing a half ounce, would contain, perhaps, ten of these documents; and in that case, 350 letters would contain the whole of them; if these letters were charged twopence each, 2*l*. 18*s*. 4*d*. would be the cost of sending these letters by post, and the additional security and certainty in sending them would put a stop to the idea of sending them by any other conveyance.

Mr. Cobden was deputed by the Manchester Chamber of Commerce to give evidence before the Committee; and the variety of details he entered into must have produced considerable effect; his opinion was, that in case the penny postage were adopted the increase would be nearly sixfold. Mr. Cobden quoted the following extracts from his notes:— "We are prevented," said one firm, "drawing bills for small amounts on our connexions in country towns by the high rates of postage." Another complains that the smallest bit of pattern enclosed should be charged double postage. "We have an instance," says the writer, "this morning of such an enclosure weighing one and three-quarter grains, costing us elevenpence, without any advantage arising to us from the same." "I sent Lobby," writes an individual, "a five-pound note, to Cambridge; it was a charity, and I could not let the bearer pay the postage; it was tenpence for the enclosed note, which, on the amount, is nearly one per cent. on transmission. There is also an injustice, that you may send a large sheet, perhaps a half-ounce weight, as single, and the smallest bit enclosed pays double postage." "Our rule," says one writer, " is never to send by post when we can avoid it." "We, ourselves," is the reply of another, "remit 180,000*l*. to 200,000*l*. by post in sums varying from 50*l*. to 200*l*., for which remittances we receive no acknowledgments, owing to the expense of postage." A third party says, "I do not doubt that four-fifths of the correspondence between Manchester and Liverpool is carried on by private hand. I often go down to Liverpool, and every trip I take I bring for my friends pocketfulls of private letters." Another says, "Many of our customers have continued for many years to send their letters to us by private hand, coachmen, guards, or travellers. On reference to our books, we have taken out one instance of many, in which an individual during the last seven years has sent us 170 orders, and 139 remittances; and in no instance through the post." A bookseller says, "In almost every coach parcel I receive, packets of letters are enclosed for individuals in this neighbourhood, totally unconnected with my branch of trade. Every traveller, whether from a publisher or stationer, has his advice letters forwarded through a bookseller's parcel; and I have frequently received thirty or forty at a time, all of which would be sent by post." One of the answers gives the opinion that "an amazing increase of letters through the Post Office would take place in connection with the lower classes; the high rate of postage compels them to find out various means of evading the postage; and it is amazing how indefatigable they are in finding out channels." "We know a firm, six miles from Manchester," writes one party, "who enclose in parcels 300 circulars, letters, invoices, &c., per week. An account was also sent to us of a railway company, the directors of which had availed themselves of a newspaper, as a medium of circulating their half-yearly report, a copy of which was thus sent to each proprietor, and the cost of postage saved." These are a few amongst a great number of similar statements which we received, all from parties bearing their own signatures; one writer says, " We should consider a general reduction of the rates of postage to one penny, as one of the greatest boons which could possibly be conferred on the trading interest; indeed, if we were asked what favour as mercantile men we should desire from Government, we should not hesitate a moment to desire the change proposed as one of almost equal importance, but of greater safety, than even the repeal of the corn laws." " I know of a house (continued Mr. Cobden) carrying on a wholesale business in Devonport, which sends all its circulars throughout the country four times a year for twopence per letter; they send 200 letters each time, and 180 of these 200 letters are sent by carrier, and twenty by post."

Lord Ashburton, formerly at the head of the great firm of Baring Brothers and Co., in answer to the question if he considered postage a proper source of revenue, said, "I have certainly always thought it a bad means of raising revenue. I think it is one of the worst of taxes. We have unfortunately many taxes which have an injurious tendency; but I think few, if any, have so injurious a tendency as the tax upon the communication by letters." In answer to various questions, his lordship said: " I think it is very hard upon family communication, and upon the social enjoyment which arises from that communication; it must affect the general diffusion of knowledge very much. Men of letters, and men of science, are the greater part of them of a class little able to bear heavy postage; and in that way it must affect the general diffusion of knowledge in the country, and to that extent affect education. As to commerce, the reduction would certainly be beneficial. I cannot doubt that a taxation upon communication by letter must bear heavily on commerce. You might as well tax words spoken in the Royal Exchange, as the communication of various persons living in Manchester, Liverpool, and London. The opinion I have expressed with respect to the present high rate of postage is an opinion I have always entertained: but I was much struck with the opinion of Mr. Hill on the subject; I thought the uniformity of the rate of postage, and the plan of stamping letters, and not making any addition for moderate-sized letters, were very good; also, I was much struck with the great facility in the delivery of letters, arising from the deliverer having no money to collect upon delivery, and the great means of simplifying the whole transactions of the Post Office, by transferring the money part of it principally to the Stamp Office, and taking away from it nearly the whole of its functions as a Board for the collection of revenue."

Let us now briefly note the result of Sir Rowland Hill's reform as it has affected the revenue and the nation. For the first three years after this change was effected there was a loss to the revenue of nearly a million sterling per annum; but each year after that time the revenue increased, and we learn from the "Treasury Minutes" of the 11th March, on the occasion of Sir Rowland Hill retiring from his post as secretary, that the gross revenue for 1863 exceeded that of 1839, the last year of the old system, by more than a million sterling, and the net revenue of last year was greater than that of 1839. The figures are, for 1839, 1,660,000*l*., and for 1863 1,790,000*l*.; so, in a financial point of view, the new system, after a period of twenty-five years, has overtaken and passed the old, and with every prospect of the distance between them being annually increased.

But we have to regard it in a much more important point of view. How it affected the revenue was, in one sense, a matter of comparative indifference; if a reduction of a penny in the pound is made in the income tax, there is a loss to the revenue of a million sterling in the year, and a relief to the country to that extent—but *nothing more*. It was quite a different matter in reference to the effect produced by the Post-Office reform; had the public not availed themselves of the benefit of cheap postage, had there not been an additional letter or newspaper carried, there would, at all events, have been a reduction of taxation to the amount of a million sterling per annum. But look at the matter as it now stands: the estimated number of letters that passed through the Post Office in 1839 was seventy-five millions; in 1863 the actual number was 700 millions—more than ninefold. The gross sum paid by the public for postage in 1839 was 2,390,000*l*., and had there been no reduction in postage, and if we could suppose for a moment that the difference in postage would make no difference in the number of letters being sent by post, the taxation of the country for postage alone would now amount to upwards of *nineteen millions sterling per annum!* But we know, as a matter of course, that if the old system still existed seven-eighths of the letters, now despatched by post, would have been forwarded to their destination through some other channel, as described by Mr. Cobden, or never have been written. The matter practically stands thus:—1st, The net revenue to the Government derived from the Post Office, after a period of twenty-five years' continued increase since the change of system, now equals the old revenue, exceeding in round numbers a million and a half sterling. 2nd, For the same number of letters which the public in 1839 paid nearly two and a half millions sterling, they pay now considerably less than half a million. 3rd, The individual or firm whose taxation for postage under the old system amounted, we will say, to 60*l.* per annum, had 50*l.* of that taxation at once struck off; and all other individuals and firms had a reduction in the same proportion. And 4thly, the revenue is now made up by two classes: the old class, who always availed themselves of the Post Office to a certain extent on compulsion, not being able otherwise to carry on their business, but who now voluntarily avail themselves of it largely; the new class comprises those who never, or but rarely, wrote letters at all.

I am considering the change of system in the Post Office strictly in a financial point of view, but there are matters relating to finance the value of which to the public is not easily estimated. In 1839 the amount of money orders paid in the United Kingdom, owing to the high charge for these orders, was considerably less than half a million sterling; in 1862 the amount exceeded fifteen millions and a half, owing, of course, to the low and graduated scale of charges. How, again, can we estimate in figures the convenience the public derive from the book post? We send a parcel (if a book or paper) from one end of the kingdom to the other in half the time and at one-fourth the cost that we can send it by railway! How can we estimate the value to the poorer classes of Mr. Gladstone's two measures that he has engrafted on the Post Office—the Savings Bank and the recent Insurance Act? The value of these different measures cannot be tested by a money standard.

I have thought it desirable, and indeed necessary for the illustration of my subject, to go into some detail as to the working of the two systems under which this great establishment has been managed; the one a sound mercantile system under which our Post Office was at a former period, as our railways are at present period, conducted, viz. to make money without any reference to the wants, the wishes, or the general benefit of the community; the other, in which the financial success was considered subsidiary to the welfare of the community.

If the Post Office had been a commercial instead of a Government monopoly, the proposition of Mr. Rowland Hill would have been too preposterous to have received a moment's attention; the revenue—that is, the Post-Office revenue—has lost by his measure not less than fourteen millions sterling; this sum remained " fructifying " in the pockets of the people, or at all events would have done so, if Chancellors of the Exchequer would have so permitted it. As it was, the deficiency was either made up from a new tax, or some other tax was not remitted that otherwise would have been. One thing is quite certain, the Chancellor of the Exchequer took care he should have his money. There was no doubt a great outcry made by interested parties some years after Mr. Rowland Hill's plan was in operation, from the alleged failure of the financial part of his scheme, and affecting to treat the loss to the revenue for the time being as an actual loss to the nation!

The Post Office is now, as it was then, a strict monopoly, and the question therefore arises, is a great monopoly necessarily an evil, or may it be rendered a great good? We have in regard to the Post Office a highly centralized system of management, extending over the whole of the kingdom, and connecting the most distant cities, towns, villages, and districts with each other and with the metropolis. We have a great dislike in a general way both to monopoly and centralization: would it be desirable, then, that the Post Office, as a national institution, should be abolished, and that the duties now performed by that establishment should be left to the operations of free trade and competition, as we find it developed in our railway companies? The Post Office has a monopoly of the conveyance of our letters on one system; the railway companies that of our persons and our property on a system totally opposite. Which is the better of the two? The duties of both are analogous. We have had certainly enough of opportunities within the last twenty years of testing the respective qualities of each. It has been somewhere suggested, that the railway system is the better of the two; and if such is the case, and the Government monopoly be abolished, we can have no difficulty whatever in tracing the course of the future Post-office companies, whenever they may be established. They would act, no doubt, as all railway or other commercial companies act—each company would charge whatever rate of postage paid it best, and taking the range of railway companies as a criterion, and the lowest charge for a single letter to be a penny, the highest would probably be a shilling. We should, no doubt, have a hundred different companies battling through the kingdom for business; they would assert their "territorial rights," they would "repel invasion," they would not submit to be "robbed of their postal traffic," and "would take measures to defeat their opponents;" they would combine against each other and the public, and the postage would rise or fall from day to day as they might be successful or otherwise in their several combinations or arrangements. The well-paying districts would be well supplied, and the non-paying districts neglected; there would be no control, authority, or combined action throughout the kingdom, nor tribunal for the redress of grievances. The public would be entirely at their mercy, and they would be served so far and no farther than suited the interests of the companies.

The truth is, that monopoly and free trade have each its separate sphere of labour, and when there is a public industrial work to be done, the first thing to be ascertained should be to which of the two departments it properly belongs. An effective competition prevents an overcharge; but if, from special circumstances, there are either no competitors in the field, or not a sufficient number to prevent their combination against the public, there is no competition, or at best it is but very partial in its operation and incomplete in its success. It is, further, a violation of the soundest principles of political economy to permit the waste of money by the construction of public works not in themselves either necessary or useful, when that object can be fully effected without either the waste of money or the injury to capitalists who have already invested their money. The English people have shown themselves in the case of the Post Office, not opposed to monopoly when it is placed under the strict control of the Legislature, for then a still greater benefit can be derived from its working than under the most enlarged system of free trade. The greatest free-trader in England would never dream of abolishing the national Post Office, nor suppose we could be as well served under any free-trade system, however perfectly it might be developed.

It is possible that the day may not be far distant when the British people will come to the opinion that a system which, in the conveyance of our letters, has been attended with such triumphant success, is not less applicable to the conveyance of ourselves and our goods; and as the Legislature have deemed the former branch of commerce so important as to keep the management under its exclusive control, so it may be hoped, when it is at liberty to deal with the latter — one which so materially affects the interests of all classes of the community—it will be equally determined to secure for the country at large all the advantages that may be derived from the proper administration of this still greater and more important branch of commerce.

CHAPTER III.

Mr. Mill on the Functions of Government—Grounds of Opposition to the Bill of 1844—The Right of a Nation to act in its corporate Capacity—Constitutional and practical Objections to Increase of Government Power and Patronage—False Issue raised to the Bill by its Opponents—Sir Robert Peel and Mr. Gladstone opposed to the immediate Purchase of Railways—The Management when possessed by the State—Their direct Management by Government not advisable—Their being leased out to Companies considered—The present Management, with some Changes, preferred—A general Board of Management to be formed from the Railway Boards—Plan analogous to that of our India Government—The Influence of Legislators in creating and forming Public Opinion.

" ONE of the most disputed questions, both in political science and in practical statesmanship, at this particular period, relates to the proper limits of the functions and agency of governments; but the general opinion in this country is in favour of restricting to the narrowest compass the intervention of a public authority in the business of a community, and few will dispute the more than sufficiency of these reasons to throw, in every instance, the burthen of making out a strong case, not on those who resist, but on those who recommend Government interference. *Laisser faire*, in short, should be the general practice; every departure from it, unless required by some great good, is a certain evil." *

Such are the recorded opinions of one of our most distinguished writers on political economy, and these opinions command almost universal assent. When a great good can be effected without the agency of Government, not only is there no necessity, but it is exceedingly undesirable, to have recourse

---

* Mill's "Political Economy," vol. ii. p. 541.

to such aid; on the other hand, when that object can be attained by no other means, it would be both foolish and absurd to deny that it is one of the most undisputed and important functions of Government to undertake that agency when its exercise becomes necessary to produce the desired good. In many cases, however, the good desiderated may not be unmixed with evil, and in some cases may be more than counterbalanced by it. Nor is it merely by material benefits to a people that the desirability of Government interference can be tested; reference must be had to their peculiar habits, and more especially their opinions as to the duties of Government. What would be not merely tolerated but recognized as the duty of a Government in one State, would be denounced as an intolerable attempt to interfere with the liberty of the subject in another. We have in this country a great dislike to a "paternal Government," and suffer the continuance of numberless social evils and much wrong-doing and injustice sooner than permit the interference of the strong hand of Governmental power. In some cases, however, the evils become so great that the public reluctance to permit the interference of Government is at length overcome, and such measures as those relating to factory children and women labouring in mines are allowed to pass. In Prussia it is one of the functions of Government to provide for the education of children. With us no such interference, under any circumstances, would be permitted. We consider those cases that occur, in which children are brought up in ignorance and vice, not sufficiently numerous to justify us in departing from the general law of nature, which declares, as a rule, that parents are the best judges to what extent their children should be educated.

" A second general objection," says Mr. Mill, "to Government agency is, that every increase of the functions devolving on the Government is an increase of its power, both in the form of authority, and still more in the indirect form of influence, and a third general objection rests on the principle of the division of labour. Every additional function undertaken by Government is a fresh occupation imposed on a body already overcharged with duties. The inferiority of Government agency, for example, in any of the common operations of industry or commerce, is proved by the fact that it is hardly ever able to maintain itself in equal competition with individual agency, when the individuals possess the requisite degree of industrial enterprise, and can command the necessary assemblage of means."

The views expressed by Mr. Mill in regard to the duties of Governments are those of the great bulk of Englishmen, and I have brought these opinions prominently forward that they may be duly considered in reference to the subject we are discussing; as it has been contended, they form an insurmountable obstacle to the carrying out of this project.

When Mr. Gladstone introduced his Railway Bill into Parliament the whole force of the opposition was directed not against what was in the bill under discussion, but what was assumed might at some future day be in some other bill on the same subject, viz., Government management. But, in reality, there is no more connection between the possession of railways by the State and their direct management by Government, than there is between Goodwin Sands and Tenterden Steeple. In popular estimation, however, it has been always held to mean one and the same thing, and that if railways became the property of the State they must necessarily be managed directly by the Government, with all the patronage, in the same manner as the Customs, Excise, or Post Office. On the Continent, wherever the railways belong to the State, they form a branch of the public service; and it appears, therefore, to be taken for granted in this country, that their ownership and management must necessarily be inseparable. Such not only is the common idea at present, but the early advocates of the purchase of railways by the State, including all who gave evidence before the Select Committee in 1844, assumed as a matter of course that the railways would, in the event of their being purchased by the State, come under direct Government management. This assumption we shall find altogether unfounded, and to it more than any other cause is to be attributed the neglect with which this subject has been treated.

As an abstract proposition, it cannot be questioned that the nation has a right to do anything in its corporate capacity which it is assumed can be better done by itself than by delegating that power to another. There are, however, many grave objections against Government taking the direct management of our railways, and I know of no argument that can be advanced in favour of following an opposite course. A very strong feeling is entertained in this country, both on practical and constitutional grounds, against entrusting to the management of Government officials more than can possibly be helped; a very low opinion is held of their administrative abilities, and there exists a belief that they are more skilled in the " way not to do it" than in the way "how to do it;" and, further, that having obtained their situations by patronage and not by merit, they have little to do, and do that little badly. Such is the popular opinion of Government officials : how far it may be correct it is not necessary for us to discuss. Another strong objection to making the management of railways a Government department, in the ordinary sense of that term, would be the vast increase of patronage it would give to Government; therefore, on constitutional grounds such a change would be highly objectionable. The prevailing policy is to diminish Government patronage, and that policy for some years past has been steadily adhered to ; but did neither of these objections which I have noted exist, there would be no necessity to have recourse to Government management.

Nothing could be more simple or clear than the object for which the Act of 1844 was passed. It was not for the purpose of having transferred to Government, at some future day, the possession and management of our railways, and with such transfer all the power and patronage therewith connected; but it was for the purpose of enabling the Legislature, after the expiration of twenty-one years, to take possession of the railways should the working of the present system not prove satisfactory to the nation. The attention of the Railway Committee of 1844 was drawn especially by more than one witness to four important facts, (1) the great superiority of public credit over private credit; (2) the comparatively small increase to a company's revenues from high fares and charges as compared with low fares and charges; (3) the certainty that that difference could be met by the saving effected in the decreased dividend paid to shareholders after the transfer of railways from them to the State; and (4) the great saving that would be effected in management by the amalgamation of all the companies. It was on these grounds, and quite irrespective of the authority to which the railways should be entrusted in the event of their coming into the possession of the State, that the committee recommended to Parliament the adoption of those measures that subsequently became embodied in the celebrated Act of 1844.

The reasons why Government did not at that time recommend the immediate purchase of the railways were clearly stated, both by Sir Robert Peel and Mr. Gladstone; they believed it possible that the necessity for such a step being taken might never arise, and that the country might possess all the benefits that railway communication could confer on it under the present system, but that, at all events, we had not then gained a sufficient experience in the working of railways, to be able to form a perfect judgment as to the expediency of such an important change, and that it was desirable to wait for a long term of years, when our network of railways would be nearly complete, and then consider its necessity when the matter should be fully ripe for discussion.

If it had so happened that the bulk of our great companies had found it to be to their interest to pursue the same policy as a few of our second and third class companies have done, viz., to carry passengers at what are considered very low fares, there would not at the present time be any occasion for legislative interference; but, unfortunately for the public, it has turned out otherwise. As we have seen, there are but two companies whose directors find it to be their interest to make so low a charge as a minute fraction more than a halfpenny per mile for first-class passengers, and the other classes in proportion, and although the companies in question pay six per cent. to their proprietors, the great bulk of our companies exercise a sound commercial policy in charging four or five times the amount of these fares to the public, and gain by so doing. The Act of 1844 was intended to provide against a contingency of this nature, by supplying a fund for indemnifying in another form the State from the loss that might be incurred by the pursuance of any line of policy that the Legislature of the time might think fit to determine on. The Act had no reference or provisions as to the future management of railways; there was left a *tabula rasa*, on which should be inscribed at a distant day the law by which their management should be regulated.

We have now to consider the different modes of administration that might be adopted if the railways were in the possession of the State. That which would most approximate to the present system, and would thereby necessitate the least change, would, *per se*, if in every other respect satisfactory, be the most desirable. The traffic of the country might still be managed by independent companies. It would, in many respects, be more in accordance with the public ideas of good management to intrust it exclusively to companies, leaving only to Government the power to enforce the agreements between them and the State. We shall therefore consider—

1. *The Contract System.*—That could be carried out by dividing the country into convenient districts, and a general tariff for passengers and goods traffic having been settled by the Legislature, leaving the working of the lines to companies

on the competitive principle. These companies would derive their revenue either from a certain percentage on the gross receipts, or a fixed sum per train mile, as might be agreed on. Many other ways for the management of our railways on the same principle might be suggested; they could be leased out to those companies that would offer the best terms, at certain fixed rentals. It is unnecessary to go into detail as to the various plans by which the railways could be managed on this system; the best would probably be, for the companies to find the rolling stock, and be obliged to keep the works in a state of thorough repair. It must, however, be remembered that when a third party comes between the Government and the public with secured rights and privileges, the railway companies would still be as they are now, in a great measure, free from legislative and popular control. One great object, however, would be attained of having a low and uniform scale of fares and charges throughout the kingdom, and many, no doubt, would be inclined to consider that if the Legislature secured that boon for the public, nothing further would be required, and the railways might be delivered over to a new class of companies under another system.

2. Government Management.—It is not necessary to discuss this proposition at any length. There is no class in the country to whom it would be acceptable, or who could be induced to assent to such a proposition. There is a belief in this country that Government signally fails in the management of public works entrusted to its hands; whether that be the case or not it is unnecessary to discuss, but there is no disposition on the part of the public to extend, in that respect, its sphere of operations. In a political point of view the objections would be insuperable; the national policy at the present time is directed by means of the competitive system to diminish Government patronage, but by giving to Government the direct management of the railways, its patronage would be increased to an enormous amount.

It now seems strange that twenty years ago, when the desirability of the purchase, by the State, of the railways was discussed in the House of Commons, the universal assumption was, that the direct management of railways by Government would be the necessary consequence of their purchase. This error was shared alike by the nation, the Legislature, the Government, and every witness before the committee who advocated the purchase of the railways by the State, nor was it till many years after that this fallacy was entirely exploded. It might just as well have been contended that a wealthy man should not purchase an estate because he might not know how to sow turnips, or embark his capital in railway shares because he could not lay out a railway or construct a locomotive. To carry out an undertaking successfully requires both capital and good management, and in every large industrial undertaking these wants are supplied by different parties; one contributes the capital and the other undertakes the management. So in regard to the State; it may, for special reasons, invest its capital in an industrial undertaking, or, what comes to the same thing, give its guarantee for the payment of a certain specified interest on a capital not its own, embarked in such an undertaking, reserving to itself the right of entrusting its management to those whom it may consider best qualified to perform the task. For many reasons Government is not the best qualified for such an undertaking; and therefore its services in this respect are never likely to be required.

3. Government Control.—This differs as much from Government management, as the shareholders in a company taking the management of its affairs into their own hands, instead of entrusting them to a board of directors, and reserving to themselves a general control over its affairs at their half-yearly meetings. Now, it must be borne in mind that without a centralized as well as a national system of management, properly conducted by those best qualified to carry out such a system, our traffic can neither be well managed nor brought under the

immediate control of the Legislature. We cannot have economy, regularity, and uniformity, if the railways should be once more in the hands of two or three score of independent companies, who would have no object in view but to make—as the old companies had done before them—as much money as they could. It is true, if the railways were leased to the companies they would not be able to alter the tariff agreed on, but the new companies would have the same motives then as the old ones have now, to use every means to force the lower-class passengers into better-class carriages; they would also have the same motives then as now, to practise in their management a cheese-paring economy, in all cases destructive of the comfort and in many cases incompatible with the safety of the public. If our present system were so far modified as to deprive our directors and managers of all motives to undue economy, and to discourage all parsimonious savings that deprive the public of what they are fairly entitled to, our railways would be the best managed in the world.

It is universally admitted, even by those who are most opposed to Government management, that a stringent Government control under our present system in the management of our railways is necessary; and, on the other hand, it will, I think, be generally admitted, that the companies' management, taken on the whole, is far superior to what we might expect if our railways were handed over to the Board of Trade, or any other class of inexperienced Government officials. The directors and managers of our companies are in general men of great experience, some of remarkable ability, and nearly all possess a thorough practical knowledge of the most economical and effectual manner of conducting railway traffic. What is wanted is not a change of men, but a change of system, to eliminate its evil qualities and conserve its good, and to confide the practical working of the new system to those who were the most distinguished in the management of the old.

The following plan appears to me to be one of the best, under the assumed circumstances, that could be adopted: Twenty-four gentlemen, approved of by Government and selected from and by the principal railway boards throughout the kingdom, such salary being given as should secure the services of the most competent, should form the general board of management of all the railways in Great Britain, to be presided over by a president and two vice-presidents appointed by the Crown, the office of one of the latter officials to be permanent, that of the other and of the president to change with the Ministry. The present railway boards should be entrusted to elect members of their own boards or principal officers, subject to the approval of the Crown, and thus a General Board would be formed well acquainted with the local traffic in all parts of the kingdom. The following detailed arrangement will more clearly define the manner in which the management I have suggested should be carried out :—

		Members from their own body, or from their principal officers.
The London and North-Western board	to elect	3
„ Great Western	„	2
„ Midland	„	2
„ North-Eastern	„	2
„ Lancashire and Yorkshire	„	2
„ Great Eastern	„	2
„ Great Northern	„	2
„ Bristol and Exeter	„	1
„ London and Brighton	„	1
„ South-Eastern	„	1
„ South-Western	„	1
„ Manchester, Sheffield, and Lincoln	„	1
„ Caledonian	„	1
„ North British	„	1
„ Glasgow and South-Western	„	1
„ Edinburgh and Glasgow	„	1
		24

As Ireland is entirely separated from England, so there should be necessarily a separate administration, subject, however, to the head of the English administration.

		Members from their own body, or from their principal officers.	
The Great Southern and Western	.	to elect	2
„ Midland Great Western .	.	„	2
„ Dublin, Wicklow, and Wexford	.	„	1
„ Belfast and Northern Counties	.	„	1
„ Ulster	.	„	1
„ Dublin and Belfast Junction .	.	„	1
„ Dublin and Drogheda .	.	„	1
„ Waterford and Limerick .	.	„	1
„ Irish North Western .	.	„	1
„ Belfast and Co. Down .	.	„	1
			12

The two establishments, however separate, could work together on a uniform system.

The above selection might be said to fairly represent all parts of the kingdom, and bring together those best qualified, both by general and local knowledge, either as directors or managers of railways, to assist in carrying out the full development of the traffic throughout the kingdom. As the Government would be responsible to the Legislature for the manner in which the carrying trade of the country would be conducted, as a matter of course the president of the board should, in all matters that might come under discussion, decide what was to be done.

All railway officials to retain their situations unless their services should not be required, and when those services should be dispensed with to receive compensation.

This plan would meet the objections of those who are not opposed to a small increase in Government patronage, but who have no faith in Government management, and would consider it unjust to any of those who are now engaged on our railways, that they should be sufferers in consequence of any change.

Two Boards thus formed of the best materials, the *élite* of the directors and managers of our principal railways in the United Kingdom, presided over by a cabinet minister who would be responsible to the Legislature for the performance of his duty, and that duty to consist in fully developing the traffic of the country by adopting the best means advised by those who were most competent to do so, should, if the principle be conceded of Government control, form an executive that ought in every respect to give satisfaction to the country. Contrast such an administration as that with what we have at present—seventy-two different boards of directors, each board at variance with its neighbour, or with others combining against the public, guided by no rule except that of expediency, and governed by no principle except that of making money by any means not absolutely forbidden by law. This mock system of free-trade, but real monopoly, is suffered to lord it over the trade and commerce of this country, forming an artificial barrier to obstruct every class of the community in the otherwise free intercourse that would exist between the most distant parts of the kingdom.

4. *The Management entirely independent of Government.*— There can be no doubt there exists a strong feeling in this country against any increase, direct or indirect, of the power and patronage of the Crown, and it would be impossible to deny that both, to some extent, would be increased by any measure that would place the management of the railways, under whatever restrictions, in the hands of Government. The opposition that the bill of 1844 encountered was, as we have seen, owing to the belief, on the part of the minority, that the purchase of the railways by the State necessarily involved Government management; nor was this proposition disputed; and it was contended then, as it would be now, that such a measure would be opposed to the spirit of the constitution, for which any material advantage the country might derive from reduced fares and charges, would afford no adequate compensation.

We are not at all inclined, as a people, to favour the principle of centralization in connection with Government management. We believe that it has a tendency to discourage individual exertion, to check private enterprise, to supersede local authorities in the management of their own affairs, and to give a power and influence to Government which might be turned to very bad account. Even supposing that the patronage of the Crown would be confined to a few of the principal appointments, many would assert that the evil of such appointments would not be counterbalanced by any benefit that would be derived from having the whole administration under the direct responsibility of the Government. Some would further be induced to fear that it would be only getting in the thin end of the wedge, and that the patronage which, in the first instance, was confined to the nomination of the principal appointments only, might, in the course of time, be extended to all offices in the administration.

In some respects the management of our railways could be more efficiently carried on by having it entirely independent of the Government. In the Post Office, however well qualified the Postmaster-General may be to perform his duty, he is, by a change of Ministry, removed from office, and another appointed in his place, entirely from political influence, who may be, and generally is, entirely ignorant of the duties of his office, and may possess no single qualification necessary for the performance of its duties. Such a system is deemed by some highly objectionable in the management of a great mercantile establishment such as our Post Office, and is not applied to other branches of the revenue, such as the Customs and Excise; the affairs of these two departments, the returns from which amount to more than ten times those of the Post Office, are managed by boards permanently appointed, chairman and deputy chairman included. The management of the Customs and the Excise has no connection whatever with politics. Many would prefer placing our railways under a Board of Commissioners selected by the directors themselves from their own respective directorates, subject to the approval of the Crown and the Legislature. In such case the management of the railways would be assimilated to that of our Customs and Excise, having not only a permanent Board of Commissioners, but also a permanent chairman, and vice-chairman, who would be quite independent of the Ministry or of ministerial changes. The general tariff would of course be settled by the Legislature, and the duty of the Board of Commissioners would be purely administrative, having merely to carry out what the law had enacted for their guidance. These Commissioners would be as independent and as free from Government control or influence as are the present directors of the companies. They would have no temptations or inducements to strain the law, either in favour of or against the public. They would be directly responsible to the Legislature for the manner in which they discharged their duties, and if, on the one hand, the Government exercised no patronage, they would, on the other, be more free than they are at present from responsibility. The situation of chairman and deputy chairman of the board would, no doubt, be offices of great trust, but there are at the present time more than two hundred members of the Legislature connected with railways, many of whom have not only held high office in the State, but are also thoroughly conversant with the management of railways. The names of at least a dozen noblemen and gentlemen will suggest themselves to any one acquainted with railway matters, the permanent appointment of any of whom would be a guarantee to the Legislature, that the administration of railway affairs would be thoroughly satisfactory to the country.

Looking, then, at the management of our railways from this point of view, and excluding entirely the political element, the whole of the Government scheme would amount to nothing more than an extension of the amalgamation principle, with the national credit pledged to the shareholders for an annual payment of many millions less than what they now receive in dividends. The shareholders would have the security of Government for payment in consideration of the benefit to be derived from having a low and uniform tariff for passengers and goods established throughout the country, and a reduction made in the present fares and charges from twenty to eighty per cent., according to the necessity of each case. No one could question, *per se*, the exceeding desirability of such a change. That the great arteries of communication throughout the country should be really opened up to the public; that the artisan, for instance, who now pays from London to Liverpool and back again, to the London and North-Western, the Great Northern, or the Great Western, one day 1*l*. 13*s*. 6*d*., and another day 12*s*. 6*d*., as it may suit their whim, convenience, or interest, should have that charge permanently reduced to six shillings and threepence, and the fares for the other classes reduced according to the circumstances of the case; and on the same principle, a corresponding reduction in the carriage of minerals, general merchandise, parcels, &c.

What necessity would there, then, exist for any special interference, or control, on the part of the executive, if all our railways were under one general management, any more than there is with the Board of Customs or Excise? In the London and North-Western Company, as we have seen, are comprised about thirty original companies at one time — all independent lines; it is now proposed to amalgamate the Lancashire and Yorkshire with this great company. The united receipts of the two companies exceeded the aggregate sum received from all the railways in the kingdom, when the project was first mooted of Government purchase, twenty years ago.

It might, perhaps, be objected that Government would refuse its support to any project to which the national credit would be pledged, without having the patronage and control that might fairly be supposed, in such case, to belong to it. But, so far from this being the case, I believe it will be found that it is this patronage question, and the supposed necessity of its exercise on the part of the Crown, which has, up to the present time, paralyzed the action of Government, and deprived the country of the full advantage that would otherwise be derived from the possession of the railways by the State.

I have noticed all these plans by which the railways could be managed, in order to show that there is no necessity that the railway department should be a branch of Government, in the sense in which that term is generally understood. It will be for the Legislature—when the proper time arrives—to fashion and mould the management of our railways to whatever it may deem most consistent with the public welfare. Probably the third plan I have sketched out would be found most in harmony with constitutional government.

One of the most important advantages to the public from the possession of the railways by the State would arise from the great saving that would be effected in their management under one general consolidated system, more especially when those who had the management of affairs were intimately acquainted with the local peculiarities of each line. Captain Laws, in his examination before the committee, laid great stress on this point, and this gentleman's opinion as to the great saving that would be effected by the amalgamation of all the railways was especially referred to by Mr. Gladstone in introducing the bill of 1844: "Captain Laws is of opinion," said Mr. Gladstone, "that if railways were placed under the general control of Government a saving of twenty-five per cent. would be effected to the public. Now this is material to consider. In the present state of the question, the elements which enter into it are rude and unformed, and the evidence, I admit, is not complete." That was in 1844. Whether or not the experience of twenty additional years in the working of our railways has, in Mr. Gladstone's mind, completed the evidence and enabled him to arrive at a definite opinion on the subject, I am unable to say.

We are opposed in this country to what is generally termed "centralization," and we have seen with what feelings of jealousy all amalgamations, or attempts to amalgamate, on the part of the great companies, are regarded by the country and the Legislature. In the last session of Parliament, we had a notable instance of this feeling—the refusal of the Legislature to sanction the amalgamation of some of the great Scotch railways, although the public would have had secured to them an immediate reduction in charges of thirty per cent.; but the parties most interested petitioned against the amalgamation, from a vague fear of what the consequences might be if the companies should have in the district the uncontrolled monopoly of conveyance, and the latter naturally refuse, without the amalgamation, to make the reduction. What a commentary this incident is in itself on our whole system! The public and the Legislature refuse to trust the companies with the power they require, and the companies naturally decline to make the reduction in charges without being allowed to amalgamate; and all parties are thus, through mutual distrust, deprived of the advantages they would otherwise possess. But notwithstanding the jealousy both of people and Legislature, the natural course of events has brought about many of these amalgamations, which in many cases have been equally beneficial to the public and to the companies. Each extension of the amalgamation system is a forward step in the progress of centralization, proceeding onward, it is to be hoped, till all the railways in the kingdom shall be comprised under one system of management. In order to form an opinion as to the manner in which amalgamation affects the public, let us look at the working of one company—the London and North-Western. This company, as everybody knows, is formed by the amalgamation of the London and Birmingham, the Grand Junction, the Liverpool and Manchester, and added to these are some five-and-twenty smaller companies; all these railways are now united under one proprietary management and central authority. How, then, would the country approve of this union being dissolved, and each of the thirty component parts of which it is formed resuming its original position as an independent company, each having its own fares, charges, and regulations, and passengers paying their fares and changing their carriages at every railway? It is only by picturing to ourselves the result of a retrograde movement, one towards decentralizing our railways, and making each independent of its neighbour, that we can form a correct estimate of the relative character of the two systems. All the companies find it necessary to carry out among themselves, so far as the law permits, a modified system of centralization; but without legislative sanction they can do little more than make arrangements for their passengers being conveyed over several lines in the same carriage, without the inconvenience of having to divide the payment of their fares among the several companies over whose lines they must pass. So far as regards the internal working of each company, the directors can make no arrangements for reducing their expenditure through the process of amalgamation, without the direct sanction of the Legislature.

It must therefore be obvious, that the more completely the amalgamation or centralization of our railways is effected, the expenditure in connection with them will be so much less, and the accommodation to the public may be made so much the greater; but, on the other hand, the more these amalgamations are allowed to extend, so also is increased the power of the companies to whom such extension is permitted, and the security of their monopoly the more confirmed; hence the jealousy with which these amalgamations are viewed, both by the country and the Legislature, and the unwillingness on the part of the latter, unless a very strong case is made out, to permit their being carried into effect.

The case would be altogether different if the railways were in the hands of the State, and, as a matter of course, under the immediate control of the Legislature. At one time in the history of this country it would have been impossible to effect such a change in our commercial policy as that provided for by the Act of 1844, but the duties of a Government have of late years been viewed in a very different light by the English people from what they were at a former period. But a few years since comparatively our Eastern Empire was managed by a great joint-stock company, subject to a "Board of Control." There was a divided authority, and consequently a divided responsibility; the merchant princes of Leadenhall Street did not at all times bow to the behests of their rulers in Cannon Row, and went even so far in some cases as to assert their independence of the wishes of their liege lords, and act in direct opposition to their views. At an eventful crisis in Eastern affairs the common sense of this country decided that, in a matter of such vast importance as the government of our Indian Empire, a divided responsibility was opposed to all sound policy, and that a joint-stock company, however intelligent and honourable its directors might be, was placed in a false position when allowed to share in the management of a great empire. The East India Company was in consequence dissolved, and the power held by it transferred to the British Government, and the patronage to the British nation. The direct management of Indian affairs was entrusted to a high officer of State, responsible, of course, to the Legislature for the way in which those affairs were conducted, and having for his advisers the *élite* of the extinct Board of Directors.

One of the changes I have suggested in the management of our railways, in the event of their being made national property, is strictly analogous to the scheme of government adopted by the Legislature in regard to our East India possessions. How far the analogy can be carried out in other respects between the two cases I am not prepared to say. Many, however, may be inclined to think that a matter involving the annual payment of the British people to the amount of THIRTY-FIVE MILLIONS sterling is not less worthy of attention than the government of a distant empire, the interests of which, however important they may be, only affect us indirectly.

The term of probation granted to the present system will

expire in 1865 ; and, in the ordinary course of events, a committee, I presume, will be appointed in the approaching session of Parliament to investigate the respective merits and demerits of the two systems, and turn to practical account the long experience we have had in the working of our railways.

Of the thirteen members of the House of Commons who in 1844 formed the General Committee on Railways, and on whose recommendation the Act was passed, there remain only two in the present House, viz., Mr. Gladstone and Mr. Horsman. That Mr. Gladstone contemplated the probability of the provisional clauses of the Act, viz., the right of purchase on the part of the State, being one day brought into operation, may be gathered from his own statement, in which he expressly declared that those clauses of the bill that authorized, under certain conditions, the purchase of railways by the Government, were the essential parts of the bill; and, notwithstanding the strong opposition which these clauses encountered, the second reading was carried by a majority of nearly two to one. Whether or not that bill is to become a dead letter, will most probably be determined during the present year.

Public opinion in this, as in every other country, is of very slow growth, and necessarily the more slow, if it runs counter to the prejudices and feelings of the people. Our commercial policy is to leave to public companies the management of our great industrial works, and however much the nation was dissatisfied with the railway companies in 1844, there was no disposition on its part to abolish the system, or adopt the organic change shadowed forth in the Government bill. It was considered by those at that time in power that, if eventually it should be found necessary to reconstruct our railway system, it would require twenty years to prepare the public for so great a change. It is not through the intervention, in the first instance, of those who are the most deeply interested in great and beneficial changes in our national policy, that such changes are generally brought about. In this, as in so many other cases, the demands of public opinion lag immeasurably behind the requirements of reason and good sense. The measures, for instance, taken for the abolition of the corn laws, so far from originating with the working class—that class most interested in their abolition—met for a considerable time with their most active opposition; had it therefore depended on the people, in the conventional sense in which that term is used, so far from the repeal of the corn laws having been carried triumphantly through Parliament, the bill would never have been even introduced.

In the discussion of the Railway Bill in 1844, there was no point touched on but the inefficiency of Government management, it being assumed throughout as a matter of course that the possession of the railways by the State necessarily implied their management by Government. That fallacy, it is to be hoped, is now abandoned, but at that time it had the effect of diverting men's minds from the subject under consideration. All the great economic truths involved in the discussion of the question were entirely ignored by the opponents of the bill; the evidence of the most eminent and experienced men of the railway world was never once referred to, and the important statistics of the Board of Trade bearing on the subject were never noticed; all these matters were passed by for the purpose of attacking the principle supposed to be involved in the bill, viz., a great increase of power and patronage to Government.

It must be remembered that at this time the subject had been but little considered in this country; our statistical information was mainly derived from foreign sources, and all the projectors who then proposed the purchase of railways by the State admitted, as a necessary consequence, that their direct management must be given to Government, notwithstanding its manifest unfitness for such a task, and the great increase of power and patronage it would thereby acquire. The charge, therefore, which ministers had then to contend with was, that under pretext of passing a useful practical measure, they were introducing a bill founded on unconstitutional principles, that should therefore be strenuously opposed.

But the expediency of carrying this Act into effect will be discussed under very different circumstances in 1865 from those in 1844.

A great deal of distress and suffering has of late years been inflicted on the lower classes of the metropolis by the extensive displacement consequent on the extended introduction of railways into London, and the recent mania for still further extension at one time threatened to increase the evil to an alarming extent. Railway companies naturally select those districts for their lines where property is the least valuable, and, consequently, those who are the most interested in it have the fewest rights to maintain, and, what in such matters is of great importance, where they are least capable of maintaining them. It is in the homes of the poorest classes that the companies attain both these objects; the great bulk of the poorer class of London, artisans and all grades from that position downward, are weekly tenants, all their "rights" are confined to a week's notice from their landlords, and at the expiration of that brief notice " they have the world before them where to choose." Their homes are broken up, and, in the great majority of cases, they are obliged to seek their dwellings in some other suburb, a considerable distance from where they follow their daily avocations; the law gives them no redress from the companies, who have only to arrange their terms with their landlords. Now, one would naturally suppose that a grievance of this sort, that may be said literally to come home to the poorest classes, would have excited a strong feeling among the public generally, and the working classes particularly, as being especially affected by these railway extensions into the metropolis. We might suppose that to avert this threatened invasion, or to indemnify them from its results, a regular organized agitation would have been got up, and that those who put themselves forward, *par excellence*, as the exclusive defenders of the rights and privileges of the poor, and are well skilled in the various ways that popular feeling is brought to bear on every grievance, would have done something on an occasion like the present. The public, however, allowed matters to take their course, and nothing was done outside the walls of Parliament. To the committee, presided over by Lord Stanley, was entrusted the important task of selecting those lines that would afford the greatest accommodation to the metropolis. This task occupied the committee to near the close of the session, and the selection of lines the committee has made appears to have given general satisfaction.

One great advantage connected with the discussion of any proposed reform in our railway system is the entire absence of all party or political feeling in reference thereto. One of the most zealous supporters of the Government bill of 1844 was Mr. Labouchere, who had been President of the Board of Trade in the former administration, and at the present time, the complaint of Lord Derby against the Government is not that they have interfered too much, but that they have not taken the initiative in those measures that might be considered necessary for the better management of our railways.

To our legislators in their individual capacity we are indebted, in no small degree, for these great reforms, constitutional and commercial, that in the course of the last thirty or forty years have brought about such a wonderful change in the state of this country. It would be impossible to refer to any great measure of reform, without identifying it with one or more members of Parliament, to whose unwearied exertions—it may have been for many years—we are indebted for the creation and formation of that public opinion through which those measures became ultimately the law of the land. To overcome the *vis inertiæ* of mankind has been in all ages and countries a matter of the greatest difficulty, and it is only when the attempt to do so proceeds from an influential quarter that there is any likelihood of its being successful.

Every word spoken by a man of eminence, either in Parliament or elsewhere, on public occasions, is noted down and circulated throughout the length and breadth of the land. All newspapers, without distinction of party, give currency to his opinions, expressed in his own words; those opinions are made the subject of comment, favourable or otherwise, as the case may be, and thus commences the growth of what we call PUBLIC OPINION. So, in regard to railway reform, it has scarcely arrived at the first stage of existence. The Government Bill, as yet, is a dead letter, but at some future day it may become a living principle; now it is a mere idea, but in the course of time that idea may develop itself into a great plan, recognized by the nation, adopted by the Legislature, and working for the benefit of the whole community through all classes of society.

CHAPTER IV.

Classification of the Groundwork of Railway Reform—The two main Grounds—Different Charges in Fares on the London and Blackwall Railway—The last Change and its Results—The Glasgow and Greenock Line—The slight Difference in the Results between high and low Fares—Evidence before the Committee of 1844 on the Subject—Railways into London—Displacement of the Poor—Cheap Morning and Evening Trains—The Earl of Derby's Resolution in the House of Lords the most important since the Introduction of Parliamentary Trains—The Effect of Government Purchase on the Money Market—*Resumé.*

THE desirability of carrying into full effect the Railway Act of 1844 rests, as we have seen, on the following distinct grounds :—

1st. In a financial point of view, it makes but comparatively little difference to a company whether, within certain limits, its fares and charges be very high or very low; these limits being three farthings per mile on the one hand, and threepence halfpenny per mile on the other for first-class passengers, and the other two classes in proportion.

2nd. As a general rule, the directors of companies find that what are called moderate charges, avoiding either extreme, are the most profitable; and twopence farthing per mile for first-class passengers, and the other classes in proportion, may be taken as the average fares on our railways, such fares being *three times* greater than those charged on the cheap lines; the latter, however, from exceptional causes, paying as high dividends as those lines on which high fares are charged.

3rd. The purchase of railways by the State does not necessarily involve either Government management or patronage; it may be a matter for discussion whether it would be desirable to have the head of the department a minister of the Crown, removable on any change of administration, or have the appointment permanent, as that of Chairman of the Board of Customs or Excise. The question of patronage would not in any case extend beyond a few appointments, and could very well be dispensed with. If railways become the property of the State, no essential change in the present management might be necessary, and such change should be confined to those measures necessary to bring the management under the effective and immediate control of the Legislature.

4th. It is a matter of the greatest national importance that a large reduction should be made in our railway fares and charges, the amount paid last year exceeding *thirty-one millions sterling*, with an annual increase of more than two millions; inasmuch as a first-class passenger can be conveyed *sixteen miles for a penny*, in a moderately loaded train and a ton of goods or minerals can be conveyed *eight miles for a penny*, the present charges are utterly disproportioned to the cost of conveyance; and so far from any likelihood existing of their being reduced, the directors are rather disposed to raise them, and a considerable rise has taken place on some of the great lines within the last few months.

5th. Inasmuch as the credit of the State is superior to that of private credit in the ratio of more than four to three, that credit ought to be made available, as contemplated by the Act of 1844, for effecting an arrangement with the shareholders, and reducing the fares and charges by at least two-thirds of their present amount.

6th. Independently of the abstract right of the Legislature to deal with all property in the kingdom, there exists on the part of the shareholders a desire to have a well-secured fixed interest for their invested capital in preference to uncertain and fluctuating dividends.

7th. There would be a great saving effected by having all the railways in the kingdom under one consolidated management, and a great benefit conferred on the public by the adoption of a low and uniform tariff for passengers and goods, &c.

The two main propositions of the foregoing ones are the 1st and 4th. On these two, in fact, the Government bill is based; and unless they are fully maintained by incontrovertible evidence, the whole scheme falls to the ground. It is necessary, therefore, to go into the evidence bearing on these two points in somewhat greater detail than we have yet done. It is to be hoped that the discussion of this national question will take a much wider range the next time it comes under the consideration of the House of Commons than it did on the last, and that all the valuable materials we now possess for investigating the merits of the two systems in all their details will be turned to good account.

At the present time there are few of those extreme fluctuations in the range of railway fares that were so common before the experience of directors and managers enabled them to settle at once the best-paying tariff. Our statistical information, therefore, on that point is principally derived from the management of railways when the subject was less understood than it is at present; there are, however, some exceptions.

The fares on the London and Blackwall line, four miles in length, were, at its opening—for first class, $4d.$; second, $3d.$ The second class was raised, some time after, to $4d.$, and the first to $6d.$ A further rise took place in September, 1841. The first class was raised to $8d.$, and the second class to $6d.$, and the same fares between all the intermediate stations, although the distance between some of the stations little exceeds half a mile. This tariff lasted only for two months, when the fares were reduced between the intermediate stations to the former rates of $6d.$ and $4d.$ Another change took place in the following March, when the fares between Blackwall and London were reduced to 6d. and 4d., and between the intermediate stations to 4d. and 3d.

The directors, in their report to their shareholders, at their half-yearly meeting held in February, 1843, thus notice the result of raising the fares in the previous year:—

"The fares of the railways were raised on the 12th of September; and the directors were much mortified to find that the result showed a very considerable diminution, not only of the numbers carried, but of the money received. The increase during the previous summer had not been inconsiderable; and in the eight weeks prior to the 12th of September, which offered the fairest means of comparison with the former year, as they go back to the opening of the Fenchurch Station on the 2nd September, 1841, the receipts show an increase of about 16 per cent. over those of the previous year; whereas those of the eight weeks following the 12th of September show a diminution of 41 per cent. in the number of passengers, and 17 per cent. in the revenue, as compared with the eight corresponding weeks."

It formed no part of the business of the directors to refer to the loss inflicted on the public by raising the fares during these two months; but the evil, in a commercial point of view, so far as regarded the interests of the company, worked its own cure, and the fares were reduced to what was considered the highest paying point. It will be seen that the directors of that day far exceeded anything that ever had been attempted as regards high fares. The directors appeared to think that all they had to do to increase the revenue of the company was to increase the fares; but when certain limits are exceeded, they soon tell their tale.

Passing over twenty years, let us now consider the last change the directors made in the fares and its results. In July, 1863, they reduced the intermediate fares on the line between *thirty and forty per cent.;* there was an enormous increase in the number of passengers, and without any increase in the expenditure; but the increase in the company's receipts for the half-year amounted only to 120*l.* The chairman stated at the half-yearly meeting, held in February, that, however profitable the reduction in fares might be to the public, the company derived no benefit from the change, but intimated that the experiment would be tried for some time longer. On looking to the company's receipts as published in the papers, for the six months ending the 30th of June, under the low-fare system, we find they amount to 46,561*l*., as compared with 45,817*l*. for the corresponding half-year under the high-fare system. This, in itself, is a mere trifle, not even affecting the dividend; and the directors will probably think themselves justified in continuing the reduction beyond the expiration of the current half-year, and not raising the fares 50 per cent.

Now here is a subject for statesmen to ponder, and we could not choose an illustration more in point of the working of the present system. The London and Blackwall Railway was constructed for the accommodation of the poorest and most densely populated district of the metropolis; the fares are moderate, three halfpence and a penny per mile, for the two classes of passengers; but considering the poverty of the district through which the railway runs, it is pretty certain, that if the fares for the whole distance, four miles, were reduced to twopence and one penny respectively for the two, they might pay nearly, although possibly not quite, as well as the present fares. The directors, no doubt, would be glad if they could accommodate the public by further reducing their fares to the level of their neighbour, the North London, if they could do so with justice to their shareholders; but instead of doing so, they may eventually feel themselves obliged to return to the old fares; it just turns on the chance of their taking a few hundred pounds less in the course of the year. The number of passengers conveyed in each train on the London and Blackwall, according to the last returns, was ninety-one; and by the North London, one hundred and fifty-five.

There were conveyed on the London and Blackwall Railway

last year, upwards of TEN MILLION passengers; yet in this densely populated district, this teeming hive of industry, where time may almost literally be said to be money, probably three times that number were obliged to travel on foot, who would have been able to pay a penny for their fare, and could have been carried at a mere nominal increase in the expense, as the trains are running comparatively empty.

One more instance. The length of the Glasgow and Greenock line is twenty-two and a half miles. There was an active competition carried on for some time between the railway company and the owners of steam-boats on the Clyde; the third-class fare by the railway, which had formerly been a shilling for the entire distance, was reduced to sixpence, and the opposition was carried on for two years; there was, of course, an enormous increase in the number of passengers, but an arrangement having been come to between the contending parties, the railway company returned to their original fares; the difference in the company's receipts, after the change, was rather in their favour, but it amounted only to *one shilling* per cent. per annum increase on their dividend.

To those who would wish to go into this branch of the subject at greater length, I would refer to the evidence laid in a tabular form before the Select Committee of 1844, in which are noted down the several variations in the fares on a number of railways, and their financial results; and it will there be found, that the most extreme case, either of raising or lowering the fares, did not make a greater difference to the shareholders than *twelve shillings* per cent. per annum. The loss to the shareholders of the Edinburgh and Glasgow Companies, which I have noticed in a previous chapter, was one per cent. per annum, in consequence of their great reduction in fares, but this took place only ten years since.

The Earl of Derby's resolution passed in the House of Lords, in the last session of Parliament, that railway companies entering the metropolis "should provide a cheap transit for the labouring classes to and from their labour by a morning and evening train," is the most important measure for the working classes that has been adopted by either House in reference to railway travelling since the passing of the Act establishing Parliamentary trains. What at one time threatened to be a serious calamity, their displacement from their homes, may be converted into the means of effecting a great and beneficial change in their habits of life, giving them a pure atmosphere for one foul and fœtid, in which they hitherto have been obliged to live when not actually engaged in their daily labour. Such a change cannot be effected without being productive of the greatest benefit to their social and moral condition.

Objection has been taken to the interference of Lord Derby, on the grounds of its being "injudicious and inoperative;" that as some of the companies have offered to do voluntarily what he proposes to secure by Act of Parliament, therefore the Act is unnecessary, "Competition," says the same authority, "can and will effect more for the public than all the Acts of Parliament in the Statute-book." It is curious to observe how the advocates of the railway interest deal with the vexed subject of "competition;" if it is proposed to make a new line, that may affect the interests of another company, nothing in that case can be made more plain, than that competition in regard to railways is totally useless, that the two companies will be sure to "unite, and so far from the public deriving any advantage from increased railway facilities for travelling, the companies will make the public pay all the unnecessary expenditure they are put to." When the public acknowledge the truth of these representations, and endeavour, to some little extent, to protect themselves by legal enactments, they are then told, in high-sounding phrases, that these do more harm than good, and the public would be better served by leaving the remedy to competition. "Means can always be found," says this writer, "of evading or nullifying public statutes." Not always, nor indeed ever where there is a large class interested in taking care that they should not be evaded; take the case most in point, Parliamentary trains—how could the companies nullify or evade the Act by which they are obliged to run them? It would be unfair to assume that they have any wish to evade the law, but it must be remembered, an Act of Parliament called this class of trains into existence, that they never would have been instituted but on compulsion, or by express agreement; and if the law compelling the companies to maintain these trains were abolished, they would at once altogether cease. The Great Western's Parliamentary train leaves London for the West of England, at 6 A.M.; and the fare to Exeter, for instance, is 14s. 3½d.; but if a traveller is unable to reach the station in time for that train, he must pay 1l. 5s. by any other train during the day. If, on the Great Northern line, a traveller miss the morning train going to York, by which he would pay 15s. 10½d., by any other train during the day he would have to pay 1l. 6s. 6d. On the Great Eastern to Norwich, the fare by the Parliamentary train is 9s. 5½d.; but by any of the ordinary third-class carriages, the fare is 14s. 3d. On the great railways, the utmost farthing the law allows is charged, nor is any additional accommodation given to what the law compels; in all this, there is no fair matter of complaint against the companies. It is quite sufficient that they obey the law; but it must be clearly understood, that were it not that the law compels the maintenance of these Parliamentary trains, the companies would immediately give them up. This will be evident, if we consider the management of the railway companies in reference to them. It must be remembered, that no small proportion of the travellers in Parliamentary trains are women and children, and to find their way in winter, at an early hour, to stations at the extremities of the metropolis, when there are no public conveyances in the streets, is very far from sufficiently meeting the wants of the working classes. The companies say with truth, that unless the hours of departure were made as inconvenient as they well can be the Parliamentary trains would be made use of by those for whom they never were intended; the policy of the London and North-Western Company is, however, an exception in this respect, to that of most other companies, as they despatch their Parliamentary trains at reasonable hours during the day.

It is impossible to over-estimate the importance of the movement made by Lord Derby in reference to the resolution passed by the Lords at his instance, rendering it compulsory on railway companies to convey passengers between the city and where they may reside in the vicinity, morning and evening, for a penny each way without reference to distance. It is to be hoped that Lord Derby intends, as Mr. Gladstone did twenty years ago, to invite the old companies to join in the movement for giving greater facility for railway travelling to the working classes. The movement cannot stop there. If one person travel on a railway paying a farthing per mile, his neighbour, who does not happen to belong to the privileged class, will not long submit to paying perhaps five or six times that fare, travelling by the same train and in the same class. The evil will in time, to some extent, work its own cure, but that is no reason why it should be unnecessarily continued.

The other subject to which I have referred as affecting the Government, and requiring perhaps some further elucidation, is the manner in which the purchase of railways should be effected, and how their purchase by the Government would operate on the money market; but we must first direct our attention to the financial position of railways, so far as regards the profit that would accrue to Government if the latter purchased the shares, giving the shareholders a bonus of 15 per cent. on the market price.

We have already had occasion to notice that the value of a

railway cannot be calculated solely from the dividends it may pay at any particular time to the shareholders; although, as a matter of course, the dividend forms a very important element in the calculation. The Manchester, Sheffield, and Lincoln Company paid, in 1863, only fifteen shillings on their 100*l.* shares; yet they could not be obtained for less than 40*l.* per share. If the dividend had been the only criterion to ascertain the value of the shares, their value would not have exceeded 15*l.*; but the shareholders considered they had good reason to expect that their dividend would be, in 1864, at least three times as much, and there is every probability of their not being disappointed. On the other hand, although the South-Eastern Company paid a dividend on their year's earnings of 5*l.* 3*s.* 4*d.*, yet the price of their shares was only about 85*l.*, whereas they should be worth 20*l.* more if the above dividend was to be the test of their value; but the public, for many reasons not necessary to notice, thought that the South-Eastern could not maintain their dividends.

In times of great prosperity, when money is very abundant, there is naturally a difficulty in finding a good investment for money. In 1844, when Consols, for a short time, were at par, investments in the best railway property would not, on an average, pay a higher interest than 4*l.* 7*s.* 6*d.* per cent.; but that time was altogether exceptional, and lasted only for a few months.

In ordinary times, with Consols say at 90, railway property can be purchased to pay 5 per cent.; but so far as the purchase of railways by Government is concerned, it would make but little difference, either to the State or the shareholders, at what time a purchase might be made, as Government stock is subject to the same influence as railway stock, and rises or falls in value, although not to the same extent, as these influences act on it.

The average difference of interest between an investment in Government stock, and an investment in ordinary railway stock,

R

may be taken at 1*l*. 10*s*. per cent., so that, after paying fifteen shillings to the shareholder, there would remain the same to Government to make up for the loss by the reduction in fares and charges; or, in other words, of the increase in the value of income derived from the conversion of railway shares into Government stock, the profit would be equally divided between the two parties. It is hardly necessary to observe that if the Act of 1844 be carried out, and the market price of shares be the basis on which they should be purchased—and it would be difficult to devise any other—a day would be named for taking prices previous to that on which the Act comes into operation.

It might, however, be supposed that to pass a Bill authorizing the Government to create such an enormous amount of stock as would enable them to purchase all the railways in the kingdom, would create such a convulsion in the money market, and cause such a depression in the price of Government stock, as might be attended by the most disastrous results. Such, no doubt, would be the case if the measure were compulsory; but nothing of the kind is suggested. Shareholders would not accept Government terms, unless they were favourable; and would continue to hold their shares till Government stock was at a better price. If a large number of companies simultaneously sold their lines to Government, and many of the shareholders realized, it would, no doubt, affect the price of Government stock; in that case the sales to Government would decrease till the market regained its natural tone.

There is but little doubt that the great bulk of shareholders would remain permanent holders of Government stock; as in the case, however, of allotments in joint-stock companies, there would be many anxious at once to realize the profits made by the transaction.

Besides the original shares in companies, there are also guaranteed and preference stock. The Legislature would deal with these shares in a different way from that in which they would deal with the ordinary stock of a company; this stock is, for the greater part, secure against risk, and the variation in the price is consequently limited. A much less premium would be sufficient for this class of stock shareholders, than for the original holders. The bondholders would probably be satisfied with a small bonus to save the Government the trouble of a loan.

The strongest argument, perhaps, that can be used to prove the possibility, in a monetary sense, of the purchase of the railways by the State, is somewhat negative in its character, viz., that during the passing of the Act of 1844, notwithstanding the strong opposition it encountered in the House, no one ever suggested a doubt as to the possibility of Government carrying out the measure, if deemed necessary at a future time by the Legislature. Nor was Sir R. Peel a man likely to sanction a Government measure about the success of which there could be a reasonable doubt.

How would such a measure affect the national credit?

If, on being brought forward and discussed, it should be found in any way to injure it, that would, of course, make an end of the project; but nothing could be more unlikely than such a result; to reduce our fares and charges to an average of one-third of their present rate, would be to reduce our payments by nearly TWENTY-FOUR MILLIONS STERLING.

The railways of the United Kingdom are managed by some seventy or eighty independent companies at the cost of about fifteen millions sterling per annum; it would be a very moderate assumption to suppose that two millions per annum would be saved in the management by their amalgamation in one general system. Taking the railway property of the kingdom as worth four hundred millions sterling, three-fourths per cent. on it would amount to three millions, and this sum, together with the assumed saving in management, would amount, in all, to five millions sterling. Whether or not this sum would be sufficient to meet the deficiency that would result from adopting the comparatively low tariff I have indicated, would be impossible for any one positively to say; but, judging from analogy, it would be more than sufficient. Looking at the account, however, in a national point of view, as there would be a saving of twenty-four millions sterling to the country if the charges on our railways were reduced to a third of their present average amount; so, whatever might be the expense incurred beyond the five millions would be deducted from the twenty-four millions, and the result would show the net gain to the nation.

It may be said that by abandoning the conservative policy of the present Parliament, encouraging competing lines, withdrawing protection, and adopting similar measures, the value of railway property would be much reduced, and Government could purchase on its own terms. Such a proceeding would be entirely opposed to the spirit of the Act of 1844, and not likely to be acted on either by the nation, the Legislature, or the Government; assuming, of course, that the companies were willing to meet fairly the views of the nation and the Legislature.

It possibly might be feared by some that, in the event of the public mind being directed towards this subject, there would take place an immediate rise in railway shares, and a successful combination of railway companies to defeat the object for which the Act of 1844 was framed. So far from that being the case, I believe it would be found that the general feeling of both directors and shareholders is in favour of some arrangement by which their property would be secured from the great depreciation to which it is so frequently subjected, and to secure this great object they would be willing to meet any fair proposal on the part of Government.

But no combination of companies could prevent the success of the scheme, provided that the country was thoroughly in earnest and determined to have cheap travelling. Let us suppose that all the companies did combine, and refuse to deal with the Government on such terms as the Legislature should determine to offer; and, remembering the formidable support the railway interest possesses in the House of Commons, we can well suppose the terms would be liberal. The result would be that all the protection that railway companies now enjoy would be entirely withdrawn, and unlimited competition would be the precursor of the downfall of the railway interest. Any supposition, therefore, of a combination on the part of the railways against the country is quite absurd. They would, no doubt, unite in an effort to get as high a price as they could, and make the best bargain in their power with Government; but, beyond that, it is hardly likely any of them would venture to go.

The *modus operandi* by which Government would carry out the scheme of purchase, would probably be somewhat after the following fashion: the bonus for the different classes of shares having been settled by the Legislature, and the day named for which the Stock Exchange quotations from the share list should be taken as the standard of prices, it would be announced by Government that on and after such a day, all companies that chose to accept the Government terms would be dealt with. The Legislature in the meantime having settled the tariff, both for passengers and goods, the Government would only require to make a temporary arrangement with the board of each company for carrying on the traffic, until the bulk of the companies came in. The process, I apprehend, would go on very rapidly. So soon as one of the great lines towards the north should signify its adhesion to the Government, and commence business on the Government tariff, it would encourage all the other companies having lines in the same direction to accept the Government terms, and thus the extension of the scheme throughout the kingdom would soon be accomplished.

CHAPTER V.

The Act of 1844 the Assertion of a Principle—Two Modes of proceeding under it—A strong Case of Necessity required to be made out—Amount of Capital in Railways—Percentage paid on it—Preference Shareholders and Bondholders—Improbability of Shareholders being disinclined to sell to Government—Approaching Half-yearly Meetings—Continued War among the Companies—Extract from the *Westminster Review*—Mr. Watkin on Government Purchase of Railways—Favours Scheme as a Director and Shareholder—Opposes it as a Senator and Citizen—His Arguments—Probable Appointment of a Royal Commission considered.

THE Act of 1844 has always appeared to me more intended for the assertion of a principle than as a special enactment by which a great measure of reform could be carried out; that principle apparently was the recognition of the supremacy of Parliament in railway matters at all times and under all circumstances. One of the principal objects the framers of this Act appeared to have had in view was to impress on the minds of railway proprietors, and especially directors, that, at the expiration of twenty-one years from the time the Act was passed, the present system should undergo a thorough parliamentary investigation, and if its working should have proved unsatisfactory, it should either be entirely abolished, or its details so modified as to make it work in harmony with the other institutions of the country.

It was evidently intended that, by the operation of this Act, or by some other Act founded on the principle contained in it, fares and freightage should be largely reduced throughout the country; and this could be effected either by purchasing up a few trunk lines running through different parts of the country, and reducing the tariff as low as the Legislature would deem desirable, which would have the effect of obliging the companies to make charges equally low; or, the other plan that might have been intended is the one I have proposed, viz. for Government to purchase all the railways, and adopt a low and uniform tariff throughout the country. Which of these two plans Mr. Gladstone had in view is not very clear, but of this we may be certain, that the bow was not drawn at a venture that sent forth the shaft destined, on the 1st January, 1866, to pierce the joints of the armour of railway monopoly. There can be no doubt that to carry out the first plan would be strictly in accordance with the Act and with the agreement entered into between the Legislature and the railway companies; but, as we have already shown, if so carried out, and a very low tariff adopted, it would bring ruin on the shareholders, and reduce the value of their property not less probably than fifty per cent. Railway shareholders would, therefore, much prefer to make the best agreement they could with the Government for the disposal at once of all their property rather than have it sacrificed in detail.

A very strong case, however, must be made out before the Government could be induced to propose, or the Legislature to sanction, a measure by which the nation, as it has been said, "would incur the enormous responsibility of increasing the national debt by some four hundred millions." We have heretofore discussed the question merely on general principles; we must now go into some detail, make the best estimate we can of the debit and credit sides of the account, and endeavour to approximate to the result.

The capital paid up by railway companies to the close of 1863 amounted to four hundred and four millions: to that sum may be added twenty-one millions, the assumed sum paid in calls in 1864; thus it would appear that the gross amount of capital invested in our railways amounts to the enormous sum of FOUR HUNDRED AND TWENTY-FIVE MILLIONS sterling, comprised under three heads, viz. :—

1st. Ordinary capital by shares	£215,000,000
2nd. Preferential capital	102,000,000
3rd. Loans	108,000,000
	£425,000,000

The nett returns of the railways for 1863 yielded within a small fraction of 4 per cent. on the invested capital. The year 1864 has been much more prosperous for railway proprietors, and the returns will probably pay a percentage of $4\frac{1}{2}$ per cent. on the capital invested. The holders of preferential stock and debenture loan notes receive on an average about $4\frac{1}{2}$ per cent. interest on their investments; and this must be paid before the original shareholders receive anything. The former class of holders are but little affected by the state of the market or the financial position of the companies: they receive their well-secured dividends or interest; whilst their fellow investors, who bore the burden and heat of the day, and took on themselves all the risk of the speculation, must rest satisfied with whatever they can obtain after the claims of the privileged class have been satisfied. In 1864 railways, as we have noticed, will pay $4\frac{1}{2}$ per cent., the highest dividend paid since 1847, so that the original shareholders at length will receive the same interest as the preferential holders.

As original railway stock pays now, on an average, $4\frac{1}{2}$ per cent., and at the market price investors can purchase at a rate that will pay them 5 per cent., it follows that the market value of the ordinary stock at the present time is 194,000,000*l*.; and if to that sum be added a bonus of 15 per cent. on the value, it will raise the amount in round numbers to 222,000,000*l*.

In regard to the preference and guaranteed shareholders and bondholders, their claims, as we have seen, on the property of the original shareholders amounts to 210,000,000*l*., about one-half of the capital invested. Now this prudent and cautious class, who have risked little or nothing, are in a very different position in regard to the amount of their claim for compensation compared with that of the original shareholders. Nevertheless, the amount is so large, their co-operation so desirable if not indispensable, and the inconvenience they would be put to so great if involved in such a projected change, that an arrangement probably could not be effected with them for a less bonus than 4 or 5 per cent., say ten millions bonus on their invested capital, which would raise the amount to 220,000,000*l.*, which may be taken at par; that is to say, a purchaser investing in guaranteed or preference stock or in loan notes would require on an average $4\frac{1}{2}$ per cent. The different companies vary very much in the degree of credit they severally possess, and consequently in the terms on which they can obtain money; but $4\frac{1}{2}$ per cent. may be taken as the average rate.

The account would then stand thus :—

Original shareholders—market value of their shares	£194,000,000
Bonus	29,000,000
Preference or guaranteed capital or loans	210,000,000
Bonus	10,000,000
	£443,000,000

Interest at $3\frac{1}{2}$ per cent., 15,500,000*l.*, proposed future payment to the present shareholders and bondholders.

The actual marketable value of the railway property of the kingdom amounts, by this estimate, to 404,000,000*l.* Investments in Consols, at the present time (December, 1864), pay nearly $3\frac{1}{2}$ per cent. interest to the purchaser. Assuming that this arrangement was made between the Government and the railway interest, that there should be an equal division of the profit between the State and the companies by the exchange of railway shares for Government stock, it would be a matter of mere detail for duly qualified accountants to arrange the exact amount for each party. The above is merely given as an approximate estimate to what it would be.

The purchase of railways by the Government would involve, it is said, "an addition to the national debt of some 400,000,000*l.*" This, however, is a very incorrect way of describing such a transaction; the term "debt" would imply that the money was spent, and nothing to show for it, as with our national debt. In the present case it would be an investment of the credit of the nation, when, so far from the money being lost, the State might make a profit, if it so thought fit, by a continuance of the present charges, of some five millions, more or less, per annum. Any one who calls that "an addition of four hundred millions to the national debt," and considers that a correct way of stating the case, must either have a strange confusion of ideas, or such a personal interest in having the matter viewed in that light as to blind his better judgment.

I do not think it at all necessary to discuss the probability of the shareholders, in the event of the nation desiring eventually to become possessed of the railways, refusing to accept whatever sum the supreme arbiter in such cases, the Legislature, should, under the circumstances, think fair and proper, nor would the opposition of interested parties be of any avail, should the public be determined on having cheap travelling and a low rate of freightage.

I believe there is no doubt that this important question, involving the proprietorship and management of railways, will at least be mooted in Parliament early in the session of 1865. It is desirable for shareholders to consider the matter well, and make up their minds as to the line of policy they will adopt. What prospect, then, does the ordinary parliamentary campaign present? Since 1847 there have not been so many projects introduced into Parliament, and that, too, at a time when money has been at a most unexampled rate of interest;

nor did the great companies ever seem more determined to carry on a fierce internecine war on the approach of any former session, than they do now. English, Scotch, and Irish seem equally determined to carry on an offensive or defensive warfare. Here we have the Great Eastern introducing its scheme again, in conjunction with the Lancashire and Yorkshire, intending to fight its battle over again, and force its way to the coalfields of the North, in spite of the determined opposition of the Great Northern and the Manchester, Sheffield, and Lincoln. The latter company finds itself in 1864 in a remarkable position: it is in the possession of a dividend of $2\frac{1}{2}$ per cent.; in 1863 it had not half that amount, and the year previous nothing whatever. So now it may be considered rich, with abundance of money to throw away. It undertakes to stop the Great Eastern on one side, and to bid defiance to the London and North-Western on the other, and with its allies, the Midland and Great Northern, purposes to force its way to Liverpool. The Scotch and Irish companies have, likewise, great campaigns before them.

But if those gentlemen who are now so actively engaged in preparing for renewed hostilities, would look around them, they would, I think, see, in the signs of the times, opinions declared, in certain influential quarters, which they would do well to ponder, and, perhaps, they might then come to the conclusion that there is another matter of much more importance to be attended to than even their Parliamentary battles, and that is the great fact that the public opinion of this country points, in a manner not to be mistaken, to the total abolition of railway monopoly; "when," according to the opinion of the *Times*, "the making of a railway will be as free to capitalists as the formation of a line of steamers."

"Existing railway companies complain," says the *Westminster Review*, "that any new company is sure, sooner or later, to get its bill, and if opposition be successful one session, it is useless the next. Let this uncertainty cease. Let it be proclaimed, that Parliament will countenance all new railway schemes, and the result will be a long truce to parliamentary contests. The real grievance of directors is competition; the grievance we deplore is uncertainty. They secretly strive after monopoly; we demand entire free trade in railways. They will consider the remedy both as an insult and an injury; its adoption, however, will immensely benefit the public. There cannot be too many railways, although there may be too few; and as regards the old established lines, they cannot possibly be so greatly damaged by rivalry as they now are by struggling for monopoly. At one time, Parliament might have determined what lines of railway ought to be made, and might have granted the necessary powers to those companies that offered to make them. Such a course is no longer possible, and we are glad of it. Had our railways been constructed under these conditions, their managers would have been justified in raising the cry of vested interests, whenever competing lines were proposed. As it is, we can afford to laugh at that cry, and can feel confident that the utmost efforts of the one hundred and fifty directors who have seats in Parliament will be baffled, should they persevere in attempting to make of some railways monopolies. Act after Act of Parliament has been acquired, in the hope that no interlopers will venture to dispute the supremacy of a company in a particular district. The chief result of that policy has been to increase the mileage of several companies, to swell their receipts, and diminish their dividends. Were the directors of the Great Western, for example, to abandon their aggressive and spendthrift policy, it is possible their fellow-shareholders would receive a more satisfactory half-yearly dividend than a quarter per cent. We are perfectly aware that the management of our railways is a public scandal; but it is no part of our duty to enlarge on the demerits of railway directors."

Many directors of railways read this article, I have, no

doubt, with great indignation, and but little anticipated that within a couple of years from that time they would see similar opinions expressed in the *Times*; and when the leading organ of public opinion in this country expresses its belief that the railway institution must be made to work in unison with all the other institutions of the country, it is quite time for every man who has money invested in the railway monopoly to endeavour to estimate the value of his property when that monopoly shall be destroyed.

I do not know what has given rise to the report that has been for some time in circulation that Government has an intention of purchasing the railways, or that it rests on any foundation beyond mere rumour; but every one should know that Government has no more power to make a wholesale compulsory purchase of the railways than any private individual. It is very true, that a year hence, on the 1st of January, 1866, there are a number of lines that Government, with the assent of Parliament, may make a compulsory purchase of; but shareholders need not be under the slightest fear—if that be the proper term—that then, or at any future time, the compulsory powers of the Act of 1844 will ever be brought into operation against them either by the present or any succeeding Government. From that quarter they have nothing to fear, whatever they may have from other quarters.

The Act of 1844 is little more than declaratory. Its framers supposed it might be possible that, at the expiration of twenty-one years, the nation might desire to take the possession and management of the railways into its own hands; and in order to be in a position to do so, if such should be its future policy, set certain limits to the demands of the shareholders; but these limits are far beyond the present value of railways.

If it should, then, be the desire of the nation to purchase the railways, it would remain with the Legislature, on the one hand, to say what price it would be willing to give the companies, and it would be with the companies on the other, to say whether they would accept it or not. *The State could itself make the railways for one third of the cost at which it could buy them*, and there is no law to prevent it doing so ; therefore, there is something inexpressibly ludicrous and absurd in any one talking of Government using its compulsory powers for the purchase of railways. Let the railway shareholders " first catch their hare." Let them wait till Government " threatens" to exercise its compulsory powers of purchase, to give not only three times the price for the railways that they could be now made for, but, in addition to that sum, give a bonus to the shareholders of 25 per cent. When Government proposes to do this, it will be quite time enough to talk seriously of Government intending to make them such an offer.

I have already stated that one of the principal objects the Government of 1844 had in view in passing this Act appears to have been for the purpose of impressing on the minds of directors that the whole system would be subject to revision or alteration in 1865. But there was also another object which the Government of that day may have had equally in view—viz., to direct the attention of the public, as the expiration of the twenty-one years would draw nigh, to a consideration of the subject of railway management generally, and of the two rival systems especially. Looking at the merits and demerits of the Act in reference to the present state of affairs, it would be difficult to say in what way it could be made operative. The same might be said of any attempt to fix by certain arbitrary rules the future price of any commodity. We have seen that at the time the Act was passed, twenty-five years' purchase on the dividends would have given the shareholders an average profit of 8 per cent. At the present time it would give some shareholders 40 per cent. beyond the value of their shares, others the exact value, some not half the value, and a great number nothing at all ! But the Act, in the end, makes it all right for both parties ; the Government is not obliged to buy in any case, nor is the company obliged to sell on the prescribed terms. A company may require a valuation in reference to *its future prospects*, which may be double, or more than double, as we shall see by-and-by, the present value; but then the Government would not give that sum, and so the matter would end. The only case in which the Act would have become really operative had reference to the limitation of companies requiring more than twenty-five years' purchase on 10 per cent. dividends.

But this Act has probably done all that its framers intended it should; it has been the means of securing the attention both of shareholders and the public, at the proper time, to the consideration of this important subject. Had not that Act been in existence, it would have been a vain expectation for any private individual to suppose he could obtain even a hearing on a subject of such magnitude. The Act of 1844 has done its duty, and done its duty well; but mixing it up in any way with the purchase of railways by the Government only embarrasses the question; it would therefore simplify matters very much if it were once more "forgotten." The attention of the public was directed to it a few months since by the *Economist* newspaper, and the result has shown what a wonderful change has taken place in public opinion within the last twenty years. Who at that time would have been listened to for a moment while advocating the purchase of railways by the State? Now we find, before even the subject is discussed, that the public takes a deep interest in the matter, and is anxious to have it thoroughly investigated.

Let us now direct our attention for a moment to railway boards. A railway board is generally composed of individuals forming two separate classes—the one wealthy, and possessing a large stake in the line; the other professional directors, that is, those who make a business of directorship, and whose time is occupied on the different boards on which they manage to get introduced, or which may seek a connection with them. These gentlemen are, for the most part, very active and enterprising, and well earn the fees they receive. It is not to be supposed that this class of directors look with much favour on any change of system that would materially affect their present position.

Not long since, the Manchester, Sheffield, and Lincoln Company held its half-yearly meeting, which was presided over by the chairman, Mr. Watkin, a gentleman of very great ability, largely connected with the railway world, and a director on some half-dozen or more of companies. Mr. Watkin took occasion very properly at the meeting to direct the attention of the shareholders to the rumours that had been widely circulated in reference to the supposed intentions of Government to purchase up the railways, " under the Act of 1844," and on that speech the *Times* had a leading article, in which the whole subject is fully and ably discussed.

But what does Mr. Watkin say to his shareholders? He is perfectly satisfied, he says, "speaking for himself, and entirely in the interest of the shareholders, and in that of the other railways with which he is connected, to express his entire readiness to hand over to Government and Government officials the property, the working of it, and all its thousand-fold responsibilities and anxieties." Now, a word in regard to the price that the shareholders of this company would under the Act receive for their shares. Twenty-five years' purchase on their average dividend for the last three years, would amount to about the *one-half* of the market price they can at any time obtain in the market for their shares; so that part of the arrangement would have to be set aside, and the shareholders be content with what two arbitrators would say was the value of the railway with reference to—its future prospects. Mr. Watkin having briefly expressed his satisfaction as a director and shareholder, at the prospect of the proposed purchase, so far as the interests of the company were concerned, immediately passed from these two characters into those of the senator and the citizen, in which he took an entirely opposite view of the supposed measure. His duties in these two latter characters unfortunately clashed with his interest in the two former ones. Whilst the director and the shareholder could do nothing but applaud and admire, the senator and the citizen could only lament and condemn. "They must consider the question," said Mr. Watkin, " not merely as railway proprietors, but as citizens, and in its bearings upon the industrial life and political independence of our people." But why *must* they, Mr. Watkin ? What was the necessity that the shareholders of the "Manchester and Sheffield" should occupy, as our cousins on the other side of the Atlantic would say, such an elevated platform. Shareholders meet, for the purpose of getting information about their affairs, and to promote every measure that will advance their interests as shareholders, and not as citizens. I have no doubt, however, that if I can point out to Mr. Watkin some mistakes he has made in the case he put before his shareholders, and that if he be able to reconcile his interest as a director, in giving up this management, with his duties as a citizen, he will feel much obliged to me. First, Mr. Watkin speaks of handing the railways over to "Government officials," thereby intimating that if Government had possession of them, their management would be handed over to the Board of Trade or some other inexperienced officers of the Government; but in the event of the change we are speaking of being accomplished, the Legislature would take very good care that, under the new administration, the services of the most able and eminent practical men of the country should be secured. It is not that the ability or integrity of those who at present manage our railways is doubted ; it is the system itself that compels them, in the execution of their duty, to set aside the most important interests of the public when they interfere in the slightest degree with the interests of their constituents as traders. Would a board composed of the most eminent directors and managers of the railway world be less active and efficient in the discharge of their duty than those who are responsible for the management of the Post Office, or Customs, or Excise branches of Government? Would Mr. Watkin cast a stigma on the leading men of our present system, and say that they would be less inclined to do their duty in the service of the State, than in that of companies? Mr. Watkin does not venture to insinuate that, but he gets out of the dilemma by intimating that their services would be altogether dispensed with, and inexperienced, and consequently incompetent, persons placed in their stead.

Mr. Watkin advanced many very pertinent reasons against handing over the railways, in the event of their being purchased by Government, to contractors. He says: "If the State owned the corpus of the railways, and the moving plant, and a contractor or contracting company worked or applied them, what a temptation would exist to run down the property and plant, in order to extract a higher rate of profit! In fact, it was found in practice that when the owners and workers were one, and had one interest, the integrity of the property was and must be more fully considered than when one party had an interest in renewals as little and the other as much as possible. A high condition of repair meant a high condition of safety, and he preferred, himself, to travel on a company's instead of a contractor's line." There would be no doubt many disadvantages in leasing out the Government lines as compared with having them under the direct control of the Legislature; there would be a number of independent companies, as there are now, each pursuing its own plans independent of the others. The directors would have then, as now, no obligation to serve the public further than suited their own interests, there would constantly be charges preferred against them, and it would require the closest supervision on the part of the authorities to prevent the contractors taking those unfair advantages which Mr. Watkin has pointed out. All that may be admitted;

but, on the other hand, as the companies or contractors would be obliged to carry passengers and goods at a fixed tariff, it would be impossible that in this most important matter they could impose on the public any more than they can do now in regard to parliamentary trains. With all the drawbacks —and I admit they would be very great—the nation would, nevertheless, derive great advantage from a change of system, even if it went no further than leasing the lines to companies.

But where would the necessity exist of the lines being let out to contractors at all? If there were a board composed of the most eminent railway men, selected from or chosen by the present boards, does Mr. Watkin mean to say that they would not form a governing body fully adequate to perform their duty and give satisfaction to the country? "There are now," says Mr. Watkin, "some 250,000 employés connected with our railways; only imagine a party government armed with the nomination and control of such a body, and able to distribute to political partisans or the incapable relatives of electioneering agents some 12,000,000l. in salaries and wages!" I have no doubt it will give Mr. Watkin the greatest satisfaction to know that this fearful picture he has drawn of the proposed scheme, which would produce such direful effects on the British constitution, and this future distribution of twelve millions a year in corrupting the constituencies of the empire, is entirely imaginary. No one, that I am aware of, ever proposed to give the patronage of the railways to the Government. The principle of competitive examinations is now so firmly established that patronage to a great extent is done away with; and if ever the railways became the property of the State, the Government in all probability will never ask, and most certainly will never be entrusted with more patronage than the Legislature may consider absolutely necessary to ensure a proper discharge of the duties of administration.

Mr. Watkin frankly admits that under existing circumstances it would be greatly for the benefit of the shareholders that the Legislature should carry out the Act of 1844, or rather the intention of its framers, and buy up the shares of all the companies. The advantages the companies would derive from such a course are, to his mind, so clear and obvious that he does not waste time in discussing them; "but, speaking entirely in the interest of the shareholders both of that and the other companies he was connected with, he would be most willing to hand them over to Government." The opinion of Mr. Watkin on this subject will, I think, be supported by every railway director in the kingdom.

It is much to be regretted that Mr. Watkin's zeal as a citizen hurried him away from this very important part of the subject, and caused him to forget that some of his fellow shareholders might be desirous to know his reasons for wishing, as a shareholder, that the Government should purchase the railways. What they were I cannot, of course, undertake to say, but the following reasons might be adduced in support of the correctness of his views:—

1st. The certainty of a great change of policy in the country with regard to railways. The success of the movement that is now being made in reference to the purchase of railways by the State depends entirely on the assent of two parties, the nation and the shareholders. It appears pretty certain at the present time that the policy of such an important step will undergo a thorough investigation, and the result may be that the nation and the Legislature will disapprove *in toto* of the scheme; or they may consider that the carrying of it out would be surrounded with so many difficulties as to become virtually impracticable; or that the shareholders require a higher price than they would be justified in paying. No matter what the cause may be, we will suppose the scheme entirely fails.

There have been two or three articles in the *Times* on this subject, and it quite approves of Mr. Watkin's views, but it notices one important omission in his speech, viz. the absence of any notice of the future policy of the country. According to that high authority, the making a railway will be as free to capitalists " as the formation of a line of steamers." The *Times* may be right in its opinion that the country will be opposed to carrying out the Act of 1844, but will insist on a perfect free trade in railways, or at least a trade so free that none but land-owners will be permitted to oppose the construction of a line. Now, if shareholders would but realize in their own minds the full import of that term, " free trade in railways," they will well understand the emphatic declaration of Mr. Watkin that he would be most willing, on the part of himself and the shareholders in the various companies he represented, to hand the railways over to the State. What would railway property be worth in five years from the present time if all protection were withdrawn, and railway companies were subjected to the same competition as any other class of traders? Notwithstanding the protection they enjoy, and the high price money has been, there will be more projects before Parliament in 1865 than in any year since 1847. In 1844 the directors refused to co-operate with those who then advocated their purchase by the State. They wished their lines to be " developed;" they would not take the value then, they would wait for the increase of trade. Within the next half-score of years they developed themselves with a vengeance, from an average dividend of about 8 per cent. down to one considerably less than half that amount. And so at the present time I have no doubt there are many inconsiderate persons who, because railways have prospered for the last few years, have come to the conclusion—without any reference to existing facts or the future policy of the country in regard to railway legislation—that they must continue to prosper, and to bear up against the competition that, under such adverse circumstances, they will be subjected to. Mr. Watkin knew better than that, and honestly acknowledges that the best policy for shareholders would be to part with their shares to the State.

Let shareholders look abroad, and then form an opinion how long the present state of things is likely to last. With the spirit of inquiry that is now spreading in every direction this bolstered and propped up system must soon come to an end, either by a compromise which would be for the benefit of all parties, and add to the present price of shares a large bonus, or by violent means, viz. by the action of unlimited competition; and it is impossible to deny, whatever the results may be to shareholders, that such a course as that pointed out by the *Times* is the one most in accordance with the general policy of the country.

One, then, might suppose, that under these circumstances, Mr. Watkin, acknowledging, as he does frankly, the benefit that would be conferred on all shareholders by the State taking the railways off their hands, would naturally be supposed to do everything in his power to promote such an object; that he, one of the great magnates of the railway world, would only be too happy to promote a project that would be so profitable to his fellow shareholders; but, so far from that being the case, we find that he will give the project his most determined opposition. He is afraid that under such a system, " England would be what France was in the latter days of Louis Philippe ;" and a " moribund Parliament he does not deem fit to meddle with the question, but he will have no objection to a properly appointed commission."

Some persons, perhaps, may be disposed to consider the course taken by Mr. Watkin and those directors who are similarly situated, to be somewhat influenced by the large emoluments they derive from office; they may not well understand why they should oppose what they admit would be so advantageous to their fellow shareholders; it is more liberal, however, to suppose that the views of these gentlemen are totally uninfluenced by any selfish consideration, and that it is a sense of high moral feeling, acting on minds peculiarly sensitive to public duty, that has produced such an extraordinary result.

It is very remarkable to notice in what opposite directions Mr. Watkin's feelings as "a citizen" cause him to act. Last session, as we all know, the Great Eastern promoted a railway to connect their main line with the coalfields of the North; and, had they been successful, it would to some extent have lessened the evils of the present monopoly of which the Manchester and Sheffield Company possess no small share. In this case, unfortunately, the zeal of the chairman overcame the patriotism of the citizen, and, mainly, I believe, through Mr. Watkin's active exertions, the scheme was defeated. The Great Eastern, no way daunted, is to make another attempt in 1865, and I am greatly afraid Mr. Watkin will offer the same opposition again, whether or not with the same success remains to be seen. Mr. Watkin, however, entertains a very different feeling towards the inhabitants of Liverpool and Manchester. There has existed, for a considerable time past, a feeling of great dissatisfaction with the railway authorities on the part of the merchants and traders of those great towns, on account of the exorbitant charges, as alleged, made for the freightage of merchandise between Liverpool and Manchester. It is only a few days since a communication appeared in the papers from the Chancellor of the Exchequer to the President of the Liverpool Chamber of Commerce, in answer to a memorial addressed to him by that body, complaining of the exorbitant rates they were obliged to pay. In his answer the Chancellor of the Exchequer stated that the matter was of great importance, and had attracted the notice of Her Majesty's Government; but, as doubtless they knew, he had no power to interfere. In this extremity, Mr. Watkin presents himself as the *deus ex machinâ* by which the merchants and traders of Liverpool and Manchester are to have their merchandise carried at a moderate rate, and he proposes to make a second line. It unfortunately so happens, however, that the trading population of these two great towns have not that confidence in Mr. Watkin and his company that perhaps they ought to have, and instead of receiving him with open arms, absolutely threaten to petition against his bill, unless they first agree about the fares and charges for merchandise. Here, now, is a great opportunity for Mr. Watkin's coming out in the character of the good citizen, and proving to the public how much may be done by private enterprise and competition, as compared with what Government could do.

The case stands thus: the Liverpool and Manchester line cost more than a million and a half, and the length is $31\frac{1}{2}$ miles; the fares are 5s. 6d., 4s., and 2s. $7\frac{1}{2}d$. for the several classes. Mr. Watkin says he can make a line for half the cost of the Liverpool and Manchester line; that reduction in the cost of construction would not enable him to carry passengers at lower fares, but the same profit on the working would give to his shareholders *double* the dividend which those of the Liverpool and Manchester Railways receive. Now, he could carry first-class passengers the entire length of his line for threepence, second-class for twopence, and third-class, a penny; and as the London and Manchester charge something more then *twenty-fold* the cost of conveyance, it is to be hoped the company finds the charges "remunerative." Merchandise can be conveyed from Liverpool to Manchester for *sixpence* per ton, and the freightage bears probably about the same proportion to the cost of conveyance as the fares for passengers do to their conveyance. Now, let Mr. Watkin make an offer in good faith to the Liverpool and Manchester people, that if they will support his line, he will consent to a tariff for passengers and goods at *one-third* of the present rates. I say, make an offer in good faith, because no man knows better than Mr. Watkin that parliamentary undertakings on the part of railway companies are not always made in good faith, either to make a line for which they apply, or keep their charges within those limits to which they had pledged their good faith to obtain their Acts. A notable instance of this kind now occurs to me. There are few companies that encountered so fierce and expensive an opposition from rival companies as the Great Northern. They were defeated in the first attempt by the combined companies; but they succeeded in their second, mainly by having had recourse to a very clever trick. The directors proposed to the committee to limit the fares for first-class to *twopence* per mile: that was a reduction of about 30 per cent. on the fares then charged by the other companies. The latter were taken quite aback by an offer on the part of their opponents to carry at "such unremunerative rates," and the committee passed the Bill. Before the line was opened, the Great Northern pointed out to the other companies the great loss they would incur by having their fares brought down by competition, proposed to the other companies to unite their parliamentary strength, and have the Great Northern's fares raised from $2d.$ to $3\frac{1}{2}d.$, the same as the other companies. This was done. It being a private Bill, it was nobody's duty to stop it, and so their Act was "amended" without opposition.

But to return to our more immediate subject. It is very remarkable that Mr. Watkin, in addressing his shareholders for the purpose of obtaining their sanction to go before Parliament, never alluded either to the cost at which he could convey passengers and goods between Liverpool and Manchester, nor the fares and rates he intended to charge. Mr. Watkin does not dispute the fact that he could carry passengers all the way from Liverpool to Manchester, or *vice versâ*, for a penny a head, or goods for sixpence a ton; nor can he assert that there would be a less profit in charging *a shilling* for a third-class return ticket between those towns, inasmuch as the cost to the company would be less than *twopence*. The working classes of these two enormously populated towns are virtually excluded from communication with each other, unless on rare occasions. The mechanic, if he intends to return now on the same day, may almost as well take a second-class return ticket, for which he will pay 6s.; whilst the double parliamentary is 5s. 3d. Now, if these two questions were pressed on Mr. Watkin, could a third-class passenger be carried for a penny from Liverpool to Manchester, and might not a single third-class ticket at eightpence, and a double ticket at a shilling, pay as well as the present fare, Mr. Watkin could not deny the possibility of such a case. But if Mr. Watkin were followed up then by the question, "Will you give an undertaking to insert a clause in your Bill, limiting third-class fares to that rate, and a proportionably reduced tariff for merchandise?" Mr. Watkin would, I have no doubt, reply at once, that he could not advise his company to undertake any such risk; and, therefore, the experiment, so far as he and his company were concerned, must remain untried. Just so, Mr. Watkin; that would be a very proper and sensible answer on your part, and perhaps you will more clearly understand now than when you addressed your Manchester and Sheffield shareholders, why it is that Government interference is necessary, viz. to try experiments which no directors of a commercial company would be justified in running the risk of incurring. I have said before, what I now again repeat, although it is not a popular doctrine, that I consider the companies have an undoubted right to exercise their own discretion, in making whatever charges they consider will pay them best; and if the Legislature thinks proper, either to alter the policy of the country, or to make experiments for the purpose of testing the desirability of altering its policy, such experiments should be made at the expense of the State, and not at that of private individuals.

There is another subject on which Mr. Watkin could give very interesting information, viz. the contest, if it might be termed such, between the "London and North-Western" on one side, and the "Great Northern" and the "Manchester and Sheffield" on the other, when they were carrying first-class passengers from London to Manchester *at a farthing* per mile. Now, it is quite possible that their profits were not so great as when they were charging two-pence halfpenny per mile. If I recollect right, what they lost by that contest amounted to about *a half per cent.* on their dividend; but it must be remembered that rate was extraordinarily low. I propose that first-class passengers should not be carried at a less average rate, according to speed, than a penny per mile; whilst the fare Mr. Watkin and his friends adopted was just the *one-fourth of that amount!*

As matters now stand in the railway world, Mr. Watkin and a few other managing directors of our great companies regulate, according to their good will and pleasure, the whole of our inland traffic, both in passengers and goods. Their word is law; they are absolute dictators; from their decree there is no appeal, and remonstrance is useless. They make "war or peace," they "contract alliances" or "dissolve unions." They plan "invasions of territory," "secure alliance," and, after a hard-fought campaign, "enjoy the blessings of peace." Such are the usual terms, in a portion, at least, of the railway press, when speaking of great railway transactions; and they are not so very inappropriate when their magnitude is considered. The only policy which these gentlemen follow is, that which each individual thinks will best promote the interests of his own company. What other interest should he look to? But how does that work in practice for the general community? One district will have very high, another very low, and another medium rates, just as the directing manager thinks best for the interest of his company. Here are all our great manufacturing and commercial towns, such as Liverpool, Glasgow, Manchester, Birmingham, and Leeds, dependent for their prosperity on a few individuals, over whom they have not the slightest control.

And this is the system that Mr. Watkin and those who act with him hold up to the admiration of the world! The "surroundings" through which these gentlemen see this system, I have no doubt, are very agreeable; but their brother shareholders, have not, I am afraid, things made so pleasant for them; and it will be for the English Parliament, when the subject comes on for discussion, to decide whether or not our present system is worthy of a great and enlightened country.

Mr. Watkin thinks "that a commission which included such names as Mill and Newmarsh, with Galton, Swift, Clarke, and Allport, ought to be satisfactory to all." On that point I think there can be no doubt. A thorough investigation into the working of our railway system is the great object that all should have in view. It should, however, be remembered that these gentlemen, however eminent they may be, cannot tell us how many passengers would travel for the next year between Liverpool and Manchester, and Edinburgh and Glasgow, and on the Blackwall, Metropolitan, or any other line in the kingdom; and that is the subject on which we most want information. It is only by a trial of the effect produced by low rates that a satisfactory result can be obtained. The same remark applies, in a great degree, to the freightage of goods; but the merchants, manufacturers, and traders in our great towns can explain to a royal commission the loss that is inflicted on them by the rates they consider exorbitant, and which they are obliged to pay; and it will be then for the commission to consider whether or not a satisfactory conclusion can be come to on the subject without first trying the fiscal results of a very low tariff for freightage.

CHAPTER VI.

Construction of New Lines laid out by Government Engineers and constructed by Contract—Constructed nearly on the present Plan—Joint Parliamentary Committees of the two Houses preferable—The Reduction of Railway Charges a National Question—Objections against its being considered so—The proper way of discussing the Question—Reduction of Charges amounts to Twenty-four Millions Sterling—Centralization—When it is advantageous—Distinction between Local Duties and those of the State—The Post Office—Objections of the Railway Press considered—Reductions on the Blackwall and Brighton Companies—Future Value of Railways—Exchange of Shares for Stock.

How our future lines should be constructed will become, at some future day, a matter of very grave consideration for our Legislature. This much, I think, may be safely predicated, that the two Houses of Parliament will never part with the right they now exercise of investigating the merits of each line for the extension of our system, and granting or withholding their assent to its construction, as the case may be.

Assuming this point to be settled, it is most likely that the success which, two sessions since, attended the experiment of the appointment of a joint committee, selected from both Houses of Parliament, to form one tribunal, to investigate local railway matters affecting the metropolis, will encourage the Legislature to continue in a more settled and permanent form a mode of legislation which was only tried for a special purpose. The proceedings and report of that committee gave, so far as I am aware, universal satisfaction; and from such an auspicious commencement there would be every reason to hope that its future proceedings would, in like manner, give general satisfaction to the country. There are several reasons why a joint committee, appointed by the two Houses, would be preferable to a tribunal composed of two separate committees.

1. It would command more respect as an authority. Now the authority is divided, and although a Bill that is thrown out by a committee of one House cannot appear before the other, there is generally a feeling of dissatisfaction on the minds of promoters when a Bill is rejected by one of the committees, and the belief is entertained by those interested that if their good fortune had brought them before the other committee, they would, in all probability, have succeeded.

2. There would be a great saving in time and labour. At present there is a great amount of useless expense incurred by the promoters, and the time of members of both Houses is needlessly occupied by the same statements being made and arguments urged before both committees.

3. As the rejected Bills do not come before the second committee, it is very disadvantageously placed; it cannot deal in any way with those Bills that have been rejected, and must either pass the Bill before it or reject it, and thus may possibly leave the district the line was intended to accommodate without any railway communication whatever.

For these reasons I think it would be exceedingly desirable that all railway committees should be composed of the members of both Houses.

In the event of our railways becoming national property, there would arise, I have no doubt, very great difference of opinion as to the system under which our future railways should be constructed.

1. They might be laid out, in the first instance, by our most eminent engineers, and, after having obtained the sanction of Parliament, the land might be purchased by Government and the lines constructed by contract.

2. The present system might in the construction of our

lines be to a considerable extent adhered to. It might be left open as now for any company to come with its Bill before Parliament with an offer to construct a line and deliver it to Government on certain specified terms, and it would be for a parliamentary committee to recommend or not that the offer be accepted. A Government board might be appointed to collect such statistical or other information as might be required, and prepare a report in each case for the use of the parliamentary committees. If this plan should be adopted, the nation would have the full benefit of competition both in the laying out and the construction of lines, rural districts would compete in getting up lines, and guarantees might be given by public bodies, as has been done in some cases in Ireland, that the line would pay a certain percentage. If Government had a satisfactory guarantee in doubtful cases that the traffic would yield $3\frac{1}{2}$ per cent. interest on the capital, little inquiry in such cases would be necessary. This plan might possibly be more acceptable to the public generally and the railway interest than the first, and would not be a very wide departure from the present system.

The last subject we have to discuss is one of the greatest importance; indeed, it may be said to be that on which the whole question hinges, and it is, therefore, necessary to consider it fully. "Unless," it is said, "it can be proved that a reduction in fares and freightage to one-third of the present charges can be effected without loss to the nation, the scheme would be a failure, as in that case the public treasury would have to make up a loss from which the general community would derive no gain." The proposition here advanced is, that a reduction of railway charges would only affect certain classes in the country, viz. those who travel, and those who pay for the carriage of merchandise; and although collectively they pay a large sum, yet the other classes who neither travel nor send merchandise by rail could not in justice be called on to contribute to make up a loss. I contend, on the other hand, that a reduction in railway charges would be equally beneficial to all classes; that a reduction to one-third of our present charges would be to all intents and purposes equal to a reduction in taxation of *twenty-four millions*, less whatever, if any, sum from the treasury might be required to make up the deficit.

The proper way, in my opinion, to discuss the matter is to suppose the railways to be the property of the State, and the present tariff for passengers and goods in operation, then to consider whether or not its reduction would be a measure likely to be called for by the public generally, and if so, whether or not a reduction should be made, and, if made, to what extent.

The principal objection made against the purchase of railways by the Government is, that it would create a vast centralized system in this country, in direct opposition to the feelings of the people; that it would abolish local government; that it would substitute official management for that of mercantile management; that it would discourage private enterprise, and initiate a new policy totally foreign to the habits of the people; that it would encourage on the part of the public dependence on Government to supply their wants, instead of leaving them to trust to their own energy, activity, and industry, to supply their wants: this is the sum of the general objections made to the purchase of the railways by the State and their management by, or under the control of, Government.

First, in regard to centralization. In matters affecting only a particular locality, it is most desirable that each community should form its own government, without any superior or controlling power. Thus, we have our municipal, parochial, and other local authorities; and these institutions, without doubt, tend in the highest degree to promote that independence of feeling, and spirit of self-reliance, and energy, so characteristic of the British people. In contrast to those local institutions so congenial to our soil, we find that in most continental countries, the people are deprived by their rulers of nearly all natural rights, and their respective Governments insist on doing everything for them, the necessary results follow; the people are without life and energy, indisposed to active exertion, and look on with a listless apathy, whilst the underlings of Government do their work.

The distinction that exists between local duties and those of the State appears so plain, that it is scarcely possible there could ever be any misconception on the subject. When there are no interests affected, except those whom the governing body represents, local government works well, and within its proper sphere; but when those boundaries are passed, and an authority, which should be merely local, manages to get hold of imperial power to exercise authority over those whom it does not represent, and by whom it cannot in any way be controlled, then there is an infringement on the rights of the subject by a power in a certain sense irresponsible, and not in any way bound to promote the interest of those over whom it rules. If people did not travel beyond the limits of their own parish, then the parish should make the line, and the parochial authorities regulate the tariff; but inasmuch as the public is entirely unrepresented at railway boards, the directors virtually exercise the power to charge what they think proper. "Taxation," we are told, "without representation, is tyranny, and ought to be resisted." We take such matters easier now; but, at all events, there is no difficulty in this case, at least, in drawing the line of demarcation between imperial and local rights. We commit as great an error in one way, in this country, as they do on the Continent in another; there the imperial power supersedes the local power, and will reign supreme in everything. Here, the local authority manages to get possession of imperial sway, and we, to avoid the Scylla, fall into the Charybdis; and whilst proclaiming our independence of the Government, we fall under the dominion of the local and irresponsible tyrant.

It has been said that the change proposed would be entirely opposed to the feelings of the people. I quite admit that would have been the case twenty years ago, and possibly may be so now, but that cannot be known till the subject is brought fully before Parliament, and thoroughly ventilated throughout the country. It is quite true a scheme may be proposed that, in a monetary point of view, would be advantageous to a people, and one, nevertheless, to which they may be opposed, and, therefore, it would be useless to discuss that point at present.

The great objection made by the railway boards to the possession of railways by the State is the "bad management of Government officials." These gentlemen are, no doubt, like most other officials, neither better nor worse; they neglect their business when they are not looked after, and perform it properly when they are. The Post-Office department is one, the employés of which come almost hourly in contact with all classes of Her Majesty's subjects, and there is no complaint of the manner in which they perform their duty; but what have Government officials, as that term is understood, to do with the present case? It can only be by Act of Parliament that railways can come under the control of the Crown, and if such an event should take place, the nation and Legislature would take care that the board that should manage the railways should be formed of the most able and distinguished men who are now directors and managers of railways, and whose high social and professional position would be a sufficient guarantee to the country for the manner in which the railways of the country would be managed.

In regard to patronage, the Legislature would, no doubt, by means of competitive examinations, and by taking necessary measures to secure each officer his fair share of promotion in the ordinary course of routine, reduce it to a very low point; still, some places would no doubt remain, and whether they should be disposed of by the board, or by the responsible head of the board, and under what conditions, it would be for the Legislature to arrange. The promotion of officers in any Government establishment to places of high trust depends on his own conduct, and any attempt on his part to advance his position through political influence would, as an immediate result, cause his name to be placed at the bottom of the list, and, therefore, an attempt of the kind is never made.

The objection that the purchase of the railways would be opposed to the freedom of private enterprise is so entirely fallacious that it is scarcely worth notice. How would it discourage private enterprise if the State would give to those who had embarked in the enterprise 10, 15, or 20 per cent., as the case might be, more than they could obtain from any other quarter, and when they would be at perfect liberty to accept the offer or not? So far from that being considered the case by those best qualified to judge, those directors who have noticed the subject admit that the purchase would be of benefit to the shareholders; they object only as "citizens."

"The English people," it is said, "will not consent that the highways of the country be handed over to the tender mercies of a Chancellor of the Exchequer and the Board of Trade, who, at any time, would have the means in their hands, by an imposition of a farthing per ton per mile on goods and on passenger fares, to replenish an exchequer however exhausted." No one ever proposed that either the Chancellor of the Exchequer or the Board of Trade should have any control over the management of the railways. The railways ought to be public property, under the immediate control of the Legislature, with rates and fares fixed, at a low and uniform rate, such as Parliament would deem necessary for the full development of the passenger and merchandise traffic of the country.

"If Parliament chose," it is said, " it could revise the maximum tolls of all the railways in the kingdom directly it met, and cut them down to the lowest figure." "In fact," says the *Railway News*, "we do not know anything which Parliament could do were the railways national property, which it cannot do just as well now when they belong to private shareholders."

Parliament has no power to do anything of the kind. The *Railway News* does not surely contend, or rather admit, that Parliament would have any moral right to compel the companies to carry either passengers or goods at a lower rate than they are permitted by their respective Acts to charge. The *Railway News*, no doubt, means that compensation should be made for any loss that would be incurred, but on the manner in which such arrangement would be carried out the *Railway News* throws no light.

"There are limits," it is said, "to the amount of capital which holders are willing to invest at 3 per cent., and there is no telling what might not be the influence of such a large issue of new Government stock as this purchase would involve upon the Government security which already exists."

There would be great force in this objection if it were proposed to pass an Act compelling shareholders to accept Government stock; and if the scheme of the Government purchase of the railways should appear to have the effect of weakening the credit of Government, it would never be attempted, nor would railway shareholders accept stock in exchange for their shares. The great bulk of railway shareholders are permanent holders for investment and not speculators, and would be as little inclined to traffic in Government stock as they had been in railway shares.

"If, at the present time," it is contended, "the Imperial Three per Cents. are readily accepted, it is because they rest on a stable foundation; but would not a different element be introduced, if these securities depended on railways which might or might not pay? We should then find Government consenting only to such extensions of the railway system as were certain to be remunerative, or else jeopardising the national revenue."

An argument somewhat similar to this I have before noticed. The Three per Cents. rest, no doubt, on a " stable foundation," inasmuch as that security consists of all the territorial property of England, and the security for the Three per Cents. issued in exchange for the railways would rest on precisely the same foundation, with the additional security of the railways for both. If the revenue fell short of what was expected, the deficiency, whatever it might be, would not be lost, but remain in the pockets of the people; so that, if the Chancellor of the Exchequer wanted it, he would know where it was, and might be very safely left to take his own measures to get back for the expenses of the country the whole, or as much of it as he might require.

"Directors are generally alive to the potency of cheap fares whenever they have reason to believe that their revenue will be improved."

That, no doubt, is true to some extent, but is far from being the whole truth. There is a natural desire in the minds of all boards to keep up high fares, and not without some reason; there is considerable risk in lowering them, as, if the low fares are found not to answer, there is often much ill-will raised against the directors by returning to the old fares, and it frequently happens in such cases that the old fares are not so remunerative as they had been formerly. But, making every allowance, the directors, I believe, in some cases, do not go as far as they might with safety. The directors of the London and Blackwall Railway, as we have seen, made a reduction of 30 per cent. in the intermediate fares about a year and a half since; they have not gained certainly by the change, but they have not lost. The directors of the Brighton Company, when a rival line against them was being contested before a parliamentary committee in the session of 1863, consented to a reduction of their fares 20 per cent. The result we shall allow the chairman of the company to state in his own words, as reported at the half-yearly meeting of the company a few days since :—" It was his duty," he said, " on the last occasion of meeting them, to announce a reduced dividend, arising from the reduction of the tariff, but he ventured at that time to express a hope that the railway traffic and the railway revenue would increase, as the revenue of the country had increased, in consequence of the reduction of duties. Those hopes had been speedily and fully realized, and it was not too much to say that not only had they a prospect of shortly, as far as the dividend was concerned, resuming their former position, but making up for what they had lost consequent on their starting on a new principle."

"Sweet are the uses of adversity." Had there been no opposition to the Brighton in 1863, the public would have had no reduction of 20 per cent. in their fares, nor would the chairman have been able to address his fellow shareholders in such congratulatory terms on the bright prospects of the company. The receipts of this company for passengers for the year amounted to about 800,000$l.$, so the passengers who travelled by that line in 1864 effected a saving of 160,000$l.$ by the gentle pressure put on the company, and the shareholders did not lose a shilling! At the last meeting of the National Association for the Promotion of Social Science, a paper was read by Mr. Chadwick, of a most interesting nature, containing a considerable number of remarkable instances of the benefit that company had derived from a great reduction of fares. At the request of the society, Mr. Chadwick has consented to have it published, and, as every one who takes an interest in the subject will have an opportunity of reading it, it is unnecessary to make any lengthened quotations from it. I shall content myself with one.

" One of the most important examples, as it appears to me," says Mr. Chadwick, " of the effect of reduced charges, was in a competition between the London and North Western Railway, in the London, Birmingham, Wolverhampton, and Stour Valley district, which includes the lines between Dudley and Birmingham, Wolverhampton and Birmingham,

Shrewsbury and Wellington. The London and North Western Railway Company were induced, much at the instance of Mr. W. Richardson Roebuck (who was then the manager of the Stour Valley Railway, but who is now at the head of an eminent trading firm in Manchester), to reduce their fares in varying rates of a fourth or fifth of the previous proportions in the district. The development of traffic was such as to astonish himself and the other local railway agents and managers, particularly the unwonted development from sparsely populated lines; and these lower fares were, in their opinion, highly remunerative, and they would have been more so if the fares had been maintained. Yet on the cessation of the competition, the company returned to the previous high rates, for which no other reason was assigned than that if the low fares were continued, the public travelling on the rest of the company's lines would be struck with the contrast, and would be dissatisfied with the high fares. And it is a matter of inquiry, on behalf of the shareholders as well as of the population, why the example should not have been extended throughout the whole of the company's lines! As one instance of the financial effect of the low fares, I am enabled to give the following results of a return to high fares. The receipts per train, at a penny fare from Shrewsbury to Upton Magna, were in December, 1858, 11$l.$ 15$s.$ 8$d.$; but on the return to 3½$d.$ in November, 1859, the receipts per train fell to 4$l.$ 4$s.$ 11$d.$ The receipts per train from Shrewsbury to Walcot were, at a penny, 14$l.$ 17$s.$ 7$d.$, and at 6$d.$ they fell, in October, 1859, to 4$l.$ 5$s.$ 5$d.$ The results of the Upton Magna case were borne out, even to a greater extent, at each station between Shrewsbury and Wellington. It is most important to observe, however, in this and other such examples, that they are examples of traffic divided between two competitors, neither running under the best conditions for a productive result. But if both lines were brought under unity of management, one might be given up to exclusive passenger traffic with increased safety and comfort, the other to goods traffic, under a consolidated management, with augmented net returns. It is further to be noted from such instances how many more are hindered from travelling by high fares than would be anticipated, *à priori*, except by reference to the economic law I have indicated as to the ratios of increase of consumption with reductions of prices."

I have, however, written this treatise to very little purpose, and failed entirely to convey my meaning, if it would be supposed that I rested my case for the necessity of Government purchase on the fact that railway boards do not make the reduction even that they might in the interests of their shareholders, although that is a most important matter to be borne in mind. The three great facts on which railway reform are based are these: — 1st. That the sacrifice of *one per cent* of a company's dividend would secure a reduction of fares 50, 60, even in some cases 70 per cent.; but as it would be preposterous and utterly unreasonable to expect that railway directors would sacrifice the interest of their shareholders and their own to the public, hence it is that only through Government interference, either by purchase of the existing lines, or the construction of lines by the State, can this nation ever derive the full measure of benefit from her railways. We have noticed in the last instances of reductions in fares in the Blackwall and Brighton lines, they may have gone as far as they can without increasing loss; if they would take off 20 or 30 per cent. more, they might very possibly find their dividends reduced by a half per cent. for some years. The second fact on which railway reform rests is the profit the nation would have by the terms of purchase being advantageous to both parties; and third, the great saving in working the lines, by their amalgamation under one management. Now, why is it that writers in the railway interest will not notice the facts, or, at least, what I put forth as facts, and either deny their correctness or show that they have no bearing on the question? Is it or is it not a fact that the three classes of passengers can be conveyed in a moderately loaded train at the rates of sixteen, twenty-four, and forty miles respectively for a penny each? Do trains convey, on an average, "not to put too fine a point on it," one-tenth of the number they are capable of conveying? Do we find that in proportion as fares are reduced, in nearly the same proportion is the number of passengers increased? Will they name any contest between two companies similar to that between the Great Northern and the London and North-Western when they carried first-class passengers *at a farthing per mile*, where the loss of dividend exceeded one per cent.? Do they think it would be a benefit to the nation if the fares were reduced to *one-third* of their present average rates? Can merchandise be conveyed on railways for about one shilling and sixpence per ton per 100 miles? Did the Great Eastern Company prove that they could bring up coals by their new line if it were granted for about a shilling per ton? Might coals be brought from the North to London, with a good profit, at 10s. per ton? Are not the contests carried on between the companies as fierce and bitter as ever? Is there the most remote probability of this or any future Parliament giving the railway interest protection against competing lines, when the most active promoters of opposition lines are the leading members of the railway body itself?

Such are a few of the topics I would suggest for the consideration of the advocates of the present system; there are none, in my opinion, who would derive so great advantage as the shareholders themselves from the change I have advocated.

"There is a broad distinction," it is asserted, "to be drawn between the reform of the Post Office, which was a purely governmental establishment, and the railways of Great Britain, which are neither indebted to the Government for any contribution towards their construction, to any aid from Parliament, but rather obstruction, nor to any extraneous assistance in their organization."

That is a distinction that every one will admit, and to refer to the difference between the two cases would be quite pertinent if it was contended that the State had any right to take possession of the railways, or that the companies should be in any way coerced to sell their property; but no one ever proposed such a course, or put forward on the part of the State any such claim; nevertheless if the companies are made an offer they should think it would be for their advantage to accept, the case of the railways and the Post Office, so far as regards the working of the two establishments, would be nearly analogous. There is in both cases the same extremely low cost of conveyance; there was in the Post Office the same fiscal restriction on the conveyance of letters, as there is now on the railways in the conveyance of passengers and goods, and we find a similar result in those cases when the railway tariff is lowered, as we have experienced by the reduction of Post-Office charges.

"The Act had become forgotten," it is said, "because the general feeling of the country never lent itself to the idea that there was any intention to take action upon the claim after the failure of every attempt to establish, by the means of commissioners and inspectors, an intrusive interference with the policy and practical working of the railways of the country."

There is some truth in this statement, so far, at least, as the "purchase claims" are concerned; but the question is, would it be for the benefit of the shareholders, bearing in mind their present position and future prospects, to make an agreement with the Government in the spirit of that Act? If they think not, that necessarily makes an end of the matter.

"The question of the 'highwayman,'" it is now declared, "is now about to be put to the railway interest—one of two things, 'unrestricted competition, or surrender your rights to the Government;' thereby meaning and intending, 'Your money or your life!' for there is no mistaking the difficult position in which the railway interest is intended to be placed by the resuscitation of the 'almost forgotten' purchase clause of 1844."

It is so far from certain of the "question of the highwayman" being put, that at the present time we have no means of judging if ever the nation will consent to the purchase of the railways on any terms whatever, and therefore the supposition is wholly gratuitous. All that can be said at the present time, so far as an opinion can be formed from the public press and from the opinions of some of the leading statesmen of the day, is, that the subject is deemed worthy of consideration. But to bring the question under the consideration of Parliament, with a view to turning it to practical account, would require the cordial assent of the railway interest; and if we are to take its press as the representative of its feelings, it does not seem much inclined to favour the project. As a matter of course, the railway press is quite right in so doing, if it considers such a change disadvantageous to the shareholders; but is it not obvious to every one, that every year the general feeling of the country is tending towards a state of perfect free trade, and at the present time the business of conveying passengers and goods through the country is the only one that can be termed a monopoly. Notwithstanding the enormous expenses the companies severally incur to maintain this monopoly, it is perfectly plain, if there is any dependence to be placed in what we see passing around us, that if the present system be not abolished, every facility at least will be given for the construction of new lines. The *Times* says, " In a few years hence people will look back with astonishment at a system that permitted interested traders to offer opposition to another set of traders who desired to compete with them in the market." The projectors of a new line will, no doubt, have to make the best terms they can with the majority of the landlords, and if there be *bonâ fide* opposition from a landowner, and he can prove that the line is not wanted, and that the opposition is *bonâ fide*, and not from another company in disguise, in such case the line would no doubt be refused. Now, I put this case hypothetically: assuming that it would appear evident, from the state of feeling in the country, that all exclusive privileges railway companies enjoy should be abolished, and unlimited competition be the future rule, would it not be for the benefit of shareholders that the Act of 1844 should be carried out?

"Are Government establishments so wisely and economically conducted," it is asked, "as to make the public place faith in the preference of Government over private administration? Are the dockyards so well conducted — the naval department so superior to private yards? Is the ordnance so cheaply and so efficiently controlled as that it may be assumed that economy and efficiency go hand in hand with Government control?"

This is the great stock argument against the possession of the railways by the State, if that can be called an argument which has no foundation whatever in fact. It affords a remarkable illustration of the association of ideas, and it seems impossible for the railway interest to disconnect Government management from the Board of Trade; there the Board sits like Banquo's ghost, shaking its gory locks at directors and railway officials, and directors and railway officials love it not. But who ever suggested that the management of the railways should be "handed over to Government officials?" or that the Board of Trade had any qualification for undertaking such a work? That Board has a number of multifarious duties to attend to, even were it qualified, which it is not, to undertake the management of our railways. There is not the shadow of a pretence for supposing that in the event of the State taking possession of the railways they would be handed over to Government officials, as that term is usually understood. The nation and the Legislature would require that the railways should be managed by a board comprised of the ablest practical men in the kingdom, selected from the existing boards, and it is only fair to suppose that the Government would give effect to the wishes of the nation. What, then, becomes of this argument that meets us at every turn about

"Government officials?" No doubt, in one sense, the gentlemen comprising this board would become Government officials; but would railway writers contend that these gentlemen, in the exercise of the duties of their office, would be less able, conscientious, and independent in the discharge of their duty on behalf of the nation than they are now on behalf of their shareholders? I hope it is the last we shall hear of the objection to "Government officials," unless the writers state to what class of officials they refer. It is very remarkable, as I before noticed, that the manner in which Post-Office officials do their duty is never held out as a warning against making railways a Government department. No doubt there are many shortcomings with them, as with other officials, but they are kept so continually under the public eye—as railway officials would be—that there is a continual check on their conduct.

"There is another course should be adopted," it is contended by the advocates of railway restriction—" that of imposing upon parliamentary committees the sacred duty of seeing that all railway powers are strictly required by the necessities of the districts which the railways promoted are professedly designed to serve, and that the promoters had not mere speculative and jobbing interests to serve."

There can be no doubt if Parliament would adopt the course suggested, and perform the "sacred duty" marked out for it, great benefit would be conferred on railway property. The task, however, would be for a committee somewhat difficult and invidious of deciding as to who were speculators and jobbers, and who were not. Here we have the directors of the "Great Eastern," in conjunction with the "Lancashire and Yorkshire" on one side, opposed to the "Great Northern," the "Manchester and Sheffield," and the "Midland" on the other; now it would be a very delicate matter for a committee to decide which boards were composed of "good men and true," and which of speculators and jobbers, and to draw the same distinction in all other applications for Bills. It would simplify matters very much, and I have no doubt give great satisfaction to the railway interest generally, if there was an Act passed making it a misdemeanor to promote a Bill for a new line within twenty miles of any existing line; such a course would put an effectual stop to competing lines.

"As no conversion could take place," it is said, "without an offer be made to repay the principal sum proposed to be converted, we believe the Chancellor of the Exchequer, who took in hand the purchase of British railways, would find that he would have to pay down a good round sum in hard cash, as well as stock certificates."

If the Chancellor of the Exchequer proposed to carry out the Act literally, and if he had to deal with a hostile proprietary, he could, as we all know, do nothing at the present time; but it is proposed to supersede the Act by a voluntary arrangement, and that the payment should be made in the ordinary Three per Cent. Stock; the shareholders would become stockholders and repay themselves, like any other stockholders, by selling out.

"Our own opinion is," says *Herapath*, "that railway travelling would not be improved by the change Mr. Galt contemplates, and that some railway properties would be victimized to a wholesale extent, while others would be fairly remunerated under a purchase by Government. How, for instance, would the Great Western proprietors be fairly compensated? It might be said, this feature might be estimated and allowed for in the private bargain. *Herapath* thinks, if Government would make an offer of 200*l*. a share—the market price being 80*l*.—the Government would have no difficulty in purchasing at such price. *Herapath's* opinion appears to be, that the value of some railway property will be so much increased that it would be unreasonable to ask the shareholders to sell at the present market price, but if sold at all it should be at the price speculative persons suppose it may be worth some ten or fifteen years hence. There is a novelty in this plan to be commended, but why should this method of purchase be confined to purchase of railways by Government? Let railway projectors show how this plan would work by giving to every one whose house or land they may require the owners' prospective valuation of the property fifteen or twenty years hence!

In Ireland, railway directors and proprietors have entertained very favourably the scheme of the purchase of railways by Government. At a meeting held in Dublin lately, in reference to this subject, Mr. Murland, chairman of the Dublin and Drogheda line, and vice-chairman of the Great Southern and Western Company, expressed himself strongly in regard to the advantage it would confer on a great number of companies, the shareholders in which, at the present time, receive no dividends whatever. Mr. Murland, it is true, stated that he did not think the public would derive as much benefit as I had calculated on from the adoption of the scheme, and in this respect he may be right; it is only by a trial the result can be tested.

Thirty years ago, a Royal Commission was appointed to report on the best plan for providing Ireland with railways. The commissioners were unanimous in opinion that the railways necessary for the country should be constructed by the State; to that report I have referred in the early part of this work. Ireland is in every respect more adapted for a railway system under the control of Government than England is. There the people do not view the interference of Government in mercantile affairs with the same distrust as is felt in this country; and whilst in one country it might be desirable to confine the experiment of low fares and Government supervision to a few lines, in the other the experiment might be extended from the Giant's Causeway to Cape Clear, and from Connemara to the Hill of Howth, with the complete assent and support of all classes and sections of the people.

CHAPTER VII.

Railway Receipts in 1865—An Agreement with the Companies to Reduce their Charges—The Justice of a Payment to the Companies for that Purpose—The Extent of Railways throughout the Kingdom—All Classes should derive Benefit from a Reduction in Fares and Freightage—Arbitrary Charges in the Tariff for Merchandise—Adam Smith—Payment to the Companies compared to the Income Tax—The direct and indirect Advantages of a Reduction in Fares and Freightage—Extract from Mr. Mill's " Political Economy "—Committee of the House of Commons—Experiments Suggested—Conclusion—Resumé.

THE amount of payments that will be made by the public to railway companies in 1865 may be calculated at thirty-six millions sterling; and we have now to consider, if the fares and rates by the companies were reduced by two-thirds, would such a reduction be equivalent, so far as the interests of the public are concerned, to a reduction of the taxation of the country by twenty-four millions; or, in other words, would such a reduction in railway charges give as much relief to the country as the total abolition of our customs duty, which amounts annually to nearly the same sum?

Let us suppose the railway companies would say to the Government, " If you make us a payment of four millions per annum, we will consolidate ourselves into one body, and reduce our fares and rates two-thirds." Would it be advisable for Government, in the absence of any other scheme, to recommend the Legislature to accept such an offer? Would the nation gain twenty millions per annum by the agreement? That is the first question we have to consider.

It will be admitted, I presume, that whether the public pays money to a company or to the State, amounts, so far as the individuals are concerned, to the same thing, as the relief is equal, if the payment be reduced, in either case. But to make that relief national it must not only be extended to every part of the kingdom, but to every class in the community; and let us consider if these two indispensable conditions are comprised in payments to the railway companies.

First, in regard to the extent of railways throughout the kingdom. One has but to glance over a railway map and he will scarcely be able to discern a village, or even hamlet, that is not provided with railway accommodation; there is not a district, however thinly populated, except in the Highlands of Scotland, that one or more railways do not run through.

Second, in regard to the classes from whom the companies receive payments. It will be found that all classes, without reference to position, would be equally relieved by a reduction in their payments to the companies. Let us take first the numbers who travel, and the payments made by the different grades of society, as represented by the three classes. The number of first-class passengers who travelled in 1863 was, in round numbers, twenty-three millions; second-class, fifty-seven millions; and third-class, *one hundred and twenty-one millions;* and the fares paid by each class severally were 3,300,000*l*., 4,200,000*l*., and 4,900,000*l*. It will be seen, therefore, that the working classes would derive their full share of advantage from a reduction in fares.

In reference to the payments to the companies for freightage, although that is paid in the first instance by the merchant, trader, or manufacturer, the charge ultimately, as every one knows, falls on the consumer; it extends almost to everything that we eat, drink, or wear, smell, taste, touch, or handle, everything, in fact, that ministers to our comforts or necessities comes under the railway tariff for " merchandise." There is in this tariff by the several companies as much difference in charges as there is for that of passengers; but inasmuch as the payments are principally confined to the trading classes,

U

it is those classes alone that know the vexatious manner in which the payments are enforced, although the general public must ultimately pay. It is in heavy articles of merchandise, such as coal, where the charge for conveyance adds so largely to the price, that the middle and working classes feel the monopoly so severely. The carriers may be said to live in a state of chronic warfare with railway directors.

It appears to me very evident that if a reduction of payments by the public to the companies be considered, either in reference to the area over which that reduction would extend, or its equitable distribution among all classes, it would be found in conformity with the doctrines laid down by our highest authorities in political economy.

Nothing, as we have seen, can be more arbitrary than the charges by railway companies, either for passengers or merchandise. What does Adam Smith say on this subject?

"The tax which each individual is bound to pay ought to be certain, and not arbitrary. The time of payment, the manner of payment, the quantity to be paid, ought all to be clear and plain to the contributor, and to every other person. When it is otherwise, every person subject to the tax is put more or less in the power of the tax-gatherer, who can aggravate the tax on any obnoxious contributor. The certainty of what each individual ought to pay is, in taxation, a matter of the greatest importance."

"It may obstruct," he says in another place, "the industry of the people, and discourage them from applying themselves to certain branches of business. All nations have endeavoured, to the best of their judgment, to render their taxes as equal as they could contrive.

"The sovereigns of China, those of Bengal while under the Mahometan Government, and those of ancient Egypt, are said, accordingly, to have been extremely attentive to the making and maintaining of good roads and navigable canals, in order to increase, as much as possible, both the quantity and value of every part of the produce of the land, by procuring to every part of it the most extensive market which their own dominions could afford."—*Wealth of Nations.*

I think it would be well to follow the example set us by the "sovereigns of Bengal, China, and ancient Egypt," and learn that as we have the best roads in the world, our work is but half done, so long as our fiscal arrangements in regard to their use by the public are of such a nature as to nullify, in a great measure, the immense advantages that the nation would otherwise receive from them.

Assuming that an arrangement could be made with the companies by a payment of four or five millions a year to make the reduction in charges we are discussing, let us examine how far such a payment would be analogous to that of the income tax laid on by Sir Robert Peel for the purpose of reducing indirect taxation.

I think it would be found that a payment to the railway companies for the purpose I have named, if we could do nothing better, would be still more beneficial to the public, inasmuch as the income tax was only laid on for the purpose of decreasing indirect taxation, whilst the payment of four or five millions a year to the companies, if such a bargain could be made, would not only decrease direct payments to *double that amount*, but also indirect payments to *a still greater amount*.

Taking our gross payments for 1865 at thirty-six millions, we might calculate on rather more than the half for merchandise; and a reduction of payments to one-third would effect a saving to the public, in round numbers, of eleven millions in direct payments on fares, parcels, &c., and thirteen millions in indirect payments on general merchandise. Thus, a person who was in the habit of paying 30*l.* a year for travelling would have that sum reduced to 10*l.*; that would be definite and distinct, and the saving he would make he could calculate to a penny. Now it is a very different matter when a reduction is made in indirect payments; it is a considerable time before the consumer derives all the profit from the change; there is generally a rise in price in the commodity itself, caused by the increased demand, then the dealer generally takes care to make something by the change, so that the consumer, often for a long time at least, makes but little by the alteration. Why is it a reduction in the income tax is always so popular? because the public—the tax-paying portion at least—have the full benefit of any reduction. So it would be with the payment of fares: every person that travels by railway—and who does not?—would have the full benefit of the reduction. But it may be said many persons do not now travel by railway. That, no doubt, is the case, but it is the result of excessive fares. Is there any class in the kingdom who either have no necessity or no wish to travel, either on business or on pleasure? Not one. From the peer to the peasant, from the wealthiest merchant to the humblest mechanic, there is no exception to the universal rule.

It might be objected that with low fares many people would not in reality save money, for many would travel three times as much as they do at present; but their doing so would be entirely optional, and if they can have the same extent of travelling for one-third of the money they formerly paid, it rests with themselves to expend more money or not, as they may think proper. At the present time many people spend more in postage than they did under the old rates, but no one, I suppose, would argue from that circumstance that the reduction of post-office charges is the less beneficial to the public.

In regard to the advantages the public would derive from the abolition of the thirteen millions of indirect payments, it would, no doubt, be more unequally divided among the population than the benefit derived from the reduction in direct payments when each individual in the community obtains his or her exact share in the reduction that takes place. In the reduction of indirect payments the person through whose hands the payments take place are naturally those who derive the greatest advantage from such reductions. This is especially the case in regard to traders when the reduction is small compared with the value of the article in which they deal; the public, for instance, derives little or no benefit from a reduction of half-a-crown in the hundredweight in the price of sugar, as the grocer considers the reduction so small that he may as well keep it to himself. So in those cases where the cost of carriage bears but a small proportion to the value of the articles carried, the general public might not gain much, yet that very large class, the mercantile community, would be very great gainers. It would be from the reduction in the carriage of heavy articles of merchandise, as coal, timber, iron, &c., the conveyance of which so greatly enhances the price, that the general public would derive the full benefit; so that, on the whole, the indirect payments of the different classes of the public would be reduced by thirteen millions, in addition to the eleven millions of direct payments.

Let us give another illustration of the benefit the nation would derive from the possession of the railways, and the adoption of the low tariff I have suggested. The nation, it is said, would by their purchase " contract an additional debt of some four hundred and odd millions." That is not a correct way of putting the case. The nation would not make any engagement whatever about the principal, but would only undertake to pay a rental in perpetuity, considerably less than the net receipts now received by the shareholders. The nation would pay, in the case I have supposed, four or five millions in its *corporate* capacity, but inasmuch as it would save twenty-four millions a year in its *individual* capacity, in the payments by individuals of whom the nation is composed, the aggregate savings of fifteen or twenty years would be sufficient to pay off the whole of the principal.

Well, then, we come back to the original question. Would the nation gain twenty millions per annum by giving the companies four millions per annum to make a reduction of two-thirds in charges ? Do these payments now made extend to every part of the kingdom ? Do they affect all classes equally ? Would the nation experience the same relief in the reduction of those charges as it would by the reduction of taxation to the same amount in the ordinary way by the Chancellor of the Exchequer ?

There is a great confusion of ideas caused by the wrong use of terms in reference to the State. Many speakers and writers use the terms "Government," "State and Revenue," as though they were synonymous; and will say, "the State incurs a loss," whereas what they mean, or at least what they should say, would be that the revenue incurs a loss. Even some of our very able political writers fall into this error. Here, for instance, is a quotation from one of our leading newspapers, a few weeks since, in reference to the Post Office :—

"The first great change in the system was all in favour of the public, to the detriment of the State. The introduction of the penny postage everybody felt directly and immediately; no relief that the Chancellor of the Exchequer could devise would come home so quickly and sensibly as this did to every man's door. The loss to the State had to be made up as far and as steadily as possible, and this could only be done by extending the business, or, in other words, multiplying the number of letters transmitted through the post."

If the writer had used the word "revenue" for that of "State," he would have been quite correct; but in the sense he used it he conveyed altogether an erroneous idea. The State would lose, and not the revenue, by the loss of a Queen's ship, or by war, or a loan guaranteed to a foreign power that the Government would ultimately be called on to repay; but the State would not lose by a reduction of taxation, although the revenue might, inasmuch as the people, who compose the State, frequently gain much more in their individual capacity than they lose in their corporate capacity. When the Chancellor of the Exchequer took fourpence per pound off tea, there was a decrease in the revenue of three or four hundred thousand pounds; and when he took twopence in the pound off the income tax there was a loss to the revenue of some couple of millions; but it would be very erroneous in either case to say that the State was a loser.

So at the present time you will hear people speak about the purchase by the State of the railways, and concerning the reduction to one-third of the present charges they will say, "Those fares will not pay, and Government will lose by it; so Government cannot undertake it." Thus the Government, the Nation, and the Revenue are all mixed up in the public mind, without any distinction or difference whatever.

It must be obvious, I think, to every one who gives the matter the slightest consideration, that the view now generally taken of the subject is altogether erroneous. It would be quite correct if Government were a joint-stock company, having no connection with the nation, and had undertaken to govern this country as a matter of speculation on its own account; but it should be remembered that the Government is but the acting manager for the country for the time being, and whatever saving is effected by its means to the different classes of society, is in every respect tantamount to a reduction in taxation.

If Government, however, in carrying out any scheme by which a great saving would be effected to all the individuals of which society is composed, should be obliged to incur some expense while acting for the nation in its collective capacity, the latter sum should be deducted from the former, and the balance shows the net gain to the nation by the transaction.

Our traders and manufacturers feel the load pressing very heavily, which railway directors are enabled, from the power they possess, to lay on them. "The cost of production," says M'Culloch, "together with the ordinary profit, may therefore be called the necessary price or value of all things made by labour and capital." But of what avail is labour and capital, it may be asked, if there is a power over them practically despotic, that can, and does to a great extent, neutralize the natural effects produced by the combination of labour and capital?

"When the cost of production is increased artificially by a tax, the effect is the same as when it is increased by natural causes. If only one or a few commodities are affected, their value and price rise so as to compensate the producer or dealer for his peculiar burthen; but if there were a tax on all commodities exactly proportioned to their value, no such compensation would be obtained. A tax on any one commodity, whether laid on its production, its importation, *its carriage from place to place*, or its sale, will, as a general rule, raise the value and price of the commodity by at least the amount of the tax. Whatever renders a large capital necessary, in any trade or business, limits the competition in that business, and, by giving something like a monopoly to a few dealers, may enable them either to keep up the price beyond what would afford the ordinary rate of profit, or to obtain the ordinary rate of profit with a less degree of exertion for improving and cheapening their commodity. There is still another consideration: the higher price necessitated by the tax almost always checks the demand for the commodity; and since there are many improvements in production which to make them practicable require a certain extent of demand, such improvements are obstructed, and many of them prevented altogether."
—*Mill's Political Economy*.

There is perhaps no class whom the railway monopoly more injuriously affects than our manufacturers, living at a great distance from our coal-fields, and obliged to submit to whatever price the companies charge, and compete, under such disadvantageous circumstances, with other manufacturers. Coal can be brought to London, and pay a good profit, at ten shillings per ton; and we all know what it costs.

It is not necessary to pursue this branch of the subject further; but when the experience of our practical men coincides with the theories of our most distinguished writers on political economy relating to a matter deeply affecting the vital interests of the country, it is surely time for the British Parliament to examine closely into the causes that have produced such a result, and devise the necessary remedy.

It must be remembered that, although the payments to the companies for 1865 may be calculated at thirty-six millions, it is impossible for any one to form an opinion as to the amount they will ultimately reach in future years. Should the Act of 1844 not be carried out, but, on the contrary, be removed from the statute book, the prognostications of the *Times* will, in all probability, prove true; and the railway system, under such circumstances, be so extended as to defy, at the present time, all powers of calculation. Mr. Watkin, it appears by his speech, does not consider our present system perfect: he thinks that "four or five large systems, bound to interchange with each other by a 'through' system of working, might be better than fifty or sixty smaller ones." This is pretty well for a beginning. It would be reforming the system, no doubt, indifferently well, but why not reform it altogether? When Mr. Watkin has got so far as to be willing to reduce the number of establishments to four—north, south, east, and west—he has only to go a little further, consolidate the four into one, obtain the increased credit that a Government guarantee would give, and then he and I are quite agreed as to the course that should be pursued.

It has been a matter of surprise to many that in France, or any other of the Continental nations where centralization is carried to such an extent, there has not been established a uniform tariff, either for passengers or goods. Although the tariff in each country has not the same diversity it has with us, yet in the different parts of each country there is considerable difference in the charges. Some years since, I was on the direction of the South Eastern Railway of Switzerland, and at one time entertained some hopes of bringing about a uniform tariff through the different cantons, but I soon had to give up the attempt; the interests were so conflicting, or they were so at least in the opinions of the different directors, that I soon found that nothing in that way could be effected.

We have been so long accustomed to deal with railways as private property, to be managed by private individuals, and that whoever manages them should make them pay, that even should the country come ultimately to the opinion that they should be in the possession of the State, it might, nevertheless, still think that the charges ought not to be reduced to a lower rate than would be met by the actual receipts—that the Government should not incur "a loss," nor seek any assistance from the Treasury. As it is not likely that there will be any legislation in the session of 1865, should even some great change be found desirable, there will be ample time to have full inquiry and experiments as to the extent that reduction in charges can be effected without " loss "—if I must use the word—before the new Parliament meet. By that time there can be collected every necessary information for legislative purposes.

Should a committee, or commission, be appointed by Parliament to consider this subject, the first matter for inquiry would probably be the actual cost of conveyance for passengers and goods on railways. Second, the additional expense, if both were largely increased, say threefold their present number or weight; and as there is no data in existence that would afford the means to form an opinion as to the amount of loss which would be incurred, the necessary information could only be obtained by an arrangement with a certain number of companies, engaging them to convey passengers and goods at such a tariff as the Legislature, acting on the recommendation of the Government, might deem desirable.

I believe there is not a company in the kingdom would refuse to co-operate with the Government in any experiment the latter might think it desirable to make, a guarantee, of course, being given for indemnification against loss; and if half a dozen or a dozen lines in England and Scotland were selected, so that all the different kinds of traffic would be represented, those lines being so isolated that they could not abstract traffic from other lines, and that tariff be continued for a year, the issue between high and low charges would be fairly determined, the public opinion of the country would be enlightened, and both nation and Legislature in 1866 would thoroughly understand and, therefore, be perfectly competent to deal with the subject.

Although the committee might recommend this course, and Parliament act on such recommendation, there would remain, nevertheless, two matters of the greatest importance the committee would have to investigate and report on, viz. the extent of reduction in fares to passengers, and in freightage on goods, it would recommend for adoption to the Legislature.

Let us now consider as briefly as we can the different recommendations in regard to the tariff for fares that would in all probability be pressed on the attention of the committee.

1. Very low fares. There are many, I have no doubt, who would recommend to the committee a reduction similar to that made in the Post Office, and contend that as, in the ordinary course of trade, the cost of production governed the price for which the article was sold, so the same principle should be acted on by Government, and as a first-class passenger could be carried sixteen miles for a penny, it would be a most unreasonable charge to make him pay a shilling in a slow train, and one shilling and eightpence in a fast train, and that the reduction should be assimilated to that of the Post Office, and that sixpence, under the circumstances, was the utmost that could be fairly charged.

It would be further contended that as the fares were decreased, so in the same proportion, or nearly so, would the number of passengers increase, until ultimately, as in the case of the Post Office, the revenue under the new system would equal that under the old, therefore, it would be argued, a very low tariff should be adopted.

I have had before occasion to remark, in regard to the financial part of this question, that, although the public good, in an enlarged sense, is the primary matter to be considered, the financial success of the scheme is secondary to it only. I have also given reasons, not necessary to repeat here, why I considered the increase in the number of passengers would not under any circumstances be in the same ratio as the increase of letters; but I will suppose that I have been in error, and that it were satisfactorily proved that a reduction could be made in fares to the *one-sixth* of the present rates without any loss to the revenue, I should, nevertheless, say that even under those circumstances it would be a sound and good policy on the part of the Legislature to charge *double* those fares.

It must be remembered that, if the railways should ever become the property of the State, the greater the revenue raised from them the greater will be the reduction in our taxation in other departments, direct or indirect, as the case may be. It is impossible for any man at present to foresee to what extent at some future time our railways may contribute to the national revenue, and, consequently, to our relief from other burthens which either press upon us, or which, from their injustice, cause considerable irritation in the public mind. The tariff which it is desirable to fix for passengers and goods should be sufficiently low to meet the necessities of all classes throughout the kingdom. In regard to passengers, I think twopence per mile by first-class express, and one penny per mile on an average of first-class fast and slow trains, and other classes in proportion, would fairly meet the necessity of the case. If we go higher than those rates, we largely decrease the traffic; but if we go lower, I doubt if the traffic would much increase.

The effect on the traffic is the sure test by which the appreciation by the public in a reduction of charges is known; and when the reduction is carried to that extent that it ceases to act with efficiency, revenue that could be easily collected is thrown away that might be usefully employed in relieving the nation from taxation of some other kind that presses heavily on it.

In regard to the proper tariff for each class of goods, I am not competent to give an opinion. Our merchants, manufacturers, and traders, would of course give all the information to a commission necessary to enable it to form a right judgment of the extent to which it should be reduced.

It is impossible to calculate, with any pretension to accuracy, the increase of passengers that would take place under the tariff I have proposed, or any other low tariff. We are, at present, to a great extent, groping our way in the dark, with only such glimpses of light to guide us as the fortuitous collisions of hostile parties occasionally furnish us with. We are, in fact, profoundly ignorant of the effect on the British people of a full development of our traffic as it would be when freed from its present fiscal restraints, not merely in reference to their commercial prosperity and physical well-being, but also to their social and moral progress. If I might venture to borrow the beautiful simile of the greatest of our philosophers, when illustrating a far more important subject than that we are now discussing, we might compare ourselves to children picking up pebbles by the seaside, with the sea itself stretching out before us, its depths unfathomed, and we profoundly ignorant of all that those depths contained.

What is the obstacle, then, to prevent our legislators from dealing practically with the railway question in the session of 1865? Simply a want of the necessary knowledge pertaining to the subject, and until this is acquired it is utterly impossible that the Legislature can, in any way, deal satisfactorily with the matter. The specific knowledge the Legislature mainly requires, is the extent to which the nation would avail itself of a low tariff for passengers and goods. We know pretty accurately the cost at which a train of carriages with passengers, or trucks with goods, can be conveyed per mile, and we likewise know that with a small addition to the cost of passenger trains three times the number of persons might be conveyed by each train; but we require more specific knowledge. Especially in regard to the conveyance of coal and other minerals, and to the weight that could be conveniently sent by goods trains, and the increased cost of sending large loads, we require additional knowledge.

Nor is it even positively ascertained that a reduction of the tariff on passengers and goods to one-third of the present rates, would have the result of increasing the number of travellers and the quantity of goods in the ratio say of 5 to 2. The principal subject for inquiry is to ascertain, on the one hand, the increase in expense, and, on the other, the profit the State would derive from the decreased payment to the shareholders, and by the saving in expense by the consolidation of the railways under one management.

We have had, it is true, many contests between railway companies, to some of which I have drawn attention, carried on for considerable periods, at *one third* of the fares I have ventured to suggest, as those that in our ordinary tariff might be adopted, without more loss in the dividends than the profit of the State would make up. These cases, however, cannot be depended on beyond a certain extent; they do not form a class from which a general rule can be drawn, as the reduction of fares on the several lines was only carried out on part of them.

That the world at large is reaping the greatest advantages from the improved, or rather newly invented facilities for locomotion can be doubted by none; they are the means whereby the most distant provinces are closely connected with their respective capitals, and not only that, but they are breaking down the barrier that separates nation from nation, uniting the capital of one country with that of another, and thus tending rapidly towards one of the great ends of human existence, the knowledge of our fellow man. And so it is: those two mighty powers of civilization and science, the steam engine and the railway, are day by day entering on new tracks, and penetrating regions hitherto almost unknown; confined to no hemisphere, indigenous to every soil, careless under what Government they exist, onward are they marching with giant strides, through the wild forests of America, along the romantic banks of the Rhine and the fertile plains of Lombardy; and in the same proportion as the wise design of Providence becomes more and more appreciated, that all should consider themselves as members of one great family, in the same proportion should we use our best exertions to extend the use of those means which seem destined to accomplish this great end.

There are other considerations connected with this subject, which I need not do more than glance at. That knowledge would be extended, and religion and morality advanced, by an increased facility of communication with those densely populated parts of the country where ignorance and vice most prevail, cannot be doubted by any thinking man. The influence which a comparatively free means of communication might be expected to exercise in abolishing these evils, have been thus forcibly described by one of our great departed statesmen:—

"The steam engine and railroad are not merely facilitating the conveyance of merchandise from one part of the country to another, they are doing more, they are sealing the intercourse between mind and mind, and they are creating demands for knowledge, sending the desire for that knowledge into all the recesses of this empire, tending powerfully to the cultivation of the mental as they are improving the physical capabilities of the country."

I have now completed, to the best of my ability, the

task I have undertaken, and, however inefficiently it may be done, I hope that I have said enough to prepare the public mind for that thorough investigation of our railway system which in the parliamentary session of 1865 it will probably undergo.

I shall now, in conclusion, make a brief *resumé* of the main facts and arguments I have brought forward in the course of this work to prove the importance and practicability of a thorough reform of our railway system.

It has been stated, in express terms, by a committee of the House of Commons:—

1. "That the highways of a country are as necessary to a people as the air they breathe," and I have endeavoured to show that our railways have become these highways; that the Legislature, in delegating the trust involved in their management to private individuals, gave up one of its most important functions, and abandoned, for the time being, to irresponsible parties, that power which should be exercised by the State alone.

2. That the present system, so far from being definitely adopted by the Legislature and the country, is avowedly on its trial; that Parliament, in 1844, acting on the recommendation of the Government of the day—Sir Robert Peel being the first Minister of the Crown, and Mr. Gladstone President of the Board of Trade—passed a general Act, whereby all railways constructed in the United Kingdom from that time forth should, after the expiration of twenty-one years from the date of their respective Bills, become national property, whenever the Legislature should so determine.

3. That, in the Act of 1844, the exact terms were stated on which the railways should be purchased.

4. That this bargain was made by the President of the Board of Trade with the representatives of the railway interest, and that the Bill passed the third reading without opposition.

5. That the purchase of the then existing railways was recom-

mended by "men of the highest commercial position and greatest experience;" and the Government, whilst fully admitting the importance of the subject, thought it desirable that the settlement of the question should be deferred for twenty-one years, when, as might be expected, our railway system should be nearly completed, and the public in a much better condition to judge of the merits of the question than they were at that time.

6. The main argument in favour of the State exercising its right of purchasing the railways is founded on the fact that the companies who hold them have virtually in their hands the monopoly of the traffic of the country, and raise and lower the fares and charges at pleasure. How this power is exercised by the companies is proved by the great variation in their tariffs, both for goods and passengers; although the cost of transport is reduced, by means of railways, to less than the one-twentieth part of what it was by common roads, yet the charges are not reduced, on an average, to one-half of what they formerly were; they vary all over the kingdom, being double, treble, or even quadruple in some places, to what they are in others; the directors' powers in this respect being practically unlimited, they naturally choose those charges that pay best, without reference to the interests of the public.

7. It is shown that the variation in fares, within certain limitations, viz. from three farthings to threepence per mile for first-class passengers, and from one farthing to one penny per mile for third-class passengers, makes but comparatively little difference in profit to the shareholders; but, as a general rule, what is termed moderate fares, viz. about twopence farthing per mile for first class, and the other classes in proportion, are found to pay best; and it is shown that, in some cases, when, from opposition or other causes, the fares have been reduced 70 per cent., the dividends to the shareholders were not, in any case, reduced more than at the rate of *one* per cent. per annum on their capital.

x

8. It is argued that as no right exists, either legal or moral, to call on railway proprietors to reduce their fares and charges lower than what they find most conducive to their interests, there is no probability of any great reduction taking place, and that therefore, under the present system, the same high and irregular charges must continue to exist throughout the kingdom.

9. It is endeavoured to be shown that our system has been as detrimental to the interest of the shareholder as to that of the public; and that competition being the only means to which the public can look for a reduction in charges, it must, if the system be not altered, prove ruinous to railway proprietors. It is shown, by a comparison of dates and dividends, that railway property has been reduced by competition to little more than half its former value.

10. A reaction having, within the last few years, taken place, and railway property being considerably improved, it is argued that the present would be the best time for railway proprietors to evince their readiness to come to an arrangement with the Government for the purchase of their railways on fair and equitable terms, according to the spirit of the Act of 1844.

11. It is contended that the improvement in railway property arises from two causes, wholly exceptional: the conservative tendency of the present Parliament in railway matters, evinced in the discountenance generally given to new projects, and the attention of the public being directed at this time to other modes of investment. It is noted, as prejudicial to existing interests, that there is a yearly-increasing tendency, on the part of landowners, to promote, in every way, the construction of new railways; therefore, it is argued that it would best suit the interest of the shareholders to sell their property to the State so soon as a public opinion in this country was created and formed, that would enable the Government and the Legislature to carry out such a project.

12. Sir Rowland Hill's plan of reform, in reference to our Post Office, is quoted as a precedent for the carrying out of a

plan somewhat analogous in regard to our railways. It is shown, by the Post-office returns, that the gross revenue is increased fifty per cent., and that the net revenue is equal to what it formerly was, although the postage on each letter has been reduced to an average of *one-sixth* of its former rate; and it is contended that a reduction in railway charges to *one-third* of their present rate might be expected to produce, in many respects, similar results.

13. The mode suggested for the purchase of the railways is, that an equivalent be given in 3 per cent. stock on the market value of the shares at the present time, with such bonus as the Legislature may consider fit. It is assumed that the Legislature would offer such liberal terms as to induce the companies to accept Government stock in exchange for their shares; that the purchase, or rather conversion of railway stock into Government stock, would be gradual; and that the operation, being voluntary, would in no way disturb the money market or the general commercial state of the country.

14. The difference between the interest paid by Government and the dividends derived from investment on the best railway unguaranteed stock is about $1\frac{1}{2}$ per cent.; and it is contended that as the shareholders would take a much less interest, secured by the State, than that which they now receive from the railways, the Government would have at their disposal a sufficient sum to make up the loss that would be caused by a great reduction in fares or charges.

15. It is proposed that as each railway would become the property of the State, a low and uniform tariff for passengers should be adopted : by ordinary trains, first-class passengers at three farthings per mile, second-class one halfpenny, and third-class one farthing per mile, with higher rates for fast and express trains; and that for excursion trains half the rates of ordinary trains should be charged.

16. The very low cost of conveyance of passengers and merchandise on railways is proved by calculations founded on

the traffic returns from the Board of Trade and the companies. It is shown that a passenger, taking an average of the three classes, can be conveyed a hundred miles when an engine is fully loaded, as in excursion trains, for fourpence; that charge covering not only every direct expense, but also a fair percentage added for the general expenditure of the establishment. A ton of merchandise can be conveyed a hundred miles for little more than a shilling. The tariff for the different kinds of merchandise, as at present charged, is given, whereby it is seen that the general charge is, in many cases, more than twenty times that which it costs the companies.

17. The injurious effects of such a system to the mercantile interests of the country are pointed out, and it is contended that in proportion as the impediments to free communication throughout a country are removed, in the same proportion must that country prosper; and it is further submitted, that impediments of a fiscal nature to extended intercourse throughout a country, in the form of what may be termed a hostile tariff, have, to a great extent, just the same effect as physical impediments.

18. The pernicious working of our railway monopoly is especially noted in regard to the supply of coal to the metropolis. It is shown, by the accounts drawn out for a special occasion about ten years since, by the chairman of one of the companies, in answer to a charge made against him that he was conveying coal at "unremunerative rates," that although, during a short opposition, he charged only a farthing per ton per mile, even at that low rate the carriage yielded 200 per cent. profit! It is further shown, by a report from a committee of the House of Lords published last year, that a railway but a few miles in length, in the proximity of London, has the power of stopping the coal traffic by railways from the North of England to a large district in London, and practically exercises it by making an enormous charge. Especial notice is directed to the fact that a Bill for completing railway com-

munication between the Great Eastern Railway and the North of England was thrown out last Session of Parliament. Although the price of coal at the pit's mouth is only six or seven shillings per ton, and the company could convey it to London at the rate of eightpence per ton, and the price of coal in winter in London is frequently more than thirty shillings per ton, the committee considered that, under the present system, the public would derive no advantage from this line being constructed, and its construction would inflict a loss on the Great Northern Company.

19. Attention is drawn to the great benefit that would be conferred on the community by the conveyance of parcels and packages throughout the kingdom at a low and, to some extent, uniform rate. The present charges by the principal companies are given. The proposed rates are, by passenger trains, parcels not exceeding 3 lbs., 4d.; above 3 lbs. and not exceeding 7 lbs., 6d.; above 7 lbs. and not exceeding 10 lbs. 9d.; and not exceeding 14 lbs. 1s.; and 6d. for every additional 7 lbs. or fraction of 7 lbs. For packages not exceeding 1 cwt., to be conveyed by luggage trains, when the distance does not exceed fifty miles, 1s.; exceeding 50 and not exceeding 200 miles, 1s. 6d. ; and exceeding that distance, 2s. per cwt.; one-fourth to be added to these several charges for each additional quarter of a hundred or fraction of that weight. All to be without booking charges.

20. Great stress is laid on the fact that there are heavy fiscal burdens under which the country labours in regard to its railway payments, that in 1865 it is calculated they will amount to the enormous sum of THIRTY-SIX MILLIONS STERLING, and the annual increase is now about two millions; it is endeavoured to be shown that the whole of our commercial policy for twenty-two years past has tended towards decreasing the charges on the necessaries of life, of which the conveyance of passengers and goods is one of the greatest.

21. A comparison is instituted between the benefits the

nation would derive from the total repeal of our customs duty and a reduction of two-thirds of the present fares and rates, and the conclusion drawn is in favour of the latter measure.

22. Railways, it is contended, must—from their intrinsic superior excellence—monopolize the great bulk of the traffic of the country, and therefore all attempts to apply to their management the laws which govern the operations of free trade must signally fail. It is, however, shown that, for the want of a more efficient remedy, the feeling is spreading in the country that railways should not be favoured by protection more than any other interest; and that when the majority of landlords, in any district, is favourable to the construction of a railway, the Legislature is bound to permit it. It is contended that the construction of unnecessary lines involves the country in a great loss of capital; and, although not without considerable use, are totally inefficient in giving the public the full benefits that might, by a proper system of management, be derived from them. That it is only by bringing the railways under the absolute and complete control of the Legislature that this object can be effected.

23. It is asserted that the strong feeling that exists in this country, and that hitherto has prevented the subject being fairly discussed, arises from the erroneous assumption that if the railways become the property of the State, the present system of management must undergo a complete change, and that they must be handed over, from the time of transfer, to the immediate charge of Government. It is contended that such a change is altogether unnecessary, and that a slight modification of our present system would effect every necessary purpose. In order to avoid any extension of Government patronage, it is suggested that the present principal directorates should elect from their own body twenty-four members whom they may consider best qualified to form a Board of General Management, such board to be presided over by a Minister of the Crown, as in the case of the East Indies and the Post Office,

and all future appointments to be made on the competitive system, or that the management should be assimilated to that of the Customs or Excise, viz. a Board of Management, with a Chairman and Vice-Chairman permanently appointed.

24. It is contended that to realize all the advantages that this country should derive from her magnificent network of railways, the principle which formed the groundwork of the Government Bill of 1844—should be carried out in its full integrity; that all our railways should be consolidated under one general management; that a low and uniform tariff for the different classes of the people should be established throughout the country; that the carriage of all descriptions of minerals, goods, general merchandise, and parcels, should be reduced in a like proportion; and that virtually, under the present management, with such modifications as circumstances may require, all the innumerable advantages that a comparatively free transit throughout a country bestows, should be made available to the British people.

25. The statement made by Mr. Watkin, Chairman of the Manchester and Sheffield Company, at the late meeting of the shareholders, is fully discussed, as well as those of writers in the railway press. It is argued that these gentlemen have altogether evaded the points at issue, and not noticed a single argument brought forward in favour of railway reform.

26. Finally, it is submitted that as contemplated by the Act of 1844, the time has now arrived for a revision of our railway system, and for that purpose a Royal Commission will probably be appointed to inquire into the working of our system; it is contended that after that inquiry shall have been completed, and the Commissioners have made their report to the Crown, it would be desirable, in order to render such inquiry effectual, and to ascertain the extent to which the traffic of the company in passengers and merchandise would be developed, that Government should be entrusted with such powers as may be necessary to make arrangements with those

companies it may think proper to select to convey passengers and merchandise at such fares and rates as it may think sufficiently low to meet the wants of the country, and by this means it is contended the Legislature in 1866 will be in possession of the necessary knowledge that will enable it to deal satisfactorily with the question.

APPENDIX I.

THE RAILWAY SYSTEM.

"The system of British Railways, whether considered in point of utility or in respect of the gigantic character and extent of the works involved in their construction, must be regarded as the most magnificent public enterprise yet accomplished in this country—far surpassing all that has been achieved by any Government, or by the combined efforts of society in any former age."—SMILES' LIFE OF STEPHENSON.

CHAPTER I.

Thomas Gray the first Projector of Railways for the Conveyance of Passengers and Goods—His Scheme for a "General Iron Railway" for the Kingdom—His Endeavours to have it adopted—His Failure and Death.—The celebrated Article in the *Quarterly Review* of 1825 on Railways—The Injustice done to the Reviewer—A *Resumé* of the Article.

As more than twenty years have now elapsed since public attention was directed to our railway system, it has struck me that a sketch of that wonderful system—its rise and progress—would not be unacceptable to the general reader. I may as well state at the outset that this Appendix is intended for perusal by those only who have no special knowledge of the subject: the facts here narrated, and the statistics entered into, are perfectly familiar to the railway world.

There lived some fifty years ago, in the town of Nottingham, a poor mechanic named Thomas Gray, and this man was the possessor of an "idea." Before railways were ever dreamt of, further than being the means of transit for coal from the pit's mouth to the place of embarkation, Gray had devised a great national scheme for supplying Great Britain and Ireland with railways, and steam as the motive power.

Gray's idea was either not sufficiently matured, or he had not the means of publication, till 1819, when he produced his "Plan of a General Iron Railway." This pamphlet has been for many years out of print, and his prospectus of a railway for carrying passengers and goods was the first ever published. It is, therefore, of considerable interest, and we shall allow the author to introduce his own project.

"The great exertions," said Gray, in the introduction to his work, "that have been made to relieve the necessities of the poor of this country have no doubt in some instances succeeded; but generally speaking, particularly in all manufacturing districts, the accounts always before the public show too plainly that the evil seems to increase, and to threaten us with its concomitant, vice, in all its most appalling features. The hand of charity has been extended in a most unparalleled manner, but still we find, unless some employment be prepared to draw off the overwhelming number of applicants, these liberal contributions apparently tend to prolong the life of misery rather than afford any permanent relief to the object. It is to be hoped that some great national work will be hit on which by affording labour may reduce the number of poor within the means of support of each parish, and at the same time answer the end proposed; for there can be no well-grounded hope of success except the public be attracted by a scheme that promises benefit to those who may be inclined to promote it, as nothing short of individual interest can ensure national prosperity."

Gray having thus appealed to the country for a friendly hearing for a plan he is about to propose to relieve the national distress by finding employment for the people, proceeds then to state the nature of his proposition.

"It has frequently occurred to me of late that an iron railway from London to Edinburgh, passing through all the commercial towns of Leicester, Nottingham, Sheffield, Wakefield, Leeds, &c., with branch railways to Birmingham, Bristol, Manchester, and Liverpool, would be productive of incalculable advantage to the country at large. And here I would suggest the propriety of making the first essay between Manchester and Liverpool, which would employ many thousands of the distressed population between Manchester and Liverpool.

"This would serve for the conveyance of all merchandise as well as persons by steam waggons and coaches, or by waggons and coaches built to run on the railway drawn by horses; in which latter case the quantum of horse power required would be infinitely less than by the present road: consequently the country must derive incredible advantage from the superior speed of conveyance, and the great saving in horses.

"The conveyance of the inland mails might be effected at a very trifling charge compared with the present enormous expenses of mail coaches, as one coach upon a proper construction would take all the mails on the line of road between London and Edinburgh.

"The introduction of fresh fish into the interior of the kingdom would open a source of trade to an immense number of individuals, and very essentially contribute to the improvement of our fisheries, as well as to the establishment of new ones.

"Very great benefit would arise to all estates in the direction of the railways by the very easy and cheap conveyance to market towns, but more especially to the metropolis, where provisions and vegetables of all kinds might be sent from distant parts of the kingdom.

"After an Act of Parliament is obtained, the sum of money required might be raised by shares of fifty and one hundred pounds."

Gray enters then into considerable detail on the many benefits his "General Iron Railway" would confer on the country. "If the conveyance," he says, "of mails across the channels by steamboats prove so highly important, how much more so the early distribution of the foreign and inland mails in all our commercial and manufacturing districts by royal mail steam carriages; the safe and expeditious conveyance of passengers by steam coaches, and the rapid transport of merchandise of every description, of steam-caravans and waggons."

Accompanying Gray's work were plates and maps illustrating his plan. He proposed there should be laid down a trunk line from London, to each of the following towns, viz.:—Edinburgh, Liverpool, Bristol, Falmouth, Devon, and Norwich, with branches to the principal towns on the respective routes. The length of railway comprised in his plan for Great Britain appears to have been about two thousand miles; and for Ireland he proposed that trunk lines should be laid down from Dublin to Belfast, Cork and Galway, with branches to the smaller towns on the respective routes, the entire length being about seven hundred miles. When looking over Gray's well-defined plans, one cannot help lamenting that there appeared no one in England capable of appreciating his great scheme for laying down his "Iron Railways," having the will or power to assist him.

"I shall take," he said, "the sum of one thousand pounds per mile for the single railway; the present plan, as above mentioned, requiring six railways, will consequently cost six thousand pounds per mile; and if we take the draught of the plan for Great Britain as given in this pamphlet for our guide, and allow for a few branch railways which may still be added thereto, the number of miles will be about two thousand, which, at the rate already stated, will amount to twelve millions sterling; supposing that double or even treble this sum be demanded, it would be found that the present revenue drawn from the public roads, the great expense of their repairs, and the enormous sums of money expended in the purchase and keep of horses, will sufficiently demonstrate the abundance of wealth the new scheme will yield to the subscribers. It may in all probability be urged that the capital required for the full execution of this plan can never be raised by subscription; however this may prove, I should wish so to convey my ideas to the public on the subject, so as to leave no point untouched relating thereto; for I feel assured that the total expense of the purchase of horses might be completely saved, and that the annual expense of their keep alone would more than provide for the steam engines necessary for this new projection, as well as defray the whole annual expense of repairs on the General Iron Railway."

"When Thomas Gray first proposed his great scheme to the public," said the Chevalier Wilson, in a letter to Sir R. Peel, in 1845, "people were disposed to treat it as an effusion of insanity. Had he chanced to live in the days of monkery and Galileo, he, like him, would doubtless have been incarcerated, and as the astronomical philosopher, to save himself, condescended to recant, saying that the sun did revolve round the earth, so also might the mechanical economical philosopher of our days have found it convenient to confess that stage-coaches and canals were the *ne plus ultra* of carriage velocity and convenience. Such, however, were his imperturbable convictions, such his enthusiastic impregnation with the grand idea, that I recollect, in 1820, he entered my room one day precipitately, saying, "I have gained my cause; travelling will be performed by steam. Now I can reply; now people will wish to read; they will read and be convinced."

Thomas Gray was, undoubtedly, the projector of our railway system, but he was mocked as a visionary when he first introduced his great scheme. Despite all his discouragements, and his subsequently neglected or unanswered memorials explaining his plans, and soliciting their examination and adoption, addressed to British Ministers of State, to boards of trade and agriculture, to the corporations of London and Liverpool, to public men and capitalists throughout the empire, and despite the continuous rebuffs of contemptuous incredulity with which everywhere he was treated, his persuasion was not the less unabated and unrepressed; but he failed in all his efforts to have his great scheme carried out, and had the mortification to see others step in and carry it out in detail.

A small sum of money was raised by subscription for Gray some time before his death, which I believe took place about the year 1850.

In March, 1825, appeared in the *Quarterly Review* the famous article "On Canal and Railway Communications," from which has been quoted some hundreds of times by historians and eulogists of the railway system, the well-known passage deprecating the absurdity of expecting the realization of a rate of speed which we should now regard as most tedious and insufficient. The popular impression of the tenor of the article, being solely derived from this isolated passage, which so many have uncandidly extracted without any qualifying allusion to the character of its context, is an extremely erroneous one. The article was, on the whole, highly favourable to railways; in fact, it was written with the express and avowed object of allaying the apprehensions about them then so rife, equally in interested as in antiquated quarters, and it represented the views of the most enlightened section of the educated portion of the community at that time. We doubt not that the great majority of the contemporaneous readers of this article looked upon its prophecies and anticipations to be quite as visionary and baseless as readers of 1865 would be disposed to regard its conclusions as characterized by extreme moderation, and indeed laughable timidity. Not for the mere purpose of vindicating the reputation of a Quarterly reviewer—in all human probability long since passed away—but because I could not possibly select a better or more favourable exemplar of the views of the very foremost minds in England, current about railways forty years ago, I present a long analysis of this article.

The object of the article was twofold—having for its purpose to give a moderate support to the Liverpool and Manchester scheme, then for the first time before Parliament, and to reprobate the enormous charges and exactions of the monopolist canal companies, and their interested opposition to the new-fangled invention. The article commences with a very humorous satirical treatment, rising sometimes to the tone of grave moral rebuke, of the host of speculative schemes brought before the public in the memorable years 1824 and 1825; a period of our commercial history which has only been equalled by the epochs of the South Sea Bubble, in the last century, and the Railway Mania, in our own times. Amongst other objects of serious or comical denunciation enumerated, are stone breakwaters and iron chain piers; bridges suspended over rivers, and tunnels bored under them; steam engines of all sizes, and for all purposes; steam vessels, steam coaches, steam cannons, steam ovens to hatch chickens, and steam kitchens to cook them in; steam hothouses to ripen grapes and pineapples at Christmas, and steam laundries, " to wash, *and to wear*," linen. And amongst other items of the long list of the schemes ridiculed, some with indignation, but most with a good-natured badinage, are milk companies, fishing companies, " for catching *gudgeon* in London and Westminster;" and coal-gas companies for whirling through the clouds at the rate of forty miles an hour, or to bowl along a turnpike road, at the rate of twelve miles an hour, with relays of bottled gas, instead of post-horses. And after citing, among other impracticable monstrosities, "a necropolis or two along the sloping sides of Hampstead and Highgate," the Reviewer winds up with an absurdity, that he has evidently deferred to the very last as the culminating climax of unattainability—" a ship canal cut through Nicaragua, or the Isthmus of Panama,"—which is probably the very earliest great triumph of engineering skill likely to be effected in our more favoured days.

After some more introductory matter of a similarly mixed serious and playful description, the writer proceeds to say : " But it is high time that we should advert to the more immediate object of this article—a discussion of the merits of an old invention, newly revived, which is become an object of almost as eager and feverish speculation as the mines or the loans. It is one, however, in which the commercial and agricultural, and, indeed, every class of the community are most deeply concerned; we need hardly say that we allude to the projected improvement in the internal communications of the country, by which a more speedy, certain, safe and economical conveyance of passengers and property is expected to be accomplished." After a summary of previous improvements in travelling in England, arising from the Turnpike Acts, the substitution of waggons for packhorses, the introduction of stage-coaches and postchaises, and of canals; " the rage for which became so vehement, that in a few years, the whole surface of the country was intersected by these inland navigations, and frequently in parts of the island where there was little or no traffic to be conveyed;" the writer proceeds :—

" Nothing now is heard of but railroads; the daily papers teem with notices of new lines of them in every direction, and pamphlets and paragraphs are thrown before the public eye, recommending nothing short of making them general throughout the kingdom. Yet, until these few months past, this old invention, in use a full century before canals, has been suffered, with few exceptions, to act the part only of an auxiliary to canals, in the conveyance of goods to and from the wharfs; and of iron, coals, and limestone, and other products of the mines, to the nearest place of shipment."

Alluding to the warm countenance and support given by Mr. Huskisson, the President of the Board of Trade, to George Stephenson and the new invention, the Reviewer proceeds, in reference to a then recent meeting " to consider the proposal of a monument to James Watt,"—" These, and many similar sentiments of the Ministers of the Crown, were cordially re-echoed by Mr. Wilberforce, Sir James Mackintosh, and Mr. Brougham, which occasioned Lord Liverpool to observe, ' that where the arts were concerned, there could be nothing like party in the country.'"

Among the general conclusions of the Reviewer, the following are the principal. He asserts that the canal proprietors had not the least ground for complaining of a grievance; and that the public were interested in any rivalry that should coerce them into a reduction of the charges for the conveyance of merchandise, which were extremely burdensome to the trading community, and so productive to the leading canal companies as to return them 100 per cent. dividends. But here the writer inserts a careful caveat:—" We are not the advocates for visionary projects that interfere with useful establishments; we scout the idea of a ' *general* railroad,' as altogether impracticable; or as one, at least, which will be rendered nugatory in lines where the traffic is so small that the receipts would scarcely pay for the consumption of coals. As to those persons who speculate on making railways general throughout the kingdom, and superseding all the canals, all the waggons, mail and stage-coaches, post-chaises, and, in short, every other mode of conveyance by land and by water, we deem them and their visionary schemes unworthy of notice." Then the pro-railway arguments are resumed on these further grounds—the great disadvantages of canals as compared with railways, from frost in the winter and drought in summer; the impossibility of the application of steam to canal traffic (a difficulty which, in more recent days, the invention of the screw propeller has pretty successfully overcome) from the washing down of the banks by the agitation of the water; the impossibility of increasing the number of canals in populous trading districts, beyond the fixed limit of the natural supply of water, as in the case of the water communication between Liverpool and Manchester, which was quite incapable of further augmentation; and, lastly, the "greater certainty, safety, and economy" of railway conveyance. In illustration of this important advantageous point of contrast, some startling facts were cited. It was stated, for example, as a well-known fact, that the loss of goods embarked on the barges running from Manchester to Liverpool, from the carelessness and dishonesty of the servants of the two canal companies, was so great as to constitute a most important diminution of the profits of the merchants and manufacturers engaged in the trade. In consequence of these frauds, all the valuable wool that went down to the West of England for manufacture into the superior broadcloths, for which that district was so famous, had to be conveyed at greatly increased cost by road. The canal servants had got into the habit of abstracting portions of wool from the bales entrusted to their care, and then saturating the remainder with a sufficient quantity of water to restore the exact weight withdrawn. Hence there was no immediate means, on the receipt of the deficient packages, of bringing home the culpability to the peculators.

The "General Railroad" referred to by the Reviewer was the scheme proposed, as we have seen, by Gray some years previously.

Shortly after this candid, and, on the whole, highly favourable—and considering that it was written forty years ago, before a single passenger or bale of goods had been conveyed by steam anywhere in England, save on a most moderate scale and in a remote nook of the kingdom, *very* favourable—summary of the advantages of railways, the well-known passage which is so frequently and so unfairly quoted, without any of the modifying context, occurs, and is as follows:—

"It is certainly some consolation to those who are to be whirled at the rate of eighteen or twenty miles an hour, by means of a high-pressure engine, to be told that they are in no danger of being seasick while on shore; that they are not to be scalded to death nor drowned by the bursting of the boiler; and that they need not fear being shot by the shattered fragments, or dashed in pieces by the flying off, or the breaking, of a wheel. But, with all these assurances, we should as soon expect the people of Woolwich to suffer themselves to be fired off upon one of Congreve's *ricochet* rockets, as trust themselves to the mercy of such a machine, going at such a rate; their property, perhaps, they may trust; but while one of the finest navigable rivers in the world runs parallel to the proposed railroad, we consider the other 20 per cent. which the subscribers are to receive for the conveyance of heavy goods, almost as problematical as that to be derived from the passengers. *We will back Old Father Thames against the Woolwich Railway for any sum.*"

The article concludes, very sensibly, it will be admitted (under the then circumstances), thus:—" We have purposely abstained from that part of the question which regards the conveyance of *passengers*. There is no doubt that a diminished weight may be conveyed with an increased speed and equal safety, as far as the strength and stability of the engine are concerned; but we think it would be expedient to waive all thoughts of this part of the subject for the present, until the roads and the engines have acquired that degree of perfection of which they are capable, and such as will remove all apprehension of danger."

I have quoted at some length from this article, and summarized its general conclusions, because, so far as I am aware, it is the first recognition on an important scale, and in a friendly tone, which the great railway enterprise obtained from periodical literature of the highest rank in this country. It brings vividly before us the exact feeling of the better class of the public towards the new invention at the time of its first appearance; and it forms a most convenient starting point, from which we now proceed on our short journey, the purpose of which is to present in a concise and non-scientific form a few sketches and statistical gleanings, illustrative of the history of the railway system, from its commencement about forty years ago down to the present time.

Another, and a special, reason has induced me to remain a little longer in the pleasant company of the Reviewer, than I might otherwise have been inclined to do, even on the grounds and for the purpose just specified. It is impossible for those dwellers in England of to-day who are not old enough to depend upon personal recollections of the character of transit in the ante-steam days, to estimate fully the advantages derived from the successive discoveries and inventions in relation to the use of steam for the purpose of traction on iron roads, without having a clear conception of their nature, and how they have developed themselves in the creation and improvement of our railway system. It is not my purpose to describe at any length the mode of constructing our railways or locomotives; the subject at the present time does not possess much interest, and any detailed description would therefore be entirely out of place; a brief narrative, however, may not be unacceptable.

In regard to steam carriages on common roads, great hopes were at one time entertained by their several constructors that they would succeed in overcoming the difficulties they had to contend with, and eventually render them of practical service. The obstacles, however, were too great to be overcome; the roads were too rough, and the friction consequently too severe for the delicate machinery of the locomotive, and so the ingenious inventors necessarily failed in their plans.

CHAPTER II.

The Construction of Railways—The Smooth Tracks in Northern Italy—First Tramroads in the Neighbourhood of Newcastle—Tramways at the Close of the Seventeenth Century—Roger North's Description of them to his Brother Lord Guildford—Derivation of the word "Tram"—George Stephenson—The Narrow, the Medium, and the Broad Gauges—History of the Locomotive.—The Marquis of Worcester—Watt—Trevithick.

THE course of successive discoveries and inventions which have led to the matured and composite result to be witnessed to-day on any of our great leading trunk lines has been twofold—the successive improvements in the roads upon which the locomotive steam-engines, with their attendant trains of trucks and carriages, run, and in the carriages themselves, and especially in the engines—those carriages which contain, elaborate, and economize the motive power. The history of the railway system, therefore, so far as its mechanical, engineering, and structural departments are concerned, naturally divides itself under these two heads—the history of the road, and the history of the engine. The railroad was in existence long before the locomotive, or even the stationary steam-engine. We therefore introduce, at this stage, a few notes on the history of rails, as appliances in mitigation of the labour and cost of traction.

At the present day the traveller, in certain of the magnificent cities of Northern Italy, may observe smooth tracks of hard marble in the ordinary paving of the streets. These have been laid down for many centuries; but they cannot, properly speaking, be called *rails*, as this term involves the essential principle of being raised above the surface, and, as some would hold, the further appliance of the "flange" of the wheel for its guidance and the conservation of the continuity and steadiness of its course. The invention of the rail, strictly so called, is of a considerably more recent date, and is solely to be claimed by England. Roads with wooden rails were first laid down in the neighbourhood of Newcastle, for the purpose of conveying coals from the pit's mouth to the sea or river side. Nicholas Wood, the author of the admirable "Practical Treatise on Railways," who was a pupil of the elder, and the instructor of the younger, Stephenson, says that it was some time between 1602 and 1649 that the first rough beginning of the railroad came into being. Some acute observer, now unknown to fame, seeing that the rut of the common road rendered the work of the cattle easier, acting on this observation, placed logs of wood in parallel lines, and thereby enabled each horse to draw at least double its former burden from the mouth of the mine, and with much less fatigue. It is certain that, ere the close of the seventeenth century, this plan had come into general operation in the north of England. The earliest literary record of its existence, so far as I have been enabled to discover, is the following. Roger North, describing a visit of his brother, Lord Guildford, to Newcastle while on circuit, says, that among the curiosities of the place were "way-leaves." "When men," he says, "have pieces of ground between the collieries and the rivers, they sell leave to lead coals over their ground, and so dear that the owner of a road of ground will expect £20 per annum for this leave. The manner of the carriage is by laying lines of timber from the colliery down to the river, exactly straight and parallel, and bulky carts are made with four romlets fitting these rails, whereby the carriage is so easy that one horse will draw down four or five chaldron of coals, and is an immense benefit to the coal merchants." No further improvement seems to have been effected until 1738, in which year we learn, from the "Transactions of the Highland Society," iron rails were substituted for wooden ones; but, owing to the old waggons continuing to be employed, which were of too much weight for the cast iron, they did not completely succeed on the first attempt. However, about 1768, a simple contrivance was attempted, which was to construct a number of smaller waggons and link them together, and by thus diffusing the weight of one large waggon over many, the principal cause of the failure in the first instance was removed, as the weight was more divided upon the iron.

In 1800, Mr. Benjamin Outram, of Little Eton, in Derbyshire, used stone props instead of timber in supporting the ends and joinings of the rails. These roads became known thence as "Outram Roads," and, by a further contraction, as "Tram Roads." Another, but as it seems to me a less supported derivation of the term, is, that long before Outram's time, the coal waggons in the northern counties were known by the provincial name of "Trams," and that the roads on which they ran were called after them.

About the time when, from whatever source, the term "tramroads" became common, and their use considerably extended, Lord Kenyon congratulated the Duke of Bridgewater upon the then established success of his canal; the prescient peer, entertaining an uncomfortable foreboding about the prospects of the new invention, and with wonderful foresight apprehending its future rivalry, replied—"Yes, we shall do well enough if we can keep clear of these accursed tramroads—*there's mischief in them !*"

The first rails in the Liverpool and Manchester Railway weighed 50 lbs. per yard, being constructed with reference to the conditions of the well-known contest in which the *Rocket* won for Stephenson his great and decisive triumph as an engine builder, which were a total weight of six tons to the engine, ten miles an hour speed, 50 lbs. pressure per inch, an aggregate load of 20 tons, including tender, and a level railway. These rails were what is technically termed "fish-bellied," *i.e.* deeper vertically at the points of support than at those points over the sleepers. The error here was the assumption that the sleeper was a movable fulcrum instead of a yielding point. It was afterwards remedied by the device of parallel rails. The thin lower end of the rail also got damaged in the chains, which were of cast iron, fixed by an iron key, and fastened down to a stone block or wooden cross sleepers. To remedy this, Mr. Joseph Locke devised the double-headed rail, which answered the twofold purpose of preventing crushing by affording a larger bearing in the chair, and of enabling the rail to be reversed when the surface first employed had become worn.

The phrase "permanent way" came into use thus: engineers devised a cheap *temporary* rail for the use of contractors in the *process of construction* of railways, which was afterwards removed after the formation of the earthworks and the laying down of the ballast. The rails then laid down were called by comparison and contrast the "permanent way." The "temporary way" was light, weak vertically, shallow and single headed, but with a wide foot, so as to stand upright without the necessity of chairs, on the temporary cross sleepers. The Ohio and Baltimore line, the first railway constructed in the United States, was laid in flat tire-bar rails on longitudinal timbers. This plan was soon discovered to answer very badly. The rail ends turned up as the trains rolled over them, and forming what were called "snakes' heads," absolutely speared the passengers through the floors of the carriages! And as the railway system began to extend in America, passengers, where there was an option of two routes to reach their destinations, would select one line in preference to another, even if involving a considerable *détour*, on the alleged ground of it having a smaller risk of "snakes' heads" than its sister channel of communication! The Americans afterwards substituted the English temporary way, which they used as their permanent one, endeavouring, though with but small effect, to atone for the want of iron by a compensating quantity of cheap wooden sleepers. "They were scarcely better than on private colliery lines," says Mr. Bridges Adams, to whose discursive, but entertaining "Roads and Rails" I am mainly indebted for the notes I here reproduce.

In England, two systems of Gauge, known as the "broad" and "narrow," have prevailed. In Ireland, at one time, there were no less than six or seven gauges, or different breadths of line. It has been jocularly stated (but possibly with some considerable grain of truth incorporated in the statement) that the diverse Irish gauges were assimilated thus :—All the various gauges being added up together, the mean was taken. Thus second-hand rolling stock was prevented being palmed upon Ireland from England. The Irish standard is now 5 ft. 3 in. The Indian gauge is 5 ft. 6 in.; and the Spanish national gauge the same. The English standard narrow gauge is 4 ft. $8\frac{1}{2}$ in. People have been puzzled why a measure containing a fraction should have been selected, but the explanation is very simple. The original cart track of five feet *outside the wheels* was taken as the standard for the gauge of rails, which were measured outside also. The width of each rail being $1\frac{3}{4}$ in., gave exactly 4 ft. $8\frac{1}{2}$ in. as the wide measure. When the rails were subsequently widened, that greater strength might be gained, they were widened outwardly, as the flange of the wheels could not be altered. Accordingly, the inner gauge has remained stationary, while the outer gauge has increased $\frac{3}{4}$ in. each rail over the old 5-feet cart standard.

The Great Western.

The 7-feet gauge employed by Brunel on the Great Western was based, in the first place, on his assumption that the time would never arrive when lines running north would come into communication with lines running west, and when, accordingly, any inconvenience could arise from diversity of gauge ; and, recently, he argued that so great a breadth of gauge would lower the centre of gravity, and increase the size of the wheels by placing them on each side instead of beneath the carriages, as in the case of the narrow gauge, and also give ample space for large engines. This innovation rendered necessary corresponding alterations in the character of the line. Bridge-rails, which are hollow bars with flanges at the sides, secured to the timber by nut-head screws on the outer flange, and by notch-head screws on the inner flange, to keep them out of the way of the wheel flanges, were employed; and felt was laid under the rails to keep them soft to the movement. The substructure on which these rails reposed was of this character:—timber piles were driven into the earth along the line, at distances of 15 feet; to these were fastened half balks of timber, connected in pairs; on these again were spiked planks of oak an inch thick, which joiners, working on their knees on the line, planed to a perfect level. As the whole structure, both of carriages and way, was an entire novelty, it is neither very much to be wondered at, nor much to the discredit of Brunel, that that did occur which might have been expected, viz., that the previously untried experiment necessitated an almost endless series of alterations and renovations, ere it could be made to answer. The engines, in place of possessing the requisite superior power to those used on the narrow gauge, turned out to be weaker. Horse-boxes, designed to carry horses sideways to the engine, which the greater width permitted, had to be cut in two, and carried their tenants, as on the narrow gauge, with their noses to the engine. As concerned the road, it was discovered that the timbers and rails played up and down from their oak and felt cushions between the piles, and striking occasionally in water lying below the timbers, they splashed it over the carriages. The passengers bumped rather than rolled over the piles, and the carriages being too short, the irregular motion was very great. Successive remedies were applied; longer carriages were substituted; the piles were removed, and the longitudinal timbers were framed together by cross transverses, and laid on the ground ladder-wise, being secured no otherwise than by their own weight. Further expedients, such as using bolts instead of screws, enlarging nuts, and boarding across the longitudinal timbers with short planking, have been added; and so, by a succession of such addenda and substitutions, the Great Western, with its tributaries, stands now in that final form and condition with regard to which we read that "at the present day there is not left upon the line a single construction—either engine, carriage, waggon, wheel, or spring—as originally designed."

One of the most important minor inventions in connection with the permanent way, was the "fish joint." Originally, the double-headed rail was fastened to the sleepers by cast-iron chairs, both at the joints and intermediates. The joints were about two inches wider than the intermediates, so as to receive the adjoining ends of the rails. But they rapidly worked loose, being only fastened by timber keys; consequently, the ends of the rails were hammered and crushed. To remedy this, the inventive genius of Mr. Bridges Adams hit upon the fish joint, in which, in place of one joint serving in common for two rail ends in contact, the rail ends were brought almost, but not quite, in contact, and suspended, not upon one joint supporting them in common, but upon two, a little apart, each supporting only one rail, and being connected together in a chair at their respective bases. This made the rails continuous bars, which was exactly what was wanted. A great gain was effected at once in the ease and the safety of travelling.

INCREASE IN THE WEIGHT OF ENGINES, AND ITS RESULTS.

The *Rocket* and the three competitors against which it was pitted, thirty-five years ago, in Lancashire, weighed only twenty tons, with their laden tenders. The weight of engine and tender now frequently amounts, especially on the broad gauge, to three times that amount. This has, of course, necessitated a proportionate strengthening of the rails, which now often weigh nearly 100 lbs. in place of 50 lbs. to the yard, and the chairs weighing from 14 lbs. to 42 lbs., there is thus formed an aggregate weight of about 100 tons per mile. Nevertheless, it turned out that not even this large augmentation of solidity and strength successfully averted great destruction of rails and sleepers. An attempt was made to *remove* the cause of this, but, latterly, efforts have been made rather in the direction of mitigating and counterbalancing it. The means now generally adopted is to place a cushion of wood at the bottom of each chair, which receives and neutralizes the blow of the rail loosened by the enormous weight and pressure. A more permanent remedial mode of treating the evil would be theoretically more eligible, and would have been preferred by railway engineers, but for the fact that, practically, the paramount consideration with them is " how to replace a worn or damaged rail with the greatest facility." Convenience has been preferred to mechanical accuracy.

SINE QUA NONS IN A GOOD RAIL.

These are, briefly, the following:—It must possess sufficient depth to distribute the load it has to bear over a considerable extent of space; it must possess sufficient lateral strength to secure the trueness of the gauge; the base must be considerably wider than the elevation; if the rail be supported in its base, depth is to be avoided; but if suspended from the other table, nothing more is required than the mere connection of the top and bottom tables. The rails must be so connected as to form a continuous beam, not merely by "fish joints," to give vertical support, but also so as to furnish lateral support. The metal must be homogeneous—neither imperfectly welded, nor likely to break into fibres under a heavy engine. To attain this latter end it is more than probable that steel will be eventually substituted for iron. Nor will considerations of cost prevent this result, as the weight of steel rails may be safely made very much less than those of iron.

Sleepers.

"What are the best sleepers?" is a relative question; or rather a question to be responded to by relative or conditional replies, according to circumstances. Stone, timber, cast iron, or wrought iron may each be the best in certain situations, and under varying conditions. The question of cost has much to do with this. Where good timber—for example, as in virgin countries—may be had for the cutting, at convenient sites along the route, and where it may be replaced from time to time for the mere cost of labour, it would be the grossest and most needless extravagance to employ anything else. Again, in climates where heat and moisture alternate, as in the Gulf States of North America, metal is, for obvious reasons, preferable. The general argument in favour of timber, on account of its elasticity, is more specious than sound. For if there be elasticity in the rails, it can only be in the intervals between the chairs, which are only of the length of three feet, and whatever elasticity there be will necessarily involve a corresponding and instantaneously reiterated rigidity. Sleepers are plastic rather than elastic, which is proved by the chairs steadily sinking into them without any indication of resurgent spring, and by the fact that they wear out mechanically and not chemically. Where elasticity is wanted—as well upon a highway as upon a railroad—is in the vehicle, and not in the way. On these and similar grounds no absolute and unfailing dictum can be laid down about the inherent preferability of one description of sleeper over another. You may have as hard substances as possible as the three constituents of your way—the rail, the chair, and the natural bottom, even if the latter be of rock—but you must have no "looseness" between the three connecting parts. Each must be immovably connected with the others by what is called an absolute and unmistakable "engineer's fit." Another simple way of accomplishing this end—

of elasticity of the whole, but of no one part—is to lay rails embedded longitudinally in timber, and bolt the timber down to a paved sub-surface.

THE EARLY HISTORY OF THE LOCOMOTIVE STEAM ENGINE is so much more generally attractive than the history of the road, and has been so much more popularized in connection with the lives of the earlier engineers, than with their construction of railways, that we may condense our remarks under the above heading within a very small compass.

The story of the Marquis of Worcester, the ingenious and speculative author of the "Century of Inventions," seeing Solomon de Caus confined in the Bicêtre in Paris, in 1641, as a madman, because he had insisted to the Cardinal Minister that he could construct a carriage which would propel itself by steam, is well known, and to be found in all the popular compendia of the subject. No result followed the discovery, or intuition, or lucky surmise of this unfortunate victim of the superstition which is the antithesis of science, and his existence has no more to do with that chain of causes which leads to ultimate successful invention, with the *ultimate application to the uses of man* of the steam engine, still less of the locomotive, than had the ingenious contrivance of the well-known steam tug at Alexandria.

Black's discovery of the power of latent heat was the scientific harbinger of those experiments of James Watt, which resulted in his production of these two important results, which for the first time enabled man to use steam in the uninterrupted supply of the motive power, and a continuous rotatory motion. It was about 1759 that Watt began to devote his mind to the question of the practicability of forming a stationary engine which should move, and generate motion, by virtue of his novel discovery. He, and many others, began further to speculate upon the possibility of the formation of steam engines to move along roads, as well as stationary ones to propel machinery. But the idea of connecting locomotion with railroads had not yet occurred. And it was not until 1784, that William Murdoch, the friend and assistant of Watt, produced the model of a steam carriage to run upon common roads. "One night," says Mr. Smiles in his "Life of Stephenson," "after returning from his duties in the mine, at Redruth, in Cornwall, Murdoch determined to try the working of his model locomotive. For this purpose, he had recourse to the walk leading to the church, about a mile from the town. The walk was rather narrow, and was bounded on either side by high hedges. It was a dark night, and Murdoch set out alone to try his experiment. Having lit his lamp, the water shortly began to boil, and off started the engine with the inventor after it. He soon heard distant shouts of despair. It was too dark to perceive objects; but he shortly found, on following up the machine, that the cries for assistance proceeded from the worthy pastor of the parish, who, going towards the town on business, was met on this lonely road by the hissing and fiery little monster, which he subsequently declared to be the evil one *in propriâ personâ.*"

Singularly enough, the next stage of inventiveness in the direction of a locomotive to run on common roads, was attended with a similar ludicrous incident. Trevithick, a Cornish miner, invented a locomotive in, or shortly previously to, 1802. But whereas the latter was content with the production of a miniature model, Trevithick constructed an actual engine. He determined to transport it to London, for the purpose of the introduction of his invention to the *savans* and commercial magnates of the metropolis, and started with his engine on the road to Plymouth, where he intended to embark with his valuable freight. Coleridge relates that whilst the vehicle was proceeding along the road to the port, at the top of its speed, and had just carried away a portion of the rails of a gentleman's garden, Andrew Vivian (who was Trevithick's cousin, and the "capitalist" in the production of the engine) descried ahead of them a closed toll-gate, and called out to Trevithick, who was behind, to slacken speed. He immediately shut off the steam ; but the momentum was so great, that the carriage proceeded some distance, coming dead up, however, just on the right side of the gate, which was opened like lightning by the tollkeeper. "What have us got to pay here?" asked Vivian. The poor tollman, trembling in every limb, his teeth chattering in his head, essayed a reply, "Na-na-na-na!" "What have us got to pay, I say?" "No-noth-nothing to pay! My dear Mr. De-devil, so drive on as fast as you can! Nothing to pay!"

For forty years, Watt, Symington, Trevithick, Blenkinsop, Chapman, Brunton, and others, had striven to discover methods of propelling carriages by steam upon common turnpike roads, and upon railways; but after numerous failures, the whole class of machine makers seem, about 1812, to have made the discovery that a simple-hand wheel could not exercise a sufficient amount of friction upon a road surface, to cause the carriage to advance. For many years the efforts of steam carriage builders were directed to alleviating this imaginary difficulty, and rachet wheels, jointed levers, and mechanical legs of every shape and form, were introduced, to the detriment of the roadway, and the diminution of the useful power of the engines. At last, in 1814, Stephenson constructed one bearing two cylinders, seated upon a boiler mounted upon wheels, and immediately above the axles of these wheels, which have cranks connected with the piston heads of the cylinders, and were made to revolve in unison by Vaucassen chains working over barrels in the respective axles. This was the true road out of the difficulty, and it is essentially the germ of the locomotive steam engine of to-day.

The various improvements that have been effected in its construction, from that time to the present, we shall not attempt to describe; those who may wish to enter more fully into the subject will find in Lardner's "History of the Steam Engine" every necessary detail.

CHAPTER III.

The Nineteenth Century—George Stephenson—Mr. Smiles' "Life of Stephenson"—Killingworth High Pit—The Stockton and Darlington Railway—The Liverpool and Manchester Railway—The great Difficulties to be overcome in its Construction—"Navvies"—Trial of Locomotives on the Liverpool and Manchester Line—Lord Brougham's Speech on its Opening—The Success of the Undertaking established.

THE nineteenth century has been emphatically a century of engineers and engineering. Not more essentially was the fifth century one of anchorites and monasticism, or the thirteenth one of crusading, or the sixteenth one of courtly pageant and trans-Atlantic conquest, or the eighteenth one of philosophy and criticism, than has the nineteenth been illustrated and distinguished by the splendid triumphs won by the keenest and most assiduous, the most unflinching and indomitable human minds over the hardest resistance that can be offered by the most stubborn material inertia in its most ponderous, defiant, and apparently invincible forms. Long since, Carlyle wrote that the keynote of the modern epic is, not "*Arms*," but "*Tools*, and the man I sing." This fact has been reflected in our recent popular biographies. It is the workers, not the warriors, whose lives are now celebrated by our most gifted biographical and critical pens, and about whom the highest curiosity of the public is displayed. Probably there has been no one man about whom the millions of modern readers have cared to learn so much, and have actually learned so much during the last ten or twelve years, as George Stephenson, the father and the founder of the railway system. This is largely to be attributed to the excellent biography by Mr. Smiles, a gentleman who is himself honourably distinguished by his eminence in a high field of railway administration, and who, by his "Life of Stephenson," and his other works, has achieved the position of *facile princeps* in the rich and important field of industrial biography. Mr. Smiles has made Stephenson's name a household word in the homes of England and the civilized world. All of us now know the man in his most intimate, private, and domestic relations, as well as in the locomotive factory, on surveying expeditions, and on the line of the completed railway. We watch his slow and arduous steps, from the humblest beginnings to the most splendid ends. We follow him sympathetically through each successive grade, from his humble cowkeeper's position at twopence a day to his promotion to turnip hoer at fourpence, stone-picker at sixpence, until he obtains the sumptuous remuneration of eightpence per diem as gin-horse driver. Then we find him engine fireman at a shilling a day, and then engine driver and plugman at twice that wage, when he innocently believes that his fortunes are secured, and exclaims, "I am now a made man for life!" We watch with sympathy his laudable efforts at self-education; his touching wooing, wedding, and early widowhood; his devotion to the one pledge of affection that his beloved Fanny Henderson left behind her—the future author of the great bridges over the Wear, the Menai Straits, and the ice-laden St. Lawrence. And, following his earlier career through its subsequent stages, we at last arrive at that period of it when his achievements fit into our narrative, in connection with the progress of the development of the locomotive.

The year 1810 was the turning point in George Stephenson's career. "Killingworth High Pit was clean drowned in water." An atmospheric pumping engine had been at work twelve weary months, incessantly eating up coal, but producing no more effect than if it had been operating on the pitchers of the Danaïdes. All the pit doctors in the district had tried their hands, but unavailingly. At last Stephenson was applied to, and in a week after his engine was set to work the mine was dry. This and subsequent achievements within the next two years led to his appointment as engine wright to the Killingworth Colliery at 100*l.* a year.

Trevithick had progressed somewhat further with his invention than merely to frighten the Cornish turnpike keeper with fears of diabolic presence. He had made a great advance on his predecessors. He had for the first time caused steam to drive the piston both ways, got rid of the condensing tank, and attained a minimum of lightness not hitherto approached. In 1804, he had actually run a locomotive on the Merthyr Tydfil Railway. In 1812, he constructed an engine for Mr. Blackett, an enterprising and far-seeing coalowner of Northumberland, and immediately afterwards built the famous *Black Billy*. Trevithick then left engine-building, when he had almost grasped substantial success. Stephenson struck in where Trevithick left off. Northumberland, with its longheadedness, seized the prize which the fickle Celt of Cornwall missed. Stephenson knew he could beat *Black Billy*. In 1814, he turned out a locomotive, the first made with smooth-tired wheels, which drew thirty tons up a slight ascent at the rate of four miles an hour In 1815, he built another, being a further improvement upon its predecessor. Next year he devoted himself to rails and wheels. Gradually his invention took to itself form, fitness, and final finish.

THE STOCKTON AND DARLINGTON RAILWAY
was the first in England which was regularly used as a locomotive line for the conveyance of passengers and goods. Stephenson was appointed its engineer at a salary of 300*l*. a year; and he persuaded Edward Pease, the principal shareholder, and his brother directors, to change it from a horse to a locomotive line, and also to permit him to lay down malleable instead of cast-iron rails. In 1822, the first rail was laid, and in three years after it was opened for traffic. Edward Pease had the insight to discover the genius of Stephenson. He united with him in establishing an engine factory at Newcastle. George Stephenson was so much engaged with his duties in the railway, that his son Robert, who was barely twenty years of age, had nearly all to do with the establishment of the factory, and was admitted as a partner. The son was only twenty-three years his father's junior, and was regarded by him rather as a younger brother than a son. The strength at once of George's affection and admiration for Robert is well displayed by a circumstance like this, as well as by the fact that when the plans of the Stockton and Darlington went before Parliament, Robert's name, when he was only eighteen, appeared as engineer. This was the father's mode of bringing his son into notice, and a clear proof that even so early his position was so well established that he could afford to fall into the background and accord his son the prominence.

THE LIVERPOOL AND MANCHESTER RAILWAY
was first broached in 1821, and revived in 1824. In that year a pamphlet was published under the authority of Stephenson, which drew forth a document from a hundred and fifty Liverpool merchants, calling for the execution of the scheme. A deputation having been sent to examine the Killingworth locomotives, a company was at once established for the construction of a double line. Stephenson was appointed engineer. His surveys, in which he was assisted by his son, were pursued under the greatest difficulties. The canal companies were up in arms, and all the local magnates on the route, the Earls of Sefton, Chesterfield, Derby, and Wilton, united in offering the hottest and most determined opposition.

He had to execute his survey on some estates by trespass, and was afterwards sued for damages. He surveyed when the watchers posted to warn him off were at dinner, and by night with the assistance of dark lanterns, and at the risk of being shot for a poacher. At last the bill came before the House of Commons, on the 21st of March, 1824, Stephenson being the only combatant on the one side, and a whole array of counsellors and "civil engineers," who scornfully repudiated Stephenson as a mere "mechanical engineer" on the other. "All the regular-bred engineers," says Mr. Adams, "disliking the presumption of the untaught man in setting himself up to thrust aside their preconceived notions and formulæ, were enlisted as willing evidence on the part of the opposition; and George Stephenson, alone, unaided save by our old friend Nicholas Wood, and a mechanical engineer, a builder of steam engines at Stourbridge—one John Urpeth Rastrick, afterwards the maker of the 'Brighton Direct'—had to enter upon the contest. The untaught man, with imperfect utterance, ignorant of the methods of schools, had to be baffled and browbeaten by a host of technical schoolmen and practical men, who had gone over and examined and measured at their leisure the course of the line, which he could only get at by glimpses. All sorts of evidence were brought forward—that the railway would stop the milk of the cows, the growth of grass, would poison the game, would burn down the farms, would frighten horses, would cost 270,000*l.* to get through four miles of Chat Moss, would be utterly unsuccessful, and yet would ruin the stage-coaches; and so, after a two months' contest of unscrupulous opposition, the bill was finally thrown out, though the preamble was passed."

At last, however, by dint of the large support given by many members of Parliament, and even of the Ministry; by buying off some of the most potent opposition; by the representatives of the Bridgewater canal property becoming large shareholders in the railway, and so carrying their eggs in two baskets; and lastly, by sinking George Stephenson's name, appointing the Messrs. Rennie engineers, and so making a humiliating concession to professional superciliousness, the bill was passed in 1826. George Stephenson was, of course, at once reappointed engineer, and the work of forming the line entrusted to his hands.

The Difficulties of the Line

were to construct the way over Chat Moss, and to bore the tunnel through the sandstone rock on which Liverpool stands. Both were with great labour overcome. The latter was done by Joseph Locke, who here for the first time appears in the history of railway engineering. Over Chat Moss a road of hurdles and heather was constructed, with a covering of earth to steady it. And when this showed a tendency to sink below the level into the abyss of bog, the moss was laden on each side of the track to balance it. When the water still oozed through, a new kind of drain pipe, formed of waste tallow casks, headed together, was invented.

George Stephenson and the railways called into existence a new class of manual labourers—the navvies. The word navvy is an abbreviation of navigator; the term having been first applied to the artificers of canals, or systems of inland *navigation*, a generation or two before the inception of railways. These navvies were, and are, splendid specimens of the bone and muscle which English bread, beef, and beer will produce. The staple and nucleus of the navvies were men born on Blackstone Edge, the great mountain ridge on the confines of Lancashire and Yorkshire, men " with stomachs like ostriches, with gizzards capable of cramming and digesting any amount of flesh, meat, and bread, and turning it into bone and muscle, to do any amount of work." So much, indeed, was *feeding* an element in the powers of the navvies, that in later days of railway engineering and contracting than those at which we have now arrived in our survey, when contractors had to dismiss any number of men on account of the diminution of work to be performed, they invariably parted with those whom they had observed to display the smallest gastronomic and digestive capacities. Two pounds of beef-steak was an ordinary allowance for a navvy's dinner, and condiments, solid and liquid, were consumed in fair proportion. Once when Mr. Brassey had a contract in France—I think, for the Paris and Orleans Railway—he resolved, from very proper and considerate motives, to employ native labour. Having collected a gang of the most strong and able-bodied field labourers whom he could find, he told them that he would fix their remuneration at the same scale, and expect the same rate of work, as he had been accustomed to in England. And, he added, that to enable them to accomplish this work, and earn this wage, they must needs eat the same quantity of food as his English workers. The delighted Frenchmen made the attempt heartily, but wofully failed. They found that they could not possibly absorb the requisite alimentary sustenance. This shortcoming was proportionately reflected in the amount of labour performed. Mr. Brassey had to bend to circumstances; and the pay-rate had to be conformed to the rate of food eaten and work done. The navvies

" earned their money like horses," and spent it like children; ofttimes the victims of the tommy-shop; caring little for lodging; helping one another in distress, to the sharing of the last shilling; imposed on by public-house keepers, and submitting to it though knowing it, and with a peculiar custom of persecuting the cheating publican by concealing from him that their contract was out on the line, and then eating and drinking his house empty and dry at a final feast, and clearing out without paying—a sort of balancing up of the general items of cheating they had suffered."

When the Liverpool and Manchester line was completed, the question remained, what motive power should be employed, and if steam, how should it be employed? Most were in favour of stationary engines; only the Stephensons, father and son, and Joseph Locke, were in favour of locomotives. The directors were at last so far convinced that the latter were preferable, that they advertised a trial of competitive steam engines, with a prize of £500 to the victor. There were four competitors; and one of them was the *Rocket* built by Stephenson at his Newcastle factory. The *Rocket* performed well all the conditions of the contest, and signally distanced the other three competitors. When the *Rocket* arrived at the platform at the close of her day's successful run, Isaac Cropper, one of the directors favourable to the fixed-engine scheme, lifted up his hands and exclaimed, "Now is George Stephenson at last delivered!"

Lord Brougham at the dinner given by the directors on the opening of the line, thus eloquently commented, on the great event:—"When I saw the difficulties of space, as it were overcome; when I beheld a kind of miracle exhibited before my astonished eyes; when I surveyed masses pierced through, in which it was before hardly possible for man or beast to plant the sole of the foot, now covered with a road, and bearing heavy waggons laden, not only with innumerable passengers, but with merchandise of the largest bulk and heaviest weight; when I saw valleys made practicable by the bridges of ample height and length which spanned them; saw the steam railway traversing the water at a distance of sixty or seventy feet perpendicular height; saw the rocks excavated, and the gigantic power of man penetrating through miles of the solid mass, gaining a great, a lasting, an almost perennial conquest over the powers of nature by his skill and industry; when I contemplated all this, was it possible for me to avoid the reflections which crowded into my mind? not in praise of man's great success, not in admiration of the genius and perseverance he had displayed, or even of the courage he had shown in setting himself against the obstacles that matter offered to his course—no! but the melancholy reflection that these prodigious efforts of the human race—so fruitful of praise, but so much more fruitful of lasting blessings to mankind—have forced a tear from my eye by that unhappy casualty which deprived me of a friend, and you of a representative." These words were addressed to the inhabitants of Liverpool, which had been represented by Mr. Huskisson, who was lamentably killed by the *Rocket* while conversing on the line of rails with the Duke of Wellington.

The first report of the directors was one continued swell of triumph. In the first fortnight the passengers had averaged eight hundred a day, and immediately after they rose to twelve hundred. The journey was performed in an hour and a half, in place of two hours, as had been undertaken. "Thus," stated the report, "in a few months was produced a new and effective system of intercommunication, highly important to the interests of a mercantile community, and so extraordinary and complete as to form an era in national improvements, and an epoch in mechanical science. The company have not been required to wait for gradual and partial transition." Although the winter was one of extreme severity, in no one day were the trains prevented from running. A dividend of eight per cent. was paid. Remarkable discrepancies between the estimates and the actualities of traffic appeared. Goods which were expected to give a return of £50,000, did not produce £3000; coals, estimated at £20,000, figured for less than £1000. But, on the other hand, the passenger traffic, which had been put down for £10,000, produced above £100,000. The aggregate net income, which had been estimated at £62,500, was over £83,000. The expenses, which had been estimated at 33 per cent. on the receipts, turned out to be 62 per cent. Similarly, the cost of the construction of the railway, which had been estimated at £510,000, reached £1,200,000. After the issue of the first report, the £100 shares rose to £200. In 1835, the annual number of passengers had risen to 473,000, being an increase of 117,000 in four years.

CHAPTER IV.

Progress of Railway Enterprise—The London and Birmingham Line—Great Difficulties in its Construction—The Kilsby Tunnel—Robert Stephenson—Brunel —The Electric Telegraph—Compensation for Land—Charges against Landowners—Their Answer—Mr. Pease—Robert Stephenson lectures before the Institute of Civil Engineers—The Grand Junction Railway—Contractors—Thomas Brassey—The various Developments of the Contract System—Sir Morton Peto.

FROM 1825 till 1830, railway enterprise was depressed, sharing in the general languor which affected all commercial operations after the crisis of the former year. But as trade began to revive, new lines of railway were projected. In 1829 an Act was passed for a line connecting Newcastle and Carlisle, but it was not opened till ten years after. There had sprung up in the meantime a desire to have great trunk lines from the metropolis. The line between London and Birmingham had been surveyed in 1825, but the project was abandoned after the panic. In 1830 it was revived. Two rival routes, one by Sir John Rennie, the other by Mr. Giles, were proposed. George Stephenson was appointed by the projectors to adjudicate between the two. He decided in favour of the line by Coventry, and against that which was proposed to proceed by way of Oxford. Stephenson and his son were appointed the engineers. The latter personally surveyed the whole line, walking some twenty times the whole distance between London and Birmingham, back and forward. The first crude idea embraced only a single line of rail, and the cost was estimated at £6000 a mile. The capital was a million and a quarter, and the shares were soon at £10 premium. More matured thought suggested a double line, which so frightened the investing classes that the shares fell to a discount. The directors were sneeringly denominated "a patriotic party of speculators, coming forward for their country's good." The company issued their first circular in January, 1832. Their total estimate of expense was £2,400,456, and the estimated revenue £671,102, divided in nearly equal proportions between passengers and goods. The discussions about this line showed, in a marked manner, the gradual progress of opinion since the Liverpool and Manchester was first mooted. Mr. Hardman Earle, who had been a strenuous opponent of that line, voluntarily came forward, and said that all his unfavourable opinions had been falsified. He had experienced no inconvenience from the trains passing through his grounds. The smoke was not offensive, and the noise not disagreeable. "The passage of the carriages was a pastime rather than a nuisance." The Earl of Derby, who had so strongly opposed the Liverpool and Manchester, manfully made a similar recantation, and supported the London and Birmingham. Still the old cries were revived, and prejudice and selfishness found expression in the form of discontent. Such expressions as the following were flying about, "the railway will be a drag on the country;" "the bridges and culverts will be antiquarian ruins;" "it will not take tolls sufficient to keep it in repair;" "the directors are making ducks and drakes of their money;" and "every hill and valley between the two towns will behold falling arches and ruined viaducts." One wiseacre wrote:— "Long before the London and Birmingham is ready, such are the improvements now making in canals, that not only may the charge be expected to be many times less than the railway, but the time of transit will be considerably saved." And another said, "Our estates will not only be deteriorated, but destroyed. It is not a question of pounds, but a question of principle." Probably no bill, with the exception perhaps of the Great Northern, ever sustained so much opposition as the London and Birmingham. The grounds of one clergyman, who was also a landowner, were surveyed by stealth, while he was performing his clerical duties on Sunday. The most extortionate demands for compensation were made. One piece of land, which had its value increased 20 per cent. by the railway, was purchased for £3000, with £10,000 "consequential damages." One proprietor demanded four bridges, which was agreed to. Then he thought that half the money which the bridges would cost would be more serviceable to him, and he made a representation accordingly to the company. They entertained it, and paid the money on the basis of this compromise. After a tremendous amount of opposition before Parliament, the bill was passed; the land requisite having been purchased at three times its fair value at least, opposition being thus bought off.

"It is well known," says Sir Francis Head, "that one of the results of Mr. Robert Stephenson's elaborate investigation was that the London and Birmingham Railway ought to pass by the healthy and handsome town of Northampton. The inhabitants, however, urged and excited by men of influence and education, opposed the blessing with such barbarous fury, that they succeeded in distorting the line *viâ* the Kilsby Tunnel, to a point five miles off." The contract for the making of this tunnel was let to a contractor for 99,000*l.* A quicksand stopped his progress, he was compelled to relinquish his contract, and the vexation killed him. Mr. Robert Stephenson took up the reversion of the enterprise. Though the difficulties were so great that the directors proposed to abandon the task, he persevered. He set in operation all the available resources. He had at work 1250 men, 200 horses, and 13 steam engines. And by their aid, he raised 1800 gallons of water night and day for eight months; he so thoroughly infused his own energy into his workmen, that it is said when one of their number was killed, they simply threw the body out of sight, and went on with their work. On the 17th of September, 1838, the railway was opened. The capital had been increased from 2,400,000*l.* to 4,500,000*l.*

Every part of the line had been carefully examined by Robert Stephenson beforehand, and it was begun in several places at once. The elaborate plans and drawings which he made were afterwards borrowed by Brunel for the Great Western, and became generally the model of all subsequent railway operations. The relations between Stephenson and Brunel were of the most creditable character to both. Mr. Jeaffreson, in his recently published " Life of Robert Stephenson," says,—" The relations that subsisted between him and Brunel could not have endured between rivals endowed with merely ordinary generosity. Continually as they were pitted against each other, much as the reputation of the one was exalted by the failures of the other, they not only preserved strong mutual affection, but in their gravest periods of public trial were always ready to assist each other with counsel and support. When Robert Stephenson, with fearful anxiety, was watching the floating of the first enormous tubular bridge to the piers, Brunel stood by his side; and when Brunel was heroically contending with the gigantic difficulties of launching the *Great Eastern*, Robert Stephenson disregarded the claims of failing health, in order that he might be on the spot to encourage and advise his brother engineer. Two nobler adversaries the world never witnessed."

Mr. Stephenson was intimate with Mr. Wheatstone and Mr. Cooke, the inventors of the electric telegraph, and he procured for them the opportunity of fixing their first wires of communication upon the line from Euston Square in the year before its public opening. The first important occasion on which beneficial uses of the electric telegraph were brought forcibly before the general public was the case of Tawell, the murderer. This man poisoned his unfortunate victim near Slough. She learned that she was poisoned—contrary to his expectation—ere she died. The piercing shriek which she uttered on making the horrid discovery alarmed her neighbours, who ran out of their cottages and saw Tawell in the act of flight. He was not captured, however, before he succeeded in taking unobserved his seat in a carriage at Slough of the up London train. But long ere he arrived at Paddington, the following telegram had been received :—

"A murder has just been committed at Salthill, and the suspected murderer was seen to take a first-class ticket for London by the train which left Slough at 7.42 P.M.

"He is in the garb of a Quaker, with a brown greatcoat on, which reaches nearly down to his feet. He is in the last compartment of the second first-class carriage."

On arriving at the terminus, he took a city omnibus, the conductor of which, he little thought, in his fancied security, was a policeman in disguise. After Tawell, probably with the object of proving an alibi on the night of the murder, had entered one coffee-house after another which he was in the habit of frequenting, he went finally to a City lodging-house, and just as he was opening the door, the policeman, who had never left the trail, calmly accosted him, and said, "Haven't you just come from Slough?" Confusedly answering, "No!" he was taken into custody, tried and hanged. A countryman, who travelled in the same carriage with Sir Francis Head from Paddington a few months after, is recorded by that entertaining writer to have ejaculated, looking at the telegraphic wires, "Them's the cords that hung John Tawell!"

It was in connection with the London and Birmingham line that what its projectors termed "the scandalous cupidity of landowners" was first displayed. They favoured the introduction of projected railway bills only that they might oppose them in Parliament until they had exacted their own terms. Sums of five, six, ten, thirty, and even so much in one case as one hundred and twenty thousand pounds were extorted, nominally for slips of land, but really to buy off opposition. In one narrow neighbourhood it was necessary to buy off opposition at a price which at the ordinary rate of railway profits would necessitate the raising of 15,000$l.$ per annum additional tolls, a sum equal to the fares of sixty thousand third-class passengers per annum to the neighbourhood in question.

The details of the occurrence just referred to are the following.

When the Eastern Counties came to be planned, it appears that a few miles of the line would pass through the estates of a noble lord and a right honourable gentleman who were indisposed to favour the project: the first entered into a contract with the provisional committee of the company, stipulating that, in the event of his not opposing the bill, he should receive £120,000 for the land required —a strip of some five or six miles. After the bill was passed, the directors demurred to paying the money, and his lordship at once applied to Chancery, and got an injunction against them. The company applied to Parliament for an amended Bill, but his lordship entered into an alliance offensive and defensive with his neighbour, the right honourable gentleman in question, and the directors were compelled to pay the peer not only the £120,000, but interest for nearly two years in addition. The commoner obtained £35,000. It is only just pleasing to record, that the son of the latter, many years afterwards, refunded £15,000 to the company, when he learned that his property had not been so much deteriorated as his father alleged it would.

The directors of the Glasgow Lunatic Asylum asked £44,000 from the Edinburgh and Glasgow Railway Company. The company determined to carry the question before a jury. Before the trial came off, the Asylum directors reduced their claim to £10,000. The jury awarded exactly £873.

Mr. Pease, of Darlington, who took a very active part in conjunction with George Stephenson in the promotion of railway enterprise, when he was once examined before a committee of the House of Commons, testified that when the Stockton and Darlington Company purchased more land, some years after the line was first opened, the very men who had received large compensation for the injuries anticipated to be done to their estates, clapped on 50 per cent. additional as enhanced value by the opening of the railway on their estates. And, on one occasion, a land valuer was giving evidence to prove how much a certain property would be deteriorated by a projected line, when the counsel for the company put in his hand a newspaper containing an advertisement drawn up by the witness, extolling the increased value of the property to be traversed by the new railway.

Robert Stephenson, in an address read by him before the Institute of Civil Engineers, thus pithily expressed himself about the peculiar claim for the depreciation of the value of land denominated by the legal term of "severance." "Parliament has never, on any occasion, considered improvement [*i. e.* of land] as an element *in favour* of a railway; but it has always been ready to tax a railway company on account of possible depreciation. The extent to which claims on account of depreciation have been carried is well known. Great was the ingenuity of the agent who discovered the use of the word "severance." To railway companies, constant repetition has made that term but too familiar. In every case in which the line passes through an estate, a claim is set up for compensation on account of "severance;" which means simply that a property having been previously in what is called a ring-fence, it becomes, by the passage of a railway through it, less convenient for the purposes of cultivation. Agents of the highest respectability make the claim, on the ground that it is customary, admitting that there is no substantial reason whatever for it. In one recent case, a claim for compensation for "severance" was made by the owner of some marsh land in Essex, *whose whole estate was taken by a company*, but who claimed for "severance" on the ground that the loss of his marsh land on the Thames was injurious to an arable farm which he possessed many miles distant. I carefully abstain from introducing anything approaching to political controversy in this sketch. But this at least may be said, without transgressing the limit which I have prescribed, that the railway interest has suffered in a much higher degree than any other form of property or description of enterprise from that relic of feudalism still imbedded in English law, by which land is considered as differing from all other kinds of estate, and hedged round with peculiar privileges and immunities; and that for these privileges and immunities enjoyed by land and its possessors, shareholders are paying at this day.

Ere I leave this department of the subject—the artificial, excessive, and exorbitant elements of expense of the construction of railways—I may add a few figures of authenticated statistics which speak far more forcibly than any amount of general description.

The following represent the cost per mile for outlay of this description paid by four of the leading companies:—

LAND AND COMPENSATION.

London and South Western	£4000
London and Birmingham	6300
Great Western	6300
London and Brighton	8000

PARLIAMENTARY EXPENSES.

London and South Western	£650
London and Birmingham	650
Great Western	1000
London and Brighton	3000

LAW, ENGINEERING, AND DIRECTION.

London and South Western	£900
London and Birmingham	1500
London and Brighton	1800
Great Western	2500

I may contrast with this the expenses of—with the exception of Mr. Bower's line in the county Donegal—the most cheaply constructed railway in the United Kingdom, the short branch of the North British, a little more than twenty miles long, connecting the pretty country town of Peebles with Edinburgh. This line was projected during the railway mania, the expenses were estimated at the then prevailing rate, and the claims of the landowners, of whom there are about a dozen or so on the whole line, were what is called exorbitant after the prevailing mode. The result was that the project never came to anything, and the shareholders were glad enough to receive back 12*l*. 10*s*., or exactly one fourth of the 50*l*. shares, after the enormous preliminary costs had been defrayed. Years brought prudence, both to the proprietors of the land and the commercial and residential parties interested in the success of the line. The measure was reintroduced, and a single line only was laid down, without a single landlord offering opposition. The required land was obtained at thirty-five years' purchase agricultural value, severance value being fixed by arbitration. The turnpike-road trustees made no claim for damages, and the Act, which was procured in 1853, cost only 650*l*., not a single penny being paid to counsel. The whole Parliamentary expenses up to the obtaining of the Act came to only 1569*l*. The total charges for land and compensation amounted to 21,222*l*., or at the rate of 1131*l*. per mile. Seven stations were built, the average cost, including the termini, being 1200*l*. The works cost 3600*l*. per mile. Thus the total cost per mile was little more than 6000*l*.. One need not wonder that it was not long ere a five per cent. dividend was reached.

It is only just towards the landowners of that period to record their defence against the charge of extortion made against them by the railway projectors. "These works," they said, " are private speculations, in which the State takes no part—a class of speculators wish to take our lands from us, convert it to their own use, and give us no higher price than if we were voluntary sellers in the market—their only object is to make money; they expect to make enormous fortunes by getting possession of our land, run up their shares to a high premium, get ten or fifteen per cent. interest for their money, and the profits arising from these transactions they wish to exclude us from entirely; they are not called on by any public duty to make railways for the country, nor do they profess to be moved by any patriotic motive; if they don't like the terms on which we are willing to sell our land, why do they buy?—nobody asks them; they complain of the high prices extorted on the Liverpool and Manchester line by landowners for their land, but, notwithstanding the 'high prices' charged, the speculators have made about 150 per cent. by the transaction; and had they shared 1000 per cent. clear, they would not give us a single shilling more than they could help. If from any circumstance a sudden rise takes place in the price of sugar, cotton, or any other commodity, does the Liverpool or Manchester merchant or manufacturer say, 'I will take no advantage of this rise—the old price allows me a sufficient profit, and I should consider it highly immoral to make a profit by this sudden and unexpected demand.' When mercantile men hold this language, and act on these principles, it will be quite time enough for them to lecture us on taking advantage of our position."

There are always two sides to a question, and we shall not stop to discuss which of the parties had the better of the argument. One story, as the proverb goes, is good till the other is told. I certainly never heard of any case where our speculators offered to share the profits with the landowners.

We now resume, after this episodical *abrégé* of the history of compensation, &c., in the construction of the earlier lines, the narrative of the successful construction of the great railways of the kingdom. We left off at the period of the opening of the London and Birmingham, the first great *unassisted* triumph of Robert Stephenson. I say his first great unassisted triumph in this sense —that it was the first great work of which he had the whole control. But, it appears, quite as much from the biography of the father by Mr. Smiles, as from the life of the son by Mr. Jeaffreson, that very much of the credit due to George for the construction of the locomotives purchased by the Liverpool and Manchester line, and of the road on which they ran, is to be divided with his well-beloved and proudly regarded son.

The Grand Junction was formed to connect Birmingham with Manchester and Liverpool, and thus to complete the chain to connect the two latter towns with London. The title was not original, there having existed many years before the Grand Junction Canal, designed to constitute the same requisite link in its day as the railway was in a later. The Grand Junction had been first brought forward in 1824, but, having failed to propitiate the "interests," was unsuccessful. A second application, in 1826, also failed. In 1832, it was again introduced, and then, for the first time, under the title by which it was subsequently known. This time there was no opposition, and the Act was procured without any difficulty. The line was opened for public traffic in 1837. Very little excitement had been created by the progress of this line—as little was caused by its completion. The country was getting accustomed to railways now; the novelty was beginning to wear off. And yet it was one of the most important ever formed—perhaps even more important than its two great predecessors. It passed through a hive of industry, and equally affected commercial and manufacturing interests. Connecting as it did the coal, iron, and pottery districts with the great emporium of the carrying trade and the cotton manufacture, it formed the remaining link necessary to connect Manchester and Liverpool with London. Its bearings upon social progress, national wealth, and the industrial interests of labour, must be considered as even of higher importance than the Manchester and Liverpool, or the London and Birmingham Railway. But, perhaps, the true view is to attribute no preponderance of importance and value to either of the three vertebræ of this great spine. Each derives the highest measure of its strength and tenacity from its association with its fellows. This circumstance was recognized some years afterwards in form as well as in fact, and the three companies were incorporated into one, the London and North Western. The completion of the Grand Junction furnished the first of those great triumphs of postal communication for which we are indebted to the railways. The Liverpool merchant, and still more the private individual of humbler station or less busy habits, were astounded to find letters sent from London at eight in the evening in their hands the following morning; and the rough and grimy Birmingham worker in iron regaled himself for the first time in his life on the unwonted luxury of fresh seafish, served to him as wholesome and as cheap as they were to the dwellers on the estuary of the Mersey.

About this time the important system of *contracting*, which has played such a large and leading part in the history of railway construction, first began to assume considerable proportions. On the Grand Junction line Thomas Brassey took a contract for the construction of ten miles. The beginnings of contracting were thus but humble. In the early days, about half a dozen miles of earthworks, fencing, and bridges formed about the average of responsibility undertaken by a single contractor; but ere many years it was comparatively common for one man to hold himself answerable for the construction of an entire railway, and deliver it over complete to the company. Then, of course, the system of sub-contracting, and yet again sub-contracting, to an indefinite extent, followed. Great capital is necessary, and large profits earned, by the great contractors. Probably never in the history of the world has any one class of traders or manufacturers, for they belong equally to both classes, so rapidly risen from such small beginnings to the possession of great wealth as the leading contractors of the world— the M'Kenzies, the Brasseys, the Petos, and the Salamancas.

One peculiarity about the nature of the business of contractor is especially worthy of notice. So long as he remains in business, he cannot for any considerable period permit his capital to lie idle, for his plant is so enormous that were it long to remain idle, it would eat away very much of the profits of even his most successful ventures. Hundreds of earth-waggons and horses, scores of miles of rails and sleepers for "temporary way," several locomotive and several stationary engines, tools of countless numbers and endless variety—these, in addition to enormous accumulations of timber, brick, stone, rails, and a host of other materials, all vociferously call for more employment. And although the mere " hands "—the Titanic navvies—can be gradually diminished as works approach completion, and involve no eating up of capital when the work is done, the contractor must have a very large staff of scientific, commercial, and skilled *employés*, whom he must keep in permanent employ or pay, else the whole work of superior organization and drill would have to be re-undertaken when every new enterprise was inaugurated. This, of course, would be as impossible as it would be irksome and costly, and hence it is that contractors are constantly pressing forward new undertakings; being willing frequently, so long as they can only secure employment for their brains, capital, and staff, to accept in very large proportion shares of new enterprises in part repayment of their services and expenditure. The same inducements produce this other result—that they themselves project undertakings, use parliamentary influence to have them legalized, and employ their private influence among their own circles of connections and dependants to have sufficient shares taken up to induce Parliament to pass bills. Thus, in very many cases, has the original relation between the contractor and the promoters and proprietors of a given measure been just reversed. They now inaugurate, and endeavour to induce the public to follow and participate, in place of the public promoting and then calling in the contractor's services for the realization of the project promoted. This diametrical change does not appear on the surface of affairs; but it is not the less practically true.

This second development of the contracting system has proved as far removed from an unmixed good as it has from an unmixed benefit. On the one hand, this restless stimulating desire for employment has doubtless facilitated the accomplishment of many enterprises whose course otherwise would have been far less smooth, or whose inauguration might have been delayed till long after the period of their actual accomplishment, or even which might not have been heard of to this day; but, on the other hand, it must be borne in mind that this insatiate, and, I add and admit, *inevitable*, craving for contracts has precipitated many enterprises prematurely, forced in others fitter for the next century than our own, and still others which the inhabitants of many homes have too much reason to fear will never be remunerative at all. A writer in the *Edinburgh Review*, under date of October, 1854, says,— " The most gigantic project which private enterprise has yet dared —a project of which, unfortunately, there is now no hope—originated with a distinguished contracting firm."

It was not long ere Mr. Brassey extended his operations to a much higher scale than his small beginnings in the Grand Junction. Before he was forty-five, he thought nothing of contracting for the construction of a thousand miles of rail, or of undertaking responsibility to the extent of many millions on his own account, and equally large sums in conjunction with two associates. Now, being about sixty years of age, he is said to have contracts in hand amounting to the enormous sum of sixty millions. The following authenticated incident is recorded of Mr. Brassey, and remarkably illustrates that indomitable perseverance and high sense of honour which have equally conduced to his astounding success. He had a contract for the construction of the line between Rouen and Hâvre, and had built a bridge of twenty-seven arches, costing 30,000*l*. During the progress of the work he repeatedly protested against the quality of the material supplied to him. The bridge fell down, the bad foundations of the bridge being the best proof of the good foundations of his complaints. His friends assured him that there was not the slightest moral claim on him for its reconstruction, and his lawyer told him that there was an equal absence of any legal responsibility; but he said, " I have contracted to make and maintain the road, and no law shall prevent Thomas Brassey from being as good as his word." He rebuilt the bridge out of entirely new materials; and although sixteen millions of bricks were necessary for its reconstruction, fourteen millions of which had to be made on the spot, the work was completed in seven months.

Another great magnate amongst the contractors is Sir Samuel Morton Peto. His earliest railway work of large bulk was the Cambridge portion of the Eastern Counties, constructed about 1843. Sir Morton Peto did not commence life, or even business, as a railway contractor. Although the nephew and successor of one of the largest builders in England, he was taken from school at an early age, and regularly apprenticed as a working builder. He was barely a journeyman when he became the head of the firm, which, in addition to the ordinary routine of the building trade, undertook large contracts: such, for example, as for the Hungerford Market and the Houses of Parliament, besides such various structures as clubs, theatres, prisons, castles, and docks. But in 1834, Mr. Peto, fascinated' with the splendour of the career opened up by railways, gave up his purely building trade, and determined to risk all in the new calling of railway contractor. His first work was the Wharncliffe Viaduct, and he early became distinguished, like Mr. Brassey, afterwards his some time partner, by the courage with which he singly undertook pecuniary responsibilities from which even companies shrank. Mr. Peto soon became honourably known to the public by the kind and assiduous care which he took of the welfare of his huge gangs of labourers. He shortened the period of the payment of wages, so as to relieve them from usurious exactions, and set his face dead against the truck system. He lent them books, established sick clubs and savings banks, and built temporary cottages for them on the line of the works going on. While carrying on a large contract in the diocese of the excellent Bishop Stanley of Norwich, known as the author of the best book on British Birds that ever was written, and as one of the best prelates that ever was ordained, the Bishop thus spoke of Mr. Peto:—

" Mr. Peto was a dissenter; and he envied the sect to which he belonged the possession of such a man, and he would gladly purchase him at his own price ; and heartily he prayed that ere long he would become a member of the Church of England. He (Bishop Stanley) was a Churchman, and holding a high office in the Church, and believed that in that Church was the purest faith; but he was still a catholic Christian, and, as such, he would hold it a dereliction of his duty if he did not express his approbation, respect, and regard for the exertions used for the moral benefit of railway labourers by Mr. Peto. All down the line he had met with his agents, and had found them not merely giving directions and instructions, but also giving to the men religious and school books, for the education of themselves and their children; and thus showing them that education can civilize the mind, reform the habits, and elevate the understanding. The gin-shops were left deserted, and the schools were full. The good and exemplary conduct of Mr. Peto's railway labourers under this system deserves to be recorded; and let it be noted as a fact, that not one labourer in the Norwich district had been guilty of misconduct that made him amenable to the law."

Sir Morton Peto is one of the largest employers of labour in the kingdom; the number of persons at present in his employ is said to amount to thirty thousand.

CHAPTER V.

Railway Taxation—Its Impolicy and Injustice—The Great Western—The London and South-Western—The London and Greenwich—The South-Eastern—The London and Croydon—Parliamentary Contest for the Brighton Line—The London and Woolwich—The London and Essex—The Eastern Counties.

It was in 1832 that the Government first determined to tax the railways. In that year a tax was imposed to the amount of a penny a mile for every eight passengers, or half a farthing for each, being the eighth part of the fare subsequently paid by the passengers by "parliamentary trains," and mulcting the whole passenger traffic of the three kingdoms of a sixteenth part, or six per cent. of its gross takings. The good policy of imposing this tax was doubted at the period of the imposition, and it will be recollected that it underwent some modification some years since at the instance of Mr. Gladstone. The general opinion is that it is impolitic for Government to tax any means of communication between one place and another, and railways should form no exception to the general rule. It must be recollected that it is a special and exceptional imposition laid upon railways. In other and ordinary ways the companies pay precisely their proportionate share of the burdens of the country, in the form of property tax to the exchequer, and of assessed contributions to the local rates of every town, county, parish, and union through which they pass. They represent the only description of fixed property in the country which pays property tax and another and a more onerous tax to boot. Or if you regard them in the light of traders, they represent the sole department of commercial enterprise which is taxed, and of which the natural development is thereby impeded.

Besides those considerations of morality and justice on which I have been dilating, another argument, one of governmental expediency, applies with equal strength against this impost. One of the most cogent arguments used in favour of the reduction of the rate of postage (and it has been amply confirmed by the result) was this: even if the revenue were to sustain a loss by the reduction, the commerce of the country would receive such an impetus, the interchange of commodities would be so increased by the stimulus given to commercial inter-communication, that the excise and customs department would largely profit by the increased consumption of duty-paying articles. This argument applies equally to railways. Cheaper travelling of persons must necessitate greater transit of commodities, many of them duty-paying. And it must not be imagined that because the Government imposed the railway tax as a poll tax on persons, it therefore follows that railway companies derive the means of paying the tax collectors out of their passenger fares. The burden falls generally upon the whole traffic, and, in some cases, it is more than possible that it is the goods that pay the tax, for the companies are bound down by a parliamentary edict to at least a minimum fare, and that forms an arbitrary standard from which they cannot very well make their higher tariffs deviate except at the fixed, understood, and now uniform scale of difference. In other words, if the railway poll tax were taken off, it is possible that the public would, in some cases at least, reap the advantage in the reduction of the charges for the conveyance of goods. The exchequer must necessarily feel the direct beneficial benefit of the increased consumption of articles not coming within the strict categories.

It is questionable, in fact, whether the revenue does not suffer considerably more than it gains by the railway tax. No doubt, to some extent, and partially at least, the railways recoup themselves by the sums they receive from the Post Office. Were no bill sent in from Downing Street to Euston Square and London Bridge, it is asserted by railway companies that Euston Square and London Bridge would not present quite such large accounts for settlement at St. Martin's-le-Grand; and, in confirmation of this view of the case, they state that immediately the tax was laid on in 1832, the Liverpool and Manchester directors boldly announced that, "in consequence of the above tax, the company's charge for conveying the mail between Liverpool and Manchester would be three-halfpence per mile, instead of one penny as heretofore." These statements of the companies must, however, be taken *cum grano salis*.

I now turn to the establishment of the Great Western line, which was many years ago called, and may be justly still termed "the most gigantic work, not only in Great Britain, but in the entire world." The well-known battle of the gauges, on which all England was divided, being waged not only between engineers, mechanicians, and men of science, but by hosts of pamphleteers, in the leaders of morning journals, and in all places of public resort, was waged about this line. But there was another fierce battle to be waged before the battle of the gauges—*i.e.* was there to be a line at all?

The first prospectus was issued in 1833, Reading only being then proposed as the terminus: 3,000,000*l.* was first named; but this was considered alarmingly great, and in deference to the money interest, the proposal was reduced to 2,500,000*l.* The bill was applied for in 1834. The old style of opposition was at once renewed—opposition, indeed, as valid as that which had assailed the Liverpool and Manchester, and much more irate then the antagonism which had assailed the London and Birmingham. But this was no indication that the railways were receding in popular favour, or that men were becoming less sanguine as the novelty wore off. The fact was very simply explained. The London and Birmingham had gone to a large extent *through*, and at all events *to*, a great centre of trade and industry. The Great Western proposed to invade one of the most luxurious, sleepy districts in England. It did not propose to open up any hive of collieries, mining, melting, spinning, or exporting enterprise. The valley of the Thames was a very different locality. It was not to be wondered at that the courtier, peers, and squires, living under the very shadow of the flag that waved over the Palace at Windsor, or that plethoric tutors of Eton, should have been horrified at the prospect of the assault of the iron monster.

The old cries were raised without the slightest variation or novelty. "It was a mere speculation of engineers, attorneys, and capitalists." "The river would beat the rail." Tunnels would smother one-half the passengers, and those who escaped suffocation in the bowels of the earth would be burned to death by the cinders, or scalded by the steam in the open æther. Every gentle slope was magnified into precipices, and whole trains were to be dashed into the abyss below. Eton College violently opposed the scheme, as certain to be the destruction at once of the morals and the discipline of their pupils. They said, "anybody who knew the nature of Eton boys would know that they could not be kept from the railway." A farmer knew that his cows would be killed, if they passed under a certain archway; and one squire coolly stated that no amount of national benefit could compensate for the destruction of the beauties of his estate. Another wiseacre warned the public that the water in the Thames would be materially decreased to supply the boilers, and drew a mournful picture of sacred royalty itself at Windsor finding no response from the tap. An attempt was made to propitiate the benevolent, by urging the circumstance of the cruelties inflicted by the drivers bringing cattle up to London from the west, and those of less fine feelings were reminded that their cattle were thus depreciated in value, to the value of many thousands per annum. But it was all of no use — the bill was rejected.

One objection urged against the bill—and it had some reason in it—was, that a railway going westward to stop at Reading was a very poor and incomplete affair. The directors profited by the objection, and reintroduced the measure extending the line to Bath and Bristol. The objectors, who had objected that they had not proposed so distant termini at first, now alleged, that, "though the Great Western may reach as far as Bath from Bristol, after having, like a mole, explored its way through tunnels long and deep, yet those who travel by it will be so heartily sick, what with foul air, smoke, and sulphur, that the very mention of a railway will be worse then ipecacuanha." However, on this occasion, in 1835, the bill was passed. The capital was 2,500,000*l*., and powers to borrow 833,333*l*. were granted. The usual enormous donations had to be given to opponents, ere success was achieved. Supplementary bills, in years immediately following, increased the capital by one-half, and the borrowing power in the same proportion.

I have already, in a preceding page, in that part of my narrative which briefly describes the history of the mechanical contrivances of the railroad, briefly noted the difference between the broad and narrow gauges. It was in the interval between the first and second parliamentary struggle for the Great Western, that Mr. Brunel, the engineer of the company, conceived the idea of enlarging the width of the rail, on scientific grounds, specified in an earlier page. He was a man capable of the propagandism of honest opinion, as well as of great practical ability, and he persuaded the directors to fall in with these views. Now these, in fairness to the memory of Mr. Brunel, must be tested by the light, not of *this*, but of *that* day. He fancied that certain great lines should rule over certain definite and mutually distant districts, and that there would be little or no necessity for intercommunication between these districts; and his conclusion was, that each company might choose its own gauge as it liked. The proposal was a magnificent one to the imagination. The whole plan, with its concomitants, assumed grand and colossal proportions; and Mr. Brunel being, as we have said, a man of fine sympathies himself, and with fine powers of awaking the sympathies of others, enlisted a great deal of enthusiasm on his side. A supplementary Act, authorizing the necessary alteration of the plans, was passed, and the programme had to be further modified in this particular. Originally the arrangement had been that the Great Western should join the London and North Western at the outskirts of the town, and use in common with it its Euston-square terminus. The alterations of the gauge rendered this impossible. And not only was the company thus obliged to build its costly station at Paddington, but to its permanent loss, was obliged to content itself with an inconvenient and remote corner of the metropolis.

Independent of the real issue involved, and its actual merits, I do not think there is any finer specimen of perseverance under difficulties, and a high, hopeful, and persevering courage, altogether unaffected by circumstances, than the position taken by Mr. Brunel throughout this extraordinary controversy. The whole railway world was against him; only one engineer of any standing was on his side. And this, unfortunately, was his own second in command, and was maliciously pooh-poohed as Sancho to Don Quixote. The press, generally ignorant of the scientific question, cried him down, or at least endeavoured to do so, and the general masses, although it could not affect them in any way, whether successful or not, grew absolutely afraid of it. The carriages could not run round the curves, the axles would be broken, and, horror of horrors! the shareholders would be ruined.

The event was, that the last-mentioned prediction seemed but too likely of fulfilment. As the scheme was new and untried, Brunel had to begin experimentally, and unfortunately for him, just in the midst of the storm, his first experiment signally failed. The whole timbers of the rail would not answer, and had to be relaid; and a bridge expressly built over the Thames at Maidenhead to show how the river might be curved by two arches instead of six, as hitherto, actually fell down twice. Amid all this outcry and calamity Brunel maintained his ground unruffled, and, by the very force of his indomitable courage, and, we may add, equally indomitable good temper, eventually gained his point.

In 1832, the London and Southampton line was first presented to the notice of the public. It was received with a general feeling of surprise. A railway between great commercial centres like Manchester and Liverpool, or Birmingham and London, it was said, could be understood; but what possible traffic, it was asked, could reimburse the outlay of a railway to a small and obscure port, as Southampton was then? A few, however, there were far-seeing enough to descry the position which Southampton would attain as the great mail-packet emporium; and Sir John Easthope, the leading promoter of the line, received valuable support, first from Scotland, and, to a still greater extent, from Lancashire; the Stock Exchange followed suit, and the capital was obtained. The further difficulties with which the company had to contend were of its own making, as its Act, or rather Acts, were procured with comparative ease. Unfortunately, however, the construction of the line was entrusted to a number of small contractors, unprovided with capital, and whose efforts were paralyzed by the slightest engineering difficulty. Matters accordingly got into a complete state of confusion, and the shares fell to a great discount. The Lancashire shareholders sent up a deputation to learn what the matter was, soon discovered the source of the evil, found money to complete the undertaking, appointed Mr. Locke engineer in place of the gentleman under whom affairs had gone wrong, and thus brought the project to a satisfactory issue. One great means of the extension of the London and Southampton (or as we know it better now by its title of South Western) from its difficulties was the adhesion of Mr. Chaplin, the head of the great carrying firm of Chaplin and Horne. Knowing the South Western would get a large portion of his business, he saw it to be the part of wisdom to make common cause with his destroyer, and, it is believed, in the end reaped a benefit to which his wise liberality of view eminently entitled him. The line was opened throughout in May, 1840, and its success was soon established. A newspaper writer, of five years' later date, thus expresses himself:—" This is one of the early lines, and furnishes a good example of the difficulties, discouragements, and disasters encountered by the enterprising men who at that date undertook the arduous duty of constructing, from private capital, these great public works, unaided, even discountenanced, by the Legislature and the Government; regarded with hostility, and even with hatred, by the owners of the land they were destined so materially to benefit; and considered, even by juries of their countrymen, in these days, as proper objects of unlimited and legitimate plunder."

Much of the success of this line is to be attributed to Joseph Locke, who, with the exception of Robert Stephenson, was the favourite and most distinguished pupil of the elder Stephenson. Among his many achievements, the following are some of the chief. He largely helped at Chat Moss, and still more largely in the Liverpool tunnel. He was the engineer of the Grand Junction, and the great tunnel on the Manchester and Sheffield is his. He was the first to introduce passenger traffic into Spain, and the chief portions of the lines that connect Paris with the Provinces are his. Perhaps the most meritorious fact that can be stated about the engineering career of Mr. Locke is, that he always kept his works within the estimates.

The construction of the following lines followed quickly upon the successful triumph of the South Western over so great and apparently insurmountable difficulties:—the London and Brighton, London and Greenwich, South-Eastern, London and Croydon, London and Blackwall, London and Essex, or, as it was afterwards called, the Eastern Counties, and now, as the result of amalgamation with smaller companies owning lines in the same district, the Great Eastern. It will be impossible, within my limits, to make any but a passing illusion to the origin and early fortunes of these lines.

Among the numerous instances of reckless Parliamentary expenditure which the history of the English railway records, the history of the London and Brighton takes high rank. No less than five contending schemes for communication between London and Thackeray's London-super-Mare, were brought forward; and their projectors fought for each of the five valiantly. The mere preliminary expenses of Rennie's line cost 72,000*l.*, Stephenson's 54,000*l.*, Cundy's 16,000*l.*, Gibbs's 26,000*l.*, and that of the South-Eastern, 25,000*l.* Ultimately, the most direct, but the most difficult way was selected. Earthworks, bridges, viaducts and tunnels were all characterized by an unusual scale of expensiveness. It is not accordingly to be wondered at that, although the directors only estimated the cost of construction at 23,000*l.* per mile, the estimate was exceeded by more than 14,000*l.* a mile.

The short line between London and Greenwich inspired its proprietors with the highest hopes. It was to be a well-paying, as well as a useful and practical, line. Its dividend was to be secured by the profits of the trips which the curiosity of the three millions of annual visitors to London would induce them to make, the promoters forgetting that just as the railway system became developed throughout the land, the curiosity would abate in proportion to the diminution of the novelty. It was certainly preposterous to expect that any curiosity would induce a visitor to London to make experiment on an extremely reduced scale of a mode of conveyance which had already carried him to London from his distant provincial home. It is true that the London and Woolwich was one of the first projected railways, and, indeed, was the first completed line which had its commencement in the metropolis, and persons old enough to recollect the occurrence, talk to this day of the extraordinary crush, curiosity and excitement of the opening day. Not only did the London and Woolwich depend upon this necessarily temporary and evanescent department of traffic, but they dwelt with great satisfaction upon the prospect of tolls from pedestrians, and on letting out at large rentals its scores of large arches as warehouses. These latter anticipations proved equally fallacious, the ardent hopes of the proprietors were disappointed, and it was not very long ere at once their importance and their identity were swallowed up by amalgamation with the South Eastern.

The South Eastern was first projected in 1833, and proposed to connect London with Dover. It had a very hard struggle with the rival plans of the Mid-Kent and Central Kent, but at last procured its Act in June, 1836. Sundry supplemental Acts empowered deviations and addenda, and much money was expended, with ultimate but deferred success, in the endeavour to procure the right of extension to Brighton.

For some time previous to the stage at which I have now arrived much public scandal had been created by reiterated allegations that the promoters of rival schemes personally canvassed members of both Houses of Parliament with shameful pertinacity, and, what was worse, were wont to enforce their importunities by promises of direct pecuniary advantages in the form of preferential and other shares. So much was said of this, and the honour of the House of Commons was becoming so decidedly compromised, that its members were compelled to take formal notice of the report. It was in 1836, and in connection with the South Eastern, that the alleged conduct of a member of the House, whose name it would serve no good purpose now to exhume, was brought before the Commons. The said member admitted that he had greatly exerted himself in his legislatorial capacity in favour of the line; further, that he had done so, not so much on public grounds, as at the solicitation of one of the directors, for that "he owed him a debt of gratitude." He further admitted that the director had, out of reciprocal regard for the member's services, conducted a negotiation in his (the member's) name and for his behoof in the sale of shares of the company, by which he benefited to the extent of three hundred pounds. But the member decidedly denied that any condition had been offered or exacted, previously to the rendering of his parliamentary services, by which any pecuniary recompense was stipulated. The committee of the House, which had been appointed to inquire into the transaction, felt bound to report that they accepted the truthfulness of the member's representation; but, though they did not suggest that any censure should be expressed, they felt " obliged to direct the attention of the House to this circumstance."

" The London and Essex Railroad" was first projected in 1831. The career of this line has probably been the most chequered and unfortunate of any in the three kingdoms. Few, if any, lines were ever projected with greater hopes of success, and certainly none, during one period of its career, has had to suffer so much public condemnation, or such a succession of the most unfortunate accidents. The leading expectation of personal profit and public advantage which the promoters of the London and Essex entertained was in connection with the supply of the London food market. The following is from the first prospectus :—" By the proposed railroad, places thirty or forty miles distant from London will be brought within a two hours' journey. The whole country will become contributory to the London market; the first necessaries of life will be supplied in greater abundance; competition increased, and a reduction in prices the necessary consequence. All descriptions of persons will be enabled to participate in many articles, the produce of the soil, from which the poor, and even the middling classes in a degree, are now precluded, from high prices, occasioned by expensive cultivation in the immediate vicinity of the town.". In such articles as fish and coal the public was especially expected to benefit. "Every shareholder," it was stated, " would in a few years save the cost of his share in fuel." Further elements in the hope-suffused picture were the following :—The London markets of all kinds would be no longer dependent on westerly winds and adverse tides: Holland and Hamburg would be brought next door to us; the nature of the country would require neither viaducts, tunnelling, nor much embankment. The picture was summed up in the concise promise of " large dividends and gradual return of the capital."

Spite of this seductive appeal, the matter remained in abeyance for three years. Unfortunately the picture had appeared without the credentials of its limners, and in the absence of the guarantees of respectable—or, indeed, any—names, the public did not extend their support. In 1834, the Eastern Counties Railway Company, with a repetition of the same proposal, came before the public, and came before it in a possibly more prosaic but much more business-like attitude. The estimates contained the following as their chief calculations:—Cost of the line, 1,500,000*l.*; annual expense of working, 150,000*l.*; gross returns over 400,000*l.*, leaving

B B

a nett profit of 267,000*l.*, or fifteen per cent. These estimates were faulty, both on debit and credit side. The estimate of revenue made no allowance for computed increase of traffic between London and the Eastern Counties and their ports; taking as data only their then existing trade line, and then calculating how much of it the railway was likely to appropriate. And this, although it was even then known that the traffic between Liverpool and Manchester had increased six-fold, and that between Stockton and Darlington in the marvellous and almost incredible ratio of twenty-fold! On the other hand, no allowance was made for compensation to landowners, an error which the company had bitter reason to remember, and on which I have already remarked in a former page. The line was violently opposed. The solicitors were met by the taunt that "by their own superior intelligence they had ascertained that the landed and commercial interests of Norfolk, Suffolk, and Essex were quite ignorant of their own concerns." "The nursery of our best sailors, it was asserted, would be destroyed by the railway, our maritime glory would decay, and England's sun would set for ever." One advantage this company had—there was neither canal nor rival railway scheme to oppose it. Nevertheless, the mere local, landed, and maritime opposition proved so formidable that the promoters rested on their oars, and withdrew their scheme for a while; in the meantime maturing a new campaign, searching for new and influential support, buying off interested opposition, and the like. A new and much more weighty direction, embracing the authoritative names of Thomas Gibbes, Sir Thomas Harvey, Desanges, Wood, Butler, &c., was formed. The ranks of the assailants had been well fortified in the interim. The promoters endeavoured, with equal legitimacy and tact, to enlist the support of the rural population to the scheme, on the ground of the notorious diminution of poor rates which had been effected in every English district to which railways had penetrated. "Wherever railways abound most," said the second prospectus, "there the greatest rise in the value of land has been observed, and the most rapid strides have been made in agricultural, manufacturing and commercial prosperity. They have not only materially reduced the poor rates of every district they intersect, by furnishing profitable occupation to large numbers of the unemployed poor, but have still further relieved the old ratepayers by contributing largely towards the reduced rates; and, while thus conferring incalculable benefits on the community at large, they have yielded to their proprietors a quicker return in the capital invested than was ever obtained from any other description of public undertaking."

Unexpectedly, the Eastern Counties now experienced opposition from rival companies; but as these all proposed going northwards, in the direction of Scotland, and they therefore had no fair ground of antagonism, their opposition was not formidable. I have already recounted how, in the two cases of opposition, of which so much has been heard, the bill was opposed, and at how great a cost it was bought off.

The 120,000*l.* paid to the Essex peer almost wrecked the bill, for it so excited the hopes of others in a position to oppose it, that there was some appearance of its being thrown out in the Upper House after it had passed the Commons. "But," says the directors' report, "the directors, by meeting the parties with the same promptness and in the same fair spirit which had carried them successfully through their previous negotiations, effected amicable arrangements with them." What the nature of the transactions euphemistically denominated "amicable arrangements" was, it is hardly necessary to discuss.

The bill was passed. The hopes of the company may be inferred from these clauses extracted from a long and cumbrous sentence of self-congratulation, uttered at the first meeting of shareholders: "From the Continent will flow in return to the eastern counties ample supplies of every commodity, foreign or domestic, of which it is the great storehouse; because the fisheries of our eastern shore freed from every restraint on their abundance, will become ten times more productive than ever; because the ports of the eastern counties will once more be rendered the favourite points of ingress; because this railway must bring with it whatever can give vigour to industry, make commerce active, or render a people happy."

Notwithstanding the confidence with which the directors looked forward to the future success of this undertaking, it proved eventually one of the most unremunerative of our great lines. When at its lowest ebb, Mr. Hudson, then at the zenith of his power and fame, undertook, unfortunately for himself, to raise its fallen fortunes, and in giving certain instructions to the secretary in reference to the accounts, said he "wished to make things pleasant," a phrase now classed among our household words.

CHAPTER VI.

Railway Legislation—Mr. Morrison's Motion—The Session of 1836—The first of the two Railway Manias—The *Edinburgh Review*—How Schemes were got up—The Reaction—Committee of the House of Commons, in 1837—Lord Seymour's Act—Mr. Gladstone's Act of 1842—The Clearing House—Railway Department of the Board of Trade—Accidents—The Act of 1844—The Mania of 1845 and its Results.

THE first attempt at legislation for the railways on a general scale was made by Mr. Morrison in 1836. He moved, " That in all railway bills it be made a condition that the dividends be limited to a certain rate, and that Parliament reserve to itself the power of fixing periodically the tolls on passengers and goods. " He obtained leave to bring in a bill, but the ministry did not support it, and Sir Robert Peel added the great weight of his name to the strong opposition of the railway interest. Mr. Morrison was obliged to withdraw his proposal after the first reading of the bill.

In the session of 1836, no fewer than twenty-nine new lines received the sanction of Parliament. The total length of these lines was nine hundred and ninety-four miles; in the following year, Government introduced what was considered by the railway interest a most arbitrary and dictatorial measure, compelling the railways to perform all services required of them by the Postmaster General. The whole railway interest was up in arms. The bill was not rejected, but many of its provisions were considerably modified. As amended, it enacted that the companies should carry the mails at such hours as the Post Office should direct, that remuneration was to be according to agreement, and that any difference that might arise was to be settled by arbitration.

All the while, new companies were being projected with the most amazing and dangerous celerity. The country had arrived at the portals of the first " railway mania. " Money was plentiful, interest low, and there were few legitimate channels of investment. It was in the latter part of 1836 that the rush into railway schemes, possible and impossible, fairly commenced. "There is scarcely, in fact," said the *Edinburgh Review*, " a practicable line between two considerable places, however remote, that has not been occupied by a company; frequently two, three, or four rival lines have started simultaneously." It is impossible for me to dwell in detail upon the successive incidents of the increase of the mania and its subsequent collapse; nor is it necessary, for the history of all such manias is almost identical, the difference being only that it is now shares in one commodity or enterprise, and at another time shares in some other, that constitute the adored El Dorado of the hour, and lure their victims on to their inevitable fate. The whole public attention was engrossed with the subject of railways; this may be observed from the circumstance, that it was at this stage of English history that the English language received certain adjuncts from the railway system. Now it was for the first time that men began to talk, when they wished to indicate preparations for an enterprise, of " getting up the steam, " or if they wished to indicate a belief that any person or project was advancing too rapidly, they spoke of him or it as "going at railway speed." The shares of all the five opposition lines to Brighton were at a premium. In a single London parish no fewer than sixteen schemes were afloat. Lord Londonderry said, that in his country there were three schemes suggested, all running in parallel lines; of the three, he said, only one was at par, the second bankrupt, the third could never pay. One man proposed to propel his engine by sails, and started a company to carry out the plan; another proposed to drag forward his trains by firing off a succession of rockets, and believed, or professed to believe, that he would thus attain a speed of a hundred miles an hour.

Still the mania was not altogether without check, opposition, or warning. The highest terms were, as usual, exacted for land. Although the great majority of the newspapers were infected by the prevailing fever—and to them, at least, it brought great profit—there were certain worthy exceptions; and the reviewers and pamphleteers of the so-called economic school frequently sounded the note of alarm. The latter endeavoured to establish the doctrine, that too great and sudden an embarkation of the surplus national capital in the railways would divert it from other legitimate channels. The great demand for labour, it was urged, would unduly increase wages and prices. Turnpike landholders and coach proprietors piteously petitioned against the newly projected lines.

Nevertheless the fever continued to rage. The grossest dishonesty, it afterwards appeared, when the poor dupes made enraged but tardy inquiry, was mixed up with many of the schemes. When a subscription became necessary, men of straw filled in their names for enormous amounts. In one company a man, receiving a salary of 60*l.* a year, signed for 35,000*l.* One railway purchased signatures for ten shillings a head. In another, which had obtained its Act, only 235*l.* had been actually subscribed, and not one penny of this sum had been paid by any one of the directors.

At last the reaction came. The Bank, as usual, gave the *coup de grace.* It raised the price of discount to five, and the bubble at once burst. Consols fell 4 per cent., and articles of trade 40. The customs receipts sank nearly a million in one quarter. All this meant ruin to thousands of those who had believed themselves to be rich, and absolute destitution to those who had already been poor. Nearly half the mills of Lancashire were shut up, and in Manchester and its immediate neighbourhood 50,000 hands were unemployed. Numbers of the working people of Glasgow and Paisley must have died but for the compassion of the benevolent.

Even on those railways of a legitimate and sound character, the effect was more than proportionate. It became necessary to make large demands upon shareholders who with the greatest difficulty could procure money for their current and necessary business expenses, and to contract loans at a time when lenders were peculiarly anxious to hold secure what they had. The London and South-Western shares, with 40*l.* paid up, were unsaleable at 13*l.* The cheques of the Great Western were refused, and shares with considerable sums paid upon them were given away, with a premium in cash to boot.

A committee of the House of Commons was appointed in 1837 to inquire into the mania and its worst aspects. One result of its deliberations was the discovery of the sham character of many of the companies. To prevent similar impositions on the public for the future—at least to the same extent—it was ordained that no railway bill should be introduced unless a tenth part of the proposed capital were paid into the hands of Government. This expedient acted well at first. It was so far successful in stopping measures, that not a single railway bill was introduced in the following year, but in a subsequent session the required deposit was reduced to five per cent.

About this time a strong feeling of dissatisfaction with the tax on travelling began to prevail very widely. Especially the nature of its incidence was objected to. It pressed with peculiar heaviness upon the poor traveller; for the proportion of the tax levied from the first-class passenger's fare was only three and a half, while from the third-class passenger's it was twelve and a half per cent. This tax in the year 1835 amounted to 39,570*l*., and in 1840 it had risen to 72,176*l*. In this year another railway bill, familiar to railway shareholders and the public as " Lord Seymour's Act," was passed. It was the first of a number of successive measures to confer upon the Board of Trade those controlling and regulating powers which now belong to that committee of the Privy Council. The bill gave to the Board of Trade the right of inspection of all lines, and a power of veto in all bylaws of the companies. As has just been shown by the enormous increase in the amount of the railway tax from 1835 to 1840, a very large number of railways were completed and opened in the latter year. In that year, it was said, " every important district might be reached by the new mode of travel." From 1826 until 1839, a hundred and three railway Acts had been passed by Parliament.

A bill supplementary to Lord Seymour's Act was introduced in 1842 by Mr. Gladstone, then Vice-President of the Board of Trade. It did not introduce any very important change. He declined to license engine drivers, as had been suggested, thinking it much better to leave the general responsibility of securing proper servants with the railway directors. The bill provided for more efficient inspection of lines before they were opened. Punishments for misconduct on railways were enacted, and greater authority in case of accidents was given to the board. This bill occasioned great discussion. The companies opposed it with all their weight, suggesting compromise or modification at least; but the Government would not flinch from any clause which had regard to the safety of the public. Mr. Plumptre opposed the bill on another ground, introducing an amendment, that the clause should be added—" That no railway should be used on any part of the Lord's day." This was rejected, and the Government bill carried intact.

In 1842 was founded the railway clearing-house, established on the model of the clearing-house of the London bankers. Although the amount of work effected by this most ingenious instance of what may be called composite account-keeping was not one-third as great when Sir Francis Head published his " Stokers and Pokers " as it is now, yet the plan then adopted is still in use, and the intricacies to be overcome then were of the same character, though not of the same amount, as now. I therefore make no apology for extracting a few detached sentences from Sir Francis' description of the clearing-house and transferring them to my pages.

"The next operation," says Sir Francis, "is, by a consideration of all these balances, to determine what the clearing-house, as the representative of all the creditor-companies, is entitled to receive from the debtor-companies. The final result of all these operations is exemplified by a monthly return forwarded by the office to each of the forty-seven companies, showing separately to each, for each of its stations, the weights, the mileage proportions, the terminal expenses, and, lastly, the balances, whether due to it or by it, on the traffic from each of its stations to all other clearing-house stations to which goods had been sent, or from which received. . . . All tickets collected at all the clearing-house stations from *through* passengers are transmitted daily to the London clearing-house, from whence, after being examined and compared with the returns of the tickets issued, they are sent back to the respective companies. . . . Returns are also sent *daily* from all the clearing-house stations on all the lines of railway, by the servants of the respective companies, of all foreign carriages arriving and departing from each of the said stations. From these returns the London clearing-house is enabled to trace the course of all waggons and passenger carriages travelling on what are termed "foreign" lines, and to debit and credit every company with the sums it has respectively incurred for mileage, as also what is due from and to the respective companies for demurrage per day of waggons or of passenger carriages. Sheets covering waggons are in like manner all checked at the junctions by the men placed there by the London clearing-house, as also by returns forwarded to the office from the various stations at which the waggons stop to be loaded or unloaded; and thus the charge of one-tenth of a penny per mile for the use of these tarred coverings is divided according to its proper proportion among the respective companies over whose lines they have travelled.

The first report of the railway department of the Board of Trade was very satisfactory. It especially dissipated the vulgar delusion that railways were more dangerous than stage coaches. Mr. Laing, who drew up the report, said—" If, then, stage coaches were attended with as little personal injury to the public as railways, the following would be near the proportional number of casualties :—

Passengers killed from causes beyond their own control	1 in	833 years.
Killed from their own folly, negligence, or misconduct	1 ,,	1250 ,,
Persons run over in the road	1 ,,	500 ,,
Coach servants	1 ,,	125 ,,

The year 1844 witnessed a still more important piece of legislation at the instance of the Board of Trade than any which I have in this Appendix hitherto chronicled. In May, Mr. Gladstone proposed that the amount of deposit on projected railways should be reduced from ten to five per cent.; and in spite of the objection of Mr. Hume, the proposal was carried. But this measure was of very secondary importance to a bill introduced by ministers later in the year—to elucidate which this volume has been written; a cursory notice of it, however, is here necessary,—a measure which met with the most determined resistance, and which the Government had in considerable degree to modify ere they could effect its enactment. The most important provisions of the Act as it finally stood were the following:—

If after twenty-one years from the passing of any Act for a railway, the profits should exceed ten per cent. per annum, the scale of tolls should be revised, and a new one fixed, such revised scale to continue for twenty-one years.

The Lords of the Treasury to have the right of purchasing any future railway after the expiration of twenty-one years, upon payment of a sum equal to twenty-five years' purchase of the divisible profits, estimated on the average of the three preceding years; but should the proprietors think their prospects more favourable than such average, the amount of purchase money to be decided by arbitration.

Existing railways to be exempt from the Act, and branch lines not longer than five miles not to be considered as new railways.

No purchase of a line to be made without an Act of Parliament, and three months' notice to be given.

A "Parliamentary train" to run at least once every lawful day, at a speed of not less than twelve miles an hour, including stoppages —to stop at every passenger station; the carriages to be seated and protected from the weather; the fare not to exceed a penny a mile.

Parliamentary trains to be exempt from the passenger poll-tax.

The electric telegraph to be established on all lines of railway.

Such are the chief, but by no means the whole of the stipulations of this most valuable Act. I doubt if it be not, next to Free Trade, the greatest boon ever bestowed on this country. The two names worthily associated with this measure are those of Peel and Gladstone, who, when it passed, were respectively Premier and President of the Board of Trade. Not the least debt of gratitude owing by the working classes of England to Mr. Gladstone is that combined comfort and cheapness of travelling which the companies twenty years ago made no attempt to confer, and which accordingly legitimately demanded the salutary interference of the Government.

I have already remarked, in my short summary of the leading features of the first railway mania in this country, that every commercial mania or fever of speculation is so much akin to every other as to present an almost absolute identity of aspect. It will not, therefore, be necessary to do more here than allude to the mania of 1845, which I have noticed at some length in the body of this work; it had filled the minds of the many nine years before, and a precisely similar catastrophe descended in 1846 as had done in 1837. It was in the three summer months of 1845 that the mania was at its height. A novelist has described with no more than fair artistic exaggeration the then condition of men's minds. "The whole country from coast to coast was to be traversed and dissected by iron roads. Wherever there was a hamlet or a cattle track, a market or a manufactory, there was to be a railroad; physical objects and private rights were straws under the chariot wheels of the Fire King. Mountains were to be cut through; valleys were to be lifted; the skies were to be scaled; the earth was to be tunnelled; parks, gardens, and ornamental grounds were to be broken into; the shrieking engine was to carry the riot of the town into the sylvan retreats of pastoral life; sweltering trains were to penetrate solitudes hitherto sacred to the ruins of antiquity; hissing locomotives were to rush over the tops of houses."

One distinguishing feature of this second railway mania was the enormous increase of the railway press. An entirely new—or, at least, a greatly augmented—department of journalism started into existence. Most of the publications had a short life, but it was a merry one. The ordinary daily papers frequently came out with entire double supplements crammed with advertisements of railways alone. Some of the exclusively railway papers netted 700*l.* or 800*l.* each publication, and two daily papers were started dedicated to the railway interest alone.

The crash came in the usual way. Discount was raised, the rein tightened, and the catastrophe came which many of the readers of these words remember; and of those who are too young to do so many will suffer the results of it during the course of their lives.

APPENDIX II.

STATISTICAL AND FINANCIAL SKETCH OF OUR RAILWAYS.

I HAVE already carried the strictly chronological plan of sketching the establishment of the institution of the English railway as far as seems to me necessary. This method of treating the subject may have sufficient interest to engage a reader so long as he is tracing the faint beginnings and early romantic difficulties of a new undertaking; but we have now arrived at a stage of the narrative when it must be considered that railways have attained their maturity, and when it would be no longer possible to associate any trait of heroism or romance with the story of their further development. I propose, therefore, to dedicate my concluding pages to the presentation of a brief general view of the existing condition and development of the principal railways of the United Kingdom, in alphabetical order, taking them as typical and representative of the inferior lines, whether these be auxiliary to, or isolated from, the great trunks.

Referring to the last published authoritative reports at the time these words are written, we find that there are now five hundred and thirty-two separate railway establishments on the earth's surface, of which no fewer than three hundred and seventy-five exist in the United Kingdom. This fact is, perhaps, the most splendid and triumphant proof of the superiority of our civilization. But we must not here, nor in any similar cases, be misled by a mere general description. There is a peculiar and delusive vagueness in the term "railway establishment," which simply means, separate company, or proprietary body. Some of our "railway establishments" represent merely a colliery line of some two or three miles. The very first company mentioned, for example, in the alphabetical list of English railways, the Aberdare Valley line, has but the modest capital of 12,000*l.*, and its length is but a mile and a half. Whereas, on the centralizing Continent, where the Governments possess and regulate, more or less, the railways, or in the wide stretches of India or the United States, such modest and miniature establishments do not exist. But, after all, if the standard of mileage, which is the only fair and decisive one, be taken, we shall be found, as might be expected, far in advance of any other nation.

Out of the five hundred and thirty-two "railway establishments" in the world, three hundred and seventy-five, as already noticed, are British and Irish, one hundred and ten are Continental, five are on the continent of Africa, of which three are in our Southern Colonies, one in Egypt, and one in Algeria; three are in Australia, nine in British North America, thirteen in India, exactly the same number in South America, fifty-seven in the United States, and seven in the West Indies, of which three are in our possession, and no less than four in the single island of Cuba.

Beside the English railway companies, railway shareholders very fairly rank a certain number of other companies, numbering in all twenty-two, as "auxiliary associations." Of these, the chief are the various Telegraph Companies, the British and Foreign Railway Plant, the General Rolling Stock and the Lancaster Waggon Companies, &c. &c.

We shall now notice briefly, in alphabetical order, the names of our principal railways, and a few particulars of general interest in reference to each.

The returns given as "capital expended" are from the last report of the Board of Trade, and are made up to 31st Dec. 1863. The receipts are for the year 1864.

The Belfast and Northern Counties line supplies railway accommodation from Belfast to Portrush, a seaport town in the extreme north of Ireland; there is also a branch to Cookstown: the length of the line is one hundred and thirty-six miles. Capital expended, 7,011,803*l*. Receipts, 110,101*l*.

The Blythe and Tyne Railway, incorporated in 1852. Length, twenty miles from Blyth to Percy Main on the North Shields line. The railway runs through a coal district. Capital, 484,330*l*. Receipts, 98,110*l*.

The Bristol and Exeter Railway is one hundred and twenty-one miles in length, Act obtained in 1836. This line is on the broad gauge, and is a continuation of the Great Western. Capital expended, 4,246,839*l*. Receipts, 351,600*l*.

The Caledonian is the largest and most important of the Scotch lines, and perhaps it is the most signal example of the vicissitudes of fortune that the history of British railways records. At one time persons (if of responsible position) were offered Caledonian shares gratis, with a money payment of thirty shillings added to tempt them. Now, the Caledonian shares are among the highest in the market, at a premium of more than thirty per cent.

The Caledonian commands 230 miles of country, but much of this territory it has gained by amalgamations and working arrangements. After long and protracted litigation about the conflicting interests involved in leases, preference shares, &c., an agreement was finally arrived at and incorporated in an "Arrangement Act," passed in 1851. Shortly after this the Caledonian, in her then crippled state, made arrangements to receive the powerful assistance of the London and North-Western; and the result is what I have recorded. The amount of capital expended 31st December, 1863, was 9,987,084*l*. Receipts, 920,500*l*.

The Charing Cross Railway Company was incorporated on the 8th of August, 1859, "for making and maintaining a line from the South-Eastern at London Bridge to Charing Cross." Subsequent powers were applied for, and granted, to effect communication by a second bridge across the Thames with the City, at Cannon Street. This is a thorough representative of what may be termed the costly intramural metropolitan lines, costing over a million a mile, or a larger sum than would be represented by paving the line with an undisturbed succession of golden sovereigns. The bridge of this company at Hungerford is declared, on the excellent authority of Mr. Bridges Adams, to be without exception the very strongest railway bridge in the world. This company has been incorporated with the South-Eastern Company.

The Cornwall line is sixty-five miles in length, and is a continuation of the South Devon from Plymouth to Penzance and Falmouth, and was incorporated in 1846. Capital, 1,648,588*l*. Receipts, 80,987*l*.

The Dublin and Belfast Junction is the second link in the chain connecting the metropolis of Ireland with the capital of the north, and is a continuation of the Dublin and Drogheda line. Length, sixty-three miles. Capital, 1,011,537*l*. Receipts, 72,602*l*.

The Dublin and Drogheda Company was incorporated in 1836, and the length of the line is thirty-two miles. This line is celebrated for its viaduct over the Boyne at Drogheda. Capital paid up, 1,168,112*l*. Receipts, 90,760*l*.

The Dublin, Wicklow, and Wexford line is not yet completed,

although its Act of incorporation was obtained in 1846; for some time past, however, the works have been in active progress, and it is expected will be completed in 1865. Capital, 1,300,630*l*. Receipts, 142,213*l*.

The Edinburgh and Glasgow was the first railway established north of the Tweed. Its first capital was very humble, being only 900,000*l*. in shares, and 300,000*l*. by loan. In 1848 it was incorporated with the Union Canal, which connects the rivers Forth and Clyde, with branches to Edinburgh and elsewhere. The company was reincorporated and consolidated in 1852. It possesses 169 miles of productive mileage, including 32 of the Union Canal. The receipts of this company are now included in the North British. Capital expended, 5,550,000*l*.

Furness is 50 miles in length, is used principally for the conveyance of minerals from Dalton and Kirley mines, commencing at Barrow, and forming a junction with the Whitehaven line at Foxfield. Incorporated in 1844. Capital, 1,271,453*l*. Receipts, 162,371*l*.

Glasgow and South-Western is one hundred and ninety-eight miles in length. The main line from Glasgow to Ayr was opened in 1843. The remainder with completion of the Dumfries line in 1850. Capital, 4,840,114*l*. Receipts, 455,906*l*.

The Great Eastern, in its final and present form, was incorporated on the 7th of August, 1862. It comprises what were formerly known as the Eastern Counties, Norfolk, Eastern Union, East Anglian, East Suffolk lines, and various subsidiary undertakings. The Eastern Counties, the predecessor if not the progenitor of all the others, has two great arteries, one running to Colchester, the other to Cambridge. By a recent Act this company is authorized to run steamboats between Harwich and the north-western ports of the Continent. The total mileage is $662\tfrac{3}{4}$, besides $67\tfrac{3}{4}$ miles " worked " by the company. The total capital, including nearly five millions of mortgage debt, is 23,220,308*l*. Receipts, 1,591,106*l*.

The Great Northern, an amalgamation of the London and York and Direct Northern, was first incorporated in 1846. Its total parliamentary powers represent $335\tfrac{1}{2}$ miles. The amalgamations, powers of working, &c., of the Great Northern, are very numerous; affecting its relations with the Great Eastern on the one hand, and extending as far as Cheshire on the other. Its relations with the North London, the Edgware and Highgate, &c., secure its connection with all parts of the metropolis. The total capital is 12,689,416*l*. Receipts, 1,627,242*l*.

Great Southern and Western (Inland) is now, with its various amalgamations and extensions, three hundred and eighty-seven miles in length. The Act of incorporation was passed in 1844 for a line from Dublin to Cork, passing by or near Portarlington, Tipperary, and other towns on the route. Capital paid up, 5,661,793*l*. Receipts, 429,746*l*.

The Great Western was remodelled in 1863, by Acts authorizing the amalgamation with it of the West Midland and South Wales. The Great Western proper had previously amalgamated many minor lines, such as the Berks and Hants, Cheltenham Union, Wilts, Somerset and Weymouth, Birmingham and Oxford, &c. Mutually beneficial arrangements have been entered into with the South Devon, the Metropolitan, the London, Chatham and Dover, &c. The mileage of the Great Western is 1225 miles, and its capital 40,666,111*l*. Estimated receipts, 3,285,000*l*. The year was not completed till the 1st February, but the receipts may be estimated at 3,410,000*l*.

Inverness and Perth Junction. Incorporated 1861. Length, 119 miles. Capital, 962,767*l*. This line has not been opened a year; the receipts for the half-year ending 31st December are 55,144*l*.

The Irish North-Western (formerly Dundalk and Enniskillen). Incorporated 1845. The length is one hundred and forty-five miles. Capital paid up, 866,187*l*. Receipts, 90,513*l*.

The Lancashire and Yorkshire is an amalgamation of the Manchester and Leeds, Manchester, Bolton and Bury, Liverpool and Bury, Huddersfield and Sheffield, Wakefield, Pontefract and Goole, West Riding Union, and East Lancashire. The present title was conferred by an Act passed in 1847. The productive mileage is 395¼ miles. The Manchester and Leeds, the parent line, was opened as far as Normanton on the 1st of October, 1844. Capital, 19,931,571*l*. Receipts, 1,890,186*l*.

The London and Blackwall Company obtained their Act in 1836. Length, 5¾ miles. This line is one of the most expensively constructed in England, the line passing through a densely populated district. Capital, 2,224,255*l*. Receipts, 112,047*l*.

The London and Brighton is an amalgamation of the Croydon and Brighton, under an Act of 1846. Various subsequent Acts have legalized a large number of branch lines. The Mid Sussex, Lewes and Uckfield, East Grinstead, &c., have been incorporated. Capital, 11,708,793*l*. Receipts, 1,024,086*l*.

The London, Chatham and Dover, was formerly called the East Kent. On its main line there are 81 miles in operation, and on its metropolitan extension seven miles. The Kent Coast line is leased to this company. Capital expended, 8,835,000*l*. Receipts, 346,847*l*. This company have just completed their bridge over the Thames at Blackfriars.

The London and North-Western is the greatest company in the kingdom, and is an amalgamation of the Manchester and Birmingham, Grand Junction, and London and Birmingham. The Grand Junction itself had been an amalgamation of the Liverpool and Manchester and four other lines. This company is further interested, by subscription or lease, in several lines, such as the Birmingham, Wolverhampton and Stour Valley, the Preston and Wyre, Lancaster and Carlisle, &c. The total capital is 38,360,364*l*. Receipts, 5,205,619*l*. The receipts of this company nearly equal what were the receipts of all the companies in the kingdom twenty years ago.

The London and South-Western was first known as the London and Southampton. In an earlier page, I have described the first difficulties of the undertaking. There are branches to Chertsey, Guildford, Farnham, Richmond, Hampton Court, &c. Lines to Portsmouth and elsewhere are leased. Capital, 13,201,406*l*. Receipts, 1,289,407*l*.

London, Tilbury, and Southend. Incorporated in 1852. Length, 45 miles. Capital, 794,244*l*. Receipts, 73,939*l*. This line was constructed by Messrs. Peto, Brassey, and Betts, and they guarantee the shareholders 6 per cent. per annum on their capital till 1876.

The Manchester, Sheffield and Lincolnshire is an amalgamation of the Sheffield, Ashton-under-Lyne and Manchester, the Great Grimsby and Sheffield Junction, the Sheffield and Lincolnshire, the Sheffield and Lincolnshire Extension, and the Great Grimsby Dock Companies. The mileage in operation is 181¼ miles. A beneficial arrangement has been negotiated with the Midland. This company is also interested in one way or other in the Cheshire, Midland, Oldham, Ashton and Guide Bridge, &c. The capital is 9,753,768*l*. Receipts, 806,178*l*.

The Metropolitan extends from Paddington to Farringdon Street, with powers of further extension City-wards. It is associated on friendly terms with the Great Western. Its works are not yet completed, its capital account is not yet closed. Capital, 1,729,000*l*. Receipts, 112,423*l*.

The Midland is one of the most prosperous railway properties in the kingdom. It is an amalgamation of the North Midland, Midland Counties, and Birmingham and Derby. The total amalgamated length is 641 miles. The following companies have been incorporated with the Midland since its first amalgamation :—The Bristol and Gloucester, and Birmingham and Gloucester (95½ miles), Sheffield and Rotherham (9¼), Leicester and Swannington (16), Leeds and Bradford (43), and many others. The capital is 23,377,447*l.* Receipts, 2,316,425*l.*

The (Irish) Midland Great Western connects Dublin with Galway, Sligo, and Athlone. Its total length is 259 miles. The capital is 3,418,954*l.* Receipts, 241,144*l.*

Monmouthshire. Incorporated 1845 for a line from Newport to Pontypool. Length, 44 miles. Capital, 1,182,161*l.* Receipts, 131,929*l.*

The North British is an incorporation of the original North British with the Edinburgh, Perth and Dundee, and Edinburgh and Glasgow, along with their respective feeders. Its total mileage is 615 miles, of which 193¼ are single line. The main line is from Berwick, by Edinburgh, to Perth, with very many branches running inland. The North British line is also further interested, in one form or other, in the Carlisle and Silloth Bay, Peebles, Selkirk and Galashiels, Border Union, Border Counties, West of Fife, &c. The capital is 15,570,678*l.* Estimated receipts, 1,063,000*l.*

The North-Eastern comprises the York, Newcastle and Berwick, Leeds Northern, and Malton and Driffield, which were amalgamated in 1844. Since that date, sundry additional amalgamations have taken place. The company now comprises the Hartlepool Dock and Railway, the Dearness Valley, North Yorkshire and Cleveland, Bedale and Leyburn, Hull and Holderness, Newcastle and Carlisle, and Stockton and Darlington Railways. A very large number of new works, such as the Lanchester Valley, Market Weighton and Beverley, &c., have, since the first amalgamation, been added. 1095 miles in length. The total capital is 30,017,800*l.* Receipts, 2,693,896*l.*

The North London Railway is one of the lines we have made frequent reference to as being one of the cheapest carrying in England, although one of the most expensive in construction. It traverses the northern and eastern suburbs of London, and by junctions with the Great Northern, Great Eastern, and the Blackwall at Stepney, passes into the heart of the City and the Steam Packet Wharf at Blackwall. Capital, 2,125,030*l.* Receipts, 160,288*l.*

North Staffordshire obtained their Act of incorporation in 1846;

the length of miles open is 258, but that mileage includes a canal. Capital, 5,656,849*l*. Receipts, 422,673*l*.

The Scottish Central obtained their Act in 1845 to construct a line from Falkirk to Perth. Other works followed, and their mileage at present is 113 miles. Capital, 2,813,241*l*. Estimated receipts, 246,000*l*.

The Scottish North-Eastern is formed by the amalgamation of several companies, viz. the Aberdeen, the Alrath, and Forfar, and some other lines. The length is 138 miles. Capital, 3,214,294*l*. Estimated receipts, 268,000*l*.

South Devon. Incorporated 1844 for a broad gauge line from Exeter to Plymouth. Length, 75 miles. Capital, 2,764,360*l*. Receipts, 196,447*l*.

The South-Eastern was first incorporated as the South-Eastern and Dover. 306 miles are now completed. The original scheme commenced at Reigate and terminated near Dover. Subsequently extensions were legalized to Dover, Canterbury, Maidstone, Ramsgate, Folkstone, &c. The company was also authorized to subscribe 300,000*l*. to the Charing Cross line. An amicable arrangement has also been made with the London, Chatham, and Dover. The capital is 13,846,703*l*. Estimated receipts, 1,202,000*l*.

Taff Vale. Incorporated in 1836 for a line commencing at Merthyr Tydfil, in Glamorganshire, to the docks at Cardiff. Length, 57 miles. Capital, 1,534,198*l*. Receipts, 280,282*l*.

The railway receipts for 1864 fell very little short of THIRTY-FOUR MILLIONS sterling. In the previous year they amounted to 31,156,397*l*., and the additional receipts as reported in the papers amount to 2,683,830*l*., but in the returns by the Board of Trade there are included some additional railways, so that the gross amount will be found to be little short of the sum which I have stated.

It will be seen from the foregoing summary, which is confined to our principal railways, and is condensed from Bradshaw's Railway Guide, the Board of Trade Returns, and the railway papers, that our thirteen first-class companies, the returns from which we are accustomed to see reported separately every week, have received, in round numbers, no less than twenty-five millions sterling; the twenty-four second-class companies have received five millions; and the remaining four millions have been received by the shoal of small companies.

In 1863 the percentage on the gross receipts for each class of traffic was as follows :—

	Per Cent.	
First-class passengers	11	
Second-class ,,	13	
Third-class passengers	16	
Season and periodical ticket holders	1	
Excess of luggage, parcels, carriages, horses, and dogs	4	
Mails	2	
By passenger trains		47
Coal and other minerals	17	
General merchandise	34	
Live stock	2	
Luggage trains		53
		100

The proportion per cent. of receipts from the passenger traffic and the goods traffic for the years 1861, 1862, and 1863 are respectively as follow, viz. :—

	Passenger Traffic.	Goods Traffic.		
1861	46·65	53·35	=	100
1862	47·76	52·24	=	100
1863	46·61	53·39	=	100

The returns for 1864 are not so complete as to enable us to calculate exactly the proportionate receipts of the two kinds of traffic, but there appears to be about the same ratio between goods and passengers as in 1862.

It may be remarked that in the winter months the goods traffic far exceeds the passenger traffic. We find, for instance, in the returns for the week-days, 31st December, the percentage on goods on the thirteen great railways exceeded that of passengers by ten per cent., whilst in the summer months the passenger traffic exceeds the goods traffic by seven per cent.

From a number of other miscellaneous statistics of the railways of the United Kingdom I select the following. And first as to the number of railway employés. But I may premise that the last return made does not come down to a recent date, and that therefore the railway employés of all classes must be by this time very considerably augmented.

Secretaries or managers	221
Treasurers	26
Superintendents	398
Accountants or cashiers	201
Station masters	2,471
Ticket collectors	404
Guards or brakesmen	3,716
Switchmen	3,263
Engineers	150
Storekeepers	198
Draughtsmen	156
Foremen	1,335
Enginedrivers	3,503
Stokers	3,644
Artificers	21,337
Platelayers	8,260
Inspectors or timekeepers	997
Clerks	8,712
Gatekeepers	1,998
Policemen or watchmen	2,349
Porters or messengers	17,091
Labourers	26,285
Miscellaneous	2,885
Total	109,660

Being at the rate of 12·263 employés of all classes per mile on the mileage of the railways of the United Kingdom. It is a year since the date of these returns, and there has been a great increase since. And it must also be recollected that under the head of "artificers" is not included all the artisans of this country who are engaged in the manufacture of railway stock and other railway plant. A very large percentage of the rolling stock, and especially of the trucks or waggons, is not the property of the railway companies, but of various joint-stock bodies whose business it is to hire out their waggons to the railway companies and the public. And besides, thousands of coal and other trucks are the property of the owners of collieries, mines, &c. Again, many of the canals are now the property of railway companies. To the list of their employés must therefore be added a considerable proportion of the various workers concerned with our inland navigation; and still further, even of the rolling stock which is the property of the companies, it is only a part, and a small part, which is manufactured by themselves. If the great companies have their great factories and veritable towns of industry at Crewe and Wolverton, there are also the great private firms of the Stephensons, the Hawthornes, and many others. I think the male adult inhabitants of the two isles who derive directly their living from the railways may be set down at a quarter of a million; and to this must be added thousands indirectly maintained by the railways—cabmen at stations, shopkeepers at places like Crewe, railway hotel keepers and their servants, and a host of others. Then, again, there are the workers in wood and iron in their first crude states, who would not have been so employed but for the railways. Add all together, and increase in the usual proportion for members of families; and I doubt if it be an excessive estimate to say that a million and a half of British mouths are filled! and British backs clad by the railways of England, Scotland, and Ireland. Even this possibly is an under-estimate; for it must be recollected, that new railways are being constantly constructed; and there seems no likely limit at present to the continuance of these new constructions. All the artificers of every kind engaged in the construction—the floating and migratory navvies, and all their more skilled but less sinewy collaborateurs—must be added. Any person living in the metropolis during the last few years, and witnessing the wholesale construction of railways in London and its neighbourhood, can form an approximate idea, in his imagination at least, how large an increase to my estimate must be made under this head. Still further, it may be urged that scores of thousands of the building trades are employed by such railways as those recently constructed or now being constructed in the metropolis. For the wholesale demolition of tenements which they effect necessitates an equal reconstruction of houses (the amount of reconstruction *ought to be at least* equal); hence numberless masons, carpenters, bricklayers, and builders' labourers find employment which would not exist but for the railways. But it would be endless to follow out the various ramifications into which any one would be led who should endeavour to assess the total amount of employment created by the railways. It is enough to say, in a word, that if they have enormously enhanced the value of land and trebled the profits of the trader, they have also added millions to the annual wages fund of the working man, while they have at the same time cheapened the cost of the commodities in which his wages are expended.

An interesting table from the Board of Trade returns shows the average length of journeys undertaken in the three countries by passengers of each class. The average of the three countries is the following :—First-class passengers travel on an average nineteen, second-class fourteen, and third-class twelve, miles each journey; the general average of the three (the aggregate number of journeys being taken into consideration) being thirteen miles each journey.

Some years since the receipts of the three classes contributed in a proportion nearly equal; first-class paying about 30 per cent., second 35 per cent., and third 35 per cent. of the whole.

On the future effects and further development of the railway system much more might be said, and it would be easy to fill as many pages on the future of the iron road and the locomotive steam-engine as have been occupied with their past history. I commenced this sketch by quotation and condensed summary of the well known *Quarterly Review* article of March, 1825. I conclude by citation from the same eminent source. And I quote, not the reviewer, but a quotation made by him, and with which he concludes his article. My readers will be able to judge for themselves, how far the fanciful and exaggerated anticipations contained in the following sentences have been realized, and how much of them, so far as they are feasible and seriously meant, remains yet to be effected. The reviewer thus concludes his lucubrations :—

" We have purposely abstained from that part of the question which regards the conveyance of *passengers.* There is no doubt that a diminished weight may be conveyed with increased speed and with equal safety, as far as the strength and stability of the engine are concerned; but we think it would be expedient to waive all thoughts of this part of the subject for the present, until the roads and the engines have acquired that degree of perfection of which they are capable, and such as will remove all apprehension of danger; without waiting, however, till they are brought to that enviable state which is contemplated by a very sensible but somewhat whimsical advocate for railroads, with an extract from whose work (*The Fingerpost*) we will close our observations for the present :—

" ' It is reasonable to conclude that the nervous man will, ere long, take his place in a carriage drawn or impelled by a locomotive engine, with more unconcern and with far better assurance of safety than he now disposes of himself in one drawn by four horses of unequal powers and speed, endowed with passions that acknowledge no control but superior force, and each separately momentarily liable to all the ills that flesh is heir to. Surely an inanimate power, that can be started, stopped, and guided at pleasure by the finger or foot of man must promise greater personal security to the traveller than a power derivable from animal life, whose infirmities and passions require the constant exercise of other passions united with muscular exertion to remedy and control them. To combat the inconvenience his senses are anticipating, I must ask him to indulge his imagination with an excursion some twenty or thirty years forward in the regions of time; when the dark, unsightly, shapeless machine that now offends him, even in idea, shall be metamorphosed into one of exquisite symmetry and beauty, glittering with all the pomp and circumstance the pride of wealth knows so well how to bestow, and as superbly emblazoned with heraldic honours as any that are now launched from the floors of Long Acre; a machine that shall regale his nostrils with exhalations, not from pit coal and train oil, but from some more genial produce of the earth, whose essence may be extracted at an insignificant cost by the same principle that creates the power which moves him, and its fragrance left in the breeze for the sensitive traveller's gratification; a machine which, in place of the dull monotonous ache-engendering rumble of modern coaches, may delight his ear with the concord of sweet sounds, the lever-wheel of the engine proving the mainspring of harmony; and last, though not least, a machine that may minister to his palate in a style somewhat superior to the comforts enjoyed by a mail-coach dinner-party in eighteen hundred and twenty-five. But a truce to fanciful imaginings: I am aware they are least of all calculated to serve the principle I advocate; they may stand, however, to exemplify the poet's sentiment, that let a man learn what he will, still must he die with half his lesson unlearned; and this caviller may rest assured that neither his olfactory, his auricular, his ocular, nor any other nerves he possesses, are likely to suffer from the change.'"

The "nervous man" may certainly take his place now in a railway carriage with less danger to fear than he formerly did in a four horse coach, but so long as railway directors neglect to take necessary precautions against accidents *because* the percentage now killed or maimed on railways is less than what it formerly was by coach, so long will the public have reason to protest against their inefficient arrangements.

APPENDIX III.

CLAUSES OF THE GENERAL RAILWAY BILL OF 1844
RELATING TO
THE PURCHASE OF RAILWAYS BY GOVERNMENT.

1. WHEREAS it is expedient that the concession of powers for the establishment of new lines of railway should be subjected to such conditions as are hereinafter contained for the benefit of the public; be it enacted, by the Queen's most excellent Majesty, by and with the advice and consent of the Lords Spiritual and Temporal, and Commons, in this present Parliament assembled, and by the authority of the same, that if at any time after the end of twenty-one years from and after the first day of January next after the passing of any Act of the present or of any future session of Parliament, for the construction of any new line of passenger railway, whether such new line be a trunk, branch, or junction line, and whether such new line be constructed by a new company incorporated for the purpose, or by any existing company, the clear annual profits divisible upon the subscribed and paid-up capital stock of the said railway, upon the average of the three then last preceding years, shall equal or exceed the rate of ten pounds for every hundred pounds of such paid-up capital stock, it shall be lawful for the Lords Commissioners of Her Majesty's Treasury, upon giving to the said company three calendar months' notice in writing of their intention so to do, to revise the scale of tolls, fares, and charges limited by the Act or Acts relating to the said railway, and to fix such new scale of tolls, fares, and charges, applicable to such different classes and kinds of passengers, goods, and other traffic on such railway, as in the judgment of the said Lords Commissioners, assuming the same quantities and kinds of traffic to continue, shall be likely to reduce the said divisible profits to the said rate of ten pounds in the hundred, and so from

time to time at the expiration of each succeeding period of twenty-one years: Provided always, that no such revised scale shall take effect, unless accompanied by a guarantee, to subsist as long as any such revised scale of tolls, fares, and charges shall be in force, that the said divisible profits, in case of any deficiency therein, shall be made good to the said rate of ten pounds for every hundred pounds of such capital stock: Provided also, that such revised scale shall not be again revised or such guarantee withdrawn, otherwise than with the consent of the company, for the further period of twenty-one years.

2. That *whatever may be the rate of divisible profits in any such railway*, it shall be lawful for the said Lords Commissioners, if they shall think fit, at any time after the expiration of the said term of twenty-one years, to purchase any such railway, with all its hereditaments, stock, and appurtenances, in the name and on behalf of Her Majesty, upon giving to the said company three calendar months' notice in writing of their intention, and upon payment of a sum equal to twenty-five years' purchase of the said annual divisible profits, estimated on the average of the three then next preceding years: Provided always, that if the average rate of profit for the said three years shall exceed the rate of ten pounds in the hundred, it shall be taken at only ten pounds in the hundred, for the purpose of calculating thereon the amount of such purchase-money: Provided also, that if the average rate of profits for the said three years shall be less than the rate of ten pounds in the hundred, it shall be lawful for the company, if they shall be of opinion that the said rate of twenty-five years' purchase of the said average profits is an inadequate rate of purchase of such railway, reference being had to the prospects thereof, to require that the rate of purchase, instead of being calculated upon such average rate of profit, *shall be taken at a valuation*, to be determined, in case of difference, by arbitration.

3. (A.) That nothing herein contained shall be construed to subject to the said option of revision or purchase any railway made or authorized to be made by any Act previous to the present session; and that no branch or extension of less than five miles in length of any existing line of railway shall be taken to be a new railway within the provisions of this Act; and that the said option of purchase shall not be exercised as regards any branch or extension of any existing railway, without including in the purchase the existing railway; also in case the company of proprietors of the same shall require that the same be so included.

4. (B.) And whereas it is expedient that the policy of calling into exercise the powers of revision or purchase hereby reserved, or either of them, should in no manner be prejudged by the provisions of this Act, and should remain for the future consideration of the Legislature, upon grounds of general and national policy: and whereas it is not the intention of this Act, that under the said powers of revision or purchase, if called into use, the public resources should be employed to sustain an undue competition against any independent company or companies; be it enacted, That no such notice as hereinbefore mentioned, whether of revision or purchase, shall be given, until provision shall have been made by Parliament, by an Act or Acts to be passed in that behalf for authorizing the guarantee or the levy of the purchase-money hereinbefore mentioned, as the case may be, and for determining, subject to the conditions hereinbefore mentioned, the manner in which the said options or either of them shall be exercised: Provided always, that before any application is made to Parliament for the powers to exercise the said options or either of them, three months' notice shall be given by the said Lords Commissioners to the company or companies to be affected thereby, of the intention so to apply.

5. That from and after the commencement of the period of three years preceding the period at which the option of ransom or purchase becomes available, full and true accounts shall be kept of all sums of money received and paid on account of any railway within the provisions hereinbefore contained (distinguishing, if the said railway shall be a branch railway, or one worked in common with other railways, the receipts, and giving an estimate of the expenses on account of the said railway from those on account of the trunk line, or other railways) by the directors of the company to whom such railway belongs, or by whom the same may be worked, and of the purposes and things for which such sums of money shall have been received and paid; and every such railway company shall once in every half-year cause a half-yearly account in abstract to be prepared, showing the total receipt and expenditure on account of the said railway, for the half-year ending the 30th day of June and the 31st day of December respectively, or such other convenient days as shall in each case be directed by the Lords of the said Committee, under distinct heads of receipt and expenditure, according to such form as may be required by the Lords of the said Committee, with a statement of the balance of such account, duly audited and certified under the hands of two or more directors of the said railway company; and shall send a copy

of the said account to the Lords of the said Committee on or before the last days of August and February respectively, or such other days as shall in each case be directed by the Lords of the said Committee, in each year; and it shall be lawful for the Lords of the said Committee, if and when they shall think fit, to appoint any proper person or persons to inspect the accounts and books of the said company; and it shall be lawful for any person so authorized, at all reasonable times upon producing his authority, to examine the books, accounts, vouchers, and other documents of the company at the principal office or place of business of the company, and to take copies or extracts therefrom.

6. Companies to provide one cheap train, each way, daily. And with respect to all railway companies subject to these obligations, which shall be open on or before the 1st day of November next these obligations shall come into force on the said 1st day of November; and with respect to all other railways subject to this obligation, it shall come into force on the day of opening of the railway, or the day after the last day of the session in which the Act shall be passed, by reason of which the company will become subject thereunto, which shall first happen.

7. That if any railway company shall refuse or wilfully neglect to comply with the provisions of this Act, as to the said cheap trains, within a reasonable time, or shall attempt to evade the operation of such order, such company shall forfeit to Her Majesty a sum not exceeding 20l. for every day during which such refusal, neglect, or evasion shall continue.

8. Board of Trade to have a discretionary power of allowing alternative arrangements.

9. That no tax shall be levied upon the receipts of any railway company from the conveyance of passengers at fares not exceeding 1d. for each mile, by any such cheap train as aforesaid.

10. Certain companies to convey military and police forces at certain charges, 5 & 6 Vict., c. 55.

11. Railway companies to afford additional facilities for the transmission of the mails, 1 & 2 Vict., c. 98.

12. And whereas electrical telegraphs have been established on certain railways, and may be more extensively established hereafter, and it is expedient to provide for their due regulation; be it enacted, That every railway company, on being required so to do by the Lords of the said Committee, shall be bound to allow any person or persons authorized by the Lords of the said Committee, with servants and workmen, at all reasonable times to enter into or upon

their lands, and to establish and lay down upon such lands adjoining the line of such railway, a line of electrical telegraph for Her Majesty's service, and to give to him and them every reasonable facility for laying down the same, and for using the same, for the purpose of receiving and sending messages on Her Majesty's service, subject to such reasonable remuneration to the company as may be agreed upon between the company and the Lords of the said Committee, or, in case of disagreement, as may be settled by arbitration: Provided always, that, subject to a prior right of use thereof for the purposes of Her Majesty, such telegraph may be used by the company, for the purposes of the railway, upon such terms as may be agreed upon between the parties, or, in the event of difference, may be settled by arbitration.

13. That where a line of electrical telegraph shall have been established upon any railway by the company to whom such railway belongs, or by any company, partnership, person or persons otherwise than exclusively for Her Majesty's service, or exclusively for the purposes of the railway, the use of such electrical telegraph for the purpose of receiving and sending messages, shall, subject to the prior right of the use thereof for the service of Her Majesty and for the purposes of the company, and subject also to such equal charges, and to such reasonable regulations, as may be from time to time made by the said railway company, be open for the sending and receiving of messages by all persons alike, without favour or preference.

14. And whereas, by an Act passed in the fourth year of the reign of Her Majesty, intituled, "An Act to regulate Railways," power is given to the Lords of the said Committee to appoint any proper person or persons to inspect any railway and the stations, works, and buildings, and the engines and carriages belonging thereto; and in order to carry the provisions of this Act into execution, it is expedient that the said power be extended; be it enacted, That the said power given to the Lords of the said Committee of appointing proper persons to inspect railways shall extend to authorize the appointment by the Lords of the said Committee of any proper person or persons, for such purposes of inspection, as are by the said Act authorized, and also for the purpose of enabling the Lords of the said Committee to carry the provisions of this and of the said Act, and of any general Act relating to railways, into execution; and that so much of the last recited Act as provides that no person shall be eligible to the appointment as inspector, who shall, within one year of his appointment, have been a director, or have held any office of

trust or profit under any railway company, shall be repealed: Provided always, that no such person shall exercise any powers of interference in the affairs of the company.

15. Repealing provision of 3 & 4 Vict., c. 97.

16. Board of Trade may direct prosecutions to prevent railway companies from contravening or exceeding the provisions of their Acts.

17. Notice to be given to the company. Prosecutions to be under the sanction of the Board of Trade, and within one year after the offence.

18. And whereas many railway companies have borrowed money in a manner unauthorized by their Acts of incorporation or other Acts of Parliament relating to the said companies, upon the security of loan notes or other instruments purporting to give a security for the repayment of the principal sums borrowed at certain dates, and for the payment of interest thereon in the mean time; and whereas such loan notes or other securities issued otherwise than under the provision of some Act or Acts of Parliament have no legal validity, and it is expedient that the issue of such illegal securities should be stopped; but such loan notes or other securities having been issued and received in good faith as between the borrower and lender, and for the most part for the lawful purposes of the undertaking and in ignorance of their legal invalidity, it is expedient to confirm such as have been already issued: be it enacted, That from and after the passing of this Act, any railway company issuing any loan note or other negotiable or assignable instrument, purporting to bind the company as a legal security for money advanced to the said railway company otherwise than under the provisions of some Act or Acts of Parliament authorizing the said railway company to raise such money and to issue such security, shall for every such offence forfeit to Her Majesty a sum equal to the sum for which such loan note or other instrument purports to be such security: Provided always, that any company may renew any such loan note or other instrument issued by them prior to the passing of this Act, for any period or periods not exceeding five years from the passing of this Act.

19. That where any railway company, before the 12th day of July, 1844, shall have issued or contracted to issue any such loan notes, or other unauthorized instruments, the company may and shall pay off such loan notes or other instruments, as the same may fall due, subject as hereinbefore provided; and until the same shall be so paid off, the said loan notes or other instruments shall entitle the holders thereof to the payment, by the company, of the principal sum and interest thereby agreed to be paid.

20. That a register of all such loan notes or other instruments shall be kept by the secretary, and such register shall be open, without fee or reward, at all reasonable times, to the inspection of any shareholder or auditor of the undertaking, and of every person interested in any such loan note or other instrument desirous of inspecting the same.

21. Remedy for recovery of tithe rent charged on railway land.

22. Communications to and from Board of Trade, service of notices, &c.

23. Penalties.

24. That where the word "Railway" is used in this Act, it shall be construed to extend to all railways under the powers of any Act of Parliament; and when the words "Passenger Railway" are used in this Act, they shall be construed to extend to all railways constructed under the powers of any Act of Parliament upon which one third or more of the gross annual revenue is derived from the conveyance of passengers by steam or other mechanical power; and whenever the word "Company" is used in this Act, it shall be construed to extend to include the proprietors for the time being of any such railway; and that where a different sense is not expressly declared, or does not appear by the context, every word importing a singular number or the masculine gender shall be taken to include females as well as males, and several persons and things as well as one person or thing.

25. That this Act may be amended or repealed by any Act to be passed in this session of Parliament.

APPENDIX IV.

MR. GLADSTONE'S SPEECH, JULY 8, 1844,

ON THE

SECOND READING OF THE GOVERNMENT RAILWAY BILL.

MR. GLADSTONE.—Sir, I am glad the time is at length arrived when the statements of the promoters and opponents of this Bill may be compared in equal debate on the floor of this house. It is not a question of party, on which the Government can appeal to the sympathy of their supporters; it is not a question of popular interest, in which the passions of persons out of doors would be largely interested in our favour; we have stood, as I think, on the ground of reason alone, while every means that the most assiduous and manifold solicitation could bring to bear against us has been employed in organizing an opposition to this Bill. I lament that the statements by which this Bill has been opposed have been in many particulars entirely at variance with its real nature. Now it is most material to look, in the first place, to the circumstances under which this Bill originated. This Bill is at once the Bill of the Government, the Bill of the Board of Trade, and the Bill of the Committee. I ask, in the first place, any gentleman connected with railways, in what spirit the Railway Department of the Board of Trade has hitherto administered its duties. I ask whether, under the administration of the right hon. gentleman opposite, that department was actuated either by a spirit of hostility or a disposition to interfere with the concerns of railways. Not to travel on this point to cases more remote, I will remind the House that at the time I proposed this question to the House, so anxious was I to secure to Railway Companies every description of full and fair representation, that in the list of the committee I proposed there were the names of four gentlemen who were actively engaged as Railway Directors in different parts of the country; but the feeling of the House was so distinctly expressed, on the nomination of that committee, against what they conceived to be undue partiality towards railways, that I felt it my duty to withdraw two valuable names, that the inquiry might not at the outset be liable to suspicion. Such were the circumstances attending the appointment of the committee, and I refer to them merely to bring to mind, what it is impossible to omit in a case of this kind, that the gentlemen out of whose deliberate examination this Bill has arisen were gentlemen whom no man can venture to assert were other than favourable to railways in this country. Now, I will go step by step. Having started with the appointment of the committee, I will not allude to the names composing it in detail. No person, I believe, has found fault with the committee on the score of the parties actually selected. In short, the list of the committee was graced by the names of almost all who were interested or known to be conversant with railway matters.

My next position, therefore, is that the committee were, except the hon. member for Reading, substantially unanimous in favour, not of the precise Bill I have laid on the table of the House, in compliance with the views of a majority of the committee, but of interference at least as extensive. An hon. gentleman opposite has said it was a question in the committee whether the power to be taken over future Railway Companies should be a power of purchase only, or a power of purchase combined with a power of revision. The hon. gentleman himself advocated the plan of purchase. My noble friend, who voted in the minority, also advocated the plan of purchase, and his objection to the present proposal was, that it did not go far enough. I believe that others took the same view, and thought that at least as much interference as this was absolutely necessary. I think I shall hardly be contradicted when I say that, except the hon. member for Reading, who, from the first day the committee sat, has, in the most straightforward and candid manner, expressed the strongest opposition to any and every interference of this kind—with that exception not a single member of the committee but agreed that something analogous to the main provisions of this Bill, if not its actual main provisions, was absolutely necessary in the present state of things. [Mr. GISBORNE dissented.] The hon. gentleman means to differ from me, but I believe the hon. member did propose a plan according to which it would have been recommended to Parliament that a power of purchase should be taken on behalf of the State, with reference not only to future but to all railways. The present Bill has reference to future railways only, and I think, therefore, the hon. gentleman's objection was not that we went too far, but that we did not go far enough, and that the proper measure would have been to assume a compulsory power of purchase over all railways whatever. [Mr. GISBORNE again dissented.] I find it so here, and of course I can only go by the printed minutes of the committee.

I now come to the charges in the petitions, and I really cannot tell how those who framed them (I do not say the railway companies, because they were not framed by the companies) could descend to the assertion that the evidence taken was *ex parte*. Why, we should deprive words of all meaning, if we sanctioned such a use of them. I know not what is meant by saying it is *ex parte* evidence, unless indeed they mean that it is evidence much more on the side of the railway companies than on the other. What are the facts? Twelve witnesses gave evidence on the general question; out of these one, Mr. Laing, was an officer of the Board of Trade, and another, Mr. Galt, was known to have strong preconceived opinions, but the other ten were railway directors, and were they chosen with reference to this particular scheme? Let us read. There was Mr. Glyn, chairman of the London and Birmingham Railway; Mr. Hudson, connected with some half-dozen railways; Mr. Baxendale, chairman of the South-Eastern Railway Company; Mr. Swift, agent of the Grand Junction Railway Company, and one of the cleverest men in the country; Mr. Saunders, worthy, in this respect, to be classed with Mr. Swift; Captain Lawes, manager of the Manchester and Leeds Railway Company; the Member for Clitheroe, of whom I will say nothing in his presence; Mr. Wilkinson, chairman of the Croydon Railway Company; Mr. R. Hill, known chiefly for his connection with another subject, but also a director of the London and Brighton Railway Company; and Mr. Harding, secretary of the Glasgow and Greenock Railway Company. This is the evidence which is called *ex parte* against railways. My hon. friend proposed that the companies should be allowed to call evidence, and I understand he made a proposal which I should think he must have been aware could not have been acceded to—namely, that the minutes of evidence should be submitted to parties out of the committee, contrary to the express rule of the House. But my hon. friend was in the committee as the representative of the railway interest. At all events he was there. I do not mean deputed; we all know what he is; but he was active, able, and energetic in their behalf.

The hon. member for Leicester also took a prominent part; but did these gentlemen, or any one else, tender a single witness to the committee who was refused? No such thing. The hon. member for Nottingham suggested several additional points in their favour, which were acceded to, because he was known to be conversant with the subject. These hon. gentlemen have not said that it was *ex parte* evidence, and I am sure I may claim their assent when I say this accusation is not only an unfounded, but a ridiculous and absurd accusation.

So much, then, for the inquiry; but now I want you to understand what we are discussing.

The QUESTION, however, of the whole Bill, is the PURCHASE or option on the part of the GOVERNMENT. If we agree about that, we shall not quarrel about the rest; on the other hand, if we differ about that, it will be a question for our consideration whether we will take the rest or postpone the whole till a future period. Now, here it is I complain of the gross misstatements which have been made to the world with regard to the nature of this Bill. The statement which has been published is this, that the effect of the Bill is to enable the executive to purchase or reduce the tolls of future railways on certain terms, if they think fit so to do. All the arguments against the Bill are arguments of the impolicy of enabling the Government so to interfere with railway companies, and taking out of their hands powers which it is contended they have used beneficially and wisely. I see an hon. gentleman opposite is under the same delusion in this respect as other parties. I see another hon. gentleman, also a railway director, who appears to be also under the same delusion, but I will prove the Bill does nothing of the kind. Another hon. gentleman, a railway director, says it does. These gentlemen, cannot surely have read the Bill. If it did give to the executive power to purchase railways at discretion, or even one railway, I would vote against it. That would be to foreclose the question which it is the whole object of this Bill to open. The Bill gives the Government no power to purchase either future or existing lines. The companies will have power to make agreements which would bind them, but they will have no right or power to make agreements which would bind the State. An opinion may be entertained that even that course is not desirable. But the proposition I mean to contend for is, that Parliament ought to have that discretion—that, with respect to existing railways, Parliament is excluded from the power; and that, with respect to future railways, it is the bounden duty of Parliament to reserve to itself that power. Are there any gentlemen within these walls under the impression that it is in the power of the Executive Government to purchase any or to receive the tolls of any railway under this Bill, without resorting to Parliament? Because, if there are, I feel confident they are wrong. But if they had read the Bill, and the effect of it is to convey such an intention or such a meaning, I will join with them in amending the Bill, so that no such meaning shall be apparent. But it may be said that, although the Bill does not give this power to determine the question, whether it would be politic for the State to sanction the purchase or revision, yet when the time arrived that that point should be submitted to Parliament, the question, although the mere mechanical and formal parts had been reserved, would be looked upon as settled. If gentlemen will read that report, they will find that the ground taken by the Committee was this, that even if it were considered politic to purchase or revise, we were not in a condition to do so with respect to existing railways; we were barred from that question. The point may be proper to be considered when it is actually proposed that the State should take these powers, but now it is beside the question. With railways the Legislature are dealing with a new system, producing new results, and likely to produce unforeseen effects. Is it not wise, then, to make provision for the future? Is it wise to trust ourselves to all the changes which the next ten or fifteen years may produce with regard to public communication by railway, without a thought for providing for the difficulties that might arise? Is it wise to place ourselves in a position in which, whatever might be the exigency, we shall be debarred from any interference, because now, before these new companies have obtained their powers, it has been neglected to obtain proper powers to enable the question to be entertained?

With respect to the *purchase of railways at the present moment*, gentlemen of great experience and intelligence had recommended that it should be so. I do not think the committee were prepared to concur in that view. And I say, that I would at the present moment vote against a plan for the purchase of railroads. I would do so because in the present state of the system there are not grounds for coming to that conclusion. But it is a very different question whether I shall reserve a free agency for either the purchase or revision at any future time in case such a measure should appear advisable. I cannot see that this is determining the point whether such purchase at a future time would be politic. What I desire to show is this, that the whole foundation of the complaint

against the Bill as to the option of purchase was swept away, for nothing is to be done except reserving a discretion ; and the distinction I mean to draw is not a mere technical one, but a real *bonâ fide* one—to enable the State, after a term of years, to purchase railroads, if the judgment of the Legislature should be such as to render such a measure politic and expedient. The intention of the Bill is to remove the preliminary bar which exists on the ground of public faith, to leave the question entirely free and open, and unfettered by the numerous and complicated considerations which now beset it. An hon. member referred me to clause 7, but is it not obvious that that merely placed the Bill in the form that would be requisite for the purpose if Parliament should determine upon granting the power ? The Government cannot purchase railroads without money: and Government could not get money without coming to Parliament: and Government could not come to Parliament for such a purpose without strong grounds of policy on which to justify their demand. I have shown that the Bill does not enable the Executive to purchase or revise, because it cannot do so without the money. But it has been said that the measure fetters and ties up the judgment of Parliament. Then, I say, invent any declaration, however authoritative, that shall leave the judgment of Parliament obviously free, and I will join in it. The committee say :—
"In this state of things the committee would deem it unwise to enter into any engagements which should tend to restrain the free action of the Legislature or the Government in future times, as it is impossible to judge what amount of inconvenience might thereby be entailed ; but they would propose that such powers only should be taken as, even though they may fall short of the full extent of the occasion when it arrives, may be either exercised for some substantial advantage, or, at the worst, left in abeyance without detriment."
This was the full purpose of the committee, and the present Bill does not give full power to the executive to deal immediately with railways. I will now revert to the main point in issue. I shall refer to what was stated by Captain Lawes, an able man, when under examination. He is of opinion that, if railways were placed under the general control of Government, a saving of 25 per cent. would be effected to the public. Now this is material to consider. In the present state of the question, the elements which enter into it are rude and unformed, and the evidence, I admit, is not complete.

The committee felt some of the difficulties. They examined particularly into the *case of the carriers,* and some peculiar difficulties presented themselves. They ascertained that carriers had been placed by the railways in a very peculiar situation, and they entered into the nature of these new relations between the traders and the railway companies. The railway companies have in fact come amongst them, like tritons among minnows, and the effect of this collision has been to produce inconvenience in many cases to individual traders. The carriers showed that their arrangements were greatly affected, not only on the lines, but off the lines; and they showed that their ordinary course of business was completely altered and controlled by the railways. I do not mean to say that these cases are ripe for decision, but there is no doubt the committee saw and felt that great difficulty existed in the case of the railway companies and those great traders who carried on business along the different lines of railway, and that this difficulty mainly arose from the want of a power to deal with such difficulties. And it is our expectation that as the country becomes covered with a network of railways, these difficulties will increase, and that we shall be reduced to this alternative—namely, to take one of two courses, either to say to the private trader, " Your case we admit is a hard one, but neither the law nor the Legislature can help you;" or else we must say that Government is bound to assume to itself a general power of interference with the carrying arrangements of railways, in order to secure justice to the complaining traders. This has been suggested to us—to take into our hands the power of control over railways, which in the case of carriers would certainly prove a relief; but then the course is open to this objection, that such a control will involve an interference with the powers and privileges which railway companies now possess. We saw that a grievance—not a general or a national grievance, but a grievance of a limited nature—existed, and that we were unable to suggest a remedy; and at the same time we saw that if grievances of this sort became numerous and weighty, they would furnish material considerations why Parliament would be justified, and would be required, to deal with the question.

The next point is, as to the probability of *economizing the means of conveyance*. This is a question which will become one of great importance, on account of the large scale on which the matter rests. The payments by the public to the railway companies are now not less than five or six millions a year; but I do not think it will be a very extravagant estimate for me to assume that in fifteen or twenty years the payments by the public will reach to fifteen millions a year. If these statements and opinions are true, which I do not mean to assume to be true, because we have not all the evidence before us yet—but if it be true that the experiment is likely to produce a large reduction of fares, then it is right for Parliament to have the power to enter upon the consideration of how this can be carried into effect so as to afford immense relief to the public with the smallest possible loss on the aggregate receipts of the railways. It is this consideration which makes it important that we should not vote at once for the purchase of railways, but have the power and means of purchasing them at some future period without breach of faith. I do not think we can expect from the railway companies any such general economical system. *Foreign railways* are managed on a principle different to our railways. Belgium, for instance, has gained much more by railways than England. I do not mean to say that the Belgian railways are as good as ours—they are, however, very much cheaper. I believe the charges are not more than one-third of our charges. We must look at this subject in all its vastness and all its bearings. It may be said that England is the richest country; but because this country is rich it is no sound reason why the public should pay the railway companies more than necessary, or that cheap travelling should not be provided for the public. But there is no likelihood that *the great experiment of the greatest possible cheapness* to the public will be tried under the present system. Some hon. gentleman may reply, "You have it tried on the London and Greenwich Railway; it may be tried on the railway from Glasgow to Greenock, and also the railway of that spirited company to which the hon. member belongs—the London and Dover line." But the effect on these lines will prove nothing satisfactory. You must have it tried on the great lines, and on such a scale as to have the whole of the effects properly developed throughout the country. The experiment must be tried in some large district; but you will not find in the large companies universally a disposition to try the experiment; for you must recollect that we are dealing with a number of independent companies. The boards of directors of these companies are bound to produce the largest dividend to their shareholders—they have no national objects to promote; and therefore if you come to deal with nine or ten railway companies in this matter, nine out of ten may be disposed to try the experiment, but then it will be found that the tenth is able so to order matters as to baffle the experiment. To secure to the House the right of purchase or revision with respect to newly formed railways, it is necessary that it shall possess a great portion of the control over such railways, only to be exercised at a befitting opportunity.

The next question which it is necessary to solve is, how did it happen, that, although this Bill is *only to affect the new railroads*, the only opposition it meets with is from the old railroads, that cannot be affected by it? What objection can they have to it? We raise the right against the railway companies now in progress—they say nothing, but the old railway proprietors are the complainants. It cannot be because any attempt has been made to control them, of which we are too much afraid, lest it should be said we are in the habit of treating too lightly the idea of an engagement so seriously entered into. But I have learned that the reason given for their objection is, that they conceive that they will at last fall within the scope of the Bill, and that Government will finally compel them to come into its proposals. This, I know, forms a part of the paper which they have dignified with the appellation of Reasons for their opposition. I should advise the writer—seeing that to force them to accept our proposal, if ours it were, must be impossible—to amend that paper, for reason it is none. And let them, in so amending it, substitute the word " Legislature " for " Government." Now, when they would urge in opposition to this Bill that the conditions forced upon the railway companies would be ruinous and oppressive, they would charge, not the Government, but you and the Legislature, with the attempt to ruin and oppress them. Now, what danger there can be of their being injured or ruined by you, I am at a loss to conceive. I really must say the railway interest is too diffident of its strength. It is by far too modest. I would recommend the adoption of more confidence in the strength it possesses within these walls. Its power is only too great.

I believe the subject resolves itself only into two considerations : the first is, the question of the option to purchase or revise; the second is a question of time. I admit that if you were now pressed to acquiesce in the reservation of the right to purchase or to revise, the objection as to the time would be strong. In such a case there must of necessity be estimates made out, a reference to long accounts, *and very probably to arbitration.* That, however, was not the case now. You are not in that state, and therefore the objection as to the time so far falls to the ground. But it is said the Blue Book, containing the evidence upon the subject of the Railway Committee's investigation, has been on your table only three weeks. Sir, I would rest with confidence in this instance upon the report of the committee. I do not, I confess, think that the House in this instance stands in want of evidence. I wish it to be understood that we did not see it in the light of a desirable investment. Our view was, that the reserving of your discretion and option was an object of public policy. Indeed, *so much am I persuaded of it, that if the blue book, all the evidence on the subject, and the report of the committee were lost, I should still recommend it to adoption as wise and politic.* The question, as I have observed, is, in the first instance, one of option, or of revision. Now, I would remind the House, that the report on which we proceeded was made on the 13th of March last, and that since the 3rd of April following the Bill has been in the hands of hon. members, which is above three months since. One hour's attentive reading of the measure would have sufficed my hon. friend to obtain a competent general knowledge of its provisions, and of its propriety as a political measure in relation to railways. During that long period, not a voice has been raised against the Bill throughout the country. *Approbation of the measure has proceeded from the railway publishers, and every print in their interest has expressed its admiration of the moderate, wise, and cautious tone of the proposal made by the Government in this Bill as far back as three months ago.* I recollect it was assumed by an hon. friend of mine engaged on the committee, that our third report, he expected, would make a noise. That expectation was only so far realized that we only heard from the railroad organs renewed approbation of the liberality of the provisions of the Bill towards the railway interests. And yet some hon. gentleman said to you, "Does it not raise universal alarm?" Now, sir, I shall dispute that proposition. But with respect to this plan, when it has been discussed on its own merits, there exists no alarm whatever; but there is, on the contrary, every disposition to accept the plan as a wise measure. I am now going to complain of a misrepresentation on the part of the London and Birmingham Railway Company. I take an extract of their petition:—" That the Select Committee, upon whose reports the Bill is founded, have been sitting during the greater part of the present session; and although they have made short reports from time to time, the last and most important of those documents was only laid upon the table of the House on the 24th day of May last, and the printed evidence, which is very voluminous, was not published until a fortnight afterwards." Now, I say I complain of misrepresentation. Sir, the meaning of that paragraph, and the meaning and intention of the man who wrote it, was, that it should be understood, that though there had been minor reports made before the 24th of May, yet the report on which the Bill is founded came out on the 24th of May. But the Bill relates only in minor points to the report of the 24th of May; the main question of the option and discretionary power of Government is wholly dealt with in the report of the 3rd of April. Yet this misrepresentation bears the seal of the company. I say it was drawn up by some solicitor, and that the seal of the company is set to the words! I know that the members of the direction would repudiate such a misstatement. I now refer to a passage in the third report:—" It appears, therefore, to your committee, that the present moment, while Parliament still retains in its own hands an entire and unimpaired discretion, with regard both to the incorporation of new companies, and the enlargement of the powers of old ones, affords an opportunity more favourable than any that can be expected hereafter to recur for attaching beforehand to the legislative sanction, which is sought by these parties on their own behalf, the conditions which may be deemed necessary for the public good, and which may realize and apply such conclusions as an experience of the railway system up to the present time may be deemed to have been sufficiently established." Now do not say that you have been taken by surprise by this Bill, because I show you the report of the committee, which was moved for by me as a member of the Government, and which points out the present moment as the moment at which Parliament should legislate on the subject, and that the consequences of delay would be disadvantageous in the extreme.

I ask, what would be the result if this Bill was postponed till the next session of Parliament? At the beginning of the session there would be, perhaps, sixty or eighty applications for railway Bills; general legislation upon other great measures would overthrow the discussion on this particular subject, and in July next year you would come to the second reading of the Bill, and if you did, you would arrive at the discussion under increased disadvantages.

But what is the opposition to this Bill? It is composed of different elements, and that is a curious and instructive part of the case. I shall state my view of it, and that with reference to facts. One portion of the opponents of this Bill are those directors of railways who adopt a very high tone against the interference of the Parliament. My hon. friend the member for Reading (Mr. Russell) is the chairman of the Great Western Railway Company, and he is a chieftain amongst the class of persons. He stood alone in the Select Committee—he adopted that high tone, and was averse to any attempt to lay down general rules for railway legislation, and to applying any legislative restrictions as to future railway Bills. Those gentlemen who, like the hon. member for Reading, have their particular mode of consoling the public on railway matters, say, " *Oh, trust to competition.*" *I would no more trust the railway proprietors on railway matters than I would Gracchus speaking of sedition!* I know of nothing more chilling than the hope which the directors of these railways hold out from the competition. If you do not shut your eyes to facts, you will draw important conclusions from what has been passing in relation to this competition, to which your attention must have been directed, and which I trust I may mention as a short episode. There has been going on during the spring a very notable affair. The London and Birmingham and the Grand Junction Railway Companies have been at deadly feud with each other; and what was the result? There was a most flourishing prospect for the public. The public were to have the choice of a new line. The public have already a new line between Birmingham and Liverpool, and between London and Birmingham. The London and Birmingham Company were engaged in the purchase of the Chester and Birkenhead Railway, and they proposed to make a line from Birmingham to Shrewsbury, and the distance from Chester not being great, parties saw there would be a line to Shrewsbury from that place, and then the public were to go down to Liverpool by this route; and this was a delightful prospect for the public: but the Grand Junction Company had as much public spirit. They thought there would be no objection to the two lines at the north end of the line, but they thought that there should also be two at the south end, and the Grand Junction proposed a line from Stafford to Bedford, and so accomplished a line all the way to Bedford. These companies are now singular philanthropists; nay, they are like lovers. No sooner had they quarrelled than reconciliation followed, and they remind one of the saying of Mr. Fox, " Breves inimicitiæ; amicitiæ sempiternæ." One of these lines, however, has gone to the land where all things end. I state this as an instance of the hopes which are to be entertained from competition amongst the railway companies. I wish to show Parliament the doctrines held by those of the high school of non-interference on the subject of existing railway companies, and the part which Parliament ought to take with respect to those which shall spring into future existence.

It is perfectly untrue that the old companies would be subject to the option of purchase or revision of the Government; they are exempted from it. But, sir, there is a deeper power at work in this opposition. I say it is *the power of Parliamentary agents and railway agents.* Yes, I know not why I should not speak out plainly. They are the great opponents of this measure. I say with them has originated this effective opposition. Why did they allow the Third Report to remain a dead letter? Why did that report remain still-born? Because it makes so great alterations as to the expenses, and consequently diminishes the prospects of the Parliamentary agents. They are the parties who know how to get up an opposition in this House. But I have shown you by dates that the Third Report was published on the 3rd of April, and I have shown you that there was no opposition raised to it worth naming. But when I come to the Fifth Report, which is called by the London and Birmingham Company the longest part of the report, the committee having at considerable length stated their reasons for thinking that something founded on a system of railway legislation is required—will hon. gentlemen say there is any dispute on that subject? Well, then, will you deny that the time has come when we should lay the axe to the root of that tree? It is one of the objects of this committee to lay the axe to this root. Therefore, it is right that these new schemes should be examined by an impartial authority. I was no party to the concluding recommendation of the committee, that these matters should be referred to the Railway Department of the Board of Trade; and I should be glad if these powers were vested in some other public authority. But this House's sittings being limited to six months of the year, and the railway schemes being prepared during the other six months, it is impossible that this House can have the officers or the machinery requisite to get parliamentary matters connected with railway Bills prepared for the judgment of this committee; but the committee recommend a preliminary reference to the Board of Trade in these cases, involving most important subjects where public questions were raised. All the evidence of Captain Lawes, of Mr. Glyn, Mr. Baxendale, Mr. Cardwell, Mr. Swift, and Mr. Wilkinson, goes in favour of this preliminary reference to the Board of Trade. The Third Report contains the present Bill, and I will show you that the Third Report was assailed by no disapprobation for two months. The Fifth Report was presented on the 26th of May, and was delivered on the 8th of June; and on the 11th of June—two days after it was sent out—a circular was sent out, signed "Hunt and Co.," addressed to railway agents and solicitors, calling upon them to consider what measures should be taken in consequence of the proceedings of the committee. I have written to ask their authority to petition against the Bill, and whether they were authorized by the companies. They say they were, because the meeting was called by circular, inviting the parties to come together and consider the provisions of the Bill. Now this is wonderful, because the article was written on the 11th of June, and the Bill was not presented until the 20th of June, and was not printed and published until the 24th of June. I have shown you that it was not when the committee recommended the enactment of this power of revision or purchase that the petition arose. It was not then that any shock was given to the proprietors of railways, and it was not then that the secretaries and others became alarmed, and the lobbies became crowded with parties immediately employed by the railway companies to solicit members for their votes,—it was not then this plan came out. No, sir; it was when we advised that the Bills should be referred to the Board of Trade, and when the committee intimated an opinion that that reference would cheapen the proceedings before Parliamentary Committees. This is the powerful element of the opposition, and of all that has taken place to render the Bill unpopular. I have pointed out *the secret source* from which this movement has arisen. The hon. member for Reading and other hon. members will understand that I do not speak of them. They have been the opponents of the Bill from the first. I speak of those from whom the movement derives its organization; and I say, that those gentlemen who came here, on a misrepresentation of the nature of the Bill, to oppose it, *are made the unconscious instruments of maintaining a lavish, and extravagant, and discreditable system of private-bill legislation* before this House. I am sorry I have been obliged to detain the House so long, but there is one other subject on which I wish to make a few remarks, and it is the last topic on which I shall trouble the House. The Bill is represented as an attack upon railway property, and the hon. member for Sheffield intimated that it had given a great shock to that property. It is really a farce to make use of such an expression; for there has been no shock to railway property. Even at this moment there has been no shock to railway property, and there has not been even as much as a dull day in the railway market. I have been taunted to-night with having said that I thought the consent of railway companies an essential condition to a satisfactory arrangement. I believe I have gone nearly that length. But I have the strongest impression that if the relations of Parliament and railway companies are to be satisfactorily carried out, they must be founded upon the discretion and moderation of both parties. I shrank from a contest with railway companies. I would have foregone any measure founded upon popularity, if the justice and necessity and policy of it had been capable of a doubt. I knew the power of railway companies in the House, and was satisfied, with justice on their side, they would be perfectly resistless; but being persuaded that justice is not with them, but against them—being persuaded that they have misjudged the interests of those on whose behalf they are appointed to act—being persuaded that the clamour which has been got up within the last three months against the plan which, three months ago, was published, and of which everybody approved, is misplaced—being satisfied that it is requisite we should reserve the power which it is now proposed to reserve, I do not shrink from the contest. I contend that this measure, so far from being a measure of violence, of an extreme or doubtful character, is a measure of the utmost importance, and that the option of revision and purchase is characterized by the utmost temperance and moderation; and feeling that we have right and justice on our side, I say that, although the railway companies are powerful, I do not think they have mounted so high, or that Parliament has yet sunk so low, as that, at their bidding, you shall refuse your sanction to this Bill.

The Second Reading of the Bill was carried by a majority of 88:
viz.:—In favour of the Bill 186
Against the Second Reading . . . 98

4

www.ingramcontent.com/pod-product-compliance
Lightning Source LLC
Chambersburg PA
CBHW021233300426
44111CB00007B/524